Baudrillard

A Critical Reader

Edited by Douglas Kellner

BLACKWELL
Oxford UK & Cambridge USA

First published 1994
Reprinted 1995

Blackwell Publishers, the publishing imprint of Basil Blackwell Inc.
238 Main Street
Cambridge, Massachusetts 02142, USA

Basil Blackwell Ltd
108 Cowley Road
Oxford OX4 1JF
UK

Library of Congress Cataloging-in-Publication Data

Baudrillard : a critical reader / edited by Douglas Kellner.
p.   cm.
Includes bibliographical references.
ISBN 1–55786–465–9 (HB : acid-free paper). — ISBN 1–55786–466–7
(pbk. : acid-free paper)
1. Baudrillard, Jean.   2. Sociology—France—History.
I. Kellner, Douglas, 1943–
HM22.F8B3818   1994   94–1736
301'.0944—dc20   CIP

British Library Cataloguing in Publication Data

A CIP catalogue record for this book is available from
the British Library.

Typeset in 10 on 12 pt Sabon
by Graphicraft Typesetters Ltd., Hong Kong
Printed in Great Britain by Hartnolls Ltd, Bodmin, Cornwall

This book is printed on acid-free paper

CONTENTS

NOTES ON CONTRIBUTORS

Steven Best is Assistant Professor of Philosophy and Humanities at the University of Texas, El-Paso. With Douglas Kellner, he is co-author of *Postmodern Theory: Critical Interrogations* (Macmillan and Guilford). He is also the author of the forthcoming books *The Politics of Historical Vision: Marx, Foucault, and Habermas* (Guilford) and *Murray Bookchin: Philosopher of Freedom* (Cassell).

William Bogard is Associate Professor in the Department of Sociology at Whitman College, Walla Walla, Washington. He is the author of several essays on Baudrillard which have appeared in *Sociological Theory, Philosophy and Social Criticism*, and *Philosophy and Literature*.

Deborah Cook is Associate Professor in the Philosophy Department at the University of Windsor. She is author of *The Subject Finds a Voice: Michel Foucault's Turn towards Subjectivity* as well as of numerous articles on Nietzsche, Merleau-Ponty, Derrida, and Adorno. She is currently working on a book dealing with Adorno's theory of mass culture.

James Der Derian teaches international politics at the University of Massachusetts at Amherst. Most recently, he is the author of *Antidiplomacy: Spies, Terror, Speed, and War* (Blackwell) and editor of *International Theory: Critical Investigations* (New York University Press and Macmillan).

Jonathon S. Epstein is a doctoral candidate at Kent State University and a lecturer at Youngstown State University. His interests lie in the broad areas of media and youth. His work has appeared in *Deviant Behavior, Popular Music and Society*, and *The Journal for Studies on Alcohol*. His first book, edited for Garland Press, is entitled *Adolescents and Their Music: If It's Too Loud, You're Too Old*.

Margarete J. Epstein is a graduate student in Sociology at the University of North Carolina at Greensboro. Her research interests include social network theory, childhood socialization and postmodernism.

Gary Genosko wrote, at York University, a Ph.D. on Baudrillard which he is now preparing for publication. He has taught at the McLuhan Program in Culture and Technology in Toronto and has been a Research Fellow at Goldsmiths' College, University of London. He is currently working on French receptions of McLuhan.

A. Keith Goshorn has published essays on Jean Baudrillard, *"Repoman and the Punk Anti-Aesthetic"* and other essays on cinema. He is currently working on issues arising from the feminist critique of the "meta-phoricization of the feminine" by contemporary theorists, in comparison with the role of traditional metaphorical figures of masculinity.

Mark Gottdiener is Professor of Sociology at the University of California, Riverside. He is the author/editor/co-editor of nine books, including the forthcoming *Semiotics and Postmodernism* (Blackwell). His book *The Social Production of Urban Space* (1985) is now in a second edition (1994) with a new preface. Gottdiener's main interests are in social theory, semiotics and cultural studies, political economy, and the new urban sociology.

Douglas Kellner is Professor of Philosophy at the University of Texas at Austin and is author of many books and articles on social theory, politics, history, and culture, including: *Camera Politica: The Politics and Ideology of Contemporary Hollywood Film* (co-authored with Michael Ryan); *Critical Theory, Marxism, and Modernity*; *Jean Baudrillard: From Marxism to Postmodernism and Beyond*; *Jameson/Postmodernism/Critique* (editor), *Television and the Crisis of Democracy*; *Postmodern Theory: Critical Interrogations*; (with Steven Best) and *The Persian Gulf TV War*.

Timothy W. Luke teaches political science at Virginia Polytechnic Institute and State University. His most recent book is *Shows of Force: Power, Politics, and Ideology in Art Exhibitions* (Duke University Press, 1993).

Mark Poster teaches at the University of California, Irvine. He has recently written *The Mode of Information* (1990) and *Critical Theory and Poststructuralism* (1988).

Kim Sawchuk is an Assistant Professor in the Department of Communication Studies, Concordia University, Montreal. She has written on feminism and media studies, marketing research, and telecommunications. She is currently co-editing an anthology entitled *When Pain Strikes*.

Sara Schoonmaker is Assistant Professor of Sociology at Colgate University. She is currently working on a book about the effects of technological change in computers and telecommunications on economic and political restructuring in the global economy, focusing on the case of the Brazilian computer and software industries.

Efrat Tseëlon is a Senior Lecturer in Psychology at the Faculty of Cultural and Educational Studies in Leeds Metropolitan University. She is author of articles on the social construction of self and gender. She wrote her PhD at Oxford on communication through clothing, and is currently working on a book on the construction of the woman through appearance.

Nicholas Zurbrugg is Senior Lecturer in literary and cultural studies at Griffith University, Australia. He is the author of *Beckett and Proust* (1988), *The Parameters of Postmodernism* (1993) and *Positively Postmodern – The Multi-Media Muse in America: Interviews with the American Avant-Garde* (forthcoming) and has also published articles on Beckett, Barthes, Baudrillard, Burroughs, Jameson, Dada, Futurism, and the poetics of postmodernism.

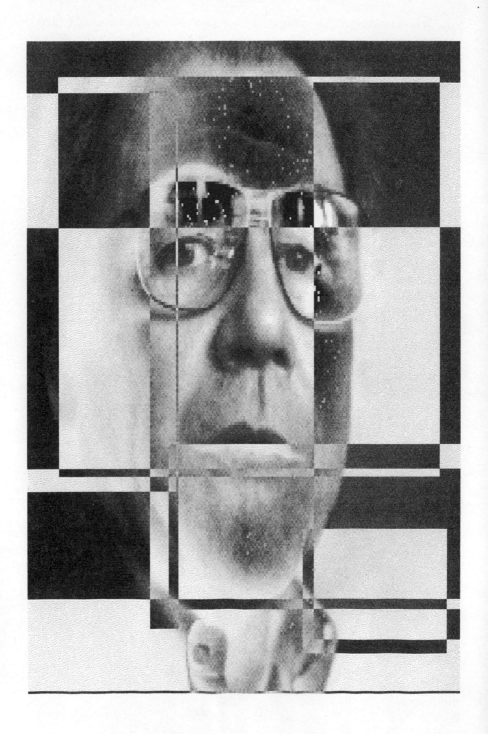

INTRODUCTION:
JEAN BAUDRILLARD IN THE
FIN-DE-MILLENNIUM

—

Douglas Kellner

Jean Baudrillard is one of the most important and provocative writers of the contemporary era. His early studies of the consumer society and its system of objects provided new perspectives on everyday life in the post-World War II social order organized around the consumption, display, and use of consumer goods. His work on the political economy of the sign merged semiological and neo-Marxian perspectives to provide important insights into the power of consumption and how it was playing a crucial role in organizing contemporary societies around objects, needs, and consumption.[1] His 1970s studies of the effects of the new communication, information, and media technologies blazed new paths in contemporary social theory and challenged regnant orthodoxies. Baudrillard's claim of a radical break with modern societies was quickly appropriated into the discourse of the postmodern and he was received as the prophet of postmodernity in avant-garde theoretical circles throughout the world.

Baudrillard proclaimed the disappearance of the subject, political economy, meaning, truth, the social, and the real in contemporary social formations. This process of dramatic change and mutation, he argued, required entirely new theories and concepts to describe the rapidly evolving social processes and novelties of the present moment.[2] Baudrillard undertook to explore this new and original situation and to spell out the consequences for contemporary theory and practice. For some years, Baudrillard was a cutting-edge, high-tech social theorist, one of the most stimulating and provocative contemporary thinkers. As the articles collected in this reader indicate, he is a highly controversial thinker who has produced a legion of fervent supporters, as well as impassioned critics. As the century comes to an end, "Baudrillard" continues to be a password for what some consider avant-garde theory that breaks with the orthodoxies

of the past and that blazes new theoretical pathways through the
mediascapes, computer networks, and information highways and byways
of the present age, as we careen toward the end of a millennium into a new
world (dis)order, as yet uncharted and frightening and confusing.

Confusion and fear produce the need for gurus who will explain the
current disorder and who offer theoretical guidance and orientation through
the morass of the present. Baudrillard has assumed such guru status and
the articles in this *Critical Reader* attempt to survey a large number of
areas in which his thought has evoked discussion and controversy. Unlike
most commentaries on Baudrillard which celebrate or attack him in often-
abstract and general terms, these studies concretely interrogate his positions in terms of specific topics, fields, and debates. The studies collected
here probe Baudrillard's works for insights into the nature and novelties
of contemporary society and culture, appraising his contributions according
to how well he illuminates the present age, while criticizing him for limitations that fail to grasp, or that ignore and mystify, salient aspects of our
current situation. Thus, the following studies take Baudrillard seriously
and undertake thinking with him, against him, or both, by engaging his
writings in salient contemporary topics, polemics, and problems.

Baudrillard himself is a provocateur and self-described "intellectual terrorist" who seeks to destroy modern orthodoxies and who periodically
attacks those who have had the most influence upon his work, thus calling
into question some of the most fashionable and influential thinkers and
ideas of our era. In each case, Baudrillard replaces the positions of the past
with his own often-novel positions, forcing his readers to decide if his
thought is a progression beyond or regression behind established positions.
Such a procedure forces us to read Baudrillard critically and, accordingly,
in this introduction I shall indicate some of the ways that Baudrillard can
be used to understand contemporary society and culture in the present era,
while many of the following papers warn against problems and limitations
in his work.

In raising the question concerning the use-value of Baudrillard, one must
recognize that he himself has attacked the concepts of use-value and
exchange-value, arguing that the current form of capitalism is organized
around configurations of sign-value.[3] For Baudrillard, people attain status
and prestige according to which products they consume and display in a
differential logic of consumption, in which some products have more prestige and sign-value than others, according to current tastes and fashion. In
a sense, it has become Baudrillard's fate to himself become a sign of the
postmodern, of the avant-garde of theoretical discourse, of the *au courant*
and faddish. He is partly responsible for this fate and has himself become
a sign of a particular mode of contemporary thought circulated and exploited as cultural capital by promoters who have fostered the discourse and game of the postmodern – or of Baudrillard's uniqueness and

importance.[4] Many studies of Baudrillard have themselves skimmed the surface of Baudrillard's texts, failing to interrogate their use and abuse, or the contributions and limitations of his writings. In the following pages, I will indicate what I think is most useful in his work, while briefly noting some of their limitations. The writings in this collection will provide a variety of different perspectives on Baudrillard and I merely want to indicate here some of the ways that one can read and use Baudrillard, as well as to provide a framework for critical inquiry into his work.

EARLY WRITINGS: FROM THE SYSTEM OF OBJECTS TO THE CONSUMER SOCIETY

Jean Baudrillard was born in Reims, France in 1929. He told interviewers that his grandparents were peasants and his parents became civil servants.[5] He also claims that he was the first member of his family to pursue an advanced education and that this led to a rupture with his parents and cultural milieu. After working hard in a French high school (Lycée), he entered the University in the 1960s, studying languages, philosophy, sociology, and other disciplines.

Baudrillard was initially a Germanist who published essays on literature in *Les temps modernes* in 1962–3 and throughout the decade he translated works of Peter Weiss and Bertolt Brecht into French, as well as a book on messianic revolutionary movements by Wilhelm Mülhmann. Opposing French and US intervention in the Algerian and Vietnamese wars, he associated himself with the French Left. Influenced by Henri Lefebvre, Roland Barthes, and the French situationists, Baudrillard started serious work in the field of social theory, semiology, and psychoanalysis in the 1960s and began a teaching career at Nanterre, one of the new universities established in Paris. Participating in the tumultuous events of May 1968, Baudrillard was associated with the revolutionary Left, though he would eventually break with his former comrades.

In his first three books, Baudrillard argued that the classical Marxian critique of political economy needed to be supplemented by semiological theories of the sign. He argued that the transition from the earlier stage of competitive market capitalism to the stage of monopoly capitalism required increased attention to demand management, to augmenting and steering consumption. At this stage, from around 1920 to the 1960s, the need to intensify demand supplemented concern with lowering production costs and with augmenting production. In this era, economic concentration, new production techniques, and the like, accelerated capacity for mass production and consumer capitalism focused increased attention on managing consumption and creating needs for new prestigious goods, thus producing the regime of sign-value.

The result was the now-familiar consumer society which provided the main focus of Baudrillard's early work. In this society, advertising, packaging, display, fashion, "emancipated" sexuality, mass media and culture, and the proliferation of commodities multiplied the quantity of signs and spectacles, and produced a proliferation of what Baudrillard calls "sign-value." Henceforth, Baudrillard claims, commodities are not merely to be characterized by use-value and exchange value, as in Marx's theory of the commodity, but sign-value – the expression and mark of style, prestige, luxury, power, and so on – becomes an increasingly important part of the commodity and consumption. That is, commodities were allegedly bought and displayed as much for their sign-value as their use-value, and the phenomenon of sign-value became an essential constituent of the commodity and consumption in the consumer society.

Baudrillard's early works are attempts, within the framework of critical sociology, to combine the studies of everyday life initiated by Lefebvre and the situationists with a social semiology that studies the role of signs in social life.[6] This project, influenced by Barthes, centers on the system of objects in the consumer society (the subject of his first two books), and the interface between political economy and semiotics (the subject of his third book). As Mark Gottdiener points out below, Baudrillard's early work was one of the first to appropriate semiology to analyze how objects are encoded with a system of signs and meanings that constitute contemporary media and consumer societies. Combining semiological studies, Marxian political economy, and sociology of the consumer society, Baudrillard began his life-long task of exploring the system of objects and signs which forms our everyday life.

In his first major work, Baudrillard argued that: "we live the time of objects: I mean that we live according to their rhythm and according to their incessant succession. It is objects which today observe our being born, which accompany our death . . . and which survive us."[7] One of the distinguishing features of his studies of the system of objects is the refusal of a moralizing critique of the consumer society. Instead, Baudrillard carries out a descriptive and hermeneutical analysis of its system of signs and consumption. In a later reflection on his first book, Baudrillard writes:

> My first book contains a critique of the object as obvious fact, substance, reality, use value. There the object was taken as sign, but as sign still heavy with meaning. In this critique two principal logics interfered with each other: a phantasmatic logic that referred principally to psychoanalysis – its identifications, projections, and the entire imaginary realm of transcendence, power and sexuality operating at the level of objects and the environment, with a privilege accorded to the house/automobile axis (immanence/transcendence); and a differential social logic that made distinctions by referring to a sociology, itself derived from anthropology (communication as the production of signs, differentiation, status and prestige).[8]

In other words, the early Baudrillard described the meanings invested in the objects of everyday life (i.e., the power accrued through identification with one's automobile when driving) and the structural system through which the objects were organized into a new modern society (i.e., the prestige or sign-value of a new sports car). Whereas his first book describes the structure and ambience of a system of objects, his second book, *La société de consommation* presents more concrete sociological analyses of the new worlds of leisure and communication in the consumer society. This book and the following *For a Critique of the Political Economy of the Sign* use semiological analysis to dissect the system of signs that produces a hierarchy of prestige and status through the differential use and display of consumer goods.

Baudrillard's early critical explorations of the system of objects and consumer society contain important contributions to contemporary social theory. His semiological optic allows one to perceive how objects are organized into a system of objects that in turn produces a system of needs which integrate individuals into the consumer society. Adding a semiological and cultural dimension to sociological theory, Baudrillard explores the life of signs in society and how what he calls sign-value produces a new world of advertising, fashion, and consumption.[9] His "political economy of the sign" provides new perspectives on consumer needs, media communication, and social integration in contemporary consumer societies. Eschewing the sometimes abstract formalism of academic semiology, Baudrillard utilizes semiological perspectives to illuminate the objects and activities of everyday life. Yet he will soon notice a dramatic mutation occurring within contemporary societies and will accordingly shift his problematic.[10]

BAUDRILLARD AS PROVOCATEUR:
THE END OF MODERNITY

Baudrillard's first three works can be read in the framework of a neo-Marxian critique of capitalist societies. One could read Baudrillard's emphasis on consumption as a supplement to Marx's analysis of production, and his focus on culture and signs as an important supplement to classical Marxian political economy, that adds a cultural and semiological dimension to the Marxian project. But in his 1973 provocation, *The Mirror of Production*, Baudrillard carries out a systematic attack on classical Marxism, claiming that Marxism is but a mirror of bourgeois society, placing production at the center of life, thus naturalizing the capitalist organization of society.

Baudrillard argues that Marxism, first, does not adequately illuminate premodern societies which were organized around symbolic exchange and not production. He also argues that Marxism does not radically enough critique capitalist societies and calls for a sharper break. At this stage, Baudrillard turns to anthropological perspectives on premodern societies for hints of more emancipatory alternatives. Yet it is important to note that this critique of Marxism was taken from the Left, arguing that Marxism did not provide a radical enough critique or alternative to contemporary productivist societies, capitalist and communist. Baudrillard, like many of his generation, was disillusioned with the organized communist Left after the failures of the tumultuous struggles in France during May 1968 to provide more radical social change. He was also reacting against the emerging hegemony of a structuralist Marxist theory, promoted by Althusser and others, that appeared dogmatic, reductionist, and excessively orthodox. Hence, Baudrillard and others of his generation began searching for more radical critical positions.

The Mirror of Production (1973) and his next book *Symbolic Exchange and Death* (1976), a major text which has only recently been translated,[11] are attempts to provide ultra-radical perspectives that overcome the limitations of an economistic Marxist tradition. This ultra-leftist phase of Baudrillard's itinerary would be short-lived, however, though in *Symbolic Exchange and Death*, Baudrillard produces one of his most important and dramatic provocations. The text opens with a Preface that condenses Baudrillard's attempt to provide a radically different approach to society and culture. Building on Bataille's principle of excess and expenditure, Mauss's concept of the gift, and Jarry's pataphysical desire to exterminate meaning, Baudrillard champions "symbolic exchange" and attacks Marx, Freud, and academic semiology and sociology. Baudrillard argues that in Bataille's claim that expenditure and excess is connected with sovereignty, Mauss's descriptions of the social prestige of gift-giving in premodern society, Jarry's theater, and Saussure's anagrams, there is a break with the logic of capitalist exchange and production, or the production of meaning in linguistic exchange. These cases of "symbolic exchange," Baudrillard believes, breaks with the logic of production and describe excessive and subversive behavior that provides alternatives to the capitalist logic of production and exchange.

Against the organizing principles of modern and postmodern society (i.e., production and simulation), Baudrillard contrasts the logic of symbolic exchange, as an alternative organizing principle of society. Against modern demands to produce value and meaning, Baudrillard calls for their extermination and annihilation, providing, as examples, Mauss's gift-exchange, Saussure's anagrams, and Freud's concept of the death drive. In all of these instances, there is a rupture with the logic of exchange (of goods, meanings, and libidinal energies) and thus escape from the logic of production, capitalism, rationality, and meaning. Baudrillard's paradoxical logic of symbolic exchange can be explained as expression of a desire to liberate himself from modern positions and to seek a revolutionary position outside of modern society. Against modern values, Baudrillard advocates their annihilation and extermination.

Baudrillard also distinguishes between the logic of production and utility that organized modern societies and the logic of simulation that he believes is the organizing principle of postmodern societies, postulating a rupture between modern and postmodern societies as great as the break between modern and premodern ones. He follows classical social theory in postulating a major divide between premodern societies, that he sees as organized around symbolic exchange, and modern ones organized around production. In theorizing the epochal postmodern rupture with modernity, Baudrillard declares the "end of political economy" and the end of an era in which production was the organizing principle of society. This modern epoch was the era of capitalism and the bourgeoisie, in which workers were exploited by capital and provided a revolutionary force of upheaval. Baudrillard, however, declared the end of political economy and thus the end of the Marxist problematic and of modernity itself:

The end of labor. The end of production. The end of political economy.

The end of the dialectic signifier/signified which permitted an accumulation of knowledge and of meaning, and of a linear syntagam of cumulative discourse. The end simultaneously of the dialectic of exchange value/use value which alone previously made possible capital accumulation and social production. The end of linear discourse. The end of linear merchandising. The end of the classic era of the sign. The end of the era of production."[12]

The discourse of "the end" signifies his announcing a postmodern break or rupture in history. We are now, Baudrillard claims, in a new era of simulation in which social reproduction (information processing, communication, knowledge industries, etc.) replaces production as the organizing principle of society. In this era, labor is no longer a force of production but is itself a "sign among signs" (p. 23). Labor is not primarily productive in this situation but is a sign of one's social position, way of life, and mode of servitude. Wages too bear no rational relation to one's work and what one produces but relate to one's place within the system (pp. 36ff.). But, crucially, political economy is no longer the foundation, the social determinant, or even a structural "reality" in which other phenomena can be interpreted and explained (pp. 53ff.). Instead we live in a "hyperreality" of simulations in which images, spectacles, and the play of signs replace the logic of production and class conflict as key constituents of contemporary societies.

From now on, capital and political economy disappear from Baudrillard's story, or return in radically new forms. Henceforth, signs and codes proliferate and produce other signs and new sign machines in ever-expanding and spiralling cycles. Technology thus replaces capital in this story and semiurgy, the proliferation of images, information, signs, overshadows production. His postmodern turn is thus connected to a form of technological determinism and a rejection of political economy as a useful explanatory principle – a move that many of the studies in this volume criticize (i.e., Gottdiener, Best, Sawchuk, Schoonmaker, etc.).

Symbolic Exchange and Death thus articulates the principle of a fundamental rupture between modern and postmodern societies and marks Baudrillard's departure from the problematic of modern social theory. For Baudrillard, modern societies are organized around the production and consumption of commodities, while postmodern societies are organized around simulation and the play of images and signs, denoting a situation in which codes, models, and signs are the organizing principles of a new social order where simulation rules. In the society of simulation, identities are constructed by the appropriation of images, and codes and models determine how individuals perceive themselves and relate to other people. Economics, politics, social life, and culture are all governed by the logic of simulation, whereby codes and models determine how goods are consumed and used, politics unfold, culture is produced and consumed, and everyday life is lived.

Baudrillard's postmodern world is also one of radical *implosion* in which social classes, genders, political differences, and once-autonomous realms of society and culture collapse into each other, erasing previously defined boundaries and differences. For Baudrillard, in the society of simulation, economics, politics, culture, sexuality, and the social all implode into each other, such that economics is fundamentally constituted by culture, politics, and other spheres, while art, once a sphere of potential difference and opposition, is absorbed into the economic and political and sexuality is everywhere. In this situation, differences between individuals and groups implode in a rapidly mutating dissolution of the social and the previous boundaries and structures upon which social theory had once focused.

In addition, his postmodern universe is one of *hyperreality* in which entertainment, information, and communication technologies provide experiences more intense and involving than the scenes of banal everyday life. The realm of the hyperreal (i.e., media simulations of reality, Disneyland and amusement parks, malls and consumer fantasylands, TV sports, and other excursions into ideal worlds) is more real than real, whereby the models, images, and codes of the hyperreal come to control thought and behavior. Yet determination itself is aleatory in a non-linear world where it is impossible to chart casual mechanisms and logic in a situation in which individuals are confronted with an overwhelming flux of images, codes, and models, any of which may shape an individual's thought or behavior.

In this postmodern world, individuals flee from the "desert of the real" for the ecstasies of hyperreality and the new realm of computer, media, and technological experience. In this universe, subjectivities are fragmented and lost, and a new terrain of experience appears that allegedly renders previous social theories and politics obsolete and irrelevant. Thus, Baudrillard's categories of simulation, implosion, and hyperreality combine to create a new postmodern condition that requires entirely new modes of social theory and politics to chart and respond to the novelties of the contemporary era.

Baudrillard's style and writing strategies are also implosive, combining material from strikingly different fields, studded with examples from the mass media and popular culture in a new mode of postmodern theory that effaces all disciplinary boundaries. His writing attempts to itself simulate the new conditions, capturing their novelties through inventive use of language and theory. Such radical questioning of contemporary theory and the need for new theoretical strategies are thus legitimated by Baudrillard by the radicality of changes in the current era.

For instance, Baudrillard claims that modernity operates with a logic of representation in which ideas represent reality and truth, concepts which are key postulates of modern theory. A postmodern society explodes this epistemology by creating a situation in which subjects lose contact with the real and themselves fragment and dissolve. This situation portends the end of modern theory which operated with a subject–object dialectic in which the subject was supposed to represent and control the object. In the story of modern philosophy, the philosophic subject attempts to discern the nature of reality, to secure grounded knowledge, and to apply this knowledge to control and dominate the object (i.e., nature, other people, ideas, etc.). Baudrillard follows here the post-structuralist critique that thought and discourse could no longer be securely anchored in a priori or privileged structures. Reacting against the logic of representation in modern theory, French thought, especially some deconstructionists (Rorty's "strong textualists"), moved into the play of textuality, of discourse, which allegedly referred only to other texts or discourses in which "the real" or an "outside" were banished to the realm of nostalgia.

In a similar fashion, Baudrillard, a "strong simulacrist," claims that in the media and consumer society, people are caught up in the play of images, spectacles, and simulacra, that have less and less relationship to an outside, to an external "reality," to such an extent that the very concepts of the social, political, or even "reality" no longer seem to have any meaning. And the narcoticized and mesmerized (some of Baudrillard's metaphors) media-saturated consciousness is in such a state of fascination with image and spectacle that the concept of meaning itself (which depends on stable boundaries, fixed structures, shared consensus) dissolves. In this alarming and novel postmodern situation, the referent, the behind and the outside, along with depth, essence, and reality all disappear, and, with their disappearance, the possibility of all potential opposition vanishes as well. As simulations proliferate, they come to refer only to themselves: a carnival of mirrors reflecting images projected from other mirrors onto the omnipresent television screen and the screen of consciousness, which in turn refers the image to its previous storehouse of images also produced by simulatory mirrors. Caught up in the universe of simulations, the "masses," the "silent majorities," are bathed in a media massage without messages or meaning, a mass age where classes disappear, and politics is dead, as are the grand dreams of disalienation, liberation, and revolution.

Baudrillard claims that henceforth the masses seek spectacle and not meaning. They implode into a "silent majority," signifying "the end of the social."[13] Baudrillard implies that social theory loses its very object as meanings, classes, and difference implode into a "black hole" of non-differentiation. But, as Deborah Cook points out in this volume, Baudrillard claims, at this point in his trajectory (i.e., the late 1970s and early 1980s) that refusal of meaning and participation by the masses is a form of resistance. Hovering between nostalgia and nihilism, Baudrillard at once exterminates modern ideas (i.e., the subject, meaning, truth, reality, society, socialism, etc.) and affirms a mode of symbolic exchange which appears to manifest a nostalgic desire to return to premodern cultural forms. This desperate search for a genuinely revolutionary alternative was abandoned, however, by the early 1980s. Henceforth, he develops yet more novel perspectives on the contemporary moment, vacillating between sketching out alternative modes of thought and behavior and renouncing the quest for political and social change.

Baudrillard concludes that the "catastrophe has happened," that the destruction of modernity and modern theory which he called for in the mid-1970s, has been completed by the development of society itself, that modes of modernity have disappeared and a new social situation has taken their place. Against traditional strategies of rebellion and revolution, Baudrillard thus begins to champion what he calls "fatal strategies" that push the logic of the system to the extreme in the hopes of collapse or reversal.[14] I will turn to Baudrillard's latest writings shortly, but first want to engage an attempt to dissociate Baudrillard from the discourse of the postmodern.

BAUDRILLARD AND THE POSTMODERN GAME

In the light of Baudrillard's powerful sketch of a new postmodern condition, one must therefore reject Mike Gane's futile attempt to separate Baudrillard from the discourse of the postmodern. In his two books on Baudrillard and in introductions to a collection of Baudrillard's interviews and the translation of *Symbolic Exchange and Death*,[15] Gane argued against assimilation of Baudrillard to the problematic of the postmodern. For instance, in his Introduction to the translation of *Symbolic Exchange and Death*, Gane opens by suggesting that the text "will be decisive" in showing that Baudrillard's position is "not postmodern." Gane, however, never eager to demonstrate his allegations, or to carry through an interpretation, doesn't indicate how the text establishes that Baudrillard's position is not "postmodern," nor does he indicate what the text shows Baudrillard's position to be. Part of Gane's problem, and part of the problem with the discourse of the postmodern, is that he never defines what "postmodernism" is and uses the term in a loose and ill-defined way to refer, among other things, to ruptures with modernity, to a new form of culture that breaks with modernism, and to a form of theory that breaks with modern theory – conceptual differences that need to be elucidated.[16]

Seen from this analytical viewpoint, Baudrillard develops a concept of postmodernity as a radical break and rupture from modernity. In *Symbolic Exchange and Death*, as argued, Baudrillard posits a fundamental rupture in history between modernity and postmodernity that was every bit as radical as the earlier break between modern and premodern societies. In other texts of the period, Baudrillard clearly associated himself with the concept of a postmodern rupture. His polemic *Forget Foucault* argues for the obsolescence of his French compatriot precisely on the grounds that the modern era that Foucault described so well is now over and his thought is thus obsolete. In "On Nihilism" – first delivered as a lecture in 1980 and then published in 1981 – Baudrillard describes "modernity" as "the radical destruction of appearances, the disenchantment of the world and its abandonment to the violence of interpretation and history."[17] Modernity was the era of Marx and Freud, the era in which politics, culture, and social life were interpreted as epiphenomena of the economy, or everything was interpreted in terms of desire or the unconsciousness. These "hermeneutics of suspicion" employed depth models to demystify reality, to show the underlying realities behind appearances, the factors that constituted the facts.

The "revolution" of modernity was thus a revolution of meaning grounded in the secure moorings of the dialectics of history, the economy, or desire. Baudrillard scorns this universe and claims to be part of a "second revolution, that of the 20th century, of postmodernity, which is the immense process of the destruction of meaning, equal to the earlier destruction of appearances. Whoever lives by meaning dies by meaning" (pp. 38–9). The postmodern world is devoid of meaning; it is a universe of nihilism where theories float in a void, unanchored in any secure harbor or moorings. Meaning requires depth, a hidden dimension, an unseen yet stable and fixed substratum or foundation; in the postmodern world, however, everything is visible, explicit, and transparent, but highly unstable. The postmodern scene exhibits signs of dead meaning and frozen forms mutating into new combinations and permutations of the same.

In this accelerating proliferation of signs and forms, there is an always-accelerating implosion and inertia, characterized by growth beyond limits, turning in on itself. The secret of cancer: "Revenge of excrescence on growth, revenge of speed in inertia" (p. 39).

Acceleration of inertia, the implosion of meaning in the media; the implosion of the social in the mass; the implosion of the mass in a black hole of nihilism and meaninglessness – such is the Baudrillardian postmodern vision. Fascinated by this void and inertia, Baudrillard privileges the scene of nihilism over the phantasy of meaning arguing that – and this is as good an expression of his postmodern position as any:

> If being nihilist is to privilege this point of inertia and the analysis of this irreversibility of systems to the point of no return, then I am a nihilist.

> If being nihilist is to be obsessed with the mode of disappearance, and no longer with the mode of production, then I am a nihilist. Disappearance, aphanisis, implosion, Fury of the *Verschwindens* (p. 39).

Baudrillard's nihilism is without joy, without energy, without hope for a better future: "No, melancholy is the fundamental tonality of functional systems, of the present systems of simulation, programming and information. Melancholy is the quality inherent in the mode of disappearance of meaning, in the mode of volatilization of meaning in operational systems" (p. 39). In fact, Baudrillard's postmodern mind-set exhibits a contradictory amalgam of emotions and responses ranging from despair and melancholy, to vertigo and giddiness, to nostalgia and laughter. Analysis of the "mode of disappearance" constitutes a rather original contribution to contemporary social theory and indeed Baudrillard has been true to this impulse to describe without illusions or regret what is disappearing in our society and culture. Indeed, Baudrillard concludes "On Nihilism" by linking his theory with "intellectual terrorism":

> If being nihilist is to take, to the unendurable limit of the hegemonic systems, this radical act of derision and violence, this challenge which the system is summoned to respond to by its own death, then I am a terrorist and a nihilist in theory as others are through arms. Theoretical violence, not truth, is the sole expedient remaining to us.

> But this is a utopia. For it would be admirable to be a nihilist, if radicality still existed – as it would be admirable to be a terrorist if death, including that of the terrorist, still had meaning.

> But this is where things become insoluble. For opposed to this nihilism of radicality is the system's own, the nihilism of neutralization. The system itself is also nihilist, in the sense that it has the power to reverse everything in indifferentiation, including that which denies it (p. 39).

Baudrillard's analysis of a postmodern break is also evident in his popular 1983 essay "The Ecstasy of Communication." In this revealing article, he describes both the rupture between his former analysis of modern objects and the new postmodern condition, as well as the "spirals" taken in his own theoretical itinerary. In the system of objects analyzed in his early writings (see discussion above), the subject lived in a "scene" and a "mirror," existing in the eyes of others and through its objects. "But today," Baudrillard declares, "the scene and mirror no longer exist; instead, there is a screen and a network" (p. 126). Henceforth, the subject becomes a "term in a terminal," dissolved in the networks of media and communications. No longer, he claims, do individuals project themselves into their objects, but command, operate, and interface with a functional network of communications. "No more expenditure, consumption, performance, but instead regulation, well-tempered functionality, solidarity among all the elements of the same system, control and global management of an ensemble (p. 127).

Using the discourse of "no more" and "no longer" to describe a "decisive mutation of objects and of the environment in the modern era," Baudrillard thus describes a postmodern rupture. As postmodern theorist, Baudrillard deploys a range of theoretical discourses and perspectives to illuminate the mutation of objects and situations in the contemporary scene. From the mid-1970s to early 1980s, he drew heavily on the discourse of cybernetics and provided cybernetic models of the new postmodern situation. This discourse is heavily saturated with scientific metaphors (i.e., black holes, fractals, DNA, and computer terminology) and presents the perspective of a high-tech, cybernetic theory on the contemporary scene. Many of his concepts from this period are extremely illuminating – as articles by Schoonmaker, Tseëlon, Der Derian, Sawchuk, and others in this reader demonstrate – though he tends to exaggerate the novelty of the present and many of his analyses are misleading and fanciful, as many authors in this volume argue.

In general, I would maintain that Baudrillard exaggerates the break between the modern and the postmodern, takes future possibilities as existing realities, and provides a futuristic perspective on the present, much like the tradition of dystopic science fiction, ranging from Huxley to some versions of cyberpunk. Indeed, I prefer to read Baudrillard's work as a science fiction, which anticipates the future by exaggerating present tendencies and thus provides early warnings about what might happen if present trends continue. It is not an accident that Baudrillard is an aviciendo of science fiction, who has himself influenced a large number of contemporary science fiction writers.

Thus, it is useful to read Baudrillard's maps as preceding the territory, as futuristic mappings of the (soon to arrive?) present from the vantage point of a possible future. Hence, in my reading, Baudrillard's simulations theory does not really represent reality as much as simulate what is to come, or what might come to pass if present trends continue and accelerate. But Baudrillard often insists that the future is already here, that we are already living in the brave new world of an already present future. Sometimes he describes this future and our present as "postmodern," yet he also continues to employ the discourse of the modern to describe the present scene.

Thus, Gane is completely wrong to claim that Baudrillard's problematic should not be interpreted as concerned with the postmodern.[18] To be sure, in an interview with Gane, Baudrillard claimed that he himself has "nothing to do with postmodernism," a quote that Gane provoked and quotes incessantly.[19] Obviously, Baudrillard wished to distance himself from the problematic of Lyotard, Jameson, Kroker, and others who were assimilating and promoting the discourse of the postmodern and to proclaim the uniqueness of his own perspectives, independent of any school or tendency. As we shall see, Baudrillard became increasingly idiosyncratic; thus he is quite right to distance himself from some other contemporary versions of postmodern theory. Yet in some texts of the 1980s he himself used the discourse of the postmodern to describe his own works; his texts indeed postulated a rupture with modernity, and he was legitimately seen as a major theorist of the postmodern. Becoming tired or disillusioned with this discourse game, however, Baudrillard began moving away from it into other discourses, which, arguably, were also connected in intricate ways to the problematic of the postmodern.

FROM PATAPHYSICS TO METAPHYSICS AND THE TRIUMPH OF THE OBJECT

In 1979, Baudrillard published *Seduction*, a curious text that represented a major shift in his thought. Whereas in *Symbolic Exchange and Death* he sketched out ultra-revolutionary perspectives as a radical alternative, taking symbolic exchange as a radical otherness to the production of goods, meanings, and value in modern societies, he now valorizes seduction as his alternative to production and communicative interaction. Seduction, however, does not undermine, subvert, or transform existing social relations or institutions, but is a soft alternative, a play with appearances, and a game with feminism, that provoked a sharp critical response, as Keith Goshorn's article in this reader shows.[20]

Baudrillard's concept of seduction is highly technical and involves games with signs rather than the activity of male seduction of women (though this seems to be included in Baudrillard's concept). Baudrillard opposes seduction as an aristocratic "order of sign and ritual" to the bourgeois ideal of production and he valorizes artifice, appearance, play, and challenge against the deadly serious labor of production. Baudrillard interprets seduction primarily as a ritual and game with its own rules, charms, snares, and lures. His writing regresses at this point into a neo-aristocratic aestheticism dedicated to idiosyncratic modes of thought and writing, which introduce a new set of categories – reversibility, the challenge, the duel, – that move Baudrillard's thought toward a form of aristocratic aestheticism and metaphysics.

Baudrillard's new metaphysical speculations are evident in *Fatal Strategies*, another turning point in his itinerary. This text presented a bizarre metaphysical scenario concerning the triumph of objects over subjects within the obscene proliferation of an object world so completely out of control that it surpasses all attempts to understand, conceptualize, and control it. His scenario concerns the proliferation and growing supremacy of objects over subjects and the eventual triumph of the object. In a discussion of "Ecstasy and Inertia," Baudrillard discusses how objects and events in contemporary society are continually surpassing themselves, growing and expanding in power. The "ecstasy" of objects is their proliferation and expansion to the Nth degree, to the superlative; ecstasy as going outside of or beyond oneself: the beautiful as more beautiful than the beautiful in fashion, the real more real than the real in television, sex more sexual than the sex in pornography. Ecstasy is thus the form of obscenity (fully explicit, nothing hidden) and of the hyperreality described by Baudrillard earlier taken to a higher level, redoubled and intensified. His vision of contemporary society exhibits a careening of growth and excrescence (*croissance et excroissance*), expanding and excreting ever more goods, services, information, messages, or demands – surpassing all rational ends and boundaries in a spiral of uncontrolled growth and replication.

Yet the growth, acceleration, and proliferation have reached such extremes, Baudrillard suggests, that the ecstasy of excrescence is accompanied by inertia. For, as the society is saturated to the limit, it implodes and winds down into inertia and entropy. This process presents a catastrophe for the subject, for not only does the acceleration and proliferation of the object world intensify the aleatory dimension of chance and nondetermination, but the objects themselves take over in a "cool" catastrophe for the exhausted subject whose fascination with the play of objects turns to apathy, stupification, and an entrophic inertia.

In retrospect, the growing power of the world of objects over the subject has been Baudrillard's theme from the beginning, thus pointing to an underlying continuity in his project. In his early writings, he explored the ways that commodities were fascinating individuals in the consumer society and the ways that the world of goods was assuming new and more value through the agency of sign value and the code – which were part of the world of things, the system of objects. His polemics against Marxism were fuelled by the belief that sign value and the code were more fundamental than such traditional elements of political economy as exchange value, use value, production, and so on in constituting contemporary society. Then, reflections on the media entered the forefront of his thought: the TV object was at the center of the home in Baudrillard's earlier thinking and the media, simulations, hyperreality, and implosion eventually came to obliterate distinctions between private and public, inside and outside, media and reality. Henceforth, everything was public, transparent, ecstatic and hyperreal in the object world which was gaining in fascination and seductiveness as the years went by.

And so ultimately the subject, the darling of modern philosophy, is defeated in Baudrillard's metaphysical scenario and the object triumphs, a stunning end to the dialectic of subject and object which had been the framework of modern philosophy. The object is thus the subject's fatality and Baudrillard's "fatal strategies" are simply an obscure call to imitate strategies and ruses of objects. In "banal strategies," "the subject believes itself to always be more clever than the object, whereas in the other [fatal strategies] the object is always supposed to be more shrewd, more cynical, more brilliant than the subject."[21] Previously, in banal strategies, the subject believed itself to be more masterful and sovereign than the object. A fatal strategy, by contrast, recognizes the supremacy of the object and therefore takes the side of the object and attempts to reproduce its strategies, ruses, and rules.

In *Fatal Strategies* and his other recent writings, Baudrillard seems to be taking social theory into the realm of metaphysics, but it is a specific type of metaphysics deeply inspired by the pataphysics developed by Alfred Jarry. For Jarry:

pataphysics is the science of the realm beyond metaphysics . . . . It will study the laws which govern exceptions and will explain the universe supplementary to this one; or, less ambitiously, it will describe a universe which one can see – must see perhaps – instead of the traditional one . . . . Definition: pataphysics is the science of imaginary solutions, which symbolically attributes the properties of objects, described by their virtuality, to their lineaments.[22]

Like the universe in Jarry's *Ubu Roi, The Gestures and Opinions of Doctor Faustroll* and other literary texts – as well as in Jarry's more theoretical explications of pataphysics – Baudrillard's is a totally absurd universe where objects rule in mysterious ways, and people and events are governed by absurd and ultimately unknowable interconnections and predestination (the French playwright Eugene Ionesco is another good source of entry to this universe). Baudrillard's pataphysics follow Jarry in inventing a version of the universe in line with the fantasies, hallucinations, and projections of its creator. Like Jarry's pataphysics, Baudrillard's universe is ruled by surprise, reversal, hallucination, blasphemy, obscenity, and a desire to shock and outrage.

Thus, in view of the growing supremacy of the object, Baudrillard wants us to abandon the subject and to side with the object. Pataphysics aside, it seems that Baudrillard is trying to end the philosophy of subjectivity that has controlled French thought since Descartes by going over completely to the other side. Descartes' *malin genie*, his evil genius, was a ruse of the subject which tried to seduce him into accepting what was not clear and distinct, but over which he was ultimately able to prevail. Baudrillard's evil genius is the object itself which is much more malign than the merely epistemological deceptions of the subject faced by Descartes and which constitutes a fatal destiny for us that demands the end of the philosophy of subjectivity. Henceforth, for Baudrillard, we live in the era of the reign of the object.

During the 1990s, Baudrillard has published *The Transparency of Evil* and *La fin d'une illusion*, which continue his excursions into the metaphysics of the object and defeat of the subject. Collecting occasional papers during the period, the books continue to postulate a break or rupture within history that conceptualizes the space of a postmodern *coupure*, though Baudrillard rarely uses the discourse of the postmodern himself. He also published a second collection of his notebooks, *Cool Memories II* (1990), and a book that claimed that the Gulf war never happened, *La Guerre du Golfe n'a pas eu lieu* (1991), a text discussed by Der Derian and Bogard in this collection.[23]

These texts continue the fragmentary style and use of short essays, aphorisms, stories, and apercus, that Baudrillard began deploying in the 1980s and often repeat some of the same ideas and stories. They contain few new ideas or perspectives, but are often entertaining. And so, we come, to another use-value of Baudrillard: humor and amusement. It is often simply amusing to read Baudrillard. Baudrillard – pataphysician at twenty – remains so and perhaps one should not take him all that seriously.[24] Or, rather, while one can read him as deadly serious, one can also read him ironically, as a grand joke on social theory and cultural criticism. One can thus either read Baudrillard as a form of science fiction and pataphysics or a form of serious social theory and cultural metaphysics. It is undecidable what Baudrillard's texts really are and it is sometimes useful to read him as making genuine and important contributions to social theory, while at other times one can enjoy the irony, cynicism, humor, and pataphysical metaphysics. Baudrillard himself, it seems, wants it both ways and thus opens the way for either a serious or a non-serious reading.

CONCLUDING REFLECTIONS

It would be a mistake, however, to reduce Baudrillard to pataphysics, or to a merely aesthetic irritation to social theory,[25] for his themes are some of the most serious, frightening, and important issues that we are now confronting. As noted, sometimes Baudrillard writes as if he is revealing the "real" conditions of our times, is articulating fundamental changes and novelties, and he is celebrated by some of his enthusiasts as a high-tech avant-garde thinker who is confronting salient, if disturbing, realities of our time.

On this reading, Baudrillard is *the* theorist of the fin-de-millennium who produces sign-posts to the new era of postmodernity and is an important guide to the new era. Yet in view of his exaggeration of the alleged break with modernity, whether to read Baudrillard's work as science fiction or social theory, as pataphysics or metaphysics, is undecidable. Baudrillard obviously wants to have it both ways with social theorists thinking that he provides salient perspectives on contemporary social realities, that Baudrillard reveals what is really happening, that he tells it like it is. And yet more cynical anti-sociologists are encouraged to enjoy Baudrillard's fictions, his experimental discourse, his games, and his play. Likewise, he sometimes encourages cultural metaphysicians to read his work as serious reflections on the realities of our time, while winking a pataphysical aside at those skeptical of such undertakings. Thus, it is undecidable whether Baudrillard is best read as science fiction and pataphysics or as social theory.

Likewise, it is undecidable whether his work should be read under the sign of truth or fiction. Curiously, Baudrillard's most recent works respond to some of the criticisms of his earlier texts, but in an often-ambiguous way that makes concessions and then proceeds to replicate his earlier positions. For example, in a 1992 lecture delivered at Essex University published in May 1993, Baudrillard says that his reflections on America are "basically a *fiction*" and he admits that his "point of view will therefore be that of a wild amateurism and a sort of cultural metaphysics," because he is not qualified to talk "about the economic, political or juridical aspects of America."[26] Yet he then repeats many of the questionable allegations about the United States and adds some new zingers. Baudrillard will thus no doubt continue to provoke controversy and debate and for this reason critical reception of his thought is essential.

IN THIS READER

In my first publication on Baudrillard in 1987, I called for the necessity of reading Baudrillard critically in the light of the emulation and celebration of his ideas by his many devotees in an uncritical fashion.[27] Since then, the critical discourse on Baudrillard has proliferated dramatically, though many of the critiques are one-dimensional dismissals of his work that have refused to seriously confront his challenges and provocations. The articles collected here, however, undertake serious critiques that enter into the heart of his problematic, think specific phenomena with Baudrillard, and then criticize him for his limitations and blindspots. Moreover, much of the voluminous literature on Baudrillard either celebrates or damns him, often in extremely general ways.

The contributors to this volume, however, appraise Baudrillard's work in terms of specific areas and topics of concern, and point out both the strengths and limitations of his thought in relation to specific topics and problems. Mark Gottdiener analyzes Baudrillard's early attempts to merge Marxism and semiology in his late 1960s and early 1970s writings. Steven Best defends Debord's neo-Marxism against Baudrillard and critically examines some of the key concepts of Baudrillard's postmodern theory, while showing that the later Debord ends up by adopting Baudrillardian positions. Mark Poster, by contrast, lays out Baudrillard's critique and challenges to the Marxian theory and defends Baudrillard against Habermas's version of critical theory.

A series of studies then examines the relevance of Baudrillard's theories in examining important contemporary disciplines and topics. Kim Sawchuk shows how Baudrillard's concepts can be used to illuminate the phenomena of marketing and telecommunications, probing both the contributions and limitations of his work. Likewise, Efrat Tseëlon examines Baudrillard's contributions to the study of fashion and signification, while Jonathan and Margarete Epstein indicate Baudrillard's contribution to a neo-formalist sociological theory of the media, a project anticipated by Simmel's sociology and McLuhan's media theory. Deborah Cook in turn provides a critical look at the analyses of media reception by Baudrillard and John Fiske, who has been a prolific and influential player in the booming field of cultural studies. Sara Schoonmaker criticizes Baudrillard's analyses of contemporary capitalism via concrete studies of electronic data transmission and political debates over its regulation. While noting the importance of Baudrillard's focus on computers and information, Schoonmaker argues that Baudrillard's theory leaves out crucial components of the contemporary form of global capitalism. Defending Baudrillard's concept of simulation, James Der Derian argues for the usefulness of Baudrillard's theory in analyzing contemporary forms of military technology and the technological/military forms of global capitalism.

Baudrillard has also deeply influenced contemporary cultural production and Timothy Luke examines Baudrillard's contributions to analysis of contemporary art and presents critical perspectives on his notions of aesthetic production and cultural politics. Nicholas Zurbrugg examines Baudrillard's interventions in the debates over modernism and postmodernism, arguing that Baudrillard's own textual productions are deeply informed by high modernism. Zurbrugg demonstrates some of the ways that Baudrillard combines modern and postmodern strategies and is best interpreted as somewhere between the modern and the postmodern.

A concluding set of essays reflect on the entirety of Baudrillard's work and influence, with focus on specific themes. Keith Goshorn analyzes Baudrillard's feminist provocations and attempts to indicate some of the ways that Baudrillard's thought can be productive for feminist theory, as well as to indicate some of the areas where Baudrillard's work would benefit from appropriation of feminist insights. Gary Genosko interrogates the theatricality of Baudrillard's literary productions and the drama of objects in his later works, which Genosko sees as playing out some of the themes of Artaud and other contemporary dramatists. William Bogard provides a set of philosophical/sociological reflections on Baudrillard's musings on history, time, and the end, defending Baudrillard against some of his critics.[28]

Together, these essays point to some areas in which Baudrillard's thought has proved to be of use in the contemporary era. Baudrillard is a highly controversial figure who excels in provocation. Influenced by modernist movements like Dada and pataphysics, Baudrillard loves to shock and outrage. Some of his antics are highly amusing and provide a level of entertainment rarely found in social theory and criticism. Some of his provocations are silly and offensive, and thus he has evoked a strong critical reaction. Consequently, a reader on Baudrillard must necessarily be a *critical reader* to distinguish the useless from the worthless, the valuable from the foolish, the important from the unimportant elements of Baudrillard's work. As we approach the end of the century, and perhaps the end of a millennium of human history (i.e., modernity), we need new theories to help us make sense of the dramatic and frightening changes that we are undergoing. Baudrillard can help us with this enterprise and thus he is of use in developing new theories and politics for the contemporary era. He can also be an obstacle and cul-de-sac, so we need to learn to read Baudrillard critically in order to appropriate his insights and avoid his limitations.

Notes

1   Baudrillard's early works include *Le système des objets* (Paris: Denoel-Gonthier, 1968); *La société de consommation* (Paris: Gallimard, 1970); and *Pour une critique de l'économie politique du signe* (Paris: Gallimard, 1972; translated as *For a Critique of the Political Economy of the Sign*, St. Louis: Telos Press, 1981). For an overview of Baudrillard's theoretical and political trajectory, see Douglas Kellner, *Jean Baudrillard: From Marxism to Postmodernism and Beyond* (Cambridge and Stanford: Polity Press and Stanford University Press, 1989). In this Introduction, I draw on my previous work, but will focus on the use-value of Baudrillard's writings, whereas previously I have often emphasized its limitations, especially of the later work.

2   These important works that articulate a postmodern turn in contemporary

society include *L'échange symbolique et la mort* (Paris: Gallimard, 1976; translated as *Symbolic Exchange and Death*, London: Sage, 1993); *L'effet Beaubourg: Implosion et dissuasion* (Paris: Galilée, 1977); translated in *October*, 20 (Spring 1982), pp. 3–13; *Oublier Foucault* (Paris: Galilée, 1977); translated as *Forget Foucault* (New York: Semiotext(e), 1987); *A l'ombre des majorités silencieuses, ou La fin du social* (Fontenay-Sous-Bois: Cahiers d'Utopie, 1978); translated as *In the Shadow of the Silent Majorities*, (New York: Semiotext(e), 1983); *De la séduction* (Paris: Denoel-Gonthier, 1979); translated as *Seduction* (New York: Saint Martin's Press, 1990); *Simulacres et simulation*, Paris: Galilée, 1981); *Les strategies fatales*, Paris: Bernard Grasset, 1983, translated as *Fatal Strategies* (New York: Semiotext(e), 1990); "The Ecstasy of Communication," in *The Anti-Aesthetic: Essays on Postmodern Culture*, ed., Hal Foster (Port Townsend, Washington: Bay Press, 1983), pp. 126–34; and *Simulations* (New York: Semiotext(e), 1983).

3 See, especially, Baudrillard, *Critique.*

4 On cultural entrepreneurs and the promotion of the postmodern, see Mike Featherstone, *Consumer Culture & Postmodernism* (London: Sage, 1991), pp. viiff, passim. On the competing discourses of the postmodern, see Steven Best and Douglas Kellner, *Postmodern Theory: Critical Interrogations* (London and New York: Macmillan Press and Guilford Press, 1991). Arthur Kroker and his associates have probably done the most to exploit Baudrillard as the key to the new postmodern universe, while Mike Gane has sought to dissociate Baudrillard from this problematic, allowing Gane to present himself as the true interpreter of Baudrillard's secrets and mana. I shall challenge Gane's readings of Baudrillard in this introduction.

5 Jean Baudrillard, *Baudrillard Live*, ed. Mike Gane (London and New York: Routledge, 1993), p. 19.

6 See Roland Barthes, *Mythologies* (New York: Hill and Wang, 1962); *Elements of Semiology* (New York: Hill and Wang, 1968); *System of Fashion* (New York: Hill and Wang, 1983); Guy Debord, *The Society of the Spectacle* (Detroit: Black and Red Press, 1970); and Henri Lefebvre, *Everyday Life in the Modern World* (New York: Harper and Row, 1971). Steven Best's article in this collection explains the basic conceptions of Debord and the situationists and their critique of everyday life.

7 Baudrillard, *Système des objects*, p. 18.

8 Baudrillard, "Ecstasy of Communication," p. 126. As we shall see below, Baudrillard will describe this modern world as one that is passing away to a new postmodern world.

9 Gottdiener and Tseëlon explore this phase of Baudrillard's thought and Sawchuk argues that in the postmodern world of marketing and telecommunications a new mode of social integration is coming into being.

10 Although there will be some dramatic shifts in Baudrillard's optic, he will continue to explore the life of objects and signs in society, thus there is a certain continuity to his work, despite some dramatic discontinuities.

11 Jean Baudrillard, *Symbolic Exchange and Death* (London: Sage Publications, 1993), translated by Iain Hamilton Grant, with an introduction by Mike Gane. Gane's introduction, as I shall argue below, fundamentally misrepresents this key text and thus blocks perception of its radicality and importance.

12   Baudrillard, *Symbolic Exchange and Death*, p. 20 (page references that follow in the text are from the original French edition and the translations are mine).

13   See Baudrillard's *In the Shadow of the Silent Majorities.*

14   Baudrillard elucidates this paradoxical conception in *Fatal Strategies* (1983), a notion discussed below in the articles by Cook, Genosko, Bogard, and others.

15   Gane's "books" are not really books at all, but series of fragments that poorly summarize his master's works, obsessively attack Baudrillard's critics, and fail to provide any innovative or illuminating perspectives of his own on Baudrillard. *Baudrillard. Critical and Fatal Strategies* (London: Routledge, 1991), the first of his texts on Baudrillard, claims to provide "essential background and context," but does so in terms of banal summaries of other players in the French theory scene, with no really illuminating analysis of Baudrillard's relation to these theories, or of his theoretical and political context. Gane then offers some highly tendentious readings of Baudrillard's relation to postmodernism, Marxism, and feminism, which are probably incomprehensible to those who are unfamiliar with Baudrillard's texts, and without establishing any positions of his own. Next, Gane offers banal summaries of some of Baudrillard's texts, omitting sustained discussion of his key text, *Symbolic Exchange and Death*, the exposition of which takes up much of Gane's next "book," *Baudrillard's Bestiary* (London: Routledge, 1991). The follow-up claims it will be an "essential guide to Baudrillard as a cultural critic," but merely provides more trite and opaque summaries of Baudrillard's social analysis, with no useful interpretive theses, few original insights, and little focus on Baudrillard as a cultural critic.

16   In previous work, I argued for the need to distinguish different family concepts in the discourse of the postmodern, distinguishing between: (1) modernity and postmodernity as historical epochs; (2) modernism and postmodernism as forms of art; and (3) modern and postmodern theory as two opposed modes of theoretical discourse and practice. See my article, "Postmodernism as Social Theory: Some Problems and Challenges," *Theory, Culture, and Society*, 5, 2–3 (June 1988) 240–69, and Best and Kellner, *Postmodern Theory*. Of course, these terms are often interrelated in specific postmodern theorists and artists, but one should be able to at least make such analytical distinctions to avoid the muddle, evident in Gane, in which "postmodernism" refers to everything and nothing.

17   Baudrillard, "On Nihilism," *On the Beach*, 6 (Spring 1984) 38. Subsequent page references in text.

18   Gane claims that my interpretation of Baudrillard as a theorist of the postmodern rests on one minor article and two interviews, whereas I am claiming that such major works as *Symbolic Exchange and Death*, *Forget Foucault*, "The Beauborg Effect," *In the Shadows of the Silent Majorities*, *Simulations et simulacra*, "Ecstasy of Communications," and other writings articulate a break between modern and postmodern epochs. While Baudrillard himself rarely adopted the discourse of the postmodern to explain this break, he did on occasion, and in any case his texts articulate a postmodern break, describe the disappearance of modernity and the modern, and systematically deploy the discourse of the "no longer" and "no more." Later, Baudrillard

would distance himself from the game of postmodernism, but can legitimately be interpreted as a theorist of the postmodern, and I would argue that much of his importance derives from precisely that problematic – as do some significant limitations and problems in his thought.

19 See Gane, *Baudrillard*, pp. 46, 47, and passim.
20 Baudrillard's celebration of seduction, his essentializing of differences between the masculine and the feminine, and his attacks on feminism and other progressive ideologies are close to the positions of Camille Paglia, though there are also obvious differences, such as Paglia's more naturalistic celebration of sexuality; see *Sex, Art, and American Culture* (New York: Vintage, 1992).
21 *Les strategies fatales*, pp. 259–60.
22 Alfred Jarry, "What is Pataphysics?," in *Evergreen Review*, 13 (May-June 1960) 131ff. See also Jarry, *The Ubu Plays* (New York: Grove Press, 1969).
23 Jean Baudrillard, *The Transparency of Evil* (London: Verso, 1993 [1990]); *Cool Memories II* (Paris: Galilée, 1990); *La guerre du Golfe n'a pas eu lieu* (Paris: Galilée, 1991); and *La fin d'une illusion* (Paris: Seuil, 1992).
24 In *Cool Memories II*, Baudrillard describes himself as "pataphysician at twenty – situationist at thirty – utopian at forty – transveral at fifty – viral and metaleptic at sixty – that's my history" (p. 131).
25 This position was hinted at in Gane's first book *Baudrillard. Critical and Fatal Strategies* where Gane occasionally presents Baudrillard as an "artist" interested in the poetics of social forms, but – consistent with his minimalist anti-hermeneutics – Gane never really works this position out.
26 Jean Baudrillard, "Hyperreal America," *Economy and Society*, 22, 2 (May 1993) 243–52.
27 See Douglas Kellner, "Baudrillard, Semiurgy, and Death," *Theory, Culture, and Society*, IV (1987) 124–46.
28 I would like to thank the contributors to this volume for responding in productive ways to the criticisms that I offered, often through several drafts. Special thanks to Jon and Margarete Epstein for providing computer-generated illustrations to the book. And thanks to Sheila Dallas for superb copy-editing and to Simon Prosser for helping to formulate the conception of the book and to advance the text smoothly through the production process.

1

THE SYSTEM OF OBJECTS AND THE COMMODIFICATION OF EVERYDAY LIFE: THE EARLY BAUDRILLARD[1]

___

Mark Gottdiener

Examination of the earlier works of a writer brings with it interesting observations, perhaps surprises, but is it the way authors want to be read? What they mean today may differ from what they meant in the past. Academic work, unlike novel writing, represents both the development and the clarification of ideas. In this essay I am less concerned with Baudrillard the subject than with using his first major text[1] to interrogate the semiotics of material culture.[2] This essay, then, seeks to retrieve some significant insights from Baudrillard's still-untranslated first writings on the semiotics of objects. By so doing, I hope to advance that inquiry.

In recovering his early work on the semiotics of objects, however, there are some interesting observations that can also be made about Baudrillard's later work. I find a critical disjuncture between the early effort to study the relationship between semiotics and the commodification of everyday life, and the later effort which abandons that project and replaces it with an impressionistic, idealized, and jargon-laden discourse that has come to be known as "postmodern" cultural criticism. The early work of Baudrillard stands out as a "reality"-based analysis of the changes in daily life that are facilitated by changes in material culture and their relation to symbolic images of consumption. Many of the concepts for which Baudrillard is known, such as "hyperreality" and "simulation" which float ungrounded through his later discourse as general conditions of humanity, are specified in concrete, useful ways in his early work. In sum, for those interested in the relation between ideology and material culture, rather than postmodernism per se, Baudrillard's Le système des objets ranks as one of the most important books of post-structuralist cultural criticism.

ANTECEDENTS: THE DISCOVERY OF STRUCTURE AND THE STUDY OF CULTURE

The influence of the Swiss linguist, Ferdinand de Saussure, was at its height in France during the 1950s. At this time the anthropologist, Claude Levi-Strauss,[4] had already applied the essential ideas of Saussure to the study of culture. In this tradition, all of culture was discovered to be structured as a language. By this was meant that cultural meanings possessed the double articulation of language and were structured according to two dimensions: the diachronic and synchronic axes. Language possesses meaning not only because the sentences we use follow strict laws called syntax (a diachronic dimension), but also because our choice of words follows another set of strict rules, called semantics (the synchronic dimension). According to the great discovery of semiotics, meaning itself was a product of the articulation or juxtaposition of these two axes.

According to semiotics, for example, the system of cuisine, or cooking, structured the meal according to diachronic laws with dishes served one after the other according to custom. In the "formal" meal, for instance, the hors d'oeuvres come first, followed by appetizers, soup, sorbet, entree, and so on. Violation of the syntax of the formal meal means a dish served out of turn or omitted. Such a faux pas would threaten group or social interpretation and sanction of the meal as "formal." In addition, along with syntax, meals are structured according to the synchronic or semantic dimension. Each dish can be prepared in a variety of ways: boiled, fried, raw, cooked, parboiled, baked, broiled, and the like. At each stage of the meal choices are exercised regarding what to serve: a hot or cold soup, a green or caesar salad, chicken or beef, and so on. Each of these synchronic choices must also conform to the diachronic dimension, i.e., the choices have to fit together as an ensemble in the normative sense, such as picking the appropriate wine to go with a particular dish. Hence the two dimensions are related to each other and together bring about a realization of that social act known as "the meal."

Saussurean linguistics as semiotics was applied to the general phenomenon of culture and became popular in France during the 1960s. As a structural method it enabled the analysis of all cultural forms as symbolic systems. Indeed, Saussure, himself, conceived of semiotics as a pan-linguistics. Early work by semioticians gave the impression, following Saussure, that cultural systems structured as a language could also communicate meanings as a language.[5] Thus, non-verbal, body language, or Kinesics and Proxemics, could communicate meanings as vividly as spoken speech. As semiotic studies matured, however, this "linguistic fallacy"[6] of Saussure was exposed and a much more modest approach to the semiotics of culture adopted.

Semioticians today follow Eco[7] and distinguish between cultural complexes that communicate intentional meanings, or systems of communication, and complexes that do not necessarily communicate intentionally but are structured as a language, or, systems of signification. All systems of communication are also systems of signification, but not the other way around. All systems of signification and, by implication, systems of communication possess synchronic (paradigmatic) and diachronic (syntagmatic) axes. Thus, for example, cuisine is a vehicle for the expression of culture and is structured as a language, but it is not a system of communication. Hence, we no longer subscribe to the linguistic fallacy of Saussure. In fact, it can be argued that the American Charles S. Peirce, who also developed a semiotics, possesses a better approach to systems of signification which avoids the linguistic fallacy.

In the 1960s Roland Barthes, the French literary critic, produced some of the most important and enduring semiotic analyses of culture. In literary criticism the two axes of meaning corresponding to the paradigmatic and syntagmatic dimensions are also known as the metaphorical (associative) and metonymical (juxtapositional/contiguous) axes. Using this distinction, Barthes extended the concept of "trope" or figure of speech to the system of signification. By speaking of literary texts using these concepts he emphasized the importance of the play of difference in the creation of meanings, because both metaphorical and metonymical tropes rely on contrasts or difference – the one associative, the other contiguous. This distinction became a core idea of deconstructionism (see below).

Barthes work has two main periods. In the first he proposed a translinguistics of culture à la Saussure[8] by which all cultural phenomena were analyzed as language. In his latter period he acknowledged the limitations of the linguistic approach. This compelled him to join the literary critics of the Tel Quel group who eventually abandoned semiotics for deconstruction.

In Barthes early, semiotic period he was particularly interested in the way systems of signification were overlaid by ideology in the form of written texts or discourse. In this way he distinguished between cultural phenomena per se that were systems of objects which did not represent communication or language, and ideologies linked to cultural processes which were discourses that manipulated the users of culture for specific purposes, such as the sale of commodities. The discourse surrounding the use of objects, such as the language of advertising, *was* a system of communication filled with the intentionality of ideology that constituted a text. By distinguishing between systems of objects which constitute modes of signification from ideological discourse involving the use of those objects, Barthes distinguished between material culture and the mode of communication used to manipulate consumer choices.

In 1967 Barthes published one of his most comprehensive semiotic analyses of a system of objects, the fashion system.[9] Barthes shows how bodily adornment is structured as language. But Barthes made the distinction between the system of dress, which functions as a mode of signification, and the system of fashion, which is a mode of communication that possesses intentionality. In particular, the system of fashion is an ideology propagated by the fashion industry and advertising for the control of appearance in order to sell commodities.

Each area of the body, for instance, from the top of the head to the toes can be a location for the articulation of styles of dress. At every location of the body, the individual has a choice regarding how to articulate with styles of adornment – whether to wear a hat or not, a necktie or not, a skirt or pants, and so on. These choices are regulated by the paradigmatic axis of the society's particular dress code. As a system of signification, the dress code regulates all fashion alternatives, such as size, shape, color, and style.

In addition, when any individual chooses body adornment, attention is usually paid to how well the individual choices of, for example, head covering, shirt, skirt, shoes, fit together as an ensemble. These contiguous items are also regulated by the society's dress code and constitute the syntagmatic axis. People can commonly violate the dictates of fashion by inappropriately mixing different combinations of clothing or adornment. In short, the dress code, which regulates appearance alternatives, is structured as a system of signification. Societies use the power of the dress code to make distinctions between men and women, young and old, caste or class differences, states of joy and mourning, and so on. These distinctions in some societies are formalized as "sumptuary laws."[10]

The dress code, however, despite its regulatory power, is not a text nor a system of communication. Barthes suggested that superimposed on this code in capitalist society, is a second system, the fashion system, which attempts to control the everyday decisions of individuals regarding appearance for the purposes of selling the commodities of the fashion industry. According to Barthes the instrumental manipulation of the fashion system, which accompanies the commodification of daily dress, operates through the texts of talk shows, magazines, advertisements, designer shows, and everyday discourse. For Barthes, the fashion system as an ideology, attempts manipulation of appearance choices through a variety of semiotic methods which he called "logotechniques." This term specifies the use of ideology for the control of consumption and refers to the general phenomenon of consumer manipulation by the commodity industries principally operating through advertising.

The fashion overlay that colonizes daily life utilizes semiotic properties of language. For example, an everyday necessity, such as waiting for a commuter train to go to work, would be metonymically conflated with the wearing of a particular fashion object, an overcoat, for example, in a visual magazine advertisement. The text which accompanies the advertisement would compound the logotechnique of visual metonymy with associations, such as the statement "A perfect coat to wear while waiting for the train." The logotechniques of fashion discourse supersede the dress code in an attempt to manipulate consumers to buy specific products, not because of need but in order to "look fashionable." Their intentionality makes the texts of fashion a system of communication.

THE SYSTEM OF OBJECTS

There is little doubt that Barthes' work on the fashion system provided the model for Baudrillard's early books. In *Le système des objets*, Baudrillard concerns himself with the way home furnishings and interior decoration have passed from an ersatz, subjective, and personalized activity to one that is highly regulated by a code of design and appearance based on the commodification of household interiors. Baudrillard introduces ideas similar to Barthes but he also generalizes his concerns by connecting to other issues popular at the time in France, such as the role of technology[11] and urbanism[12] in changing everyday life.

In contrast to Barthes, this early book provides a basis for Baudrillard's later postmodern musings, because he explicitly raises the issue of modernity (conceived as an historical epoch) and its affects on the regulation of household interiors using the design concepts of modernism (conceived as a form of art or design), a subject which Barthes ignores in his work on the fashion system. Thus, Baudrillard is less concerned with the power of ideology to control everyday life, and more interested in the general effect of cultural change under the sign of modernity (later postmodernity) which he sees as an inexorable and pervasive shift to the commodification of all cultural objects. This theme is closer to Karl Marx's analysis of the effects of capitalism than is Barthes emphasis on ideology, and Kellner[13] is correct to suggest that Baudrillard's early work supplements Marxian analysis with a semiotics of objects – an important and significant contribution, indeed, that is, unfortunately, still untranslated.

At the very same time in this study, however, Baudrillard lays the foundation for his transcendence of Marxism (which he fully accomplished later on) by demonstrating the power of cultural as opposed to economic change (conceptualized here as the movement of modernity) in the alteration of daily life. The commodification of daily life proceeds as cultural movement, as part of an effort to keep up with others and be "modern." In short, the forms of modernity causing social change operate through the logotechniques of fashion and design, through the coercive power that Saussure, Barthes and, also, Durkheim, understood to be a power of any language, just as they do through changes in "political economy" which are most often taken to be primary by Marxists.

Le système des objets is an exemplary exercise in materialist semiotics. Unlike Baudrillard's later writings, assertions are backed up by concrete examples, theory is explicitly stated, and connections are made between the author's observations and the work of others. As Baudrillard wanders through the typical middle-class household, he concretely demonstrates how a modern system of signification articulates with common everyday objects and commodifies daily life.

The book consists of three parts. The first analyzes what Baudrillard calls "functional objects," which are consumer goods associated with home furnishings. He then considers commodities as projections of the future, such as gadgets and robots, which are advertised as either "the latest" in home furnishings or the future of decor. Finally, he discusses "nonfunctional objects," the antiques, anachronistic marginal commodities and collections that are also found in the middle-class home. For each of these areas, Baudrillard describes the social shift from a traditional to a "modern" way of life which is part of a "new social order," or "hypercivilization." This is also conceptualized as a process of the disenchantment of the traditional world through the hegemonic intrusion of abstract systems of signification tied to fashion and modernist design practices. In other words, Baudrillard's interesting thesis explored in this book is that the commodification of everyday life takes place through the hegemony of the generalizing and differentiating tendencies of the fashion system, commodification and technological innovation.

The functional system

The configuration of the home and its furnishings in the traditional mode represented the domination of paternalism. We access this configuration through childhood memory of the family home which depicts "not an objective world, but the boundaries of a symbolic relation of family life" (p. 26).

The contemporary home is configured by the disenchanting effects of modernity. Each room of the house is a target for the articulation of fashion and modernist home furnishings. Each room is commodified as a separate unit. There are kitchen "sets" for the kitchen, living room "sets" for the living room, and bathroom "sets" for the bathroom. Decor and appearance are structured metonymically, as an ensemble, as well as metaphorically, as a syntagm. As with the conceptualization of "postmodernism," which came much later in Baudrillard's writings, the metonymical relation dominates the system of appearance. The modern decor is structured by the opposition "milieu/position" which is typified according to the general concept of "ambiance," or organized under the sign of ambience (p. 28), i.e., structured as a relational milieu according to the logic of interior design.

Baudrillard notes that the objects remain familiar. They are still chairs, tables, lamps, etc. Thus, the liberation of objects from traditionalism and the emotional, subjective context of daily family life by modernity "is only a liberation of the function of the object, not the object itself" (p. 26). Hence the system of household objects organized under the sign of ambiance constitutes a functional system. Modernist design's emphasis on pure form, on line, on shape, on the fit of the ensemble or decor, liberates the object from the sentimentality of traditionalism through the emphasis on function. Functionality, for example, is expressed in the shift from a "grandfather clock" or the clock as heirloom, to the abstract, functional clock designed according to a particular fashion.

As Baudrillard remarks, however, when objects are freed from affect and reduced to function, people are freed from sentimentality but become only "users" of objects. The transformative shift of modernity creates a set of functional objects as commodities and a status of humans as users or consumers. This transforms the house from the hearth of tradition and historical continuity to a showcase for consumerism and status.

Here Baudrillard draws on earlier work by the planning critic Francoise Choay.[14] The milieu of modernity reduces all meaning to the sign of function. The modern environment is "hyposignifiant," i.e., its symbolism is attenuated. But, he pushes this idea further by showing how the functional space is dominated by the metonymical (i.e., contiguous) relation "which is the basis of modernity." Ambiance is constructed through difference and relation. The modern decor signifies, not through sentimentality and affect, i.e., metaphor, but through interrelation, or intertextuality, by creating a milieu or space. The "meaning" of objects in the home passes from the code of traditionalism, with its deep-level signifieds, to the self-referencing, hyperreal system of appearances based on the play of signifiers alone. The production of meaning through metonymical differences is the mechanism by which the space of the home is structured according to modernist ideology.

Baudrillard comments on what has been lost in the shift from tradition to modernity. The nineteenth-century bourgeois home was filled with mirrors. All images are reflected back to the center reinforcing the unity of space while also amplifying space. Today the use of mirrors in the home has largely disappeared. Modern decor emphasizes separation according to the ensembles of each room. The unity of the home is broken up by modular construction, partitions, and blank walls. Along with the break-up of interior space, clocks have also disappeared. "In the petite bourgeois home the clock often crowns the mantle piece, itself often dominated by a mirror . . . . The tick-tock of a clock consecrates the intimacy of a place – it makes it resemble the interior of our bodies" (p. 33). The home, as body of the family focused toward the center through mirrors, looses its heart – the clock – as the framing piece of the living room.

Modernity transforms personal space not only through the logotechniques of interior design but also through the effects of technology and the desire for technology under the sign of progress. The practice of consumption is altered into a technological practice of the manipulation of objects. We turn things on, adjust them, calibrate them, gauge their output, and arrange them according to specifications. The arrangement of the home changes from the celebration of possession, as among the nineteenth-century bourgeoisie, to the management and manipulation of objects or, as Baudrillard suggests, "a praxis" of location.

Gadgets and the technological society

The system of objects is ruled by the articulation of the logic of interior design and the products of technological society.[15] For Baudrillard, the domination of a technological logic in modernity means the eradication of nature and its historicity or connection to the past. "The goal of a technical society is the bringing into question of the very idea of genesis, the omission of origins, of a given meaning and 'essences' of which old furniture was the concrete symbol" (p. 38). Home furnishings are no longer meant to signify continuity with the past. They are meant to be controlled, managed, manipulated, and inventoried. They can also be sold or junked when "out of style." The old, traditional order is based on the oral structures of historicity – every object has a story. The new technical, modern order is a phallic environment of calculation, functionality, and control: "everything must go together, be functional – no more secrets or mysteries" (p. 46). This phallic order of calculation disenchants the world and privileges the metonymical relation of ambiance or arrangement.

The abstraction of objects in high-tech designs brings to an end "the age old, anthropomorphic status of objects" (p. 66). Technology is an elision of the human gesture which can no longer be perceived in the design of the gadget. Traditional society produced objects that conformed to the use by the human body and were an extension of human physical abilities. Like the ancient scythe or basket, these objects were extensions of the body. Technological gadgets erase all connection to the body. Buttons are pressed, dials are turned, and the work gets done through electronic and mechanical means.

Baudrillard suggests that the functional logic of modernity is amplified by the dominance of technology in its displacement of the humanizing attributes of traditional home furnishings. He states, "Household appliances, cars, etc., require only a minimal participation. Almost as much as the workplace, the home is ruled by regularity of command gestures. The whole body used to be needed for gripping objects, but now only contact (hand, finger or foot) and control (sight, sometimes hearing) are needed.

In brief, only people's 'extremities' participate actively in the functional environment" (p. 68).

In short, the desire for gadgets helps propagate the social changes of modernity. This desire becomes one powerful way individuals are attracted to the new fashions in objects, thus guaranteeing their participation in modern society. Once introduced into the home, gadgets redefine the logic of use. Their forms and deployment are divorced from the morphology of the body. The technological object helps transform decor to abstraction and calculated ambience. According to Baudrillard, the humanized world of the traditional home is transformed into a functional milieu of technique.

The nonfunctional or marginal object

"A whole category of objects seems to escape the system we have just analyzed – the unique, unusual, folk, exotic or antique object [objet ancien]" (p. 95). According to Baudrillard, these objects are also part of modernity and they are most often acquired recently according to the practice of interior design rather than inherited as part of continuity with tradition. As Olalquiaga observes, the "momento mori" has a place in the (post) modern milieu.[16]

The antique stands outside time, hence it has the special function of signifying the passage of time. This is not "real time," according to Baudrillard, but the signifying time of fashion. It is time as cultural index. The antique object, like the system of modern objects, is subjected to a logic of interior design, but it is a separate one that structures the marginal or non-functional elements within the home.

Folk art is a variation on the antique object. The folk object stands outside both time and space. It signifies historicity and otherness. Acquisition of folk objects is the reverse phenomenon of the desire for technologically sophisticated objects by the underdeveloped world (p. 106).

The marginal object is not synchronic or diachronic, it is achronic. It represents a transcendence of the fashion system. "These objects are less objects of ownership than of symbolic intercession, like ancestors. They are an escape from dailyness, and escape is never so radical as in time, it is never so profound as in its own infancy" (p. 106). The marginal object stands outside the myth of progress embodied in modernity.

Baudrillard extends his comments on the marginal object to an explanation for the significance of the "second home." The successful, modern bourgeois purchases a second home in the country. The country home possesses a country decor. Every effort is made to preserve the image of rustic nature. The country home stands outside the timeline of modernity, of progress. "In a civilization in which synchrony and diachrony tend to organize a systematic and exclusive control of the real, a third dimension appears, that is, anachrony" (p. 114). The acquisition of the country home by the successful modern bourgeois contrasts with the desire for a modern home by the less fortunate working classes.

The marginal system: the collection

The anachronistic object stands outside the system of objects to signify the unique dimensions of space and time. The "collection" represents a separate, contrasting dimension to the system of objects. According to Baudrillard, every object possesses two functions: to be used or to be possessed. Modernity tries to reduce the object to its abstract function of use. When technology prevails we have the extreme case of the machine – pure function or pure use value. In opposition, certain objects are important because of their value as possessions. The pure object stripped of its function becomes an object in a collection.

As Baudrillard suggests, the objects of a collection are all equal. They are not distinguished by their function, only their value in the collection. The logic of collection is metonymical – we have only a succession of objects which can always be increased incrementally. You "add" to a collection, the single object never suffices. It is the same when sexual practices are transformed by the logic of possession. "The relation of love dotes on one loved one, while possession is only satisfied by a series of lovers" (p. 116). The activity of collection is a kind of promiscuity of possession and it is always pursued passionately by the collector.

Baudrillard likes the analogy between collecting and a certain kind of sexuality. In fact, he sees collecting as a stage of latent sexual evolution or transition. The formidable phase of collecting is usually during the years between seven and twelve. This corresponds to the latent period prior to puberty (p. 122). According to Baudrillard, the activity of collecting declines after puberty. But, it then re-emerges after the age of 40. This personifies the regression to the anal stage "which is expressed by behaviors of accumulation, order, aggressive retention, etc." (p. 122). In short, with the advent of middle age, when a diminuation of the sex drive is experienced by the neurotic adult, the behavior of collecting appears as a passionately pursued substitute.

The section on collecting in this book is quite entertaining reading. Baudrillard makes a succession of interesting observations about collecting and collectors. He remarks that the collector reaches the heights of passion, not through the acquisition of objects with an intrinsic worth, but through fanaticism. Furthermore, the collected object is the perfect domestic pet. It is an other that is totally controlled. Baudrillard also suggests that, because the collection is animated by the displaced sexual desire of the collector, the ultimate object of the collection is the collector him/herself. Hence, "it is better never to complete the collection always desiring another item" (p. 134). Finally, Baudrillard observes that "The deprivation of the possessive game would be as de-stabilizing to the individual as the denial of dreams. Objects help us to resolve the irreversibility of birth towards death" (p. 134). The collection, like hyperreal simulation, is a never-ending chain, like the chain of signification – the indefinite displacement of one object with another.

A BRIEF NOTE ON POSTMODERNITY

Baudrillard develops several ideas in this first book which figure prominently later on in his postmodern writings, especially the concepts of model and differance. The reduction of affect through the hegemony of interior design as ambiance is accomplished by consumerism which emphasizes decor. The integrating logic of the ensemble expresses itself through the model – the kitchen set, the model room, the model house. Commodification and consumerism imply mechanical reproduction of the object. The model is generalizable to any social status. Consumption as an act becomes the consumption of the model. It is, in short, a simulation.[17]

The hegemony of ambiance means the domination of the metonymical figure in the system of objects. To follow modern decor means relating object to object through the abstract practice of interior design. When meaning is dominated by the paradigmatic axis, it is produced by contiguity. This relation is always one of deferral. In place of the sign conceptualized by Saussure as the unity of the signifier and the signified, we have the sign of deconstruction, the endless deferral of signification, i.e., the relation of signifier to signifier to signifier, and so on.

Difference as differance is always produced by discourse. This is both the discovery of deconstruction and its great limitation.[18] We leave the system of objects and deal with the system of language: writing or speech. The process of differance or the production of meaning through the chain of signification lies at the heart of all logotechniques. Baudrillard illustrates this with regard to the expropriation of colors by the system of interior design. All colors are signified by affective states – warm, cold, cheerful, gloomy – through the discourse of fashion. Yet, the warmth of a color is a functional warmth. Its warmth does not derive from a warm substance but from its difference in relation to other colors. It is a signified warmth that can never be realized, because it cannot change the characteristics of its own matter and be "warm." "What characterizes this warmth is the absence of any heat source" (p. 51). In short, its warmth is a discursive relation. As part of the chain of signification, the discourse of decor belongs to hyperreality.

In Baudrillard's analysis of the system of household objects he shows how a fashion aesthetic that is calculating, phallic, and abstract invades the home with the commodification of everyday life through modernity and converts signifying objects into hyperreal signifiers belonging to a system of interior design. This cultural system is ruled by ambience and it replaces the sentimentality and paternalism of the traditional family home. The modern system of objects supersedes the traditional system in three respects: (a) a change in the primary function of the object from affective associations and use value to ambiance; (b) a change in primary needs from tradition to consumerism; and, (c) a change in the symbolic relation between (a) and (b) from historicity and paternalism to phallic-centered calculation and control under the sign of ambiance (p. 88).

Baudrillard sees the system of objects as being dominated by the logic of metonymy and differance. Unlike Derrida, however, he does not equate reality with the chain of signification; at least, not in this first book. Given time, however, Baudrillard fashions a vision of postmodern life that is nothing more nor less, that is equated with the hyperreal, and which is constituted, like the text of Derrida, through the metonymical play of difference. Like Barthes, something happens to Baudrillard in the 1960s, and he moves to a deconstructionist position, not because of the critique of Saussure, as in the former case, but because of an extreme vision about the commodification of daily life.

In this sense, does the belief that there exists a material world of use values which grounds the symbolic world of sign values in the system of objects belong to modernity alone, that is, to a world that is real not hyperreal? I think not. Material culture and its systems of signification exist in the present conjuncture as well. To be sure, abandoning this premise brings us to the postmodernity of the later Baudrillard.[19] If the present is postmodern, in the sense that the interplay of sign value dominates cultural logic[20] and the hyperreal has replaced reality, it too possesses its own logic of domination which nevertheless still depends on the existence of material objects, and on both their use and exchange values.[21] Sign value, or the status of objects as expressive symbols, remains linked to both the status of objects as possessing use value in daily practice and exchange value in the system of capitalist accumulation. The process by which cultural hegemony is expressed as the reduction of all objects to sign value, does not eliminate either the practices of daily life which are based on use value or the system of capital accumulation which relies on exchange value, as Baudrillard seems to suggest in his later writings. Rather, cultural hegemony is characterized best by the way use values and exchange values are exploited by the postmodern culture of consumption which privileges the image over substance.[22] In short, the transformative properties of sign value depend on materiality and the particular links between the processes of exchange, use, and signification, as Baudrillard shows clearly in this early book.

Baudrillard abandoned the style of analysis, following Barthes, of the articulation between ideology and material life, which he utilized in *Le système des objets.* However, we do not have to travel that same road which involves a journey toward idealism and reductionism in pursuit of an extreme vision – the reduction of all life to the hyperreal in the culture of postmodernity.

The Le *système des objets* is an exemplary exercise in the semiotics of material objects. According to my perspective,[23] the objects of material reality constitute a system of signification. Superimposed on this system and the discourse of daily life is the system of communication belonging to the logotechniques of consumerism and advertising. In the case of the system of household objects, sign value is specified at the connotative level and articulates with use value and exchange value which operate on the functional or denotative level. In this sense both modernity and postmodernity operate as ideologies which articulate with material culture and systems of signification. While, no doubt, there is a "political economy of the sign,"[24] there is also a more mundane political economy of commodity production. One hasn't replaced the other, as Baudrillard maintains; rather, the two are part of the same process of capital accumulation under conditions of postmodernity (or late capitalism).

For example, the needs that govern the use values of daily life are exploited by the logic of commodification because of the logic of capital accumulation which requires exchange value. But, the process of capital accumulation consists of two distinct phases. An initial period that exploits wage labor in the creation of surplus value at the place of work must be followed by a second period during which the value represented by the commodity is realized through the act of purchase. As long as surplus value remains embodied in the unsold object, capital accumulation cannot be realized. The sale of the commodity depends on its exchange value, just as the realization of surplus value depends on its exchange value. If the price of sale does not meet the costs of production, no profit is made.

Capital not only has a problem with production – one that is personified by the class struggle, and that Marx was keenly interested in as we know – but also a problem with the realization of surplus value which depends on the market. It is for this reason that sign value and the connotations of consumerism, or what Baudrillard calls in the present case the system of objects, becomes important in capitalist society. As commodification of daily life proceeds, sign values dominate the culture, and, through the hegemony of consumer culture, everyday life becomes commodified. This is a multi-leveled process that is as characteristic of postmodernity as it is of modernity.

This socio-semiotic approach to material culture has some implications for postmodern theory. The suggestion by Jameson,[25] for example, that postmodernity is a particular hegemonic mode of late capitalism, does not periodize the process of commodification, hence it lacks historical grounding. Jameson's analysis of the appearances or forms of our contemporary culture is quite fascinating, but it fails to specify, at the deep structural level, an adequate periodization of changes in the logic of consumer culture. The latter has privileged the connotative level of the sign, or the image and its symbolic rather than functional value, since the origin of mass advertising techniques during the turn of the century. The cultural dominant of commodification that is hyposignifiant, which replaces the importance of use values in daily life, already existed during modernity, as Baudrillard shows in home furnishings. The image-driven culture of late capitalism, then, is probably less a new hegemonic mode of society than a recent trend of contemporary life. Electronic media techniques and the general speed-up of information processing and assimilation, have simply amplified tendencies which already existed during modernity.

The commodification of everyday life, according to the later Baudrillard, has achieved closure in postmodernity with the collapse of all value into the sign. We no longer have a logic of difference among use values, exchange values, and sign values. As Baudrillard maintains,[26] the realization problem of capital, or the process of consumption, now dominates all political economy. This shift from the production logic of Marx, itself a reduction as Baudrillard, among others, rightly shows, to the consumption logic of Baudrillard's *Simulations*, is also a reduction. In the latter case, and in his more recent work, we are left with a fatalistic vision of postmodern life that cannot escape the modelling logic of signification and the hyperreal.

But, if the realization of capital remains grounded in the threefold process of use value, exchange value, and sign value, as I maintain, then opportunities exist to resist the logic of commodification and the reductionist culture of consumerism. The notion of resistance is counter to the fatalistic vision of Baudrillard's most recent work. Cultural resistance has been chronicled by those commenting on the struggle between capitalism and everyday life;[27] on the concepts of cultural hegemony and counter-hegemony following Gramsci (Birmingham Centre for Contemporary Cultural Studies)[28]; and on the socio-semiotics of popular culture.[29]

Much can be said about this subject, especially now when interesting differences exist among cultural analysts regarding what actually constitutes resistance;[30] however it is not possible to pursue this discussion here. By way of example, however, we can illustrate the concept of resistance. Some early critical writings on adolescent subcultures,[31] for instance, have shown how popular cultural styles of music, appearance, and recreation are not passively received by an undifferentiated mass of teenage consumers, but are worked over and fashioned into active modes of living that answer important questions about adolescent life. The Mod, Skinhead, and Teddy Boy subcultural variants in the United Kingdom, which are forms of resistance, have lasted through several generations. In the United States, Chicano low-rider subcultures resist the speed-up of fashions in the consumer society by raising the symbols of 1950s and 1960s adolescent culture in cars, appearance, and music to iconic status. Rock music "Oldies" and outdated American cars are some of the objects around which the Chicano counter-culture organizes its daily life in resistance to the emphasis on the "new" and "the latest" among the Anglo middle class. These and other examples of resistance would be dismissed by Baudrillard as already stripped of content by virtue of their force as images of resistance, yet the daily life organized with the aid of these objects by the subcultural users and the way taste differences are jealously guarded as differentiators of subcultures, such as in the case of rock music,[32] belies the waning of affect in counter-cultural social forms which resist postmodernity.

Baudrillard's *Le système des objets* describes the specific way commodification of daily life proceeds through the transformation of the home by the practice of interior design. But he fails to distinguish, as Barthes did in *Le système de la mode*, between material culture as a system of signification and the ideological discourse which regulates consumption. By conflating the logic of home decoration as use value which grounds the *modern* system of signification, and, the logotechnical discourse of interior design as fashion, which constitutes a hegemonic system of communication and an ideology of the modern, Baudrillard opens the way for the reductionist vision of postmodernity contained in his most recent writings where the real implodes and disappears in the ideology or hyperreality of the image.

Notes

1 I would like to acknowledge the assistance of Charlotte Stanley in the translation of Baudrillard's *Le système des objets* for this chapter.
2 Jean Baudrillard, *Le système des objets* (Paris: Denoel-Gonthier, 1968).
3 Mark Gottdiener, "Hegemony and Mass Culture: A Semiotic Approach," *American Journal of Sociology*, 90, 5 (1985) 979–1001; *Semiotics and Postmodernism* (Oxford: Blackwell, forthcoming; Mark Gottdiener and A. Lagopoulos, *The City and the Sign* (New York: Columbia University Press, 1986).
4 Claude Levi-Strauss, *Structural Anthropology* (New York: Basic Books, 1963). Mandel, E. 1975. *Late Capitalism.* London: Verso.
5 Roland Barthes, *Elements of Semiology* (London: Cape 1964).
6 M. Krampen, *Meaning in the Urban Environment* (New York: Methuen, 1979); Mark Gottdiener, "Postmodernism and Semiotics," in D. Dickens and A. Fontana, eds., *Postmodernism and Social Inquiry* (New York: Guilford Press).
7 U. Eco, *A Theory of Semiotics* (Bloomington: Indiana University Press, 1976).
8 Roland Barthes, *Semiology; Mythologies* (New York: Hill and Wang, 1972).
9 Roland Barthes, *Le système de la mode* (Paris: Seuil, 1967).
10 R. Konig, *A La Mode: On the Social Psychology of Fashion* (New York: Seabury Press, 1973).

11 J. Ellul, *The Technological Society* (New York: Alfred Knopf, 1964).

12 H. Lefebvre, *Critique of Everyday Life* (London: Verso, 1991 [1947]).

13 D. Kellner, *Jean Baudrillard: From Marxism to Postmodernism and Beyond* (Stanford: Stanford University Press, 1988).

14 Francoise Choay, "Urbanism and Semiology," pp. 160–9, in M. Gottdiener and A. Lagopoulos, eds., *The City and The Sign*. (New York: Columbia University Press, 1986).

15 Ellul, *Technological Society*.

16 C. Olalquiaga, *Megalopolis* (Minneapolis: University of Minnesota Press, 1992).

17 Jean Baudrillard, *Simulations* (New York: Semiotext(e), 1983).

18 See Gottdiener, *Semiotics and Postmodernism*.

19 Baudrillard, *Simulations*.

20 Ibid.; F. Jameson, "Postmodernism, or the Cultural Logic of Late Capitalism," *New Left Review*, 146 (1984) 53–92.

21 See Gottdiener, *Semiotics and Postmodernism*.

22 Ibid.; R. Goldman, *Reading Ads Socially* (New York: Routledge, 1992).

23 Which is referred to as the *socio-semiotic* approach; see Gottdiener, "Hegemony and Mass Culture" and *Semiotics and Postmodernism*.

24 Jean Baudrillard, *For a Critique of the Political Economy of the Sign* (St Louis: Telos Press, 1981).

25 Jameson, "Postmodernism".

26 Jean Baudrillard, *The Mirror of Production* (St. Louis: Telos Press, 1975).

27 Lefebvre, *Critique of Everyday Life*; M. de Certeau, *The Practice of Everyday Life* (Berkeley: University of California Press, 1984).

28 Birmingham Centre for Contemporary Cultural Studies, *Resistance through Rituals*. Working Papers in Cultural Studies, Nos. 7 & 8 (University of Birmingham, 1975); J. Fiske and J. Hartley, *Reading Television* (London: Methuen, 1978).

29 Gottdiener, "Hegemony and Mass Culture"; Goldman, *Reading Ads Socially*.

30 Gottdiener, *Semiotics and Postmodernism*.

31 D. Hebdige, *Subculture: The Meaning of Style* (London: Methuen, 1979).

32 Ibid.; Birmingham Centre, *Resistance Through Rituals*.

2

THE COMMODIFICATION OF REALITY AND THE REALITY OF COMMODIFICATION: BAUDRILLARD, DEBORD, AND POSTMODERN THEORY[1]

Steven Best

> But certainly for the present age, which prefers the sign to the thing signified, the copy to the original, fancy to reality, the appearance to the essence, . . . illusion only is sacred, truth profane. Nay, sacredness is held to be enhanced in proportion as truth decreases and illusion increases, so that the highest degree of illusion comes to be the highest degree of sacredness.[2]

Karl Marx was the first to trace the emergence and historical development of the commodity form, showing how it was the structuring principle of capitalist society. Subsequent Marxists (Lukács, Adorno, Marcuse, *et al.*) have shown how, in a "neo-capitalist" consumer economy, commodification has permeated new realms of experience and social life. In their theories, capitalism has become a reified and self-legitimating system where the object world assumes command and human well-being is defined by the (conspicuous) consumption of goods. Building on this tradition, Jean Baudrillard initially argued that the commodity form has developed to such an extent that use and exchange value have been superseded by "sign-value" that redefines the commodity primarily as a symbol to be consumed and displayed. In his later work, Baudrillard claimed that the semiotic system inscribed at the heart of the entire system of commodities took on an autonomy of its own, that political economy and the era of production were finished, and that a new, dematerialized society of signs, images, and codes had emerged that was governed by a process of "radical semiurgy." In this new postmodern world, images and signs proliferate to the point where previous distinctions between illusion and reality, signifier and signified, subject and object, collapse, and there is no longer any social or real world of which to speak, only a semiotically self-referring "hyperreality."

In his early works, Baudrillard pursued an analysis of commodities and consumer society. Until *The Mirror of Production*,[3] Baudrillard could be described, like Guy Debord, as a neo-Marxist whose project was to retain the basic theoretical framework of Marxism, while supplementing it to account for new forms of domination effected by the creation of a consumer and mass media society. Debord and Baudrillard were doing sociological studies of the new consumer society in France simultaneously in the 1960s. Just as Baudrillard was aware of Debord and his group – the Situationist International, so Debord and his group were aware of Baudrillard.[4] In one text they denounced him as a "decrepit modernist-institutionalist."[5]

But it seems the Situationists were more an influence on Baudrillard than vice versa. They disbanded in 1972, well before Baudrillard had become an important cultural theorist. Baudrillard says that the Situationists were "without doubt the only ones to attempt to extract this new radicality of political economy in their 'society of the spectacle.' "[6] At one time, in fact, Baudrillard considered himself a Situationist: "Pataphysician at twenty – Situationist at thirty – utopian at forty – transversal at fifty – viral and metaleptic at sixty – that's my history."[7] Yet Baudrillard soon rejected the Situationist analysis as itself bound to an obsolete modernist framework based on notions like history, reality, and interpretation, and he jumped into a postmodern orbit that declared the death of all modern values and referents under conditions of simulation, implosion, and hyperreality.

In this chapter I wish to respond critically to Baudrillard's assault on modern theory and modernity. I will trace a trajectory of analysis as it develops from Marx through Debord and the Situationists to Baudrillard, a movement from the society of the *commodity* to the society of the *spectacle* to the society of the *simulacrum*, paralleled by a movement from Marxism to neo-Marxism to post-Marxism. This trajectory also traces a shift from modernity to postmodernity and my discussion intends to elucidate these terms and clarify why it is wrong to speak of postmodernity as an absolute break from capitalist modernity. Where one might speak of the "commodification of reality," I wish to invert this formula to speak, equally as well, of the "reality of commodification" and the world that Baudrillard and his followers claim dissolves in the proliferation of signs.

MARX AND THE DAWN OF ABSTRACTION

A commodity appears, at first sight, a very trivial thing, and easily understood. Its analysis shows that it is, in reality, a very queer thing, abounding in metaphysical subtleties and theological niceties. (Marx)

For Marx, as for Debord and Baudrillard, capitalism represents a rupture in history, the overthrow of the medieval era by a radically secularized modern world and its utilitarian imperatives. In capitalism, we find the dissolution of organic social and natural relations in the development of a fragmenting division of labor and an unprecedented structure where commodity production is the purpose of society and maximization of profit is the purpose of commodity production. Before capitalist society, commodity production existed, but always marginally in relation to other activities. Capitalism is the triumph of the economy over its human producers.

This triumph can be interpreted in terms of inversion and abstraction. Capitalist inversion takes place on several levels beginning with the inversion of subject/object relations and the domination of the subject by the object. "The increase in the quantity of objects is accompanied by an extension in the realm of the alien powers to which man is subjected."[8] Under the capitalist mode of production, the forces of production come under private ownership, commodity production proliferates, a fragmenting division of labor spreads, and subjects are displaced from their life-activity to confront a world of alien objects. Forced to sell his or her labor-power to survive, "the worker sinks to the level of a commodity and becomes indeed the most wretched of commodities,"[9] reduced from the status of qualitative individual to mere exchange value in the form of labor power.

Marx described the alienation of the modern worker as a "loss of [human] reality" where the worker "mortifies his body and ruins his mind."[10] The creative, imaginative, and transformative praxis which defines the "genuinely human" falls into desuetude. Ultimately, the estrangement of the worker from the products and process of production leads to an estrangment from his or her own human potential and from other human beings. Life is lived only in the abstract where hostile, coercive powers rule.

Where the early Marx gave a philosophico-anthropological description of alienation and the inversions it effects, the later Marx of *Capital* described this inversion in "scientific" terms where exchange value assumes primacy over use value. Where once the goal of production was the simple satisfaction of needs, and money was a mediating element, now the realization of surplus value (profit) is the goal of the system, and commodities are mere mediating figures in the valorization of money, no longer tied to commodities except in an accidental way. Before capitalism, exchange is driven through the need for the other's use-value. Capitalism eliminates individual exchange and subordinates use value to exchange value, reversing the hierarchy of value, and establishing exchange value as an independent logic. The goal of commodity production is not the creation of use value, but exchange value, and not exchange value *per se*, but exchange in the form of commodities.

This inversion is rooted in a process of social abstraction that dissolves the concrete and the particular. Abstraction is a result of the logic that assumes hegemony in capitalist society. This logic is based on exchange value and its law of equivalence which dissolves all qualitative differences into the identity of quantitative values. Exchange value solves the problem of exchange – how to trade qualitatively unique goods in fair and equal quantitative ratios which estimate the amount of labor time necessary to produce them. This process, however, results in the quantification of qualitative relations and phenomena, their reduction to a single standard (money). An object becomes a commodity when, over and above its use-value, it assumes an exchange value which allows its trade, putting it within the realm of the quantitative.

The insertion of subjects and objects into an economic calculus transforms them, turns them into abstract entities, strips away their unique characteristics and reduces them to a numerical expression, to a quantitative sign. With the spread of money, commodification, and quantifying logic, a general abstraction process envelops society. "[J]ust as money reduces everything to its abstract form, so it reduces itself in the course of its own movement to something merely *quantitative*."[11] This is not to equate abstraction with commodification alone, for technology and technological reason also are key factors, but the commodity form constitutes an important source of abstraction in its own right and I will focus on it.

With the valorization of exchange value comes the abolition of society – social needs and values – as the aim and referent of production. The organic community, *Gemeinschaft*, is replaced by a fragmentary *Gesellschaft* ruled by exchange value, commodification, and abstract powers. Marx described this inverted world as "perverted, enchanted" and "topsy-turvy." The object of Marx's criticism, of course, was not the commodity *per se*, as a simple object in trade necessary to sustain social existence, but rather its *fetishization* in capitalist conditions of production and exchange, its magnification to the point where it subsumes and mystifies the underlying relations of production. Here, *abstractions* take over, and with them comes the danger of obscuring the nature of social reality, and so a deepening of domination.

As a result of the domination of money, the abstraction inherent in exchange value becomes even greater. In W. F. Haug's words, "As soon as exchange value has become independent in the form of money, the whole exchange value standpoint is provided with the precondition for its independence too."[12] Money provides a means to facilitate and generalize exchange, serving as "a uniform language of valuation."[13] In the most extreme, but quite common, form of trading stocks, there is no earthly referent at all. In finance capitalism, money is made out of money, profit is made through manipulation of abstract figures with no apparent connection to the commodity world already abstracted from social relations and activity.

Once the circulation of capital has been abstracted from sensuous needs and qualities, from any social referent (the referent has become uprooted, privatized, fragmented among competing private interests), once it extends beyond the factories to penetrate all cultural and interpersonal relations, it has a profound corruptive and distorting effect. The inversion that occurs in the economy, and which affects the whole of social life, is then directly transferred to the cultural and personal realm *where commodity fantasy begins*. With money, as Marx has noted, one can possess various human qualities. "That which exists for me through the medium of *money*, that which I can pay for, i.e., which money can buy, that *am I*, the possessor of money. The extent of the power of money is the extent of my power. Money's properties are my properties and essential powers – the properties and powers of its possessor."[14]

Under these conditions of abstraction, where meaning and exchange are abstracted from everyday life (at the same time that reified exchange *is* everyday life), one is able to *buy* qualities – if only in a temporary and illusory way – and the qualitative becomes a function of the quantitative. "Thus, what I *am* and *am capable* of is by no means determined by my individuality. I am ugly, but I can buy for myself the most *beautiful* of women. Therefore, I am not *ugly*, for the effect of *ugliness* – its determinant power – is nullified by money."[15] In a "topsy-turvy" society where human beings are things, things (money) take on human powers. "All the things which you cannot do, your money can do,"[16] and, conversely, what money cannot do seemingly cannot be done.

Detached from a reality of *quid pro quo* where human qualities depend on human powers, removed even from a specific commodity-body, exchange value assumes hyper-abstract powers in the form of money. As a disseminating, corrosive, abstract form, money determines the nature of reality itself and builds its empire on commodity fantasies and illusions. "Being the external, common *medium* and *faculty* for turning an *image* [or, imagination] into *reality* and *reality* into a mere *image* (a faculty not springing from man as man or from human society as society), *money* transforms the *real essential powers of man and nature* into what are merely abstract conceits."[17] Thus, just as money transforms an unreality – the absence of a power or quality – into a reality, so it transforms a reality – the presence of a power or quality – into an unreality. Real powers pale in comparison with the illusory powers one can buy; real needs go unheeded where people pursue the dominant pseudo-need, the need for money.

Thus, in the early Marx, there is already a heightened sense of the desubstantialization process thematized by postmodernists, a vivid description of the beginnings of an abstract commodity phantasmagoria, a process I will term the commodification of reality. The movement and generalization of money and the commodity form is simultaneously the fetishization, mystification, quantification, and, ultimately, dissipation of social reality. But however abstract this inversion process was, Marx understood that it emerged from concrete historical conditions, in the production and reproduction of social life. And, however unreal social reality was becoming, Marx saw that it was also becoming increasingly real, all-too-real with the proletarianization and immiseration of the masses, with "the real subsumption of labor" that mortified the mind and body of the worker. Turning now to the work of Guy Debord and the Situationists, I will trace the development of abstraction and the commodity form, and a parallel development in neo-Marxist theory.

THE SITUATIONISTS: CONSUMPTION, SPECTACLE, AND LATE-CAPITALISM

The commodity can only be understood in its undistorted essence when it becomes the universal category of society as a whole. (Lukács)

Marx astutely identified the first powerful forms of inversion and abstraction that began with an autonomous economy, a self-contained and self-valorizing system of production organized around profit and accumulation imperatives. He saw not only incipient forms of imperialism and monopoly, but also the first manifestations of an emerging consumer society. In what could be an accurate description of today's advertisers, for instance, Marx wrote that the industrial capitalist "puts himself at the service of the other's depraved fancies, plays the pimp between him and his need, excites in him morbid appetites, lies in wait for each of his weaknesses."[18]

While Marx displayed such insights into the new tendencies and developments of the commodity form, he could not have developed any concrete theory of how commodification and abstraction would mature in the twentieth century. The fetishism of commodities that Marx analyzed was only one instance of the fate of all social phenomena, corrupted and homogenized in their subsumption to the rule of exchange value.

In the shift from an early, competitive capitalism, organized around production, to a later form of state monopoly capitalism organized around consumption, media, information, and high-technology, new forms of domination and abstraction appear, greatly complicating social reality. Lukács was the first Marxist to develop a theory of this later moment in social development (although he wrote before the conjunction of consumer/media/information society).[19] Drawing from Max Weber's work, while rejecting his fatalist conclusions, Lukács argued that rationalization, domination, and reification, results of the capitalist production process, led to a greater administration of human beings, and made social relations appear as relations among things, thereby blunting workers' experience of class and the social relations of oppression. Similarly, Horkheimer, Adorno, Marcuse, and others traced the gradual bureaucratization, rationalization,

and commodification of social life. They described how the "culture industry" defused critical consciousness, providing a key means of distraction
and stupefaction, and they developed the first neo-Marxist theories of the
consumer society.

These analyses were the point of departure for Debord and the Situationist
International who saw themselves as the contemporary extension of the
Marxist project. Their program was to theoretically supplement Marx's
critique of capital and the commodity. They attempted to trace the further
development of the abstraction process inherent in commodity production
– "the becoming-world of the commodity and the becoming-commodity of
world."[20] For the Situationists, "late-capitalism" is a rupture in capitalist
organization, but it is still fully accessible to a Marxist interpretation.
Beneath the new forms of domination there is "an undisturbed development of modern capitalism."[21]

Also influenced by Gramsci, the Situationists saw the most recent stage
in social control as based on consensus rather than force, as a cultural
hegemony attained through the transformation of commodity society into
the "society of the spectacle." In this society, individuals consume a world
fabricated by others rather than producing one of their own. Paraphrasing
Marx, Debord said: "In the modern conditions of production, life announces
itself as an immense accumulation of spectacles."[22] The society of the
spectacle is still a commodity society, ultimately rooted in production, but
reorganized at a higher and more abstract level. "Spectacle" is a complex
term which "unifies and explains a great diversity of apparent phenomena."[23] In one sense, it refers to mass media society. But this is the "crudest
and most obvious" definition. More generally, it refers to the vast institutional and technical apparatus of late-capitalism, to all the means and
methods power employs, outside of direct force, to relegate subjects to the
critical and creative margins of society and to obscure the nature and
effects of its distorting power. Under this broader definition the "education" system and the institutions of "representative democracy," as well
as the endless inventions of consumer gadgets, are all integral components
of the spectacular society.

Thus, the spectacle is a tool of pacification and depoliticization; it is a
"permanent opium war" which stupefies social subjects and distracts them
from the most urgent task of real life – recovering the concrete totality of
human activity through social transformation. The spectacular society
spreads its narcotics mainly through the cultural mechanisms of leisure
and consumption, services and entertainment. This structural shift involves
a commodification of previously non-colonized sectors of social life and
the extension of bureaucratic control to the realms of leisure and everyday
life. Drawing from the Frankfurt School conception of a "totally admin-
istered" or "one dimensional" society, Debord states that "The spectacle
is the moment when the commodity has attained the *total occupation* of

social life."[24] Here, exploitation is raised to a psychological level; basic physical privation is augmented by "enriched privation" of higher needs; alienation is generalized, made comfortable, and alienated consumption becomes "a duty supplementary to alienated production."[25]

The shift to a "bureaucratic society of controlled consumption" (Lefebvre) organized around the production of spectacles can be seen as the exploitation of use-value and needs as a means of advancing profit and gaining ideological control over individuals. Throughout early capitalism, where the structural exigencies lay in the forceful exploitation of labor and nature and in defining the worker strictly as a producer, the society of the spectacle also defines the worker as a consumer and works to constitute the worker's desires and needs. In this sense, Debord claims that use-value was resurrected as a referent of production: "In the inverted reality of the spectacle, use value (which was implicitly contained in exchange value) must now be explicitly proclaimed precisely because its factual reality is eroded by the overdeveloped commodity economy and because counterfeit life requires a pseudo-justification."[26] It is not that exchange value no longer dominates, but that use-value is now deployed in an abstract and ideological way. The spectacle resolves a legitimation crisis of capitalism insofar as the stark evidence of power and misery of Marx's time becomes mystified and displaced, while the working class is sufficiently distracted and mollified by the new cultural productions, social services, and wage increases.

The advanced abstraction of the spectacle brings in its wake a new stage of deprivation. Marx spoke of the degradation of *being into having*, where creative praxis is reduced to the mere possession of an object, rather than its imaginative transformation, and where emotions are reduced to greed. Debord speaks of a further reduction, the transformation of *having into appearing*, where the material object gives way to its representation as sign and draws "its immediate prestige and ultimate function" as image.[27] The production of objects *simpliciter* gives way to "a growing multitude of image-objects"[28] whose immediate reality is their symbolic function as image. Within this abstract system it is the *appearance* of the commodity that is more decisive that its actual "use-value."

Where the image determines and overtakes reality, life is no longer lived directly and actively. The spectacle escalates abstraction to the point where we no longer live in the world *per se* – "inhaling and exhaling all the powers of nature" (Marx) – but in an abstract *image* of the world. "Everything that was directly lived has moved away into a representation,"[29] one which secures the false consciousness of enriched alienation. Debord understands abstraction in terms of the philosophization of reality. "The spectacle does not realize philosophy, it philosophizes reality."[30] The realization of philosophy, as conceived by Marx, entailed the abolition of "philosophy" – the destruction of an abstract ideology constituted above and against the concrete conditions of social existence (which none the less determine its form and content) – and the synthesis of theory and practice. The philosophization of reality, on the other hand, separates thought from action as it idealizes and hypostatizes the world. It converts direct experience into a specular and speculative universe of images and signs, where subjects do not constitute their own lives and society but contemplate the glossy surfaces of the commodity world. "The concrete life of everyone has been degraded into a *speculative* universe."[31] Mesmerized by the spectacle, subjects move farther from their immediate emotional reality and desires and closer to the domination of bureaucratically controlled consumption: "the more [one] contemplates the less he lives; the more he accepts recognizing himself in the dominant images of need, the less he understands his own existence and his own desires ... his own gestures are no longer his but those of another who represents them to him."[32]

Within the abstract society of the spectacle, the image becomes the highest form of commodity reification. "The spectacle is *capital* to such a degree of accumulation that it becomes an image."[33] But, as inverted and abstract, the spectacle is simply "the other side of money" and the social relations of capitalism. Earlier, money directly dominated society as the representation of general equivalence, allowing the exchange of incompatible use-values. In "late-capitalism," however, the hegemony of money is indirect, mediated through the production of images which allow a more generalized equivalence. "The spectacle is the developed modern complement of money where the totality of the commodity world appears as a whole, as a general equivalence for what the entire society can be and can do. The spectacle is the money which one *only looks at*, because in the spectacle the totality of use is already exchanged for the totality of abstract representation."[34] Where qualitative differences previously were erased in the serial production of objects, now they evaporate in the stratosphere of images and signs.

Debord thus emphasizes the super-reification of image-objects as a massive unreality, an inversion of reality and illusion. The spectacle is "the autonomous movement of the non-living."[35] It is based on the domination of the intangible world of unreal images over the tangible world of real forces and relations of production, "where the tangible world is replaced by a selection of images which exist above it, and which simultaneously impose themselves as the tangible *par excellence*."[36] The spectacular society is explicitly concerned with the production of illusions and pseudo-forms, with all types of "counterfeit life." It unleashes a spate of unreality – "unlimited artificiality" – whose "cumulative power ... sows everywhere the *falsification of social life*."[37] Within the spectacle, "the satisfaction of primary human needs is replaced by an uninterrupted fabrication of pseudo-needs which are reduced to the single pseudo-need of maintaining the reign of the autonomous economy."[38]

To say that images "impose themselves as the tangible" is to say that they are taken as real. Thus, the converse of the movement of the non-living is the stasis of the living. The actual class divisions of society, for example, are abolished in the spectacle and replaced with signs of unified consumption which address everyone equally as consumers. But, like Marx, Debord saw not simply the blurring of illusion and reality but the authen-tication of illusion as more real than the real itself. "Considered in its own terms, the spectacle is *affirmation* of appearance and affirmation of all human life, namely social life, as mere appearance."[39] The universalization of the commodity form is to be seen as the reduction of reality to appear-ance, its subsumption to commodity form, its subsequent *commodification*.

Along these lines, as I will show, there is a remarkable congruence with Baudrillard's key themes, specifically his notions of radical semiurgy, im-plosion, and hyperreality. But Debord was more a good Hegelian-Marxist than a proto-Baudrillardian. Like Marx, as much as Debord emphasized the commodification of reality, he also emphasized the reality of commodification. Despite the pronounced emphasis on the artificiality of the spectacle, Debord refused to abandon the attempt to interpret and change social reality. Debord peered into the abyss of a reified unreality but drew back to report and critique what he had seen; there is an "implosion" (Baudrillard) of opposites, but the separate poles retain their contradictory identity; illusion overtakes reality, but reality resurfaces precisely where it is most absent; alienation has divided the essential unity of the social and the individual, but the whole can be regained at a higher level if the historical subject – the proletariat – becomes conscious and realizes its revolutionary objectivity.[40]

It was the task of Jean Baudrillard to declare this neo-Marxist frame-work a fiction, to push the analysis of abstraction and inversion to its ultimate consequences, to obliterate the subject and embrace the object, to cross that threshold where opposites lost their identity – where truth ceases to exist, politics dies with the collapse of the social, and reality disappears altogether. This threshold point is the doorway from modernity to postmodernity.

BAUDRILLARD: DEATH OF THE REAL

> Abstraction today is no longer the map, the double, the mirror or the con-cept. Simulation is no longer that of a territory, a referential being, or a substance. It is the generation by models of a real without origin or reality: a hyperreal. The territory no longer precedes the map. Henceforth, it is the map that precedes the territory . . . it is the map that engenders the territory.
>
> (Baudrillard)

With Baudrillard we move to a whole new era of social development: beyond Marx, beyond the Situationists, beyond modernity. We leave behind the society of the commodity and its stable supports; we transcend the society of the spectacle and its dissembling masks; and we enter the society of the simulacrum, an abstract non-society devoid of cohesive relations, social meaning, and collective representation. For Baudrillard, postmodernity marks the horizon where modern dynamics of growth and explosion have reached their limits and begun to draw inward and absorb themselves, resulting in an implosive process devouring all relational poles, structural differences, conflicts and contradictions, and referential finalities.

Baudrillard's work can be seen as an attempt to assess the catastrophic fallout of the abstraction process traced by Marx and Debord. Whereas Marx described the reduction of materiality into quantitative commodities and Debord described the absorption of the commodity world into a specular empire of images, Baudrillard describes an even more advanced state of abstraction where the object is absorbed altogether into the image and dematerializes in closed cycles of semiotic exchange. Baudrillard theorizes a cybernetic society based on consumption, media, information, and high-technology where exchange occurs at the level of signs, images, and information, thereby dissolving the distinction between "superstructure" and "base" and deeply problematizing the classical theory of surplus value, no longer definable in the simple terms of the unpaid labor of an industrialized proletariat.

Emphasizing late-capitalism as a rupture in the old mode of organization, Baudrillard's work was well-distanced from classical Marxists, but much akin to the Situationists, whom he credited for having grasped consumption as the new form of domination. But the early Baudrillard broke with the Situationists on both theoretical and political grounds. He understood contemporary society not in terms of spectacle, but "sign-exchange-value," rooting the development of the commodity in the structural logic of the sign. Baudrillard sometimes spoke of the "spectacle," but only provisionally. He rejected the term for two reasons: because it implies a subject-object distinction which he feels implodes in a hyperreality, and because the Situationists theorize the spectacle as an extension of the commodity form, rather than the instantiation of the political economy of the sign, or, as theorized in his later writings, of radical semiurgy and simulation models.

In his early work, Baudrillard claims that the "political economy" theorized by Marx is first and foremost a *semiological revolution*: a massive restructuration and reduction of complex (pre-capitalist) symbolic formations to the rationalized formulae of industrialized society. "Political economy is this immense transmutation of all values ... into economic-exchange value. Everything is abstracted from [the symbolic] and reabsorbed into a world-market."[41] Abstraction occurs not in the shift from "concrete" to "abstract" labor, as Marx analyzed it, but rather in the passage from "symbolic exchange" to "production" and "work." Political economy, a reduction of symbolic ambivalence to rationalized equivalence, breaks with the symbolic organization of exchange. Its fundamental fact is not the exploitation of labor, but, more generally, the rationalization and functionalization of the entire world.[42]

Baudrillard interprets the advance of political economy as a two-sided process of increasing semiotic abstraction. The first stage of political economy (early capitalism) is the *instantiation* of the sign-form, the initial reduction of the symbolic onto the procrustean bed of economic value. This early historical form of the sign is a relatively primitive structure organized around the binary opposition of use-value/exchange value. The second phase of political economy (late capitalist consumer society) is the *generalization and complexification* of the sign form, its extension throughout the entire culture and environment and its mutation into sign-exchange value. Here use and exchange value still remain, but the commodity is produced, distributed, and consumed for its conspicuous social meaning. The object is converted into a mere sign of its use, now abstract and divorced from physical needs. The whole cycle of production, distribution, and consumption is converted into a semiotic system of abstract signifiers with no relation to an objective world. This is a new stage of abstraction, a dematerialization of the world through semiurgic (re)processing.

The structural prerequisite of sign-exchange value is the autonomization of the signifier. In this phase of political economy, the relative unity and stability of the industrial world/sign breaks apart. No longer constrained by an objective reality, or tied to some signified in a simple binary relation, the signifier is free to float and establish its own meanings through its manipulation in coded differences and associative chains (as occurs in advertizing). Freed from any stable relationship with a signified, where the sign structure points to a distinct referent in the world, the signifier becomes its own referent and this autonomization becomes the basis of semiological domination. The commodity-form is eclipsed by the "sign-form," and subsequently "bears no relation to any reality whatever: it is its own pure simulacrum."[43] Signification is now radically relativized and anything can pass as "meaning" or "reality."

The hegemony of the sign which appears in "late-capitalism" is not an extension of the commodity, as Debord saw it, but rather the unfolding of a more dominant logic of which the commodity was only an initial form and alibi. Lacking an adequate semiotic perspective, bound with Marx to the mirror of production, Debord failed to grasp "the passage from the form-commodity to the form-sign, from the abstraction of the exchange of material products under the law of general equivalence to the operationalization of all exchanges under the law of the code. With this passage to *the political economy of the sign*, it is not a matter of a simple 'commercial prostitution' of all values [as Marx says] . . . It is a matter of the passage of all values to exchange-sign value, under that hegemony of the code. That is, of a structure of control and of power much more subtle and more totalitarian than that of exploitation. *For the sign is much more than a connotation of the commodity*, than a semiological supplement to exchange value."[44]

In Baudrillard's scheme, the sign is the secret source and telos of the commodity. "All the repressive and reductive strategies of power systems are already present in the internal logic of the sign."[45] The referential world of the commodity – needs, use-value, and labor – was only a historical passageway of a radical semiurgy which aims at the liquidation of society and the real, their displacement through structural codes and signs. The real source of abstract power, then, lies not in the commodity, nor in technology, but in the autonomous development of the sign, whose genealogy Baudrillard traced in *Simulations*.

Under conditions of radical semiurgy and implosion, Baudrillard claims that not only are political economy and the era of production dead, but also more recent theorizations of the disciplinary society and the spectacle itself are obsolete: "We are witnessing the end of perspective and panoptic [disciplinary] space (which remains a moral hypothesis bound up with every classical analysis of the 'objective' analysis of power) and hence of the *very abolition of the spectacle* ... We are no longer in the society of the spectacle which the situationists talked about, nor in the specific types of alienation and repression which this implied."[46] Baudrillard's point is that the distinctions and assumptions Foucault's and Debord's analyses depended upon – the subject/object distinction, a subject of alienation or repression, and objective reality – have been obliterated. Baudrillard claims we are in a radically new situation of maximal implosion more resembling a DNA call "in which the opposing poles of determination vanish according to a nuclear contraction" programmed by the code.[47]

The inversion of illusion and reality that Marx and Debord described is now radicalized, finalized, pushed to its highest degree. Baudrillard's postmodern world could be described well in Debordian terms – "the affirmation of all human life ... as mere appearance"[48] – with the key proviso that there is no longer a real to be recovered behind the illusion (and so there is no illusion either). Here Baudrillard drew a crucial distinction between dissimulation and simulation. Both terms involve a feigning and a faking, but where dissimulation masks reality, and so ultimately reaffirms it, simulation devours the real – the representational structure and space it depends on – and, like a grinning Cheshire cat, leaves behind nothing but commutating signs, self-referring simulacra which feign a relation to an obsolete real.

The hyperreal is the end result of a historical simulation process where the natural world and all its referents are gradually replaced with technology and self-referential signs. This is not to say that "representation" has simply become more indirect or oblique, as Debord would have it, but that

– where the subject/object distance is erased, where language no longer coheres in stable meanings, and where signs no longer refer beyond themselves to an existing, knowable world – representation has been surpassed. The real, for all intents and purposes, is vanquished when an independent object world is assimilated to and defined by artificial codes and simulation models. The "precession of the model" is what "puts an end to the real."[49]

THE REALITY OF COMMODIFICATION: CRITIQUE OF DEBORD AND BAUDRILLARD

The encounter between Debord and Baudrillard is a confrontation between modern and postmodern theories. At stake is nothing less than the nature of contemporary society and the possibility of radical social transformation. Baudrillard's provocation to modern theory is the claim that the era of modernity is over and, therefore, that the theories, categories, and politics of the modern era are no longer relevant. In particular, Baudrillard proclaims the demise of political economy and the obsolescence of Marxist critique in the new era of simulation and hyperreality. As the following discussion will note, while Baudrillard develops some important insights into the nature of the current world, his positions are deeply flawed and Debord's more dialectical stance is generally superior.

Debord's concept of the spectacle contains the advantages of Baudrillard's concepts without also suffering their defects. Against Baudrillard's decontextualized analysis of hyperreality, Debord situates the spectacle within the framework of advanced capitalism and its structural imperatives of accumulation, growth, and profit. As we have seen, while Baudrillard initially interrelated the political economies of signs and commodities, he later forfeited this rich analysis to analyze signs, codes, images, and culture in general abstracted from capitalist social institutions.

Despite the proliferation of simulacra, hyperreality, and artificiality of all forms in the age of electronic mass media, I think contemporary society is better interpreted as an *intensification* of (capitalist) modernity, rather than a wholly new "postmodernity." The current social form Baudrillard tries to describe is best understood as *a generalized extension of capitalism* – a more abstract and imagistic mode of commodity production (Debord), a higher realization of fundamental structuring principles (Mandel), "the cultural logic of late-capitalism" (Jameson), or as part of a new stage of "technocapitalism" (Kellner).

Thus, the dissolution of the social and the real has its roots in the reified economy, where abstraction finds its first support and nourishment. I believe it is best to see "postmodernity" as a *specific phase* in an *inversion and abstraction process* which proceeds *through the commodity-form and capitalist social relations*, assimilating first the physical object, then the entire sphere of culture and everyday life, extending to the commodified exchange of images, signs, and events in a "postmodern" mass-media society. Thus, I believe our current era can be fruitfully understood through a *qualified* use of Baudrillard's key categories: hyperreality, simulation, and implosion. But these concepts do not require us to renounce the whole modern lexicon; we can acknowledge the conceptual advances of Baudrillard's theorizations of media and semiotics, while rejecting their hyperbolic phrasing and abstraction from political economy.

I find a useful analogy in Poulantzas' concept of "social formation."[50] This concept was meant to point out that the "capitalist mode of production" is an abstraction which masks the existence of other modes of production which exist *simultaneously* with capitalism, if only as marginalized moments. Similarly, Baudrillard is wrong when he says we are no longer within a disciplinary society, or a society of the spectacle, but are completely within a fully processed stimulatory, cybernetic, post-capitalist society where all distinctions such as between subject and object are obliterated. Just as a feudal mode of production can co-exist with capitalism, so, for example, can disciplinary or "spectacular" forms of power co-exist with the "dead power" of simulation. What we see today is not discipline *or* simulation, the society of the spectacle *or* the world of the panopticon, but a complex interplay of various mechanisms of social control that include discipline, spectacle, simulation, and the classic overt violence of the state.

As evident by the continued barrage of fashion and advertising as well as the furor over gays in the military, capitalist society continues to depend on the disciplining and normalization of identities to maintain its "moral" order. The imposition of work as a mode of discipline has advanced, rather than decreased, as the average hours of the working week increase. Certainly, the phenomena of simulation, hyperreality, and implosion are prevalent today. When Judge Wapner is accepted as a legal authority and Marcus Welby as a real doctor, when history becomes recoded in the form of docudrama, or when the doors of perception open into the disembodied world of cyberspace, it is clear that the codes of real and unreal have become confused. Perhaps more than anything else, the Gulf War showed the incredible power mass media has in constructing "reality." Although the devastating effects of the Gulf War on the Iraqi people and the environment were all too real, the true enormity of the war was buried in the barrage of media images which coded the war as the struggle of Good against Evil and helped to mobilize the public in favor of the war. The fact that "smart" bombs, so often shown hitting their target with "surgical" precision, in reality usually missed their targets was merely one overt example of the conversion of falsehood into "truth" and the sanitization of barbarism by the media.[51]

Against Baudrillard, simulation and hyperreality ultimately cannot be divorced from the larger analysis of capitalism and political economy. A postmodern implosive event such as the erasure of boundaries between news and entertainment in television should be seen not as the fated effect of some autonomous "code," as Baudrillard sees it, but rather as the effect of intense rating competition among the networks which compels them to package the news in a more visual, dramatic, and interesting way, more easily consumed.[52] Similarly, one could see the implosion of identities, gender and otherwise, as a result, at least in part, of the fashion industry and its economic and ideological function within capitalism, serving both to engulf the individual within a continuous cycle of commodity consumption (where the self must continually renew and recyle its own images) and to legitimate the society based on commodity production.

Unlike Baudrillard, who rejects *all* philosophical frameworks (save his own hyper-poststructuralism), proclaiming the death of hermeneutics in the implosion of depth into surface, message into medium, and dialectics in a cyberblitzed erasure of difference and contradiction, Debord maintains a *dialectical hermeneutics* which seeks to decipher and critique the underlying basis of a frozen history and social order.

This means Debord: (1) holds onto a "dissimulation" thesis and so thinks that referential reason and its reality principle (a knowable world existing independent of consciousness) remain intact and recuperable; (2) maintains the link between cultural production and the system of political economy determined by the capitalist mode of production; and (3) attempts to apply theory toward the revolutionary transformation of individual subjects and capitalist society.

Baudrillard, I have shown, came to reject all of these claims. He pushed the Debordian framework, where reification and mechanization are so strongly emphasized, to the point where dissimulation becomes simulation; complex, multi-dimensional reality becomes no more than a stage set; and revolution is an impossibility or strategic illusion. For Baudrillard, the reified images of postmodernity are no longer simply *abstract* capital, they move beyond capital, *beyond representation*, into the realm of pure signs, dead power, and hyperreality. Just as Aristotle thought the pre-Socratics were groping toward his conception of causality, so Baudrillard might think Debord was striving toward his conception of hyperreality, unable to make the decisive moves.

But what prevents Debord from abandoning Marxism – its commitment to hermeneutics, political economy, a reality principle, and the possibility of social transformation – is not any failure of nerve, some post-catastrophic "panic," but his sharp *dialectical sense and skills*: his dual insistence on the unreality of reality and the reality of unreality, the commodity within a distorted world and a distorted world within the commodity, the true within the false, and the historical within the eternal.

Where Baudrillard surrenders to the surface of the simulacrum, Debord seizes on the most reified aspect of the commodity *as its most revelatory source of meaning.* Just as Marx discovered congealed human value in money, and from there identified the whole social basis of exploitation, Debord critically deciphers the congealed image-object, penetrates its reified surface, and situates it within its context of social and historical relations. Debord maps out the most advanced stage in reification, but, he would argue, no object is fully opaque or inscrutable, standing outside of an impoverished social context *which it cannot ultimately refer to, betray, and be projected against.* The commodity shows us a distorted world, but "The world of the commodity is [also] . . . shown for *what it is*;"a "separate power developing in itself . . . and working for an ever-expanding market."[53]

Where Debord's strategy reminds us of the ultimately antagonistic, conflictual, and contradictory aspects of a social reality open to critique and transformation, Baudrillard's radical rejection of referentiality is premised upon a one-dimensional, No-Exit world of self-referring simulacra. But, however reified and self-referential postmodern semiotics is, signs do not simply move in their own signifying orbit. They are historically produced and circulated and while they may not translucently refer to some originating world, they none the less can be socio-historically contextualized, interpreted, and critiqued.

Through Debord's work, we can grasp a point of singular importance: *self-referentiality does not entail hyperreality.* Signs, images, and objects are not inscrutable and hermetic simply because they no longer stand within a classical space of representation. It is not that one signifer brings us a "real" world and another doesn't, but that one occludes a larger social context more than another, that contextualization may be more difficult in one case than another. However self-referential and abstract the signifers, a critical hermeneutics can uncover their repressed or mystified social content and social relations.[54]

Debord is right then to insist that "The spectacle is not [just] a collection of images, but a social relation among people, mediated by images."[55] While Debord did not provide as powerful an account of postmodern media and signification as Baudrillard did, and perhaps too closely subordinated the sign to the commodity, he was right to insist that, at some level, the spectacle is "the other side of money"[56] and so of capitalist social relations. For Baudrillard, however, the sign develops according to its own autonomous logic, and his one-sided analysis is decontextualizing and depoliticizing, serving to exonerate the "captains of consciousness."

While dialectical hermeneutics does not posit a *Ding-an-sich* discoverable beyond a historical horizon and unmediated by language, it rightly tries to recover the distinction between reality and illusion as the preliminary basis for a political criticism. It is the work of the culture industry to erase this distinction and it should be the work of radical criticism to recover it.

This hermeneutical project entails a reconstructed notion of "representation." While Baudrillard cogently problematizes certain realist views of representation (e.g., those developed in the seventeenth century, where language is seen as the "mirror of nature" or the realist fictions of our present-day media) and illuminates recent mutations in the sign brought on by media and advertising, he wrongly rejects other possible forms of "representation," such as that which Fredric Jameson has recently attempted to develop in his notion of "cognitive mapping."[57]

To pass from the collapse of modern theory to the thesis of radical simulation and implosion, from the fragmentation of meaning to the "end of meaning," is too hasty a move and obscures the ways in which we still can and must configure our world, not in an act of pictured reflection, but rather in a theoretical and critical analysis which attempts to grasp the constitutive relations of society and decode their ideological operations. In a critical hermeneutics the surface appearance of things is unmasked to reveal not the "real" itself, which remains a dialectically mediated category, but the social forces behind these appearances, the actors, groups, policy-makers, agendas, and institutions still identifiable and subject to a critically informed resistance. This suggests that "simulation" can be critically deconstructed and resolved into (mere) "dissimulation." There are different realities for different social actors: what may be "hyperrreal" for one will be patently ideological for another.

Thus, not Baudrillard's fatalistic formula – "this impossibility of isolating the process of simulation"[58] – but Godard's empowering suggestion – "trace the images back to their sources" – should be the impulse behind a critical mapping of the postmodern terrain. Baudrillard's exaggerated articulation of potentially useful concepts demands that we speak not only of the commodification of reality, the dissolution of the real through the movement of the commodity form, but *the reality of commodification and the social forces behind it.*

This critical reversal, implicit in Debord's dialectical hermeneutics, foregrounds what postmodern theory consistently obscures: *the continued existence of the capitalist mode of production, consumer society, the culture industry, and coercive violence* in the repression and determination of social being. Debord insists upon the reality of the spectacle as : (1) an institutional apparatus governed by real social classes; (2) an ideology, derived from real social conditions, which "has become actual, materially translated"[59] and which (3) possesses a real motivating force of "hypnotic behavior." Thus, Debord is able to analyze social domination and class oppression. Baudrillard, by contrast, obscures *the profound misery of the present age.* To employ Debord's useful distinction, "the reality of commodification" refers both to *privation* (the reality of physical exploitation, suffering, hunger, and homelessness throughout the world), and *enriched privation* (the impoverishment of everyday life under the power of hyper-alienated leisure and culture).

The critique of Baudrillard's postmodern thesis is necessary insofar as such extreme versions of postmodern theory conjoin with capitalism to obscure the most vicious and banal aspects of a violence no less real for being media-tized, and nihilistically renounces the capacities of active subjects. Debord's strategies can be likened to those of Marcuse who, in Jameson's words, reminds us "that salvation is by no means historically inevitable, that we do not even find ourselves in a prerevolutionary, let alone a revolutionary, situation, and that the total system may yet ultimately succeed in effacing the very moment of the negative, and with it of freedom, from the face of the earth."[60]

But this becomes a call to action, not an excuse for despair. What can give impetus to such a radical politics is the fact that while negativity is largely contained, the negation of life is still experienced, and this experience can be *strategically heightened*: "the critique which reaches the truth of the spectacle exposes it as the visible *negation* of life, as a negation of life which *has become* visible."[61] And while postmodern culture and technology portend new modes of domination, they also provide new political possibilities and structural openings (e.g., a radical appropriation of new communication technologies or the implosive erosion of traditional identities and hierarchical relations).

Thus, just as the spectacle occludes history, *history haunts the spectacle* – insofar as it can be recovered in a radical critique which exposes the deprivations of the contemporary world. The spectacle degrades social existence more than ever, but it cannot fully eclipse the experience of this degradation and so remains vulnerable to a politics of counter-memory (Foucault) and utopian projection. The recovery of a time before and after the spectacle is an important part of a renewed critical awareness.

In their cultural politics, Debord and the Situationists maintained a link to "real" or "authentic" needs. Baudrillard, of course, denied *all* needs, and saw "primary" needs as only the "alibi" of secondary needs and the consumer system produced and reproduced through the ideology of needs.[62] While Baudrillard provides a powerful critique of certain metaphysical discourses of need, such as we find in traditional political economy, and shows how use-value too can become fetishized,[63] thereby supplementing Marx and Debord's theorization of the commodity in important ways, his rejection of needs *in toto* is an idealist move which denies the physical body. His error here is a failure to distinguish between the social *mediation* of needs and the social *construction* of needs (all needs are socially mediated, but not all needs are socially constructed), and to see how historically created needs could be positive (as Marx well saw) or employed as "surplus consciousness" to subvert the commodity system.[64]

Clearly, we need not articulate a metaphysics of nature or human essence to reject the radical post-structuralist position and construct some basis for political struggle. The alienation model can receive different articulations, not all of which are metaphysical or "humanist." Insofar as we can speak of unrealized *historical* possibilities, for example, we can retain the critical concept of alienation without positing a human essence, and so retain a normative impulse which provides the power behind any vision of an alternative future. With Debord, we must assert and reassert "the *absolute wrong* of being relegated to the margin of life"[65] when human beings are capable of so much more. We must continue to see that "survival" today, where it is not in literal danger, is largely an alienated "enriched survival" of depleted subjectivity. Where capitalism has shown itself capable of buying off radical consciousness, through a slight redistribution of the economic pie, radical critique must continue to focus on the full extent of human potential, the degree to which this has been falsified under conditions of relative leisure and comfort, and how its full development requires an altogether different social order than is possible under capitalism.

For Debord, in sum, the late-capitalist world remains *accessible to interpretation* and *vulnerable to active transformation*. The power of postmodern culture is by no means assured. Where Baudrillard would have us believe in the "fantastic perfection" of the schemes of control,[66] Debord's work serves to remind us that the capitalist economy and culture is defined through cycles of satisfaction and dissatisfaction, and that commodity logic continually breaks down and has to be reinvented, commodity by commodity. "In the image of the society happily unified by consumption, real division is only *suspended* until the next non-accomplishment in consumption."[67] Accordingly, we need to remain vigilant to the "new signs of negation multiplying in the economically developed countries" that "already enable us to draw the conclusion that a new epoch has begun: now, after the workers' first attempt at subversion, *it is capital abundance which was failed.*"[68]

A dialectical analysis, for example, could seek the contradictions within commodity semiotics and locate the moments where these strategies fail and meet subject resistance. The aesthetic promise of the commodity constantly gives way to a rude *reality*, an unsurpassable lifeworld where money can*not* buy everything and mystified signifiers are irrelevant to actual human needs. Within postmodern consumer culture, subjects wear designer jeans yet remain lonely and unhappy; the spectacle is ubiquitous but people are still bored; everyday life is shit *and people know it.*

Thus, the fundamental goal of Situationist praxis was to reconstruct society and everyday life to overcome division and fragmentation in the spectacle. "With the generalized separation of the worker and his products, every unitary view of accomplished activity and all direct personal communication among producers are lost."[69] The recovery of active existence was possible only through the destruction of spectacular relations and the electronic media which fostered "unilateral communication."[70] Both Debord and the early Baudrillard thematized the loss of genuine communication and social relations in the age of electronic media and information.[71] For both, the electronic media represented a new stage in abstraction where interpersonal relations become technologically mediated. Both were concerned with authentic communication and a more vivid and immediate reality apart from the functional requirements of rationalized society. For Baudrillard, this entailed a destruction of all media, for their function is precisely to *mediate*, to prevent genuine communication, which, in a strange Rousseauian metaphysics of presence, he conceived to be symbolic and direct, non-mediated. Debord's conception of media as "unilateral communication" is similar.[72] Both essentialize media technology as inherently oppressive and unilateral, and thereby ignore the possibilities of alternative media.

Moreover, Debord included bureaucratic forms of "radical" political organization (Leninism) within the sphere of spectacular relations, seeing that non-democratic leftist structures also pacified individuals and subjected them to the rule of alien powers. In opposition to the concept of a "Vanguard Party," Debord argued for Councils as the proper mode of organization: "Only there is the spectacular negation of life negated in its own turn."[73]

Although Debord rejected some aspects of orthodox Marxism, he uncritically replicated old-fashioned workerism which privileged the working class as the revolutionary subject of history, an anachronism which New French Theorists such as Foucault, Deleuze, and Guattari rejected in favor of a more decentralized struggle of multiple groups. In *The Mirror of Production*, Baudrillard too embraced a concept of micropolitics organized around women, blacks, and other groups that he thought lay outside of the code of political economy. Baudrillard very soon abandoned any hope of political change, however, and found solace in nihilism.

For Baudrillard, there is no one to turn to, nowhere to go, and nothing to be done. Taking poststructuralism to its ultimate conclusions, Baudrillard leaves us paralyzed and without *any* ground to articulate opposition. Indeed, we cannot even draw the most elementary distinctions, such as between Left and Right. And any imaginable opposition to the cybernetic order is *a priori* rejected as alibi, simulated negativity, just another route of social reproduction. We are left with, if anything at all, the antithesis of a Gramscian politics of counter-hegemony, the "fatal strategies" of a pata-politics which asserts that the "system's own logic" is "the best weapon against it."[74] Baudrillard's work describes less the actual nature of our contemporary world than his own entombment within an increasingly bizarre theoretical orbit; the ideological perspective of a middle-class intellectual enmeshed in a very specific mode of experience divorced from the complex realities of diverse groups of people and their daily struggles; a symptom of the post-1968 disillusionment with the radical project, a French replay of the postwar conservatism of American ex-radicals. If reification is the transformation of the world into an occulted movement of objects and signs without social relations, this is precisely the task that Baudrillard's work helps to accomplish. His work erases the institutional forms of advanced capitalism which seem to have determined his discourse to such an extent as to (mis)lead him to conclude that capitalism no longer exists. Baudrillard's insistence on the hermetic nature of postmodern simulacra is better seen as the introjection and projection of the capitalist imaginary – the dream of seamless closure, complete mystification, and perfected hegemony – than an accurately descriptive thesis. Baudrillard advances a superimplosive postmodern theory which confuses *tendencies* of contemporary society with a *finalized state* of affairs.

DEBORD'S DEFECTION

Yet Debord eventually succumbs to the same problem. So far our contrast has been with the early Debord and Baudrillard. While I have shown important similarities between Debord and the early Baudrillard, I have also shown that Debord pursued a similar analysis of a society dominated by signs, images, and falsehoods to a different conclusion and did not abandon an oppositional stance. But if we turn to Debord's recent reflections on his earlier work, to his own later stance in the 1980s, writing in the same pessimistic climate as the later Baudrillard, we find an abandonment of his earlier revolutionary stance, the loss of the dialectical tension characterizing his earlier work, and the taking up of a position far closer to Baudrillard's defeatism and nihilism.

In the first decade after the publication of *The Society of the Spectacle*, Debord maintained his belief in "the inevitable fall of all cities of illusion"[75] and the possibility of revolution through the creation of autonomous proletariat assemblies. He congratulated himself that every thesis in his book remained true and nothing was contradicted by the development of historical events.[76] In his *Comments on the Society of the Spectacle*, however, written a decade later, a full twenty years after his original reflections, Debord's confidence cracked and his theses, he implies, have been falsified.

His main conclusion is that "the spectacle has ... continued to gather strength," that it has "learnt new defensive techniques"[77] and that it has largely absorbed whatever critical opposition had earlier opposed it from the quarters of everyday life. Having had two more decades to penetrate into the mass psyche, the spectacle has not only been entended quantitatively, it has also changed qualitatively, developing a new hybrid form. Earlier, Debord distinguished between two forms of the power of the spectacle: the "concentrated" dictatorial form and the "diffuse" form. The former instance found its model in Soviet Russia, or perhaps in Orwell's *1984*, and operates through overt oppression. The later instance was perfected in the USA, is aptly represented in Huxley's *Brave New World*, and involves a more subtle form of power based on libidinal and psychic control and seduction. Debord now finds that there is a third form of spectacular power, the "integrated spectacle" pioneered by France and Italy, which combines basic aspects of the concentrated and diffuse forms and therefore represents a more formidable power than either form by itself.

As its name suggests, Debord finds that the integrated spectacle has totally insinuated itself into social reality and everyday life and has abolished the distinction between the false and the true: "When the spectacle was concentrated, the greater part of surrounding society escaped it; when diffuse, a small part; today, no part. The spectacle has spread itself to the point where it now permeates all reality."[78] This development represents both the "globalisation of the false" and the "falsification of the globe." With the extension of capitalist institutions, "there remains nothing, in culture or in nature, which has not been transformed, and polluted, according to the means and interests of modern industry. Even genetics has become readily accessible to the dominant social forces."[79]

References to genetic engineering and "the spectacle's *iron heel*"[80] – a phrase which he previously could not have written, since the spectacle was by definition a means of hegemony – suggest that, indeed, Debord is describing the unified world of Orwell and Huxley. These statements show that Debord has abandoned the dialectic tension between the true and the false, history and the eternal, power and struggle, and has lapsed into a position akin to the later Baudrillard. Thus, Debord writes of the "end of history" with the loss of historical memory and the instantiation of an eternal present.[81] Taking up the Baudrillardian theme of the end of meaning and society with the implosion of meaning in the masses, Debord describes the complete dissolution of the public sphere due to "the crushing presence of media discourse,"[82] the loss of critical and argumentative skills, the increase of censorship, and the perfection of the art of propaganda and disinformation.[83] Where Baudrillard found that political scandal was merely an alibi for a system that was thoroughly corrupt, and thus served the function of suggesting that there was, somewhere, a non-scandalous politics, Debord goes even further to say that "scandal is ... archaic"[84] where no one can criticize, no one cares, and absolute power rules absolutely.

Thus, in the world of the integrated spectacle, where images and iron boots rule side-by-side, where consumer markets flourish along with techniques of state terror, there is little or no chance of social reform or revolution: "We have dispensed with that disturbing conception, which was dominant for over two hundred years, in which society was open to criticism or transformation. Not thanks to any new arguments, but quite simply because all argument has become useless. From this result we can estimate not universal happiness, but the redoubtable strength of tyranny's tentacles."[85] No more talk of the inevitability of the fall of capitalism; no more references to an autonomous and empowered proletariat; Debord now complains more than criticizes and he joins hands with Baudrillard in the solidarity of despair and resignation.

At one place Debord speaks of the *"fragile perfection"* of the integrated spectacle,[86] but this is the fragility of a ton of lead. He opens the book with a quote from Sun Tzu: "However desperate the situation and circumstances, do not despair;" but this hope proves a cryptic and ungrounded leap of faith. Debord's succumbing to the fatalism of the postmodern scene must be understood in part as a result of his identification of social change with the struggle of the proletariat, which for a long time has been neither a class-for-itself or even a class-in-itself, and his inability to find new sources of resistance in other political groups. It can also be traced, as with Baudrillard, to their initially false hope for total revolution, an unattainable ideal whose inevitable failure will naturally lead to pessimism. Political defeatism is all-too-often the flipside of ultra-revolutionary fervor.[87]

Baudrillard and Debord's recent work are responses to the "God that failed," to the collapse of Marxism, naive revolutionary ideals, and the public sphere itself. There is indeed a good deal to be pessimistic about, as the techniques of power become increasingly perfected, as ecological collapse seems immanent, as the Right continues to define the terrain of culture and everyday life, while the "Left" continues to disintegrate into special interest groups and identity politics. But the later Debord and Baudrillard both ignore the crisis tendencies that continue to threaten global capitalism and the deep dissatisfactions of everyday life that continue to erupt on occasions, such as the result of the Rodney King trials in Los Angeles, the epicenter of the spectacle. The powers of reason and argumentation are indeed ebbing (as it becomes known that at perhaps up to half of US population is functionally illiterate), but the powderkegs of anger and desire continue to burn their fuses. As Debord himself once said, these are the wellsprings of collective action and social transformation.

Notes

1 For very helpful remarks on earlier drafts of this paper, I am indebted to Joe Grohens, Robert Resch, Rick Roderick, and especially Douglas Kellner. A different version of this paper first appeared in *Current Perspectives in Social Theory*, 9 (1989).
2 L. Feuerbach, preface to the second edition of *The Essence of Christianity*.
3 Jean Baudrillard, *The Mirror of Production* (St. Louis: Telos Press, 1975).
4 For examples of Situationist texts translated into English, see *The Situationist International Anthology* (Berkeley: Bureau of Public Secrets, 1981), Raoul

Vaneigem, *Revolution and Everyday Life* (London: Pending Press, 1983), and *The Book of Pleasures* (London: Pending Press, 1983).

5 Cited in Grant Kester, "The Rise and Fall? of Baudrillard," *New Art Examiner*, November (1987) 20–3, n. 3.

6 Baudrillard, *Mirror of Production*, p. 120.

7 Jean Baudrillard, *Cool Memories II* (Paris: Galilée, 1990), p. 131.

8 Karl Marx, *The Marx-Engels Reader*, 2nd edn, ed., Robert C. Tucker (New York: Norton), p. 93.

9 Ibid., p. 70.

10 Ibid., p. 74.

11 Ibid., p. 93.

12 W. F. Haug, *Critique of Commodity Aesthetics* (Minneapolis: University of Minnesota Press, 1986), p. 18.

13 Ibid., p. 14.

14 Marx, *Economic and Philosophic Manuscripts* (New York: International Publishers, 1964), p. 103.

15 Ibid., p. 103.

16 Ibid., p. 96.

17 Ibid., p. 105.

18 Ibid., p. 94.

19 Georg Lukács, *History and Class Consciousness* (Cambridge, Mass.: MIT Press, 1971).

20 Guy Debord, *Society of the Spectacle* (Detroit: Black and Red Press), 1970 #66.

21 Ibid., #65.

22 Ibid., #1.

23 Ibid., #10.

24 Ibid., #42.

25 Ibid., #42.

26 Ibid., #48.

27 Ibid., #17.

28 Ibid., #15.

29 Ibid., #1.

30 Ibid., #19.

31 Ibid., #19.

32 Ibid., #30.

33 Ibid., #34.

34 Ibid., #49.

35 Ibid., #2.

36 Ibid., #36.

37 Ibid., #68.

38 Ibid., #51.

39 Ibid., #10.

40 Ibid., #114.

41 Jean Baudrillard, *For a Critique of the Political Economy of the Sign* (St. Louis: Telos Press, 1981), p. 113.

42 I would suggest that Baudrillard has always followed Weber more than Marx. In the *Critique* and *Mirror of Production*, he interprets political economy as

a gigantic system based on rationalized administration of all social life of which "capitalism" and industrial organization is only a moment of a larger process of rationalization. Baudrillard retained this broader emphasis in his later work where the focus shifts from consumer society to an even more intense form of control in the form of cybernetic codes and models.

43 Jean Baudrillard, *Simulations* (New York: Semiotext(e), 1983), p. 11.
44 Baudrillard, *Mirror of Production*, pp. 121-2.
45 Baudrillard, *Critique*, p. 70.
46 Baudrillard, *Simulations*, p. 56.
47 Ibid., p. 53.
48 Debord, *Society of the Spectacle*, #10.
49 Jean Baudrillard, *In the Shadow of the Silent Majorities* (New York: Semiotext(e), 1983), pp. 98-9.
50 Nico Poulantzas, *Political Power and Social Classes* (London: New Left Books, 1973).
51 For a superb analysis of the media coverage of the Gulf War, see Douglas Kellner, *The Persian Gulf TV War* (Boulder, Cal.: Westview, 1992).
52 See Steven Best and Douglas Kellner "(Re)Watching Television: Notes Toward a Political Criticism," *Diacritics*, 17, 12 (1987) and "Watching Television: The Limits of Postmodernism," *Science as Culture*, 4 (1988).
53 Debord, *Society of the Spectacle*, #27 and 25.
54 Outstanding examples of this dereification practice would include Judith Williamson, *Decoding Advertisements* (Boston: Marion Boyars, 1978); Robert Goldman, *Reading Ads Socially* (London and New York: Routledge, 1992), and the works of Mark Gottdiener cited in his chapter in this text.
55 Debord, *Society of the Spectacle*, #4.
56 Ibid., #34.
57 See Fredrick Jameson, "Cognitive Mapping," *Marxism and the Interpretation of Culture* (Urbana: University of Illinois Press, 1988), pp. 347-57.
58 Baudrillard, *Simulations*, p. 40.
59 Debord, *Society of the Spectacle*, #5.
60 Fredric Jameson, *Marxism and Form* (New Jersey: Princeton University Press, 1971), p. 115.
61 Debord, *Society of the Spectacle*, #10.
62 See Baudrillard, *Critique*, pp. 63-87.
63 See Baudrillard, *Critique* and *Mirror of Production*.
64 See Rudolph Bahro, *The Alternative in Eastern Europe* (London: New Left Books, 1978).
65 Debord, *Society of the Spectacle*, #114.
66 Baudrillard, *Simulations*, p. 40.
67 Debord, *Society of the Spectacle*, #69.
68 Ibid., #115.
69 Ibid., #24.
70 Ibid., #24.
71 See Baudrillard's essay, "Requiem for the Media," in *Critique*.
72 See Debord, *Society of the Spectacle*, #24, 28.
73 Ibid., #117.
74 Baudrillard, *L'échange symbolique et la mort* (Paris: Gallimard, 1976), p. 12.

75 Guy Debord, "Preface to the Fourth Italian Edition of the 'Society of the Spectacle,'" (London: Cronos Publications, 1979), p. 23.
76 Ibid., p. 11.
77 Guy Debord, *Comments on the Society of the Spectacle* (London and New York: Verso, 1990), pp. 2, 3.
78 Ibid., p. 9.
79 Ibid., p. 10.
80 Ibid., p. 67.
81 Ibid., p. 14.
82 Ibid., p. 19.
83 Ibid., pp. 19, 22, 48.
84 Ibid., p. 22
85 Ibid., pp. 21–22.
86 Ibid., p. 21.
87 See Douglas Kellner, *Jean Baudrillard: From Marxism to Postmodernism and Beyond* (Cambridge and Stanford: Polity Press and Stanford University Press, 1989).

3

CRITICAL THEORY AND TECHNOCULTURE: HABERMAS AND BAUDRILLARD[1]

—

Mark Poster

Since World War II, Marxist theory has confronted a conjuncture that has proven increasingly recalcitrant to its categories and analysis. Although the mode of production has remained capitalist, and therefore amenable to the critique of political economy, the locus of revolution and social protest has, within the most advanced capitalist nations, shifted further and further away from the labor process. In the period 1840 to 1880, when Marx searched the world panorama for signs of emancipatory stirrings, his eyes fixed on the English, French, and German factory workers, the proletariat that resisted the harsh discipline of the new labor process. His hopes for the transformation of civil society lay with a class that was becoming, or was sure to become, the most numerous, the most downtrodden, the most exploited, but, at the same time, the most necessary to modern capitalism.

Marx tended to overlook, or at least to downplay, the more ambiguous features of the situation. The most militant rebels came from two groups that were in transition: the artisans who were losing their independence as they moved into the factories; and the peasants, who came to the factories from the countryside, a world apart from the industrializing cities. The fact that these groups may have resisted capitalism because of the change in habits it demanded of them rather than because of its intrinsic structure was not highlighted in Marx's thinking. He attributed the revolutionary role of the proletariat to the exploitative structure of the capitalist labor process itself, which progressively impoverished the life circumstances of the workers. For Marx, the impetus to rebel against the new system came directly from the new system; the only response possible for the workers was to liberate themselves and the world from the conditions of wage labor. As the century wore on, and workers' discontent took the form of political parties and labor unions that sought to ameliorate life within the system rather than to overturn it, Marx failed to account adequately for the possibility of cooptation.[2]

Historians have posited numerous explanations for the apparent domestication (temporary?) of the working class: better wages, stratification of the labor force, ethnic and regional differences, poor leadership at the party and union levels, changes in the liberal state, and nationalism, among others. Whatever the reason, the industrial working class no longer appeared, by the mid-twentieth century, the standard-bearer of revolt. At the same time, other groups rose to prominence as centers of revolution. First the peasants of the Third World, and, more recently, students, racial and ethnic minorities, women, gays, prisoners, environmentalists, all have made legitimate claims as "proletarians," as the group most oppressed by society and most opposed to its continuation in its present form, and thus as the "revolutionary subject."

Many theoretical questions are posed to Marxism by the shifts in the locus of militancy, but there is one in particular I will address in these pages: did Marx adequately conceptualize the relationship between technology and culture, practice and consciousness, labor and symbolic interaction? It can be argued that Marx's faith in the revolutionary potential of the industrial working class was gained too easily, that he assumed too readily that material hardship and social subjugation were sufficient conditions for revolt. One finds numerous instances in his texts in which the connection between material conditions and communicational practice is drawn too closely. Given a certain structure of work, his writings contend, social agents are expected to produce a certain political outcome.

The issue at stake is not one of the neglect of ideas. In the first thesis on Feuerbach, Marx indicates that he is fully cognizant of the active role of ideas in history, of the subject as an intentional agent: "[I]n opposition to materialism, the *active* side was developed by idealism . . . ."[3] In addition, historical materialism specified a prominent role for ideology in the process of social analysis. Religious doctrines and political programs are, in Marx's historical writings, fundamental aspects of the class struggle. The difficulty in Marxist theory is not that consciousness is relegated to the backstage of the historical drama but that the categorial richness and articulation of Marxism subsumes the problems of culture to those of technology. The gap in Marxist theory may be one not of basic principle but of secondary theoretical elaboration. The analysis in Marx of the region of the workplace is subtle, differentiated, complex; the analysis of the culture of the workers is undeveloped and deficient in analytic specification. The critique of political economy explores every turn of the capitalist structure; the critique of cultural politics is general, vague, undeveloped.

The result of this uneven theoretical development is that Marxists have focussed in great detail on what the workers did: how they worked, what they were paid, what conditions were responsible for their misery, how these changed, and how they could have changed. But there has been very little Marxist analysis of the impact of bourgeois ideas and practices upon their lives and political activities; about the way the structure of the workplace facilitated or retarded their communication; about the way the worker's relations with his/her community, spouse, children, relatives, and friends influenced his/her choices and goals.[4]

Marxism provides a coherent general outline of a democratic workplace: the reorganization of labor will eliminate specific deficiencies in the capitalist factory. Whatever conundrums remain concerning the conflict between central planning and worker self-management, between consumer and producer interests, between the requirements of production and the ecological balance with nature, these are, for Marx and for most Marxists, secondary problems that can be resolved at the level of practice. Another set of questions is not so easily manageable: What forms of culture are consistent with socialist society? Does the transformation of the technological and social apparatus imply a change in the form of symbolic interaction? Are the meanings associated with capitalist production a target of political strategy?

Because Marx assumed that oppression stimulated the worker to contest capitalism he did not theorize extensively about the problems of revolutionary consciousness, language, and symbolic interaction or culture in general. Hence when the sociopolitical developments of the twentieth century did not follow the Marxist trajectory, the framework of historical materialism was put in doubt. The cloth of Marxist theory becomes unraveled as new political movements pull at the threads of the concept of the mode of production. Marxism appears unable to account for today's oppositional movements: the Kurds of Iran, the Muslims of Bosnia, the prisoners and prostitutes of France, the women and blacks in the United States, the Basques of Spain and Quebecois of Canada, the ecologists of Germany, the youth of Britain. If Marxism is to survive as the critical theory of advanced capitalism it must become more than the special theory of the (male) workers' exploitation.

These complaints about Marxist theory cannot be answered with a simple phrase. It will not suffice to follow the example of Stalin and decide by fiat that language must be promoted from the superstructure to the base. Nor can one call for an eclectic expansion of the Marxist paradigm, adding where required some Kant or Weber or Freud. Experiments in this direction have foundered when diverse concepts rub uncomfortably against each other, generating electrostatic sparks rather than theoretical light.[5] Yet there have been substantial efforts by theorists to conceptualize anew the relation of technology and culture within a somewhat revised and loosened Marxist framework. In particular the work of Jürgen Habermas in Germany and Jean Baudrillard in France has had far-reaching impact on the revival of critical theory.

In the rethinking of Marxism by Habermas and Baudrillard, the common intellectual denominator is the importance given to language as the mediator between technology and culture. In the twentieth century there has arisen a profusion of theories of language upon which to draw: Saussure's structural linguistics, Wittgenstein's theory of language games, the Russian School's formalist linguistics, Bertalanffy's information theory, Searle's theory of speech acts, Bateson's systems theory of communication, Barthes' semiology, Chomsky's theory of generative grammar, Gadamer's hermeneutics, Foucault's analysis of discourse, Derrida's method of deconstruction, Lyotard's philosophy of phrases, and other forms of language analysis.

This far-from-complete list serves to remind one of the variety and richness of recent meditations on language. Given the prominence of the question of language, it is truly surprising that so little effort has been made to account for it: why should so much attention be given to language theory in the twentieth century, especially since World War II?[6] One possibility is that language has become more central to social practice. The relation of computer language to the brain, the diffusion of electronic media bringing discourse from around the world into the home, and the spread of bureaucracy through which politics and work rely more than ever on written forms of communication, are all examples of new practices that drastically extend the role of language in everyday life. And one may argue that language is not so much central to social practice but that it is changing its character as it takes on electronic forms; that the way language solicits a subject, the way discourse constitutes positions of subjectivity, is undergoing drastic transformations. In another work I have termed this process the mode of information.[7]

In any case, for the purposes of this paper it need only be acknowledged that philosophies of language present a challenge to the critical theory of society. For there is a tendency to argue, explicitly or implicitly, that language is prior to or formative of society itself. This position of course cannot be embraced by critical social theorists because it unduly restricts the scope of social theory and often illegitimately constricts the range of possible emancipation from domination. Habermas and Baudrillard, in very different ways, have wrestled with the question of language, subordinating it to and integrating it with critical social theory. In the process, they have opened new perspectives on the relation of technology and culture, offering resolutions to the deficiencies of classical Marxism.

I

In the case of Habermas the shift toward language theory began in the 1968 essay "Technology and Science as 'Ideology,'" in which the Marxist notion of work came under attack.[8] Associated with the Frankfurt School, Habermas was extending a line of thought initiated by Max Horkheimer and Theodor Adorno in *Dialectic of Enlightenment* (1944). In that book Horkheimer and Adorno attempted to differentiate critical theory from the scientific tradition in which Marx and Engels had initiated it.[9] For Horkheimer and Adorno scientific rationality was a means of dominating nature that had also become a means of dominating men. If Enlightenment, from the Greeks to the philosophes of the eighteenth century, based its critique of social domination on reason and science, it sustained and nurtured domination in a different form, one that would, under capitalism, become the source for an insidious form of social domination. Horkheimer and Adorno pleaded for a radical critique of the culture of capitalism rooted not in the workplace but in the legitimating ideology of science. Their experience of German Fascism, in which political domination and scientific culture operated in harmony, resulted in their pessimism about the future of the class struggle and even in the efficacy of critical theory.

Far less disturbed by the gloomy events of the twentieth century than Horkheimer and Adorno, Habermas searched for a renewal of radical theory in the critique of science and technology. He traced a line of filiation between Marx's theory of labor and the conservative function of science: "At the stage of their scientific-technical development . . . the forces of production appear to enter a new constellation with the relations of production. Now they no longer function as the basis of a critique of prevailing legitimations in the interest of political enlightenment, but become instead the basis of legitimation."[10] The conservative alliance of science and class relations was rooted in structural changes in advanced capitalism. While Horkheimer, Adorno, and even Marcuse, stressed the negative prospects implied by these developments, Habermas took them as a sign of an inadequacy in Marx's critical theory. Marx was unable to present a critical evaluation of the legitimating role of science and technology because his theory did not distinguish clearly enough between emancipatory action and technique. Marx could not offer an "alternative to existing technology" because, Habermas thought, his theory of labor was itself scientistic and technical.

Habermas found a way out of the dilemma in a most surprising fashion. The political aims of critical theory were in jeopardy because it had discovered a connection between technology and culture. Technology had become a source of ideology; the successes of the production system transformed it into its own justification; matter was transmuted into ideas. This conundrum of critical theory was reversed by Habermas, who located in Max Weber's theory of action the basis for once again separating technology and culture. Weber distinguished between purposive-rational action and value-rational action, a dichotomy that Habermas employed to develop an antinomy between technical action and symbolic interaction.

Marx's theory of labor praxis was limited to the former; the ends of social action were given; the means were geared to produce results in the technically most efficient manner. What was left out or subordinated in Marx's account of work was language, communication, the means through which individuals recognized each other as subjects. Hence Marx was unable to distinguish between science and emancipation.

The problem with Habermas's double theory of action is that it is not properly grounded in critical theory. The new category is simply added on to the old with no theoretical elaboration, no "transcendental deduction." Thus Habermas writes, "I shall take as my starting point the fundamental distinction between work and interaction."[11] But this "fundamental distinction" is neither self-evidently fundamental nor an obvious starting point of argumentation. It is, instead, a conclusion, one that leads to an improper separation of technology and culture. The borrowing of the concept of symbolic interaction from Weber is not enough. It does not explore systematically the metaphysical presuppositions behind Weber's thought and it introduces an artificial, even arbitrary, distinction which sets Habermas's thought down a wandering path into the thickets of the notion of the ideal speech situation. Eventually, in *The Theory of Communicative Action*,[12] Habermas will have to reintroduce a transcendental subject that directs his thought not beyond Marx but behind him, back to Kant. Faced with the dilemma of science as ideology, Habermas might have inquired into the difficulties in the notion of a rational subject and in that way avoided the subjectivism into which he eventually fell.

Habermas treats the question of language theory as an aspect of critical social theory. He rejects in turn: (1) Chomsky's theory of generative grammar since that grounds language in an asocial notion of human nature; (2) Saussurean linguistics since that removes the study of language from active social subjects and treats it as a purely formal, objective phenomenon; and (3) Austin's speech act theory since that provides no basis on which to evaluate critically the situation of the speaker. To account for language or symbolic interaction from the point of view of critical social theory, Habermas develops the notion of the ideal speech situation. Speech is an effort to communicate and this for Habermas necessarily implies that what the speaker says is comprehensible, that what the speaker states is true, that the speaker is sincere, and that the utterance fits into a normative context. On the basis of these criteria, language becomes available for analysis in terms of the distortions introduced into speech by social modes of domination.

Habermas is aware that few, if any, conversations meet the criteria of the ideal speech situation. Nevertheless, he argues for the apodicticity of his concept: "No matter how the intersubjectivity of mutual understanding may be deformed, the design of an ideal speech situation is necessarily implied with the structure of potential speech; for every speech, even that of intentional deception, is oriented toward the idea of truth."[13] In other words, "truth, freedom and justice" are inseparable tools of linguistic analysis. Habermas is maintaining, in a somewhat Kantian manner, that the ideal speech situation is a necessary condition for the comprehension of any utterance. The degree to which speech fails to meet the criteria of the ideal speech situation signifies not an individual's failure to communicate but social oppression, ultimately the class struggle.

There are many difficulties with the notion of the ideal speech situation. To begin with, one might ask if it is possible to evaluate empirically a given conversation according to Habermas's criteria. In the flow of interchanges between a husband and a wife, as represented imaginatively, for example, in Who's Afraid of Virginia Woolf, the levels of distortion are so complex that untangling "the truth" and analyzing the structures of domination might be impossible. In fact, the concept of the ideal speech situation implies a God-like epistemological vantage point from which the foibles of everyday confusions could be sorted out. But let us set aside the empirical problems and agree with Habermas that deviations from the ideal speech situation "increase correspondingly to the varying degrees of repression which characterize the institutional system within a given society; and that, in turn, the degree of repression depends on the developmental stage of the productive forces and on the organization of authority . . ."[14] If that is so, another difficulty arises: the analysis of symbolic interaction remains a direct reflection of the mode of production and we are back to where we began, with the problem of labor.

Habermas sought to extract the notion of the ideal speech situation from the grip of the economic structure by arguing that "communicative competence" is itself an historical phenomenon. The ability of speakers to meet the ideal criteria thus depends not only on the levels of repression introduced by the mode of production but on the stage of "moral development" of the individual. Communication is depicted as an evolutionary phenomenon in its own right, one that depends on issues of socialization and personality development.

Habermas contends that "the species learns not only in the dimension of technically useful knowledge decisive for the development of productive forces but also in the dimension of moral-practical consciousness decisive for structures of interaction."[15] Just as there is progress in the evolution of modes of production, so there are criteria, provided for the most part by Piaget, by which to evaluate communicative competence. During stage one an "imperativist mode of communication" is predominant; there ensues the era of "propositionally differentiated speech"; finally we arrive at an epoch, presumably our own, in which speech is "argumentative" and fully subject to the criteria of the ideal speech situation. Changes from one stage to the next are made possible, according to Habermas, by general changes in social organization.[16] The implication of Habermas's argument is that in the next stage of social organization, the one beyond capitalism or a more democratic stage within capitalism, communicative competence will enable and social freedom will authorize the realization of the ideal speech situation. This position has led Habermas, to the chagrin of the radical Left in Germany,[17] to argue for a "public sphere" in which open debate would provide the conditions for qualitative social change.

The utopianism of Habermas's political position is rooted in the subjectivism of his theory. If speech is distorted systematically by social repression it is not likely that open debate in the public sphere would eliminate that distortion. Such an ideal speech situation would still be subject to the general forms of repression. Even in the context of "the legitimation crisis" it is difficult to see how the distortions can be eliminated, for Habermas's version of critical theory depends upon an unjustified view of the subject as "ideally" truthful. But the pressure to be truthful does not necessarily produce the truth; it might just as well lead to more elaborate lies or self-deceptions. In the end Habermas's theory leads to a demand for an ideal speech situation which is not adequately based on an analysis of the structure of communication in everyday life. To attain that sort of analysis one must posit language as an objective phenomenon, at least provisionally, and carry out an investigation of it that renders it intelligible socially and historically. This is the direction of the work of Jean Baudrillard, who frees critical theory from an unwarranted dependence on evaluating the subjectivity of social participants by which, as we have seen, the analysis of culture is divorced from that of technology.

II

Baudrillard's early works, *Le système des objets* (1968) and *La société de consommation* (1970) took their inspiration from the problematics of the critique of everyday life developed by Baudrillard's teacher Henri Lefebvre and from Roland Barthes' semiology.[18] Under advanced capitalism, Baudrillard maintained, consumerism had come to dominate the various aspects of everyday life. At this stage of his thinking, Baudrillard was happy to place the regional analysis of consumption within the broader Marxist critique of capitalism. The experience of the events of May 1968 had dramatized changes in the structure of capitalism, such as the importance of everyday life, that required analysis and critique. Where Baudrillard differed from traditional Marxism was in his use of semiological theory[19] to make intelligible in a new way the features of consumerism.

Like Habermas, Baudrillard was unwilling to accept language theory – in this case structuralist semiology – in its dominant versions. Saussure's structural linguistics, as employed by Lévi-Strauss, Lacan, and Barthes, enables the investigator to examine phenomena at a new level of complexity.

An object can be dissected into its binary oppositions, revealing a play of rules and patterns of formation, without resorting to a concept of consciousness or subjectivity. Social experience is open to analysis at a level of internal articulation: myths, kinship systems, fashion magazines, consumer objects – each constitutes a structured world of meaning that derives its intelligibility from its likeness to language. Yet the use of structural linguistics in social theory bears a certain cost: the formalism of linguistics, when carried over into social science, implies a dehistoricization and a weakening of critical powers. Structural linguistics mandates that phenomena be studied synchronically, outside time, and without reference to normative evaluations.

Baudrillard was one of the first thinkers in France to attempt to employ semiology both historically and critically. The thesis of *Consumer Society* was that in advanced capitalism a new structure of meanings had emerged whose effectiveness was based on a logic of differentiation that was subject to analysis only by a semiological theory. "The social logic of consumption," Baudrillard wrote, "is not at all that of the individual appropriation of the use value of goods and services . . . it is not a logic of satisfaction. It is a logic of the production and manipulation of social signifiers."[20] But Marxism missed its analytical boat if it rested with demonstrating that capitalism generated these signifiers to manipulate the masses into unwanted acts of consumption.[21] The point was rather that the signifiers themselves, not the products, had become objects of consumption that drew their power and fascination from being structured into a code. The code, in turn, could be deciphered not by the logic of capital but by the logic of semiology.

Baudrillard's analysis of consumption was thus fully historical because it subordinated semiology to critical theory: the production of commodities had entered a new stage that was accompanied by a new structure of signs, a new linguistic apparatus. Once this new structure of meanings was analyzed semiologically, revealing its structured code, an argument could be developed that radical change must focus on the code, and develop a practice to dismantle it and a strategy to create a new order of symbolic exchange with a new system of signs. Baudrillard's intent was double: to revise semiology so that its formalism and ahistoricity were tamed to the needs of critical theory; and to revise Marxism so that its productivism was tamed to the needs of cultural criticism. The result would be a new critical theory that captured the interdependence of technology and culture, production and symbolic exchange.

The *System of Objects* and *Consumer Society* carried out these goals by demonstrating the advantages of semiology over the Marxist concept of needs in the analysis of consumerism. If commodities are conceptualized as deriving their value from labor and their use from need, the extraordinary expansion of consumerism since World War II remains a mystery.

Why would workers exhaust themselves in labor only to purchase the products that capitalism places on the market, products whose worth may be questioned? According to Marx, human needs are not fixed, but alter with changes in the mode of production. If that is true, capitalism has successfully instituted an infinite cycle of production and consumption. But Marx's analysis overlooked, according to Baudrillard, the function of social exchange. Limited to the metaphor of production in the analysis of social practice, Marx missed the force of the social exchange of meanings that envelops commodities in a non-productivist logic. If, on the other hand, society were seen as a system of symbolic exchange, the power of the code would reveal its force.

Under advanced capitalism, Baudrillard contends, the masses are controlled not only by the need to labor in order to survive but by the need to exchange symbolic differences.[22] Individuals receive their identity in relation to others not primarily from their type of work but from the signs and meanings they display and consume. Taking his cue from Veblen and certain anthropological theories, Baudrillard asserts the importance of commodities as social signifiers, not as material objects. But he avoids the dangers of such theories of emulation by rooting his analysis firmly in the soil of the current social epoch. The shift from the primacy of production to the primacy of exchange has been facilitated by the development of new technologies, such as radio and television. The cultural significance of these technologies is that they emit a single message and constitute a new code: "the message of the consumption of the message."[23] The new media transform the structure of language, of symbolic exchange, creating the conditions in which the new code of consumerism can emerge.

From the vantage point of semiology, the new code is easy enough to decipher. An advertisement for Pepsi-Cola, for example, pictures a community of all ages, classes, sexes, and races enjoying a drink together. The message is clear if subliminal: to drink Pepsi-Cola is not so much to consume a carbonated beverage as to consume a meaning, a sign, that of community.[24] In this advertisement a value that capitalism destroys (community) is returned to society through the advertisement. In another example the code operates not as utopian realization but as pressure to conform. Brut cologne is associated with aggressive manhood. Again, to use the product is to consume the meaning, in this case a stereotype of masculinity. The implication of the advertisement is that those who do not use Brut will not be manly, thus losing out in the game of sexual conquest.

Although opposite in their strategy, both advertisements illustrate the mechanism of the code. The product itself is not of primary interest; it must be sold by grafting onto it a set of meanings that have no inherent connection with the product. The set of meanings subject to semiological analysis becomes the dominant aspect of consumption. Unlike Habermas, who sees meanings as scarce in advanced capitalism, Baudrillard discovers a profusion of meaning in the system of consumption. This difference in the two thinkers speaks to the relative value of their sources: the elitist pessimism of the Frankfurt School which, failing to find "authentic" values in mass society, rejects popular and consumer culture out of hand, and the semiology employed by Baudrillard which grants the validity of popular and consumer culture long enough to carry out a trenchant analysis of it.

In *Pour une critique de l'économie politique du signe* (1972) Baudrillard endeavored to correlate systematically his critical semiology with Marx's critique of political economy. Still remaining within a Marxist framework, at least nominally, he tested the general principles of Marx's analysis of the commodity with that of semiology's analysis of the sign. Just as Marx decomposed the commodity into use value and exchange value, so semiology deciphered the sign as signified and signifier. Baudrillard discovered a homology between the sign and the commodity: the signifier is to exchange value what the signified is to use value.[25] The parallelism at the formal level, however, masks a certain misrecognition or ideology which is the effect both of the structuralist concept of the sign and the Marxist notion of the commodity.

The structuralist concept of the sign naturalizes or universalizes what is, in fact, according to Baudrillard, a historically based semiological formation. The sign, split off from the referent and intelligible only at the level of the relation of signifier to signifier, is actually a drastic reduction of the symbolic. In a universe of symbols, signifier, signified, and referent are integrated in acts of communication. Symbols are characterized by an ambivalence of meaning as they are exchanged from one person to another. The sign, on the contrary, is full, positive, univocal.[26] It is not an inevitable truth about language, but a product of a specific semiological epoch. Programmed by industry and bureaucracy, the sign is part of the strategy of power.[27] Removed from the web of mutual reciprocity, the sign is a unilateral message, a communication without a response.[28] Signs are made possible by the new technologies of the media in which signifiers flash by potential consumers. Once signifiers have been separated and abstracted in this way, floating free, so to speak, in communicational space, they can be attached to particular commodities by the arbitrary whim of advertisers. Thus a new structure of meaning is instituted that collaborates with the requirements of advanced capitalism.

Marx's concept of the commodity never attains this level of analysis. He neglects the process of transformation by which exchange value becomes a sign.[29] Because the conceptual apparatus of Marxism is modeled on production and labor, it cannot make intelligible "the social labor of producing signs,"[30] which is based on a different logic. The circulation of signs itself produces surplus value, one based not on profit but on legitimacy.[31] At this time, Baudrillard was content to argue that his analysis of the message was parallel to Marx's analysis of the commodity. Just at the point where Marxism became "ideological" because it could not decode the semiology of the commodity, Baudrillard stepped in to enrich and improve upon historical materialism, updating it to the circumstances of advanced capitalism.

Hints of a coming break with Marx were none the less present in *Pour une critique*. The point of divergence with Marx centered on the question of the logic of production versus the logic of exchange, the materiality of commodities versus the ideality of the sign. In rejecting the structuralist separation of the sign from the world, Baudrillard argued that the world "is only the effect of the sign."[32] If individuals consumed meanings rather than products, the centerpiece of social theory was symbolic exchange, not the production of goods. Value was created, therefore, not in the labor process but in the communicational structure. In *Pour une critique*, Baudrillard's emphasis was on revising Marx rather than supplanting him but the seeds of post-Marxist critical theory were already planted.

The break with Marx came only a year later with the publication of *The Mirror of Production*.[33] Here Baudrillard presented in no uncertain terms his critique of Marx's notion of labor, systematically deconstructing the apparatus of the critique of political economy: "A specter haunts the revolutionary imagination: the phantom of production. Everywhere it sustains an unbridled romanticism of productivity. The critical theory of the *mode* of production does not touch the *principle* of production. All the concepts it articulates describe only the dialectical and historical genealogy of the *contents* of production, leaving production as a *form* intact."[34] The Marxist concept of labor, Baudrillard proposes, is too close to the liberal notion of *homo economicus* to provide a radical critique of political economy. Like the liberals, Marx reduces practice to labor and society to production. Marx discovered in use-value the radical basis for the critique of the liberal notion of exchange value. The labor that goes into the commodity constitutes for Marx its true worth, not the amount for which it is exchanged. The notion of exchange value reduces all labor to one level; it obscures concrete differences between human acts, Marx complains.

Baudrillard responds that to uncover the human essence of labor behind the capitalist shroud of exchange value is not enough. Marxism only "convinces men that they are alienated by the sale of their labor power; hence it censors the much more radical hypothesis that they do not have to be the labor power, the 'unalienable' power of creating value by their labor".[35] Like liberalism, Marx conceptualized the social field in the mirror of production, presenting back to capitalism its own image, only in an inverted form. A radical critique must rather locate the field that is obscured by liberals and Marxists alike – that of symbolic exchange.

Baudrillard locates the point at which Marxist theory becomes complicit with capitalist productivism by reviewing the stages of the relation of production and exchange presented by Marx in *The Poverty of Philosophy*.

During stage one, before capitalism, production was for use by the producers and only the surplus was exchanged. In stage two, that of classical capitalism, all production by industry was exchanged. In stage three, fully developed capitalism, not only industrial production, but everything – "virtue, love, knowledge, consciousness" – is placed on the market for possible exchange.[36] Marx views the spread of capitalist principles beyond the area of production as a "corruption" or a time of "universal venality." For Marx, stage three involves the reflection of the base in the superstructure, a secondary effect of the mode of production. Thus the basic shift for him is from stage one to stage two, stage three being conceived only as the logical working out of the system, its general extension to all social relations.

In his critique, Baudrillard wavers not between supplementing Marx and rejecting him but between rejecting him only for the analysis of stage three or rejecting him for the entire genealogy of capitalism. In the weaker critique, Baudrillard argues that Marx obscures the significance of the shift to stage three because of his productivist metaphor. Social exchange in stage three, from the semiological perspective outlined above, reveals a structurally new type of domination generated by the code or the sign, a type of domination that cannot be made intelligible through the concept of production. In this case, Marxism becomes inadequate as a critical theory only with the advent of the sign as the general principle of communication. In the stronger critique, Baudrillard maintains that the sign and the commodity arose together at the beginning of the process of the birth of capitalism and that the critique of the political economy of the sign is more radical than the critique of political economy from the outset. As a critical category, the mode of signification should perhaps take precedence over the mode of production.

Symbolic Exchange and Death[37] draws out the pessimistic implications of the theory of the code, marking a change in Baudrillard's political stance.[38] As the politics of the 1960s receded so did Baudrillard's radicalism: from a position of firm leftism he gradually moved to one of bleak fatalism. In *Symbolic Exchange and Death* he searches desperately for a source of radicalism that challenges the absorptive capacities of a system with no fixed determinations, a world where anything can be anything else, where everything is both equivalent to and indifferent to everything else, a society, in short, dominated by the digital logic of the code. Baudrillard's depressing conclusion is that only death escapes the code, only death is an act without an equivalent return, an exchange of values. Death signifies the reversibility of signs in the gift, a truly symbolic act that defies the world of simulacra, models, and codes.[39]

Symbolic Exchange and Death is flawed by the totalizing quality of Baudrillard's writing. Still, the value of the book lies in the refinements it provides of many of the themes of Baudrillard's earlier works. In it Baudrillard grapples, as nowhere before, with the problem of characterizing the structure of communication in a world dominated by the media. This important issue, too much neglected by critical theory, becomes the main-stay of his writing after 1976. Although Baudrillard treats this theme with hyperbole and vague formulations, he had initiated a line of thought that is fundamental to a reconstitution of critical theory. While this project is somewhat akin to the recent work of Habermas, Baudrillard wrestles with the communication structure of the media, whereas his German counter-part pursues the quixotic end of defining the "ideal speech situation."[40]

In *Seduction*[41] Baudrillard makes a turn toward a post-structuralist cri-tique of the hermeneutics of suspicion. Theories that deny the surface "appearance" of things in favor of a hidden structure or essence, theories like Marxism, psychoanalysis, and structuralism, now come under attack. These interpretive strategies all privilege forms of rationality. Against them Baudrillard celebrates a Nietzschean critique of the "truth" and favors a model based on what he calls "seduction." Seduction plays on the surface thereby challenging theories that "go beyond" the manifest to the latent. The model of seduction prefigures Baudrillard's later term, the hyperreal, with all of its post-modernist implications. At the close of the book, Baudrillard tentatively suggests that seduction might be a model to replace the model of production.

In *Simulacres et simulation*[42] Baudrillard extends, some would say totalizes, his theory of commodity culture. No longer does the code take priority over or even precede the consumer object. The distinctions between object and representation, thing and idea, are no longer valid. In their place, Baudrillard fathoms a strange new world constructed out of models or simulacra which have no referent or ground in any "reality" except their own. Simulations are different from fictions or lies in that the former not only presents an absence as a presence, the imaginary as the real, it also undermines any contrast to the real, absorbing the real within itself. Instead of a "real" economy of commodities that is somehow bypassed by an "unreal" myriad of advertising images, Baudrillard now discerns only a hyperreality, a world of self-referential signs. He has moved from the TV advertisement which, however, never completely erases the commodity it solicits, to the TV newscast which creates the news if only to be able to narrate it, or the soap opera whose daily events are both referent and reality for many viewers.

If Baudrillard's argument of hyperreality has a modicum of validity, the position of the New Historicists and Deconstructionists must be taken seriously. The self-referentiality of language, which they promote against materialists, phenomenologists, realists, and historicists as the key to tex-tual analysis, now in Baudrillard's hands becomes the first principle of social existence in the era of high-tech capitalism. Critical theory faces the formidable task of unveiling structures of domination when no one is domi-nating, nothing is being dominated, and no ground exists for a principle of liberation from domination. If Auschwitz is the sign of total tyranny as the production of death, the world of "hyperreality" bypasses the distinction between death and life.[43]

The pessimistic implications of *Simulacres et simulations* are brought home in *Fatal Strategies*.[44] Here Baudrillard attempts to think of the social world from the point of view of the object, a seeming oxymoron. Like the post-structuralists, Baudrillard assumes that the era of the representational subject is past. One can no longer comprehend the world as if the Kantian categories of time, space, causality, etc. are necessary, universal paths to truth. Baudrillard takes this to imply that the subject no longer provides a vantage point on reality. The privileged position has shifted to the object, specifically to the hyperreal object, the simulated object. In place of a logic of the subject, Baudrillard proposes a logic of the object, and this is his "fatal strategy." As the reader will discover, the world unveiled by Baudrillard, the world from within the object, looks remarkably like the world as seen from the position of postmodernists.[44]

Baudrillard is not disputing the trivial issue that reason is operative in some actions, that if I want to arrive at the next block, for example, I can assume a Newtonian universe (common sense), plan a course of action (to walk straight for x meters), carry out the action, and finally fulfill my goal by arriving at the point in question. What is in doubt is that this sort of thinking enables a historically informed grasp of the present in general. According to Baudrillard, it does not. The concurrent spread of the hyperreal through the media and the collapse of liberal and Marxist politics as master narratives, deprives the rational subject of its privileged access to truth. In an important sense individuals are no longer citizens, eager to maximize their civil rights, nor proletarians, anticipating the onset of communism. They are rather consumers, and hence the prey of objects as defined by the code. In this sense, only the "fatal strategy" of the point of view of the object provides any understanding of the present situation.

In a more recent essay "The Masses: The Implosion of the Social in the Media," Baudrillard recapitulates the theme of his work in the 1980s: the media generate a world of simulations which is immune to rationalist critique, be it Marxist or liberal. The media present an excess of information and they do so in a manner that precludes response by the recipient. This simulated reality has no referent, no ground, no source. It operates outside the logic of representation. But the masses have found a way of subverting it: the strategy of silence or passivity.[45] Baudrillard thinks that by absorbing the simulations of the media, by failing to respond, the masses undermine the code.[46] Whatever the value of this position it represents a new way of understanding the impact of the media. Instead of complaining about the alienation of the media or the terrorism of the code, Baudrillard proposes a way out: silence. Critical theorists will certainly not remain silent about Baudrillard's paradoxical revolutionary strategy. In fact, more suggestive approaches to the question of resistance have been offered by Pierre Bourdieu and Michel de Certeau. In *The Practice of Everyday Life*, de Certeau argues that the masses resignify meanings that are presented to them in the media, in consumer objects, in the layout of city streets.[47] De Certeau's position on resistance seems more heuristic and more sensible than that of Baudrillard.

III

Baudrillard's writing is open to several criticisms: He fails to define his major terms, such as the code. His writing style is hyperbolic and declarative, often lacking sustained, systematic analysis when it is appropriate. He totalizes his insights, refusing to qualify or delimit his claims. He writes about particular experiences, television images, etc., as if nothing else in society mattered, extrapolating a bleak view of the world from that limited base. He ignores contradictory evidence such as the many benefits afforded by the new media, for example, by promoting progressive movements concerning civil rights and the environment, by providing vital information to the populace (e.g., the Vietnam War) and counteracting parochialism with humanizing images of foreigners. The instant, worldwide availability of information has changed the human society forever, probably for the good.

Nevertheless Baudrillard's work is an invaluable beginning for the comprehension of the impact of new communication forms on society. He has introduced a language-based analysis of new kinds of social experience, experience that is sure to become increasingly characteristic of advanced societies. His work shatters the existing foundations for critical social theory, showing how the privilege they give to labor and their rationalist epistemologies are inadequate for the analysis of the media and other new social activities. In these regards he joins with Derrida's critique of logocentrism and Foucault's critique of the human sciences. Unlike these post-structuralist thinkers, Baudrillard fails to reflect on the epistemological novelties he introduces, rendering his work open to the charges outlined above. For the critical theorist, Baudrillard represents the beginning of a line of thought, one that is open to development and refinement by others.

The tendency to give priority to communication and the media rather than to labor is found in the recent work of both Baudrillard and Habermas.[48] Both have enlarged the scope of critical theory to encompass the phenomenon of language and both have placed technology in a closer relationship with culture than did Marx. The mode of signification becomes as central to critical theory as the mode of production. The ideal speech situation for Habermas and symbolic exchange for Baudrillard become the new basis of revolutionary theory. The problem of transforming the mode of production must share the attention of criticism with the problem of transforming the world of meaning, culture, and language. By taking critical theory in this direction both Habermas and Baudrillard provide a ground for incorporating into the revolutionary perspective a locus of radicality outside the workplace. Women, minorities, gays, criminals, all the oppressed subcultures, may now take part in the process of social transformation on a footing equal to that of the proletariat. Although neither Baudrillard nor Habermas systematically addresses the question of the relation of these subgroups to the mode of signification, there is the clear implication in their thought that this issue is high on the agenda of critical theory.

Although the similarities in direction of the ideas of Baudrillard and Habermas are striking, there remain fundamental differences between them. These divergences can be clarified by comparing their relationship to the Left of the late 1960s. In Germany Habermas became a focus of criticism by the New Left, who saw his notion of a public sphere as insufficiently radical. For his part, Habermas viewed the students as bourgeois children protesting against paternal authority and sexual repression.[49] The significance of their revolt was that they forced into public attention areas of life that hitherto had remained private. They had successfully broken through the shell of bourgeois ideology revealing the absence of democracy throughout society. In the advanced societies the main problem, however, was that of technology and its undemocratic character. Here the issue could be resolved only through resort to an ideal speech situation. The problem was one "of setting into motion a politically effective discussion that rationally brings the social potential constituted by technical knowledge and ability into a defined and controlled relation to our practical knowledge and will . . . . Our only hope for the rationalization of the power structure lies in conditions that favor political power for thought developing through dialogue."[50] The issue for Habermas was one of creating an institutional framework for undistorted communication. He posited the need for a new subjective basis for rationality; the ideal speech situation would produce a rational society. While appealing to honored and ancient cultural imperatives, Habermas's prescriptions do not go much beyond the contours of the Enlightenment.

Baudrillard was far more enthusiastic than Habermas about the radicalism of the late 1960s. The events of May 1968 was for him an apocalyptic smashing of the repressive code. Against the monologue of the TV, May 1968 presented a festival of symbolic exchange. The streets and walls of Paris shouted down the abstract murmurs of the sign. A new mode of signification was realized in everyday life, if only briefly.[51] The seemingly unconquerable power of the code dissolved in a volley of chatter from students and workers. The new mode of signification was created not through the dialectical maneuvers of the class struggle but in a simple explosion of expressive communication. Like graffiti, the force of symbolic exchange erupted in the semiological field in a sudden burst of meaning. The events of May 1968 confirmed for Baudrillard the poverty of the Marxist notion of revolution. It shattered in one brilliant display of semiological fireworks the notion of the party with its intellectuals, its theory, its cadre, its careful organization and strategy, and its duplication of the bourgeois world that it would supplant. The theory of symbolic exchange in Baudrillard's version thus implies a very different world from that of Habermas. The new mode of signification depends not on a new notion of the subject or a new realization of rationality. It denotes instead a new structure of communication in which signifiers would be generated directly in the course of exchange, connected closely to both signified and referent.

Although Baudrillard's critical semiology permits a deeper analysis of the communication structure of advanced capitalism than that of Habermas and avoids undue reliance on concepts of the subject and rationality, it too misses, finally, a satisfactory resolution of a theory of the relation of technology and culture. The danger in Baudrillard's notion of the code is that it accepts too easily the omnipotence of the semiological structure; it totalizes too quickly the pattern of communication that it reveals. As opposed to Habermas's subjectivism, Baudrillard's analysis errs in the direction of objectivism. In his view, floating signifiers pervade the social space without adequate recognition or theoretical account of the continuous disruptions of it by subjects. Baudrillard convincingly theorizes one side of the question – the emission of the signals – but the reception of the signals remains beyond the ken of his semiology. For reception is also an act and it is one that is discontinuous, at least partially, with emission, especially during the epoch of the sign. Revolt against the sign takes place not only in the exceptional collective outburst, such as that of May 1968. Protest and transgression are repeated daily by women who refuse to douse themselves in seductive perfumes, by gays who overtly display their threatening sexuality, by prisoners who do not accept the discipline of the panopticon, by workers who sabotage the smooth flow of the production line, by everyone who draws a line through, or erases or marks over, the imperatives of the code.

If critical semiology enables critical theory to make intelligible the domination inherent in the mode of signification, it displaces the locus of revolt, failing to present a theory of subjectivity that would account for the gaps and fissures within the system. When Baudrillard argues that escape from the code is found only in death, when meaning finally is not reincorporated into the nightmare of signs, it becomes plain that his objectivism has led to a retreat to a distant desert. None the less, Habermas and, more especially, Baudrillard have carried critical theory far beyond the boundaries of the mode of production to a more fertile theoretical field in which a resolution of the question of technology and culture can be pursued.

Notes

1 This essay is a revision of two earlier pieces: "Technology and Culture in Habermas and Baudrillard," *Contemporary Literature*, 22, 4 (Fall 1981) 456–76 and "Introduction" to *Jean Baudrillard: Selected Writings*, edited with an introduction by Mark Poster, trans. Jacques Mourrain (Stanford: Stanford University Press, 1988).

2 See Carol Johnson, "The Problem of Reformism and Marx's Theory of Fetishism," *New Left Review*, 119 (1980) 70–96 for a discussion of Marx's failure to theorize adequately the problem of revolutionary consciousness.

3 Karl Marx, "Theses on Feuerbach," in *Writings of the Young Marx on Philosophy and Society*, trans. and ed. L. Easton and K. Guddat (New York: Anchor, 1967), p. 400.

4 It could be argued that the Marxist school of historiography begun by E. P. Thompson with *The Making of the English Working Class* (New York: Random House, 1963) as well as the Birmingham School of cultural studies are exceptions, serious ones, to this charge.

5 See, for example the long history of the effort to marry the ideas of Freud with those of Marx, e.g., Wilhelm Reich, "Dialectical Materialism and Psychoanalysis" (1929); Reuben Osborn, *Marxism and Psychoanalysis* (1965); Herbert Marcuse, *Eros and Civilization* (1955), etc.

6 Martin Jay begins to address this question in "Should Intellectual History Take a Linguistic Turn? Reflections on the Habermas-Gadamer Debate," in Dominick LaCapra and Steven Kaplan, eds., *Modern European Intellectual History* (Ithaca: Cornell University Press, 1982), pp. 86–110.

7 Mark Poster, *The Mode of Information* (Chicago: University of Chicago Press, 1990).

8 The English version can be found in *Toward a Rational Society: Student Protest, Science, and Politics*, trans. Jeremy Shapiro (Boston: Beacon Press, 1971).

9 *Dialectic of Enlightenment*, trans. John Cumming (New York: Seabury Press, 1972).

10 *Toward a Rational Society*, p. 84.

11 *Toward a Rational Society*, p. 91.

12 Jürgen Habermas, *The Theory of Communicative Action*, Thomas McCarthy trans., Vols. 1 and 2 (Boston: Beacon Press, 1984 and 1987).

13 Jürgen Habermas, "Toward a Theory of Communicative Competence," in *Recent Sociology No 2: Patterns of Communicative Behavior*, ed. Hans Peter Dreitzel (New York: Macmillan, 1970), p. 144. This text is a translation of "Vorbereitende Bemerkungen zu einer Theorie der kommunikativen Kompetenz."

14 Ibid., p. 146.

15 Jürgen Habermas, Communication and the Evolution of Society (Boston: Beacon Press, 1979), p. 148.

16 Habermas provides examples of this in *Communication*, p. 112.
17 On Habermas's disagreements with the left student movement in West Germany see the first three chapters of *Toward a Rational Society*.
18 See Henri Lefebvre, *Everyday Life in the Modern World*, trans. Sacha Rabinovich (New York: Harper and Row, 1971) and *Le language et la société* (Paris: Gallimard, 1966). See also Roland Barthes, *Mythologies*, trans. Annette Lavers (New York: Hill and Wang, 1972) and *Système de la mode* (Paris: Seuil, 1967).
19 Semiology may be defined as the study of all social meanings, not just those inherent in language.
20 Jean Baudrillard, *La société de consommation* (Paris: Gallimard, 1970) pp. 78–9. In Saussure's theory of structural linguistics, signs are composed of signifiers or words and signifieds or mental images. Emphasis is placed on the relations between the signifiers, whose connection to signifieds and referents is virtually ignored.
21 For an example of that type of analysis see Stuart Ewen, *Captains of Consciousness: Advertising and the Social Roots of the Consumer Culture* (New York: McGraw Hill, 1976).
22 *La société de consommation*, p. 134.
23 *La société de consommation*, p. 188.
24 For numerous examples of analyses of advertisements see Judith Williamson, *Decoding Advertisements* (London: Marion Boyars, 1978).
25 For more extensive elaborations of this sort of homological analysis see Jean-Joseph Goux, *Economie et symbolique: Freud, Marx* (Paris: Seuil, 1973) and Marc Shell, *The Economy of Literature* (Baltimore: Johns Hopkins University Press, 1978).
26 Jean Baudrillard, *Pour une critique de l'économie politique du signe* (Paris: Gallimard, 1972) p. 181.
27 Ibid., p. 91.
28 Ibid., p. 138.
29 Ibid., p. 129.
30 Ibid., p. 132.
31 Ibid., p. 140.
32 Ibid., p. 185.
33 Jean Baudrillard, *The Mirror of Production* (St. Louis: Telos Press, 1975).
34 Ibid., p. 17.
35 Ibid., p. 9.
36 Ibid., p. 119.
37 Jean Baudrillard, *L'échange symbolique et la mort* (Paris: Gallimard, 1976). Translated as *Symbolic Exchange and Death* (London: Sage, 1993).
38 See the interview with Baudrillard by Maria Shevtsova, "Intellectuals [sic] Commitment and Political Power," in *Thesis Eleven*, 10–11 (1984/5). 166–75. Here Baudrillard presents his current views on politics. Also interesting in this regard is Robert Maniquis, "Une Conversation avec Jean Baudrillard," *UCLA French Studies*, 2–3 (1984–5) 1–22.
39 It might be noted that Baudrillard defends the notion of the symbolic against psychological theories. See his critique of psychoanalysis in "Beyond the Unconscious: the Symbolic," *Discourse*, 3 (1981) 60–87.

40   See Habermas, *Theory of Communicative Action*, Vol. 1, *Reason and the Rationalization of Society*, originally published in 1981.

41   Jean Baudrillard, *De la séduction* (Paris: Editions Denoel-Gonthier). Translated as *Seduction* (New York: Saint Martin's Press, 1990).

42   Jean Baudrillard, *Simulacres et simulation* (Paris: Galilée, 1981).

43   See Jean Baudrillard, "Fatality or Reversible Imminence: Beyond the Uncertainty Principle," *Social Research*, 49, 2 (Summer, 1982) 272–93 for a discussion of the chance/necessity distinction in relation to the world of hyperreality.

44   See Hal Foster, ed., *The Anti-Aesthetic: Essays on Postmodern Culture* (Port Townsend, Washington: Bay Press, 1983), especially the brilliant piece by Fredric Jameson. It might be noted that Baudrillard himself is a contributor to this collection. *Les strategies fatales* (Paris: Bernard Grasset, 1983). Translated as *Fatal Strategies* (New York: Semiotext(e), 1990).

45   Jean Baudrillard, "The Masses: The Implosion of the Social in the Media," *New Literary History*, 16, 3 (1985) 89. See also Baudrillard, *A l'ombre des majorités silencieuses ou la fin du social* (Paris: Utopie, 1978). Translated as as *In the Shadow of the Silent Majorities* (New York: Semiotext(e), 1983).

46   See Baudrillard's essays "What Are You Doing After the Orgy?," *Artforum* (October, 1983) 42–6; "Astral America," *Artforum* (September, 1984) 70–4, and *L'Amérique* (Paris: Grasset, 1985) for descriptions of life in the new world of the media, especially in the USA where the tendencies Baudrillard discusses are most advanced.

47   Michel de Certeau, *The Practice of Everyday Life*, trans. Steven Rendell (Berkeley: University of California Press, 1984). See also Pierre Bourdieu, *La distinction: critique sociale du judgement* (Paris: de Minuit, 1979). Translated as *Distinction* by Richard Nice (Cambridge, Mass.: Harvard University Press, 1984).

48   See Baudrillard, *L'échange symbolique* and *A l'ombre des majorités silencieuses*.

49   *Toward a Rational Society*, p. 37.

50   *Toward a Rational Society*, p. 61.

51   Baudrillard, *Pour une critique*, p. 218.

4

SEMIOTICS, CYBERNETICS, AND THE ECSTASY OF MARKETING COMMUNICATIONS

Kim Sawchuk

We know that today all material production enters into this sphere. We know that it is at the level of reproduction (fashion, media, publicity, information and communication networks) on the level of what Marx negligently called the non-essential sectors of capital . . . that is to say in the sphere of simulacra and the code, that the global process of capital is founded.[1]

Obscenity begins precisely when there is no more spectacle, no more scene, when all becomes transparence and immediate visibility, when everything is exposed to the harsh and inexorable light of information and communication.[2]

ROUTE 1: I DREAM OF JOHNNY

I used to think of you JB, as I sat at my desk in the marketing research office. I had plenty of time to let my mind wander between coding surveys. Every day was filled with mounds of them – up to the 250 a day – rife with information about consumer likes and dislikes, their memories of television, print, radio commercials, details of their use of the products of both our clients and competitors.

You crossed my mind JB, when I read my *Coder's Manual* for the first time and was told that my job was one of translation, not interpretation. My manual was very clear about my task and this process. It was my job to turn the impressions of consumers, words gathered by a team of "field workers" – or telemarketers – into numbers that eventually would be fed into a computer. I was not to interpret, but to swim along the surface of language, across the flat two-dimensional plane of meaning in a shallow pool of consumer memories.

Didn't you say that in the latest semiurgical moment in capitalism that all meaning would be liquidated, that "meaning disappears in the horizon of communication?"[3] Ironically, your words made sense to me. Excuse me for being referential, but you seemed to describe what I was experiencing as a social subject and seeing at the office: the hyperproduction of information, and the search for all possible meanings of a given image obliterating meaning and communication as a shared, social activity.[4]

You followed this with the statement that the "media" are at the locus of this disappearance, but that this disappearance itself "is always a challenge to the powers that be."[5] Not from my experience.

The disappearance of meaning might prove to be a challenge to marketers in an age of "media clutter," but this proliferation of semiotic cacophony, and hence "disappearance" of the exactitude of meanings and messages didn't upset any power structures at the office, in the various markets we were busily monitoring, or in the circulation of capital. In fact, it provided us, the marketing firm, with business – the surveillance of meaning and the monitoring of the different social statistical aggregates, both actual and potential, who not only consumed these meanings but produced, appropriated, perverted, understood, and misunderstood them in a variety of ways and from a multitude of media sources. I learned that marketers call this melange of contact points, or points of interface with consumers, a "media mix."

But let me return to my story.

Product-image-number: this became my marketing mantra, a veritable description of the journey of the product in this abstract system of documentation. I witnessed the daily metamorphoses of products from use-value, to exchange value, to pure sign-value. You were right in this respect. The least important item of that equation was the product itself, at least at this stage of the game.

I thought of you JB, and your beautiful description of "soft technologies" and ontological positions of "reversibility" for postmodern subjects turned objects, turned subjects, turned objects.... You told me: "We cannot distinguish an active manipulator from one who is passively manipulated – thus reverberating the old relationships of domination and violence into this new era of soft technologies."[6] Here I was, just a cog in the marketing wheel – or rather, a node in the marketing network – my subjectivity twirling in a tailspin of reversibility.

I contemplated this reversibility.

At once consumer and underpaid worker, I began to think of myself as an "ad cop," participating in a sophisticated form of corporate spying. I realized that I was a security guard in this "obscene" system that circulated signs – or the consumer goods that were themselves signs – from dog food to diapers, to cameras, to planes. In the world I worked in reality was only a support for the packaging.

I discovered that simulation means savings for "smart marketers" in the trade magazines that would be left around the office.[7] If changing the color of the mushroom soup convinced the Canadian shopper that the soup contained more mushrooms, then there were more mushrooms as far as we were concerned. But, as you asked, then what of the objective, discernible referent? We didn't care. If it made it on the code frame because enough people believed it was true, well it was. Truth had a particular meaning in this business. Wasn't this the epitome of simulation where signs of the real replace the real?

I sat there JB, watching the force-feeding of the population, who were being bombarded – or is that seduced? – with visual cues, sound cues, slogans, in the hope that there would be something, anything, they might hang onto – something they would re-call or remember. It was the details that counted in the statistical accumulation of consumer recall. I felt a perverse satisfaction witnessing the desperation of our corporate clients to see if the consumer could see, or cared to see, any differences between competing brands of the same products. Yet I was alarmed by the enormous resources being implemented both to monitor public opinion at the political level and ensure a continual escalation of buying. I often wondered what you would think if you were in my seat reading these surveys.

What do you do when the phone rings? Do you answer the marketing call?

ROUTE 2: MARKETING COMMUNICATIONS OR THE END OF ADVERTISING

It [advertising] is our only architecture today; great screens on which are reflected atoms, particules, molecules in motion. Not a public scene or true public space but gigantic spaces of circulation, ventilation and ephemeral connections.

Advertising signs and marketing codes

Coded similarities and dissimilarities: that is certainly the image of cyberneticized social exchange.[9]

Baudrillard's work is part of a long trajectory of social theory concerned with the role of advertising and commodity culture in the present capitalist system. As several authors have noted, since 1968, Baudrillard has expanded on Lukács's note in his essay on reification that "the problem of commodities is the central, structural problem of capitalist society in all its aspects."[10] Like other contemporary French theorists in the wake of post-structuralism, Baudrillard's analysis doesn't assume an untainted, prehistoric essential human subjectivity waiting for its liberation from capitalism. He describes our immanence in capitalism, an immanence that creates our very ontology. The "codes" of political economy, as commodity form and as sign form, do not alienate consciousness from its contents, but form the basis of our social relations "integrating the group through the very process of their circulation."[11]

While his critique of political economy has intensified in his most recent writings, for Baudrillard, the commodity has never simply been a problem in economics, but a crisis in meaning and value as well as a problem of communication.[12] By *The Mirror of Production*,[13] consumption is described as a form of labor in which individuals organize their existence and invest it with meaning. What is purchased is not simply the objects themselves – a car, a watch, a pen – but the entire sign-system of objects that imbue these functional objects with both status and signification. A particular type of car may be chosen for its color, engine size, or design, or price – all elements which create an "image" for that car and paradigmatically place it in relationship to the other cars on a market.[14] Within capitalism, "The code of political economy rationalizes and regulates exchange, making things communicate, but under the law of the code and through the control of meaning."[15] What does Baudrillard mean by code, and how does it relate to the production of meaning? Is he referring to Marx's famous C-M-C, the law of equivalence and exchange; or the structural-linguistic notion of a code which establishes a series of differences between elements in a sign system; or is the code merely a conventionalized set of meanings?

Baudrillard's fluctuating use of the term code is indicative of tensions in his relationship to semiotics and cybernetics, which, in turn, has influenced his understanding of consumer culture. *Critique* includes a discussion of "objects as carriers of indexed social significations, of a social and cultural hierarchy, embodied in their form material, colour, durability, arrangement in space." But he also draws our attention to the limitations of a code conceived of as "inventory of objects and their *significations*," Individuals and groups do not blindly follow the injunctions of such codes, but use this repertory of objects and significations "to their advantage."[16] In this same text he also explicitly criticizes the notion of the code in the transmitter-receiver model of communications for the same reason: it assumes a "univocality" and singularity of message and interpretation. "Each communication process is thus vectorized into a single meaning, from the transmitter to the receiver: the latter can be transmitter in turn, and the same schema is reproduced." It is not a scientific theory as much as "the epitome of social exchange *such as it is* . . . ."[17] In this schema the system of speech, like the system of economic exchange, reproduces itself through us. Even though there is an exchange of positions between transmitter and receiver, this oscillation is nothing but enforced feedback. As he says, "*Reversibility* has nothing to do with reciprocity."[18] Baudrillard calls enforced feedback the "cybernetic illusion."

After *Oublier Foucault*[19] it becomes clear that a subtle shift in emphasis between semiotics and cybernetics has occurred, a shift produced by Baudrillard's awareness of genetics. No longer is the "code" of political economy related to semiological codes, but to the digital code, present in some linguistic theories, but culled primarily from genetics.[20] In this model, communication is equivalent to information, and information is conceived of as a series of digital binary units (bits) reducible to ones and zeroes. A code in this model is a preprogrammed sequence of instructions biogenetically replicated. Transmission of information, rather than meaning, is the central concern.[21] In this later work, Baudrillard not only describes information theory as the dominant mode of communication, he incorporates the assumptions of genetics and information theory into his reading of contemporary culture. In part, this accounts for the transition in his work from a semiotics concerned with interpretation by subjects to an information model based in cybernetics which de-emphasizes the production of meaning in favor of the processing of signals and the reduction of noise. According to Baudrillard, this is the current "strategic model that everywhere is replacing the great ideological model which constituted political economy in its time."[22]

Cybernetics is more than a theory of information and a communications model. In ontological terms, cybernetics views all of life – whether animal, human or machine – as information processing mechanisms. In Baudrillardian terms we move from the idea that we consume the codes of political economy, to the idea that right down to our genetic material WE ARE THE CODE. Within this epistemological and ontological framework, the self is an information system which is part of a larger information system. Baudrillard expresses this sentiment precisely in the "The Ecstasy of Communication": we are "terminals within multiple networks," rather than actors or dramaturges in a theatrical space.[23] Concomitantly, we are no longer in the industrial era, or the second order of simulation, but the electronic era, or the third order of simulation.[24]

Marketing communication

... today the scene and the mirror no longer exist; instead there is a screen and network. In place of the reflexive transcendence of mirror and scene, there is a nonreflecting surface, an immanent surface where operations unfold – the smooth operational space of communications.[25]

This shift in priority in Baudrillard's work from semiotics to cybernetics, and the second order of simulation to the third order of simulation, has influenced my interpretation of how I may characterize the practice of advertising within a Baudrillardian framework. We no longer live in a capitalist productivist society, but in a "neo-capitalist cybernetic order" that, as Baudrillard stresses, aims for total systems control. "This is the mutation for which the biological theorization of the code prepares the ground."[26] The predominance of the paradigm of the genetic code, and the idea of coding itself, is no longer "limited to the lab," but our "banal, everyday life is invested by these models."[27] Goodbye advertising, hello marketing.

It is more and more common for business and business schools to refer to advertising as marketing communications. This rhetorical change indicates a shift taking place in the "operational means of power," as Baudrillard would state.[28] Advertising becomes a moment, or subsystem, in this network environment or marketing matrix, particularly as we move from a mass sales approach (or product differentiation) to market segmentation and target marketing.[29]

Yet it would be a mistake to say that the entire representational function of advertisements is no longer strategically useful to advertisers. Advertisements, as complex and dynamic image-texts, are part of a sign-system whose provisional and specifically located meanings can be charted using semiotic techniques, and whose circulation is part of an entire marketing and promotional system whose conceptual terrain is articulated in the assumptions of cybernetics. While theoretically related in some traditions of the field, cybernetics is neither equivalent to semiotics nor has it entirely replaced it within the present promotional network.[30] A more sustained analysis of advertising in relationship to marketing is necessary if we are to understand the way neo-capitalism programs a series of potential interactions in which we are given a number of limited choices – perhaps the analogy of the video game is appropriate here.

Likewise, we must re-examine the concepts of representation, simulation, and circulation. It is no longer possible to critique advertising on the basis of representation as it is traditionally conceived – that is according to the truth or falsenenss of the image in relationship to some external referent. Advertising, as marketing communications, is part of a system in which compliance does reward us, rather than one of mere "persuasion" based on a pleasing image: the recent proliferation of incentive buying schemes that award you points every time you purchase something, points which act as credit for other consumer purchases, exemplifies this new virtual architecture of consumption. Disparate commodities and corporations are merging: Shell (gas) is connected to Safeway (groceries) and Air Canada, while Esso (gas) offers you Club Z points. Electronic networking and computer software developments create a vast virtual transactional space which invites us to conduct ourselves along programmed potential routes of consumption. Image-based campaigns are part of the tactical artillery deployed against consumers in this marketing matrix. While this is a fecund terrain for critical thinking, academic work, including Baudrillard's, tends to revert to discussions of advertising, or the issue of representation, rather than marketing, or the question of circulation.

For example, Baudrillard places "ad men" at the center of the system of sign production: "The adman cannot but believe that people believe it – however slightly, that is, that a minimal probability exists of the message reaching its goal and being decoded according to meaning. Any principle of uncertainty is excluded."[31] Uncertainty is understood to be a part of the entire system. Advertisers are quite aware that the great majority of their advertisements never reach their destination, or target audiences, hence the crucial importance of marketing research which only expects to receive an approximation of what messages are getting through and how the messages may relate to buying behaviour. Marketers know that consumers may be able to faithfully redescribe an advertisement, but neither name or use the product. This is the reason for the creation of more and more elaborate systems of "monitoring, measurement and modelling" which connect television, to store, to user, to product. I will examine some of these later.[32]

Consumers and the various producers who participate in the circulation of signs, goods, and capital for exchange are part of a mobile incentive and surveillance apparatus which functions on statistical probability. As Baudrillard says in *La société de consommation*, the whole culture becomes a gigantic combinatorial machine.[33] While no one person or single corporation can be said to have ultimate control of this decisional apparatus, not everyone has the same amount of access to information and resources, or power and control. Affirming that power and manipulation exist acknowledges that the system is constructed with particular desired goals in mind: for example, profit in the case of the corporation and political control in the case of government. Yet the creation of these combinatorial structures which attempt to transport us along prescribed lines does not guarantee that people will stop to buy a product or watch an advertisement. Here I turn to Baudrillard a second time, not as an authority on the sign and commodity production, but as a theorist of communications and networks. But I do this with reservation because of two other obstacles I have encountered in his texts.

First, while he devotes a number of pages to the topic of polling and surveys throughout his works, Baudrillard tends to criticize them from two angles: one, the simplistic position that they structure replies to the questions they ask; and two, that they are not objective. He tends to view political polling and marketing surveys as the same, a tendency that is part and parcel of Baudrillard's proclivity for oppositional extremes and linear totalizing evolutionary schemas. He contends, for example, that the digital *completely* obviates the analogical, so that "the entire system of communications has passed from that of a syntactically complex language structure to a binary sign system of question and answer – of the perpetual test . . . ."[34] (1983: 117) His question-answer metaphor is a useful device for understanding how choice is presented to us in neo-capitalist cybernetic culture. Yet, while digital coding is technically outstripping analogical means of *transmitting* information, it is erroneous to think that digital communications – signalling – necessarily eliminates the communication of meanings and/or complex messages – semiotics.[35] Both are strategically valuable in setting up these spaces for consumer transaction.

Massive polling and surveillance depends upon the easy dispatch of "information," made possible by the rapid transmission rate and reliability of telecommunications signals – but the rapidity of information transfer is not enough. Polling and testing do not solely rely on electronic devices or passive forms of monitoring that are divorced from signification. Further, political polls tend to adopt this stimulus-response framework (yes-no), while marketing surveys combine yes-no responses with associational question and answer sections. I would argue that this is the difference between a poll and a survey. While language is reduced to numbers in the survey process, there is always a translation between numerical or statistical modeling and language-based communication. Not only does a field worker write down an oral response, but a coder must read these responses and assign them a numerical value. This will then be fed into a software program that draws up correspondences in the form of graphs, tables, and charts. But clients do not want huge volumes of data: the numbers and charts act in many ways as reassurance that the empirical work has been done, but a skillful marketing representative must construct a persuasive story about the meaning of these numbers for the corporate client.[36] Because of this, knowledge that lies, inconsistency, and forgetting are endemic, marketers are experimenting with automatic "passive" means to document consumer patterns of viewing advertisments and buying products – a notion that I will return to later.

Secondly, in *Forget Foucault*, Baudrillard expresses skepticism that any understanding of the media universe is possible. "Our anti-destiny is the media universe. And I don't see how to make this mental leap which would make it possible to reach the fractal or fatal zones where things would really be happening. Collectively we are behind the radio-active screen of information. It is no more possible to go behind that curtain than it is to leap over your own shadow."[37] Really happening? Behind the curtain? These are strange statements considering Baudrillard's insistence that theatricality or representation is over. Theatricality and the spectacle are, after all, the realm of ideology, where one can distinguish the true from the false, the real from its representation, not a cultural condition of third-order simulation which obfuscates these borders. It also conveys a profound nostalgia for the real.[38]

To agree with Baudrillard on this point would make it impossible for us to follow him in any of the directions he takes. If this is so difficult, why read Baudrillard at all?

Why? His words annoy, irritate, provoke, but they also resonate with my present experience as a contemporary subject/object, continually tested and probed and prodded and my past experience as a coder in marketing research. I find myself stimulated both to respond, and highlight correspondences and disagreements. In this essay I will both probe Baudrillard and *play* with his texts in conjunction with marketing discourse, rather than apply or test Baudrillard's theory against the 'empirical" reality of marketing research. Baudrillard's writings on advertising, polling, cybernetics, simulation, seduction, and communications don't give us a *peak* behind the curtain as much as a *means* to travel in the virtual transactional space of the marketing matrix. In "The Ecstasy of Communication" from *Fatal Strategies*, I find stimulating descriptions of the virtual architectures being created by corporations who are engaged in the practice not of merely advertising their products, but in promoting them in a variety of ways: a realm where the packaging is indistinguishable from the product; a realm less concerned with the question of an adequate representation of the sign to the product-referent, than the types of associations being created in the minds of viewers and consumers; a realm whose operational function collapses the spheres of wage labor and consumption, the marketplace, and the home, as home shopping and point of purchase displays make apparant; a realm absolutely interested, whose absolutist interests, lie in the convergence of all data systems into a single information highway made possible by digital processing and the promise of fiber optics. To return to the opening quote in this section: "It is our only architecture today . . . . Not a public scene or true public space but gigantic spaces of circulation, ventilation and ephemeral connections."[39] The new consumer is a veritable node in the marketing network, immanent to modern telematic power.

This scenerio and recombinant quality has been made possible by technical and economic developments, but equally because of a major post-war epistemological shift that one could argue made these developments possible. Is it coincidental that the development of the later stage of marketing research coincides with the growth of cybernetics?[40] The transformation in the ontological and operational definition of subjects as consumers, subjects who are then conceived of as "fragments in a mobile space," to borrow a phrase from Foucault, to be documented in excruciating, obscene detail, occurs within a very specific context where all beings, whether animal, human, or technological, are conceived of as information systems.[41] Perhaps Baudrillard flirts with cybernetics and genetics in his later work, not because this is a desired state of affairs, but because it is one of the crucial means by which the hegemony of consumerism is maintained in neo-capitalist cybernetic culture.

I will now examine this period more closely to distinguish marketing from advertising, to understand the evolution in abstraction from production-based economic activities to marketing based activities, and to address Baudrillard's concept of the masses, or "the silent majority," in this system before we follow him along our next pathway.

From masses to targets

The masses no longer express themselves, they are surveyed."[42]

Marketing, or the practice of promoting the exchange of commodities through door-to-door sales, promotions, direct mail, the telephone, the television, *and* advertising has become a specialized yet central part of business since the 1950s. Advertising is one subset of marketing, while marketing is a micro-instance of the macro-political economy of neo-capitalism. A 1983 article in Business *Week* draws the distinction between marketing and advertising in this simplistic, but useful, way: "As companies define marketing more clearly, they no longer confuse it with advertising, which uses media to let consumers know that a certain product or service is available. In essence, marketing means moving goods from the producer to the consumer."[43] The history of marketing often is depicted as having three stages: from production to sales to marketing, an evolution that in some respects parallels Baudrillard's description of the shift from production to consumption, and the resultant transformation of the commodity. The productivist approach coincided with the need for companies to be close to raw materials. While marketing research existed at this point, it literally was research into markets for a product which was first made. The change of emphasis to a sales orientation began to conceive of the consumer as integral to the system, and not merely a point at the end of the production line to be sold a piece of goods. Commercial research departments were established to supply information about present markets, sales teams devised to dispose of products, take care of advertising, and find out about potential markets. However, in this, the emphasis was still on the selling of the attributes of the product. This is a crucial distinction.

In the late 1950s, large companies became "total marketing companies." Since the 1950s, successful businesses have modified their strategies (general goals) and tactics (operational means by which a business implements these goals) from a sales approach to a marketing approach. Marketing is not the same as sales or selling. Selling adapts the consumer's desires to the product. In the words of marketers, a "Copernican revolution" in marketing took place after World War II, when "the consumer became the sun" around which contemporary marketing strategy would revolve.[44] Manufacturing's turn-of-the-century concern with the sales of a product to a mass market has given way to detailed studies of the lives and habits of consumers.[45] While the tracking techniques and organization of data have been facilitated greatly because of the general availability of computers, in effect accelerating the entire process, this intense focus on the consumer and their "desires" are the basis of modern marketing.

Baudrillard recognizes that desire, in this context, is neither an ontological or empirically distinct realm, nor a libidinal challenge to the status quo, but a historically shifting force. He also articulates the idea in his later work that "you are the system; you are at the center of power."[46] Ritualistic feedback is a mechanism central to system maintenance. For Baudrillard, "the mass realizes the paradox of being both a subject and object of simulation."[47] While this is a percipient point, neither individuals nor the various conglomerations of social subjects are viewed by marketers as undifferentiated, liquidating masses – they are discernible entities who can be cut up and reconfigured in multiple combinations. This move from product differentiation to market segmentation was crucial to the placement of the consumer at the center of the system.

Baudrillard critiques "productionism:" therefore it is interesting to note that in marketing terms, the idea that one markets to a mass is related to the production mentality. As a standard marketing textbook states, a mass marketing approach is a "production-oriented procedure." It focusses on the product assuming that all consumers are the same. Mass marketers do not mass market, we are reminded. Mass marketers aim at a large market area through the practice of target marketing.[48]

In other words, mass marketing has been replaced by ever-more sophisticated techniques of market segmentation in which consumer markets are identified and "targeted" to develop, produce, and market products that represent abstract wishes or hidden anxieties, particularly anxieties related to the body.[49] Although concomitant with Baudrillard's explicit observation that the masses have been "surveyed to death," and his implicit assumption that sociology has been complicit with this trend, so much for the mass as a "silent majority" or a "black hole" that absorbs all.[50] In this shift, the masses are not liquidated as much as documented and primed for travel down various marketing channels.

Marketing channels and media carriers

For finally, it was capital which was the first to feed throughout its history on the destruction of every referential, of every human goal, which shattered every ideal distinction between true and false, good and evil in order to establish a radical law of equivalence and exchange, the iron law of its power. It was the first to practice deterrence, abstraction, disconnection, deterritorialization, etc.; and if it was capital which fostered reality, the reality principle, it was also the first to liquidate it in the extermination of every use value, of every real equivalence, of production and wealth, in the very sensation we have of the unreality of its stakes and the omnipotence of manipulation ... it only multiples the signs and accelerated the play of simulation.[51]

To return to where we have been, marketing history has developed the following discourse on its own practice: marketing records ostensibly inherent desires, then creates new products (or repackages old ones) that ostensibly satisfy these desires. In doing so, there is a shift in level of abstraction. One does not sell a specific product, such as a tampon, one sells "sanitary protection," of which a tampon is one potential profitable solution. At the same time as this shift has occurred, we also are cajoled into making associations with "brand names," although the logos which are the image-text for the corporate name, complete with trademarked font and colours, do not represent a single specific product. "Porsche" no longer simply sells cars, the item that the brand name was first associated with, but pens, watches, and other designer goods whose aesthetic code – black, chrome, classically "modernist" – defines a type of "porschean" masculinity acquired through the purchase and use of these products.[52]

In this transformation to a new level of abstraction the use-value of the product is pushed from its centrality within the system, as Marx so perceptively theorized. It embodies both use-value and exchange value. But, as Baudrillard noted earlier, in the twentieth century it also is conceived of as a "sign" and not merely a symbolic status object.[53] This is reflected at the level of production – which is not separable from other aspects of distribution, consumption, and exchange in Marx – and in advertising or the sphere of reproduction. The dominant mode of address in advertising has shifted from a description of the functional use of the objects to a description of their sign-values, as indicated by the prevalence of emotional appeals in advertising and life-style advertising.[54] McDonalds is not selling fast food, but a family adventure of eating out together, intergenerational bonding, and sharing love, as their advertising campaigns reiterate over and over in various ways. Ingesting a specific food item is only one part of this total experience.

Ironically, it is this explicit demarcation of this shift that makes Baudrillard's texts appealing to advertisers. His descriptions of the effects created by the proliferation of advertising "signs" have not simply been taken as descriptions of life "such as it is," but as a justification for the right of advertisers to create symbolic meanings beyond use-value or exchange value. Baudrillard is quoted within advertising journals as proof of the necessity of an evolution from "the object to its symbol, the meaning of the sign, and from reality to image."[55] "I think advertising men and advertisers have created a new natural right to abundance, to shows, to dreams. It is their duty to defend this right through a remarkable display of the brand and its values."[56] Beyond use-value, or product attributes, and exchange value, they have a right to add imaginary values (sign-value), and brand personalities. Marketers actually say that this is not "seduction," but "love."

One could, however, argue that this is strategic reading of Baudrillard's text. With the advent of marketing, the sign is no longer about symbolic exchange[57] but acquires a new hegemonic sign-function. In neo-capitalist cybernetic culture the sign-value has an indexical, performative function; it is significant that semioticians such as Umberto Eco conceive of the sign as a "sign-vehicle," a mode of transportation from one place to another. In this, signifier and signified constantly invert and branch out into other networks of complex association where signifier and signified perpetually invert. To go back to an earlier example, seeing an image of chrome on a black pen sporting the Porsche logo links the pen to the car. But the car is not a stable signified or final referent. It is a signifier replete with the cultural codes of masculinity, codes nurtured and stabilized in the Porsche marketing strategy which features an angular masculine face to anchor the connection. Masculinity itself is connected to very specific displays of power in North America, of which the image of car driven by a man, is one. Hence the equation man + car = power becomes tautological. The signs are exchangeable one for the other. Further, the sign-product – a black and chrome pen – loses its symbolic or iconic traits, traits that point to one specific signified or referent, such as knowledge, masculinity, or power – all are invoked by this pen. The signification process is both stable and unstable, but meaning does not wholly give way to digital signal processing or conventionalized clusters of shared meanings. At the same time as redundancy and repetition in these images are key means to conventionalize meanings, and make connections between a look (chrome and black), a brand name (Porsche), and a product (pen), this instability between the sign and its referent leaves open their potential reconfiguration into other lines of products and promotions.

Shifts in advertising strategy are themselves a sign of this phenomenon of infinite recombination. In contemporary television advertising, the images and texts are triggers that can be condensed or enlarged, depending on the price of media time, into 15-20-30-60-second segments. They are repeated across a variety of media carriers during a given campaign to maximize the points of contact between image and target audiences who are literally, physically mobile. There is an increased use of paid postering in places like subways, buses, bulletin boards, streets, and even elevators – all the liminal spaces that commuting populations are temporarily stabilized in before moving to their next place. But this mobility is not simply true of the consumer, it is a systemic necessity in marketing – circulation is both a problem and a necessity. Consumers must be moved to the stores to buy the product in order for a campaign to be continued; even if the advertisement is remembered, if the product does not sell the marketing campaign will be abandoned. An advertising sign does not deliver the consumer to the product alone; the image is an indexical sign, which points us in different directions on a multitude of planes and spaces, working in tandem with other elements in a marketing matrix. This matrix is composed of the famous "Four Ps" of marketing – product, place, price, and promotion. "We develop a Product that we feel will satisfy the target customers. We find a way (Place) to reach our target customers. Promotion tells the target customers about the availability of the product that has been designed for them. Then the Price is set – after estimating expected customer reaction to the total offering and the costs of getting it to them."[58] As marketing texts emphasize, you can have all the advertising you want, but if the product is not available to the consumer when they want it, in the color or size they need, at a price or within a financial arrangement, such as systems of "instant credit," or "no down payment until ..." schemes that accommodate consumers' budgets, then it is probable that a transaction will not take place. All of these marketing elements are equally important as part of the entire architecture which creates channels to move people, goods, and images. The customer is not liquidated but stimulated along these transactional marketing highways. "Signification" is what Umberto Eco calls a "text-oriented" procedure, not a static form of codification or "grammar-oriented" procedure.[59] Textual fluidity has an important tactical function in the transactional network of marketing communications; it is not obliterated by these electronic means of communication.

ROUTE 3: REPRESENTATION, SIMULATION, CIRCULATION, OR GOING IN CIRCLES

There is no longer a machinery of representation, only a machinery of simulation.[60]

The function of the advertising image is transformed as marketing practices rely more and more on the full range of electronic media available to them. It is useful, in this context, to understand simulation in *conjunction* with representation in the process of transactional circulation in neo-capitalist cybernetic culture – for there is both a machinery of representation and simulation. Baudrillard often mentions circulation and simulation together: "Simulation is characterized by a precession of the model, of all models around the merest fact – the models come first, and their orbital circulation (like the bomb) constitutes the magnetic field of events."[61] However, the terms simulation and representation are pitted against one another in his work: one has replaced the other. Simulation is opposed to representation; it is "the radical negation of the sign as value, as meaning, as referential." In representation, "a sign could refer to the depth of meaning, a sign could exchange for meaning."[62] It had only one meaning, it could be falsified: "the sign and the real are equivalent, if only ideally." Moving into the age of simulation indicates that there is no longer a sovereign real against which to measure the model or the representation: "the age of simulation thus begins with a liquidation of all referentials – worse – by their resurrection in systems of signs, a more ductile material than meaning." Let's sift through Baudrillard's statement. How is it that signs are more ductile than meaning, if meaning is part of the sign – the signified? Is he suggesting that we are left only with signifier or pure form, and no content? This remains unclear throughout his corpus. As many have argued before, Baudrillard seems to be lamenting the loss of denotative meaning, but is this all there is to representation?[63]

Borrowing heavily from Walter Benjamin and Thomas Sebeok, Baudrillard does, however, distinguish between first, second, and third orders of simulation. He aligns their insights with technical-economic transformations. The renaissance-feudal period is characterized by representation, or simulation of the first order – a counterfeit or copy could be produced of an object, but the relationship was still singular, as the level of production still proceeds essentially by hand. Industrial production transforms this, "emancipating the sign," eliminating its "aura" as discussed by Benjamin in "The Work of Art in the Era of Mechanical Reproduction."[64] In this realm of second order simulation differences are not abolished, but meanings, like commodities, are proliferated. In the third order of simulation, the electronic era, the real is "liquidated" there is no longer theatrical illusion, but "an immanent logic of the operational principle.[65] In third order simulation: "cybernetics, control, generation from models, differential modulation, feed back, question and answer, etc. such is the operational configuration. Industrial simulacra are only operational – digitality is its metaphysical principle and DNA its prophet."[66]

Whereas in the first order of simulation a copy is made of the real, the representation is in some senses, unique; in the second order of simulation the possibility of the mass repetition of images destroys the idea of the uniqueness of the copy, yet it preserves some sense of distinction or difference between the original and the copy. Think of the difference between a picture drawn of an object by hand and an image reproduced by a photocopier which makes endless proliferation of this same image possible. The photocopier proliferates the number of copies, but still maintains generational, material differences between the original and copy. The third order of simulation breaks this down entirely because of the ability to digitally reproduce information. In this "third order," there is no original and copy: "genetic miniaturization is the dimension of simulation. The real is produced from matrices, memory banks and command modules and with these it can be produced an indefinite number of times."[67] Contrast both the reproduction of an image by hand and by photocopier with the production of images using computer software in the digital era. No first copy remains, no original exists; the image or text can be infinitely recombined with other images, the colors easily transformeed with no apparent seams or generational differences.

There are still issues to be explored in Baudrillard's delineation of the orders of simulation as they apply to the circulation of the advertising image in the context of marketing. Even if we understand the advertising image as a simulated image which has no copy, origin, and does not mimic the real, it is still possible to conceptualize simulation in dialectical terms, as the opposite or antithesis of representation. In representation the appearance tries to faithfully copy or reproduce its object; in simulation, these models or copies, not only precede the referential object, but resurrect the copy into another level of existence: the "hyperreal." Baudrillard concludes that "The essential is no longer to represent, but to circulate."[68] But, are all of the orders of simulation antithetical or are they are interdependent? How are they connected?

Think of how food is packaged and sold. A chicken advertised in a local paper is depicted to inform the consumer that it is on sale. This reproduction of the chicken as image occurs at the level of representation: the photographic image or drawing of a chicken, the chicken's referent, is supposedly the chicken in the store. One knows that the image is not unique, but cheaply reproduced and circulated to the entire region where both the newspaper is located and the store selling the sale fowl can be found. But can this bird be understood as the final referential ground upon which the advertising photo is based? Chickens, agriculturally massproduced on poultry farms, are genetically altered to create a breed of bird that grows rapidly and efficiently according to the amount of food it eats. But their alteration does not end here. After they are killed, they are injected with water to make them appear plumper. They thus visually fulfill the consumer's desire for a luscious, juicy fowl. The chicken is not "real" or "natural" but a culturally manipulated foodstuff. It is a simulated bird, a hyperreal chicken, an extension of the producer's marketing strategy. Here we can see how representation, simulation, and circulation work together in a promotional strategy where there is no firm level of the real outside of the entire system of reproduction; but we also see how, in the present order, production and reproduction are part of the same process. As a sign, the signifier (the form) and the signified (the content constantly invert). The chicken as sign is part of a vast network of reproduction and signification: the packaging is part of the very object being sold.

There are other issues to be examined here. First, in Baudrillard's scheme, simulation and circulation always occur in a self-enclosed system, like the Moebius strip he is fond of using as an example: "All the referentials intermingle their discourses in a circular, Moebian compulsion."[69] For this reason, says Baudrillard, it is impossible to rediscover an absolute level of the real.[70] Indeed, reversibility in this instance collapses the distinction in Baudrillard's work between a variety of couples including, the "subject-object" couple, "the transmitter-receiver" couple, and the "sign-meaning" couple. "Circular discourse must be taken literally: that is, it no longer goes from one point to the other but describes a circle that indistinctly incorporates the positions of transmitter and receiver, henceforth unlocatable as such."[71] Second, Baudrillard maintains that reversibility and manipulation are the hallmark of simulation: "manipulation is a floating causality where positivity and negativity engender and overlap with one another, where there is no longer any active and passive."[72] And: "It is this magnificent recycling that the universal simulacrum of manipulation, from the scenerio of mass suffrage to present day and illusory opinion polls, begins to be installed."[73] In other words, because of this intermingling and circularity, Baudrillard concludes that since there is no way to locate an origin, or reference, or the real in any "clear" sense that "there is no longer any instance of power."[74] He does waver on this point, telling us it is not power, nor even seduction, we are dealing with here, but manipulation – although I am not clear why manipulation is not a form of power in his mind. Thus we are handed more antagonist couples. Power is associated with panopticism, theatricality, and representation, and manipulation with simulation, circulation, and polling, which are located outside of power because positions are reversible.

In terms of marketing and subjects, ad men, to return to an earlier example, may also be consumers of products, dependent on wages and the targets of their own marketing practices. While they may produce the images that become associated with the products we may or may not buy, they themselves are monitored by the companies who hire them. The company is, in turn, accountable to both the corporation who may hire another independent marketing firm to monitor the results of a given campaign initiated by the firm. The brand manager for the corporation who produces the product-sign is, in turn, both assessed by the profit margins the brand garners and responsible to company executives, who are, in turn, responsible to stockholders, and so on. But are these multiple situations of power in this example merely bi-polar or reversible? Is the distribution of power within these relationships equal, or do some have more resources than others? It seems to me that as a description of the distribution of power, the metaphor of the circle is inadequate.

As a portrayal of the process of the distribution of meaning, the circle, likewise, is flawed. The metaphor of the circle does not break out of the appearance-essence distinction, or Western metaphysics: it reverses them and sends them into a self-enclosed orbital spin. This is distinct from the idea of reversibility occurring in an open network. In traditional semiotic terms, a sign (the photographic chicken-image) always refers to another sign (chicken as food) whose reading is determined because of its placement in relationship to other food items in a flyer distributed by a retailing firm that calls itself a grocery store. However, this reversibility is not circular and self-contained, but branches out into a plethora of possible combinations whose fulfillment depends on the placement of the image in a particular semantic and syntactic field and the participation or "subjects" in the sign-system. In the context of an animal rights flyer the chicken does not signify food, but the exploitation of animals for human consumption. But there is another issue at stake here.

This inability to conceptualize the sign outside of a circular reversibility, to understand it as it branches out or relays and propels meaning into different combinations, keeps Baudrillard going around in circles. In the neo-capitalist cybernetic system of marketing research, the circuits are not circular, but continually open up and mutate, moving horizontally and laterally through the body politic.

Within this invisible yet very "real" virtual architecture that manages the circulation of bodies and products and images, as Margaret Morse has noted, the car becomes the prototype for subjectivity. Consumers are "driven" to products through elaborate pull strategies which may not name products or companies yet create effects that clearly benefit those companies. For example, in a recent "pull strategy" deployed by a pharmaceutical company, symptoms for women to diagnose menopause were listed on television along with a recommendation to see a doctor. No drug treatments were mentioned. Instead manufacturers targeted doctors with drug representatives who "informed" doctors of the product's ability to treat these symptoms, anticipating that a percentage of women would tell the doctors about the symptoms. The doctors, armed with this information, then would recommend the product. Here we can see how *not* showing the product can still achieve the desired marketing effect. The consumer is not so much "seduced" by the glamour of a particular image, as *incited* to move along prescribed channels that have been strategically set up to get her, in this instance, to purchase the product. While it is "impossible" to designate a point of origin in this elaborate network – for the doctor is as much a middleman for the company as their dupe, power is nevertheless exerted – not power as violence, but, as Baudrillard says, as manipulation. It is important to recall that manipulation is not false consciousness, or the misrepresentation of sign to product, or signifier to its signified, but as travel along the lines of least resistance. Memories are triggered along certain pathways as associations are made between product, image, and usage, but these associations must be flexible. The commodity must be as protean as the consumer in the era of marketing communications. Aspirin, for example, is promoted for arthritic pain relief, to prevent heart attacks, and alleviate menstrual cramps: three very different uses, images, and target markets. But while we are encouraged to venture along these pathways, this does not mean we build the roads, or that our delivery is guaranteed.[75]

Any advertisements, whether they are in the form of print, radio, or television, do not circulate between two dialectically situated terms. Signs in neo-capitalist cybernetic culture are sign-vehicles that have the potential to move in several directions, but are often coerced and deployed along a variety of pathways throughout the marketing network. They must be malleable, and because they are, their movements must continually be documented and traced as they move through different segments of the consumer body. Does the color red remind people of danger, communism, or Air Canada? Is the airline's image hampered because of these associations? Because of their mutability, the sign-texts or images as they occur within an advertising campaign are nodal points in a vast cultural databank of potential signs. In marketing communications, the primary functions of these sign-vehicles are to trigger particular associations that will move subjects toward an initial purchase of a product, and later ensure sustained use.

The sensorial impulses of images and sounds, that make up the (im)material objects as they are presented in the electronic media, are temporary *anchors* which provide provisional meanings, but which must then *relay* us into other circuits. They activate us into consumption and into being in capitalism: this campaign is based on probability. To continue with our previous example, we must be pulled into watching the advertisement in the guise of a public service announcement, become alarmed enough to search ourselves for these signs, and decide that a trip to the doctor is worth taking. In the meantime, the doctor must be knowledgeable about the product, and prepared to prescribe it to the potential consumer/patient. Often the memory of the product for the doctor is recalled by the presence of "reminders" around the office supplied by intrepid sales representatives; the pen with the company name, a notepad with the shortened name of the drug rather than an unwieldy chemical name. The compound then must be available in the local pharmacy for purchase. The manufacturer must have targeted not only the doctors but also the druggist. This description excludes the elaborate process of getting a compound accepted by Health and Welfare Canada, and the informertial past the Advertising Standards Council. Every potential roadblock to the circulation of the product must be thought out beforehand to ensure that a potential connection can be made leading to a profit for the manufacturer, to be reinvested or put back into circulation, in the end. To put it another way, these advertising image-texts, or promotional products, are triggers which must catalyze an interaction, or act as a conduit, so that a transaction takes place.[76]

Let us unpack this further and examine how these marketing channels stimulate not only buying, but also the production of more information to create buying behavior. This propels us into another area in Baudrillard's work: the conflicting statements he makes on seduction and production.

ROUTE 4: BAUDRILLARD, FOUCAULT

Seduction/production

Something tells us, but implicitly, as if seen in a reverse shot of this writing too beautiful to be true – that if it is possible at last to talk with such definitive understanding about power, sexuality, the body and discipline, even down to their most delicate metamorphoses, it is because at some point all this is here and now over with.[77]

I wish to return to my original reservations and the text that I have been circling around: *Oublier Foucault* and the question of power. According to Baudrillard, Foucault's usefulness as a theorist of power is, like power itself, dead. Power is dead because it is "dissolved by reversal, cancellation, made hyperreal through simulation."[78] Power is now nothing more than the simulation of power. Baudrillard confuses the use of techniques of simulation by institutions that wield power with the "simulation of power," or the "death of power."

Baudrillard allies Foucault's concept of power with that of production, while, for Baudrillard, the simulation of power is a sign of the triumph of seduction.[79] Production seeks to "exterminate seduction." ". . . we must keep in mind that sex or production seeks everywhere to exterminate seduction in order to establish itself over the single economy governing relations of desire."[80] In Baudrillard's reading of Foucault, Foucault's work is a critique of power still caught within both a "productivist" model and contained within a conception of the political that displays this nostalgic longing. Baudrillard seems to understand Foucault's use of the terms production and power as transcendental signifieds, or final causes that explain all. "Power, then, is still turned toward a reality principle and a very strong truth principle; it is still oriented toward a possible coherence of politics and discourse . . . while it is no longer despotic in nature, it 'still belongs to the despotic order of the real . . . . It never ceases being the term.' "[81]

His argument with Foucault is, I believe, based on an ungenerous, selective misreading of Foucault's text. First, Foucault is explicit that the panopticon is not the model of power, but the model of power in the classical age.[82] Secondly, Baudrillard positions consumption and production as dialectically polar moments. He therefore concludes that Foucault thinks that production is more "real" than consumption. In Baudrillard's depiction of the theoretical terrain he and Foucault in habit, we are given another set of adversarial pairings: production, power, the real vs. consumption, seduction, the hyperreal. But Baudrillard is a slippery guy. While this seems to be his dominant argument in *Forget Foucault*, it is hard to pin this reading of Foucault on Baudrillard. He recants on this point in the very same essay: "What we need to analyze is the intrication of the process of seduction with the process of production and power and the irruption of a minimal reversibility in every irreversible process, secretly ruining and dismantling it while simultaneously insuring that minimal continuum of pleasure moving across it and without it would be nothing."[83] Seduction has not replaced production, nor is it merely allied with simulation, but also with representation, but not representation as the stable identity of signifier to signified.

Seduction and production are intertwined strategic moments within the marketing world. Take the coupon as an example: a coupon is an interface between the publishers of magazines, the readers of magazines and newspapers who are also consumers, and the advertisers and producers of a product. A coupon stimulates buying behavior in conjunction with an image by the promise of a discount (it must set us into motion as consumers). This is the moment of seduction. But a coupon is also a very sophisticated monitoring device coded with information that travels with you. The minute you rip out the coupon and truck down to the store, you are actually providing a company with information about which magazine you saw it in, where in the magazine, what store it was later cashed at, and when. Thus corporations not only get a sale, but a bonus: information on whether the magazine they are spending their advertising dollars on is actually circulating. The monitoring of consumers and citizens involves the process of seduction and production to generate information, particularly pertinent information, which in the words of one marketer, is power.

Reversibility, power, and surveillance

Baudrillard separates information from surveillance. "No more subject, focal point, center, or periphery: but pure flexion or circular inflection. No more violence or surveillance, but only information."[84] But how can there be information without surveillance?

It is important, at this moment, to return to the body, which is not "a large and useless object," discarded to the desert of the real, but within this schema, a hyperproductive entity: as Baudrillard notes in other places, power works not simply through visuality, but through tactility. The body is not referential "ground," but a crucial data source, hooked up to these systems and integrated into multiple feedback mechanisms. The carefully segmented consumer groups who are the target of these practices are a data source scanned with infrared light, supplying statistics for the marketing machine, more and more integrated into a global political economy.

This can be done in two ways; through integrated promotions and through passive monitoring which are thought to be more accurate than surveys which must actively engage subjects in an interpretive moment.

Promotional architectures such as Club Z use credit cards to follow purchasing behavior, and then use this data to reward consumption. In marketing jargon, the Zeller's "Club Z" system is known as "targeted incentive marketing" because it provides "the ability to monitor and manage customer relationships through frequent buyer program." "Smart cards," such as Club Z cards, accumulate points for consumers by automatically tabulating what you buy, and what you cash in, thereby rewarding consumers for their consumption, and encouraging consumption in their retail outlets. The cards also tabulate information on customers to provide a broad demographic base to be used for the creation of new promotional schemes. Rewards to customers can be customized based on this information to increase loyalty: "If Mrs. Smith buys a certain amount of groceries and the system knows from her purchases that she has two kids, the system should reward her with child-related benefits. Those kinds of relationships are going to drive increased, loyal, full margin purchases."[85]

Each promotion in such a system is "controllable and measurable" so that one can test the effectiveness of each campaign. Again, the issue is flexibility and the ability of these networks to adapt moment by moment and from place to place. These systems must be able to dynamically change with the customer's buying behavior, which means that this behavior must be constantly monitored. Club Z has been incredibly successful. When the campaign started, their credit card base was 600,000 active cards. After three months in the program they had 1.5 million customers, and by January 1990, they had approximately 4.5 million; 71 percent of Zellers sales occur on the program, and a year after the launch, shopping frequency increased 40–50 percent.

A second future technique to eliminate active "responses" that depend upon the complicity of subjects is through systems of passive monitoring. These bypass the interpretive moment in the system by fully utilizing the digital capacity of new technologies. Corporations imagine setting up interactive devices that connect the home to the television to instigating and monitoring of purchasing behavior in a circuit of consumption and surveillance. New market-television testing systems, such as Infoscan, Scanamerica, and Behaviorscan combine people meters with scanning wands to provide information on viewing and consumption beyond the information that can be gleaned from a marketing survey. The most sophisticated system deployed by marketers so far is Scanamerica. Scanamerica electronically measures television viewing of individuals, via people meters, and tracks products purchased in panel households via an in-home portable scanner that reads UPC codes on package goods. Scanamerica now operates in Denver and was expanded nationally for the 1988–9 television season. It is important to remember that when we are talking about this infiltration it is based on a number of representative households throughout a given territory. Not everyone need be monitored – only sufficient numbers to accurately assess the probability of others following suit. Infoscan, which competes with Scanamerica, tracks consumers from 60,000 American households.[86] Within marketing communications, these monitoring devices which "reward" consumers for their consumption allow corporations to track the movements of today's postmodern consumer. As Baudrillard says: "Truth is no longer the reflexive truth of the panoptic system and the gaze, but the manipulative truth of the test which probes and interrogates, of the laser which touches and pierces, of computer cards which retain punched out signals, of the genetic code which regulates your combination, of cells which inform your sensory universe."

ROUTE 5: MARKETING IN A POST-PANOPTIC CULTURE

We are no longer a part of the drama of alienation; we live in the ecstasy of communication. And this ecstasy is obscene.[88]

While Baudrillard has been a useful guide through the ecstatic universe of marketing communications, we have had to take a few detours. (1) I have insisted on the relationship between semiotics and cybernetics within the present marketing system, and attempted to clarify the many ways that Baudrillard uses the term "code" in his work, including his later concern with genetics. (2) I have bypassed Baudrillard's theory of reversibility in a closed cybernetic circuit opting instead for a more open "rhizomatic" structure where probability and randomness never suture a circle, but create a situation of probable movement. (3) I have demonstrated some of the tactical uses of representation, simulation, and circulation in marketing communications. (4) And I argued that his reading of Foucault and privileging of seduction over production is, indeed, bumpy.

Baudrillard's writings on advertising, paradoxically enough, bring us to the end of the advertising era; or at least the pivotal position of advertising, and, in particular, the advertising image as an independent strategy of seduction separate from other processes, particularly the production of information through systems of passive monitoring, and marketing promotions. The advertising agencies that produce these sign-vehicles are only one part of the process for stimulating the circulation of commodites in our high-intensity capitalist market setting: what I have called, along with Baudrillard, our neo-capitalist cybernetic culture. These agencies are part of a marketing mix, matrix, or network, whose logic is not simply one of simulation, but production, seduction, *and* circulation.

The marketing matrix is not a closed system but is comprised of a loosely interconnected network that sets up ritualistic circuits of feedback in which the consumer is said to have ultimate control. In truth, while the consumer is at the center of the marketing circle, it is not because she/he is in control. The consumer's movements are the central concern of a vast system of observation that is post-panoptic in its methods of tracking, tracing, and seducing us into participation. This is different from saying that consumers control the process. At the same time that they make this evident, most marketing textbooks confuse these two points in their eagerness to appear democratic and "responsive" to consumer needs. As Baudrillard would say, consumers are, in a sense, "held hostages" by a system that promises easy credit, financing, rebates, coupons, incentives to buy, "lost leaders," and a whole host of marketing and promotional items, techniques pioneered by "smart marketers."

Documenting and tracing how we are encouraged to enter into this system, and then held hostage by it, is the task of a critical theory of consumerism. It is also crucial, but beyond the scope of this paper, to trace the convergence, interdependence, and complicity of our patterns of consumption in the increasingly global penetration of this marketing system. This not only produces consumers, or creates consumers as producers, but relies on the seduction of consumption as part of a strategy to maintain horrifying conditions of labor (production) in various parts of the globe. As North American subjects continually activated along these circuits, we are part of a larger web of power that needs to be explored *and* transformed.

Notes

1 Jean Baudrillard, *Simulations* (New York: Semiotext(e), 1983.

2 Jean Baudrillard, "The Ecstasy of Communication," in Hal Foster, ed., *The Anti-Aesthetic: Essays on Postmodern Culture* (Port Townsend, Washington: Bay Press, 1983) (from *Fatal Strategies*, 1983).

3 Jean Baudrillard, *Forget Foucault* (New York: Semiotext(e), 1987; translation from 1977), p. 102.

4 Jean Baudrillard, *For a Critique of the Political Economy of the Sign* (St. Louis: Telos Press, 1981; translation from 1972).

5 Baudrillard, *Forget Foucault*, p. 102.

6 Jean Baudrillard, *Fatal Strategies* (New York: Semiotext(e), 1990; translation from 1983), p. 44.

7 Jo Marney, "Sensing is not Always Believing," *Marketing*, November 26 (1990) 16.

8 Baudrillard, "Ecstasy of Communication," pp. 129–30.

9 Baudrillard, *Simulations*, p. 110.

10 See Stephen Best and Douglas Kellner, *Postmodern Theory: Critical Interrogations* (New York: Guilford Press, 1991). As quoted in Levin's introduction to Baudrillard, *Critique*, p. 5.

11 Jean Baudrillard, *Le système des objets* (Paris: Denoel-Gonthier, 1968), p. 147.

12 Baudrillard, *Critique*, p. 1.

13 Jean Baudrillard, *The Mirror of Production* (St. Louis: Telos Press, 1975; translation from 1973).

14 In *Critique*, Baudrillard is particularly interested in household furniture.

15 Baudrillard, *Système des objets*, p. 147.

16 Baudrillard, *Critique*, p. 37.

17 Ibid., pp. 178–9. See Umberto Eco, "The Death of the Gruppo 63," *The Open Work*, trans. Anna Cancogni (Cambridge, Mass.: Harvard University Press, 1989), pp. 245–6.

18 Baudrillard, *Critique*, p. 181.

19 Jean Baudrillard, *Oublier Foucault* (Paris: Galilée, 1977).

20 Baudrillard, *Simulations*, p. 56.

21 For a layperson's explanation of genetics, see William Bains, *Genetic Engineering for Almost Everybody* (London: Penguin, 1990). Bains makes the connection between genetic coding and information clear. "A gene is simply a piece of information coded on a length of DNA." (p. 20).

22 Baudrillard, *Simulations*, p. 108.

23 Baudrillard, "Ecstasy of Communication," p. 128.

24 Ibid., p. 103.

25 Baudrillard, "Ecstasy of Communication," pp. 126–7.

26 Baudrillard, *Simulations*, p. 111.

27 Ibid., p. 112.

28 Brent Stidson, "The Management and Regulation of Marketing Communication in Canada," in Donald Thompson, ed. *Problems in Canadian Marketing* (USA: American Marketing Association, 1977).

29 E. Jerome McCarthy and Stanley J. Schapiro, *Essentials of Marketing* (Illinois: Richard D. Unwin, 1983), p. 29.

30 See Umberto Eco, *A Theory of Semiotics* (Bloomington: Indiana University Press, 1979), pp. 9–14 for a listing of all of the fields engaged in semiotic analysis and of the disparate conceptions of the discipline. Baudrillard seems most influenced by Saussure, although he frequently addresses linguists such as Roman Jakobson (*Critique*, p. 178) or cites long passages from formalist and scientific semioticians, such as Thomas Seboek (*Simulations*, pp. 106–8).

31 Jean Baudrillard, *In the Shadow of the Silent Majorities* (New York: Semiotext(e), 1983; translation from 1978), p. 34.

32 These 3 Ms of marketing are described in more detail by James F. Donius in "Marketing Tracking: A Strategic Reassessment and Planning Tool," *Journal of Advertising Research*, 25, 1 (Feb/Mar, 1985) 15–19.

33 Jean Baudrillard, *La société de consommation* (Paris: Gallimard, 1970), p. 157.

34 Baudrillard, *Simulations*, p. 117.

35 See Umberto Eco "Openness, Information, Communication," *The Open Work*, pp. 67–8: "information theory provides us with only one scheme of possible relations (order-disorder, information-signification, binary disjunction, and so on) that can be inserted into a larger context ... [the scheme] is valid, in its specific ambit, only as the quantitative measurement of the number of signals that can be clearly transmitted along one channel. Once the signals are received by a human being, information theory has nothing else to add and gives way

either to semiology or semantics, since the question henceforth becomes one of signification."

36 This description is taken from my experience in a marketing research office. For a marketer's thoughts on the topic see Leo Bogart, "Advertising: Art, Science or Business," *Journal of Advertising Research* (Dec 1988/Jan 1989) 47–55.

37 Baudrillard, *Forget Foucault*, p. 134.

38 Brian Massumi, "The Simulacrum and the Real," *Copyright*, Vol. 1, No. 1.

39 Baudrillard, "Ecstasy of Communication," pp. 129–30.

40 Donna Haraway traces the history of cybernetics in sociobiology in "The Biological Enterprise: Sex, Mind and Profit from Human Engineering to Sociobiology," in *Simians, Cyborgs and Women: The Reinvention of Nature* (London: Routledge, 1991), pp. 43–71.

41 Michel Foucault, *Discipline and Punish: The Birth of the Prison*, trans. Alan Sheridan (New York: Vintage, 1979), p. 138.

42 Baudrillard, *Silent Majorities*, p. 20.

43 "Marketing: the new priority," *Business Week*, (Nov. 23, 1983) 93.

44 Robert Keith, "The Marketing Revolution," in Ben M. Enis and Keith Cox, *Marketing Classics: A Selection of Influential Articles*, 4th edn. (Toronto: Allen and Bacon, 1981), p. 47.

45 However, as one marketer put it, "not all consumers are created equal." In modern marketing terms, a market is described as "people or organizations with wants to satisfy, money to spend, and a willingness to spend it." Jeff Ostroff, *Successful Marketing to the 50+ Consumer: How to Capture one of the Biggest and Fastest Growing Markets in America* (New Jersey: Prentice Hall, 1989), p. 46.

46 Baudrillard, *Simulations*, pp. 52–3.

47 Baudrillard, *Silent Majorities*, p. 34.

48 McCarthy and Schapiro, *Essentials of Marketing*, p. 34.

49 Wendall Smith, "Product Differentiation and Market Segmentation as Alternative Market Strategies," in Howard S. Thompson, *Great Writings in Marketing* (Plymouth: Commerce Press, 1976), p. 127.

50 Baudrillard, Silent Majorities, p. 28.

51 Baudrillard, *Simulations*, pp. 43–4.

52 Theodore Levitt, "Marketing Myopia," in James G. Barnes and Montrose S. Sommers, eds., *Current Topics in Canadian Marketing* (Toronto: McGraw-Hill Ryerson, 1978), p. 39.

53 I have discussed these differences in my article "A Tale of Inscription/Fashion Statements," *The Canadian Journal of Political and Social Theory* (Winter, 1987). For more on the distinctions between these terms see Kaja Silverman, *The Subject of Semiotics* (New York: Oxford University Press, 1983), pp. 14–25.

54 William Leiss, Stephen Kline, and Sut Jhally have documented this in their text *Social Communication in Advertising: Persons, Products and Images of Well-Being*, 2nd edn., revised (Toronto: Nelson Canada, 1990).

55 Phillipe Nicholas, "From Value to Love." *Journal of Advertising Research*, 28, 4 (Aug/Sept, 1988) 7.

56 Ibid., p. 8.

57 Jean Baudrillard, *L'échange symbolique et la mort* (Paris: Gallimard, 1976).
58 McCarthy and Schapiro, *Essentials of Marketing*, p. 37.
59 Eco, *Theory of Semiotics*, pp. 138–9.
60 Jean Baudrillard, *La gauche divine: chronique des années 1977–1984* (Paris: Grasset, 1985), p. 112.
61 Baudrillard, *Simulations*, p. 32.
62 Ibid., p. 10.
63 Meaghan Morris adeptly deconstructs Baudrillard's collapsing of referent, with object, with meaning, with the real. Meaghan Morris, "Room 101 Or A Few Worst Things In The World," in *Seduced and Abandoned: The Baudrillard Scene*, André Frankovits, ed. (Glebe, Australia: Stonemoss Services, 1984), pp. 91–117.
64 Walter Benjamin, "The Work of Art in the Era of Mechanical Reproduction," in *Illuminations* (New York: Shocken, 1969).
65 Baudrillard, *Simulations*, p. 95.
66 Ibid., p. 103.
67 Ibid., p. 3.
68 Baudrillard, *La gauche divine*, p. 112.
69 Baudrillard, *Simulations*, p. 35.
70 Ibid., p. 38.
71 Ibid., p. 76.
72 Ibid., p. 30.
73 Ibid., p. 79.
74 Ibid., p. 77.
75 For a brilliant discussion of mobile subjectivity see Margaret Morse, "An Ontology of Everyday Distraction: The Freeway, the Television, the Mall," in Patricia Mellancamp, ed. *The Logics of Television* (Bloomington: Indiana University Press, 1990).
76 Barthes discussed the idea of anchorage and relay in analyzing the relationship between image and text, but I think they are useful in the larger sense that I have just mentioned. Roland Barthes, *Image-Music-Text*, trans. and ed. Stephen Heath (London: Fontana/Collins, 1977), pp. 40–1. In Eco's theory of semiotics, he outlines how the planes of expression and meaning constantly invert. In Baudrillard's terms, I think seduction and circulation can be used to understand this sign function: seduction corresponding to the moment of anchorage, circulation to the moment of relay. See Eco, *Theory of Semiotics*, pp. 55–8.
77 Baudrillard, *Forget Foucault*, p. 11.
78 Ibid., p. 12.
79 Ibid., p. 45.
80 Ibid., p. 48.
81 Ibid., p. 12.
82 Foucault explicitly denies that he is offering a general theory of power in *Discipline and Punish*; we should not take panopticism as a model of power in our century, although "power today may have some of its features." "Eye of Power." in *Power/Knowledge: Selected Interviews and other Writing, 1972–77*, Colin Gordon, ed. (New York: Pantheon, 1977), p. 148.
83 Baudrillard, *Forget Foucault*, p. 48.

84   Baudrillard, *Simulations*, pp. 53–4.
85   Arthur Smith, "Survival techniques for the Nineties," *Marketing* (Jan 22, 1990)
     20–2.
86   See the 1989 report of the Advertising Research Foundation for more infor-
     mation (Chicago: American Marketing Association), 7, 77. For information
     on "fingerprinting" read Jonathan Sims, "VCR Viewing patterns; An Elec-
     tronic and Passive Investigation," *Journal of Advertising Research* (April/May,
     1989) 11–17.
87   Baudrillard, *Simulations*, p. 49.
88   Baudrillard, "Ecstasy of Communication," p. 130.

5

FASHION AND SIGNIFICATION IN BAUDRILLARD

——

Efrat Tseëlon

My concern in this chapter is with an analysis of the history and theory of fashion in terms of Baudrillard's concepts and ideas. I start off with an analysis of Baudrillard's "orders of simulacra:" imitation, production, and simulation. I proceed with a historical account of sartorial signification which I analyze in terms of Baudrillard's system. The classical stage corresponds to the order of imitation, the modern stage corresponds to the order of production, and the postmodern stage corresponds to the order of simulation. I then contrast Baudrillard's position on the difference between modern and postmodern fashion with the position of fashion theory. I show that his earlier (Marxist) analysis of fashion is antithetical to contemporary theories of fashion which view post-industrial fashion as reflecting a democratization process. Baudrillard argues, however, that it is the ideology of consumption which creates an illusion of democratization by promoting the myth of universal meaning of fashion, accessible to all. His later, postmodern, analysis, goes further – beyond meaning of fashion, beyond signification. However, several currents can be discerned regarding postmodern fashion. Essentially they fall into two perspectives: either challenging the meaning while reaffirming the code (a signification system), or challenging the meaning as well as the code. Baudrillard's position belongs to the latter.

Finally, I critique his contention that postmodern fashion transcends the code (beyond signification) by pointing out that his account commits the same logical error that he ascribes to those who reject fashion altogether. Because "while it is true that one can always escape the reality principle of the content, one can never escape the reality principle of the code. Even while rebelling against the content, one more and more closely obeys the logic of the code"[1]

THE "ORDERS OF SIMULACRA"

In his "orders of simulacra" Baudrillard identified three orders of sign value.[2] The first order, that of *imitation* characterizing the classical period, presupposes dualism where appearances disguise reality. In the second order, *production*, appearances create an illusion of reality. In the third order, *simulation*, appearances invent reality. No longer concerned with the real, images are reproduced from a model. And it is this lack of a reference point which threatens the distinction between true and false. It is a reality captured by the following lines from a recent article in *The Independent on Sunday* about MTV (music video): "Rock videos give you a sense that you could switch off the real world with your TV remote control: reality is just another channel."[3]

In structural linguistics the process of signification is carried out through a system of signs. The meaning of signs according to de Saussure is made up of two elements: *signifiers* (sound-images) which index the *signifieds* (concepts) "I propose to retain the word *sign* [*signe*] to designate the whole and to replace *concept* and *sound-image* respectively by signified [signifié] and signifier [signifiant]."[4] De Saussurian structural linguistics is based on two principles: a metaphysics of depth and a metaphysics of surface. The metaphysics of depth refers to meaning as based on the link between the signified which underlies the signifier (for example, in fashion imagery, soft materials stand for sensuality). A metaphysics of surface implies a relational concept of meaning. It is the notion that signs do not have inherent meaning but gain their meaning through their relation to other signs (for example, in fashion the "soft" gains meaning against the "severe," the "elaborate" against the "austere," and the "feminine" against the "masculine."[5])

In terms of signification relations the three orders can be summarized as follows: the order of imitation involves direct signifier-signified links. The order of production involves indirect signifier-signified links. The order of simulation involves signifier-signifier links, i.e., links between signifiers that are divorced from relations to signifieds. These links subvert signification in favor of a play of signs.

I would like to illustrate Baudrillard's stages of simulacra with a signification analysis of the history of European fashion. Drawing on contemporary theories of fashion a correspondence can be established between Baudrillard's orders of simulacra and my analysis of the stages of fashion signification such that the order of imitation corresponds to the classical stage, the order of production corresponds to the modern stage, and the order of simulation corresponds to the postmodern stage.

THE ORDERS OF FASHION

Throughout European history, dress has divided people along class lines. From the Greek and Roman periods through Byzantine and medieval eras, but particularly since the fourteenth century which marks the beginning of fashion,[6] the costliness of materials or workmanship involved in the production of garments distinguished courtly from common. Throughout the history of dress it was the principle of scarcity of resources which symbolized rank in dress. Natural scarcity provided "guarantee of exclusivity."[7] Scarcity took either the form of rarity in nature (as in the case of the furs of certain animals, or of gold and precious stones), or in the man-made resources (as the case of silk which, up to the fifteenth century, was imported from the East). All the above meant that economic constraints effectively guarded the social order since those expensive materials were only within reach of the nobility. Servants and workmen used more wool, no silk or dyed cloth, and less ornamentation than their masters.[8] Coarse and common furs were used by the lower classes, while finer, smaller, and more rare ones were worn by the wealthy.[9]

A historical examination of the symbolic aspect of dress within the framework of the orders of simulacra yields the following:

Imitation: the classical stage

The first order of simulacra (*imitation*) which characterizes the classical stage is based on the religious belief in transcendental value.[10] In sartorial terms, clothes would be seen to reflect the order of nature without ambiguity. In the Middle Ages where class order was rigid and appeared ordained, dress reflected the God-given subordination of the lower orders to their superiors. Thus, for example, medieval dress recreated the social order by assigning the more elaborate and rich garments to the elite. As long as the class system was stable and undisturbed there were few fashion changes among the lower classes. The system was challenged when, in the fourteenth century, the expansion of trade, and the prosperity of the wool and weaving industries, brought previously expensive materials within reach of the emerging urban middle classes "the urban patricians began to manoeuvre into positions of equality with the old feudal nobility."[11] These developments threatened to blur and to break down the hierarchical society of feudal times.

The process intensified after the end of royal absolutism (in the French Revolution).[12] A petition to King Edward III from the House of Commons complaining that common men had begun to wear fabrics which did not fit their rank or income resulted in the legislation of the first sumptuary law defining precisely the type and quality of fabrics which could be worn by various classes. Similar laws continued to be passed until the sixteenth century with severity but little success. The sumptuary laws which attempted to regulate clothing practices along status lines, did not relate to style since rank was manifested in the quality of fabric, in the details, and in the choice of decoration rather than in different styles.[13]

Up until the fourteenth century the shape of the garments remained almost unchanged. It was in the second half of the fourteenth century that clothes began to take on new forms. Since styles were not sanctioned by law, "Imitating their masters in dress and manners was a constant accusation levelled at servants."[14] After 1600, when the nobility began to allow its servants to follow the fashion more closely, critics claimed that "if servants were allowed to be fashionable it became impossible to tell who was the mistress and who was the maid."[15] The aristocracy could thus only distinguish itself by the speed with which it adopted new styles. A cycle of differentiation and emulation developed where the wealthy were the first to adopt the new styles. The lower classes, who could not afford them, adopted the new styles only later, in less luxurious materials, or with cast-off garments from their masters. As soon as the new style was copied by the lower classes, the upper classes moved on to a new one.[16]

Production: the modern stage

The second order of simulacra (*production*) characterizes the (industrial) modern stage. Its shift to secularism is based on a code of the immanent rather than the transcendent. Thus, according to Sennett, Victorians believed appearances to have personal meaning that can be revealed involuntarily. Therefore their desire was to disclose as little as possible through their own (while learning as much as possible about others). At the same time the technological developments that characterized industrial capitalism, such as the invention of the sewing machine and washproof dyes, increased the democratization of fashion. It reduced the price of materials and brought colored fabrics (once an aristocratic preserve) within the reach of the mass market.

The industrial revolution created the city, the mass society, and encouraged the taste for anonymity in cosmopolitan life "and behind uniform fronts the road was open to create illusions."[17] It created the distinction between public and private zones unknown in the Middle Ages.[18] This separation between the public and the private gave rise to a distinction between a private self and public personae, and a need to keep the private self secret behind an "art of dissimulation and disguise."[19] The cosmopolitan city was a world in which physical appearance had no certainty. For this reason it became important to establish whether people unduly transform economic achievement into the social category of a "gentleman," and whether a respectable looking woman was not in fact "loose." Thus, when clothes ceased to be indexical of status due to homogeneity of style, a subtle expert system of status differentiation through appearance accessed only to initiates has evolved. This system coded the minutiae of appearance, and *commodity fetishism*, a term assigned by Marx to the process of mystifying material objects of consumption by investing them with human qualities, turning use-value into exchange value. Clothes were attributed symbolic meanings that reflected the person's character or social standing.

Technological advances increased mobility and the pace of life, and multiplied social roles. A new order was created in which work rather than lineage determined status. Uniforms were introduced to the work place to denote rank as dress no longer reflected the rank order but defined time of day (daywear, eveningwear), type of activity (work, leisure), type of occasion (formal, informal), gender – even an individual mood. Fashion kept pace with the increasingly compartmentalized, multi-role life of the bourgeoisie.[20]

These threats to the traditional social order encouraged the development of an alternative, more subtle, system of demarcation. In an attempt to distinguish the aristocracy by lineage from the nouveaux-riches, this system anchored certain sartorial practices to moral values. For example, the concept of "gentility," developed in the nineteenth century by the landed gentry to distinguish the "genuine" from the "pretend," encapsulated this code of ethics of noblesse oblige. This code held that to be a "lady" was a standard of conduct which included rules of etiquette, elegance, and subtlety. "Those of birth and education learned to discriminate between good taste and sham."[21] Bright tints and clashing combinations were vulgar by their breach of certain rules of harmony and propriety. Such sensibility is illustrated, for example, by Bernard Shaw's flower girl in *Pygmalion*. Eliza Doolittle, who comes to discuss her elocution lessons with Professor Higgins, turns up for a morning appointment vainly clad in her best clothes, and wearing a hat decorated with a garish combination of orange, sky-blue, and red ostrich feathers. "The knowledge of . . . manners, language, and dress, became an artificial dividing-line, separating the Ins from the Outs."[22]

Simulation: the postmodern stage

In both *imitation* and *production* the signifier indexes an underlying meaning, either inherent, or constructed. In contrast, the third order of simulacra (*simulation*) refers to the principle of the postmodern dress.

Postmodernism appeared to reflect a radical break with the dominant culture and aesthetics.[23] In architecture, where it has been most acutely addressed, it represented romantic subjectivity, plurality of forms, fragmentation of styles, and diffuse boundaries. Thus it substituted disunity, subjectivity, and ambiguity, for the modernist unity, absolutism, and certainty.[24] In the sciences, it was evidenced in a Western "crisis in representation," concerning their authority and universal claims. This challenge to the "correspondence theory of truth" resulted in replacing the "master narratives" which mirror the world, with a plurality of "narrative truths" which reflect, instead, the conventions of discourse.[25]

The postmodern cultural shift has left its mark on the fashion world through its self-referentiality (lack of reference to an outside world), indifference to traditional social order, and its preoccupation with shifting multiple identities expressed in diversity of styles. This emphasis on individual diversity, and the variability of styles,[26] resulted in diminishing shared agreed meanings of styles.[27]

Last, the reading of each kind of signifier is also different: *Imitation* marks an obliged sign which refers unequivocally to a status. It signifies "the natural order of things." *Production* references not "the law of nature" but "the law of exchange." Its meaning is not fixed to a particular signified but is open to struggle (e.g., as when environmental awareness to Green issues turns fur, once a symbol status of the rich, into a symbol of the morally insensitive and environmentally irresponsible). *Simulation*, by virtue of its being referent-free invites a reading of a different order: it is a perpetual play of the code.

Baudrillard actually presents a very similar scheme himself when he regards the meaning of clothes as a transition from a semiology where meaning resides in "natural" signs, through a semiology where meaning resides in arbitrary (structuralist) signs, to a new (post-structuralist) semiology where signs transcend meaning. It is a change from *dress* which is pure disguise – to *fashion* – a disguise which is a signifier of social distinctions – to *post-fashion* which is a pure signifier "a deconstruction of both the form of the sign of fashion and the principle of signification itself."[28]

MODERN AND POSTMODERN FASHION: BAUDRILLARD VS. FASHION THEORY

Having shown that the history of fashion signification can be coded in terms of Baudrillard's "orders of simulacra," I wish to examine the relationship of modernism and postmodernism to fashion from two contrasting perspectives. On the one hand, fashion theories identify a move from elitism to democratization in sartorial representation. On the other hand, Baudrillard's Marxist theory of consumption, espoused in his *Critique*,[29] argues that power relations are always inscribed into the very production of objects.

Early modern theories of fashion viewed the fashion process as reifying the social hierarchy, and as a site of struggle for social supremacy. They assumed the elite's desire to preserve the social order to be the single point of origin for fashion. Thus, in *The Theory of the Leisure Class*,[30] Veblen developed the notion that the increasing wealth of the leisure class gave heed to the display of conspicuous consumption of leisure and waste. Conspicuous consumption is coded into clothes through their superfluousness, decorativeness, and non-functionality.

The notion of fashion change as a dynamics of the upper classes' desire to keep a clear demarcation line between the classes, and an opposite desire of the lower classes to emulate the upper classes, was first put forward by Simmel.[31] In his "trickle down" model of fashion, Simmel postulated an upward spiral in which the upper classes adopt a style that differentiates them, and as soon as this is copied by the lower classes, the upper classes discard it in favor of a new style. And along similar lines the conspiracy theory of fashion assigned the authoritative voice of fashion to its creators (designers) and manufacturers (industry).[32]

In the 1960s, this early conception was contested by the assumption of a "trickle across" process.[33] According to this formulation, the emulation of the upper classes has broken down in the twentieth century because mass production made similar styles available simultaneously to all classes. Other democratization theories argued that fashion styles were not dictated by the fashion houses. Rather they originated in a mass movement,[34] in the high street,[35] or in subcultures,[36] whereupon they were appropriated into mainstream fashion. Thus, modernist analysis regarded fashion as reflecting social movements or social change.

In contrast, Baudrillard has pointed out that an analysis of the social function of objects is at the same time a critical analysis of the political function of the ideology of consumption. Drawing on Marx's notion of products as "instruments" (reflecting a functional logic of use-value), and "commodities" (reflecting an economic logic of exchange value), Baudrillard argued that when products move from the referential to the representational realm, they become carriers of social meaning "objects never exhaust themselves in the function they serve, and in this excess of presence they take on their signification of prestige."[37] Baudrillard thus extends the framework of "the logic of consumption" to include sign-value. Baudrillard's notion of sign-value is based on an analogy between a system of objects (commodity) and a system of signs (language). He argues that a system of objects regulated by sign value homogenizes desires and reproduces the power structure of the political economy.[38]

Thus the transition from use-value and exchange value to sign-value includes "symbol" (reflecting the logic of a gift), and "sign" (reflecting the logic of status). From this perspective, when products move from the realm of function (use-value) to the realm of signification, they become "objects." This transformation involves two levels. First, the change from a "product" to a "symbol" is commodity fetishism: a mystification of the product which conceals a signifying function (e.g., status)with a utilitarian gloss (e.g., need fulfilment). This is achieved through a dual mechanism whereby every non-utilitarian product (e.g., decorative, superfluous) disguises behind an aura of functionality, while functional objects are assigned with symbolic meaning. Secondly, the change from a "symbol" to a sign is what Baudrillard calls "semiological reduction" whereby an ambivalent symbolic object (an outward manifestation of some inward quality) becomes a univocal flat image. Thus the ideology of consumption is expressed in appropriating the product as a sign, while masking the labor, exploitation, and power relations that go into its production. Baudrillard's position is antithetical to fashion theory which views post-industrial fashion as reflecting a democratization process. His is a conspiracy theory of a different sort. From his perspective, democratization theories fall into the trap of confusing the ideology of consumption with consumption itself. This ideology creates the illusion of democratization. It promotes the myth of the universal meaning of fashion – right down the social scale, and masks the social inequalities behind a democracy of leisure. The ideology of consumption creates the appearance of a social change while being, in fact, a game of social change. It is a "theatrical sociality." It is subversive, recycling past models in new forms, yet it is controlled by the fashion industry and does not really change the essential order.[39]

However, the Marxist analysis of signification is not Baudrillard's last word on the matter of fashion. In other writings[40] he extends the paradigm of simulacra to a paradigm of seduction. The notion of seduction operates in two ways. On the one hand it is an elaboration of postmodern simulation (including fashion). On the other hand it is an alternative metaphysics which replaces the Marxist power principle and the Freudian pleasure principle with the seduction principle.

Seduction, according to Baudrillard, substitutes symbolic (seductive) power for real power, and replaces the psychoanalytic psychic economy of drives, desires, and the unconscious with a different libido; one which feeds on competition, challenge, risk, provocation; one which is secretive but not repressed, a "catalystic impulse," a "deeper energy" of fission, rupture, and vice, a compelling energy which is enigmatic, luring, hypnotic and enchanted; it is not a passion for desire, but a passion for games and rituality; one which is dual but not polarized, reversible but not dialectical. Thus if in *Critique* he defines fashion as "a kind of meaning drive" to innovate signs,[41] in *Seduction* he talks about a system where reversibility puts an end not just to the stability of the sign. It also marks the end of the principle of opposition itself as a basis for meaning "a theory that would treat signs in terms of their seductive attraction."[42]

Seduction is based on the attraction of the void – presence which hides absence. As a metaphysics it is a feature of modern as well as postmodern fashion. It is a feature of modern fashion both historically (since it was a common courtly game from the Renaissance to the eighteenth century,[43] and metaphorically. For it substitutes an *appearance* of democracy for *absence* of real social change. Seduction is also applicable to postmodern fashion where signs are used randomly, playfully – and where an *attempt for meaning* (such as is evidenced both in fashion magazines and fashion analyses)[44] masks a *meaning void*.

But if in a postmodern culture the signifier is not fixed to a particular signified, and the same fashion item can be read in any number of ways,[45] can the fashion sign still be said to have meaning, or is it, as Baudrillard argues "beyond meaning"? By way of an answer, postmodern theory offers two contrasting visions: *postmodernism of reaction* and *postmodernism of resistance*.[46] The former characterizes fashion theory, and the latter characterizes Baudrillard's position.

"Postmodernism of reaction" is strategic: it repudiates modernity and exploits cultural codes only to reaffirm liberal humanist values. From the perspective of fashion theory, postmodern fashion, with all its playful nihilism and cannibalization of styles, still alludes to a reality of signification. Within this framework the very concept of postmodern fashion becomes a status marker, as can be illustrated by two paradigmatic features of postmodern fashion: fake jewels and nostalgia clothes. In the world of jewelry, a conscious and deliberate use of non-precious materials is made, without the low status connotations associated with such materials; quite the contrary. This is exemplified by a fashion article in *The Independent on Sunday* which plainly talks about an addiction to "fabulous fakes" but points out that *"It is never a matter of not being able to afford the real thing*. We actually prefer the non-precious. Costume jewelry, unlike most real gold and real jewels, is shaped by fashion, designed to complement the clothes of the moment."[47]

Another hallmark of postmodernist fashion is imitation and integration of an eclectic mixture of styles and periods into a new discourse (or montage, or collage, or bricolage).[48] Despite its seeming uprootedness, such nostalgic fashion need not be taken at face value. Alternatively, it can indicate that fashion does not cease to signify even when it removes itself from the market forces. For Jameson, imitation of bygone styles lends historical depth to a world of surface signifiers, and shows "a desperate attempt to appropriate a missing past." For Baudrillard,[49] bygone objects derive their value from affirmation of craft-value and repudiation of the stigmata attached to industrial production. And according to McRobbie,[50] second-hand fashion is used by those who can risk looking poor in a stylized way which marks out their distance both from conventional dress and from real poverty. In different ways, the above examples show how repudiation of the stylistic values of representation expresses yearning to these values.

"Postmodernism of resistance," however, is engaged in a different project: it deconstructs modernity and questions cultural codes in order to critique liberal humanist values. Baudrillard's "postmodernism of resistance"[51] would rule out the above interpretation as he negates the idea of representation altogether. Moving away from the logic of consumption he points to a "deconstruction of the principle of signification;" a breakdown of the notion of objects as an index of differentiation. For him, simulation replaces signification: it is a playful spectacle, a carnival of appearances. It empties traditional signs of their signification (e.g., the use of religious symbols as ornaments, or expensive materials in common contexts), and is completely self-referential "fashion for its own sake." For him, the effacing of "real history" as referent leaves us nothing but empty signs and marks the end of signification itself.

CONCLUSIONS AND CRITIQUE

I have analyzed Baudrillard's argument regarding fashion and signification. I have shown how he views fashion, like any order of signification, as a transition from a purely referential function which encodes meaning of (a) differentiation and (b) distinction – to a purely self-referential function which marks the end of meaning. In a nutshell, the argument goes as follows: as simulation substitutes for production it replaces the linear order with a cyclical order, and frees the signifier from its link to the signified. This, in turn, results in fashion as a form of pleasure taking the place of fashion as a form of communication, subverting the visual code from a language to a spectacle.

William Golding once said that myth is truth that can only be told in a story. To me this is the value of Baudrillard's insights. Their sign-value is given, not in their accurate depiction, but in their mythical perceptiveness encased in a poetic format. And like any complex thinker, Baudrillard's theory is not woven of a single thread, but with various – sometimes – dissonant ones. It is our task, therefore, to subject these insights to reality testing, or theory testing. Therefore, in the final section I would like to take issue with the limitations of the notion of fashion as the end of signification.[52]

Baudrillard articulates in a single stroke two contradictory accounts of fashion. Modern fashion, where aesthetic passion hides a *myth of change*, reproduces the power relations of industrial capitalism. And in postmodern fashion, real *change* marks an end-point in the relationship between signs and meaning. Postmodern fashion is a stage "beyond meaning" where "fashion is pure speculative stage in the order of signs. There is no more constraint of either coherence or reference."[53] The two accounts not only represent two stages of development; they are structurally different. The account of modern fashion regards fashion as a signifier of a wider social process within industrial capitalism "modernity is a code, and fashion is its emblem."[54] The account of postmodern fashion, however, falls into the trap of the same self-referentiality it attributes to postmodern fashion itself. This account falls short of acknowledging that whatever happens *inside* fashion does not necessarily affect its signifying function as an emblem of a social process. It also mistakes fragmentation of the code with its disappearance.

In discussing postmodern fashion Baudrillard develops a number of assumptions in a way which is not always justified, and is not even always compatible with his own argument.

1   His assumption of the indeterminacy of the code and the instability of signifier-signified relationship brings him to doubt the possibility of a referential function. This predicament is neither logically necessary, nor corresponding to actual behavior. From a theoretical viewpoint, a looser signifier-signified relationship can simply mean fragmentation of society into smaller units of relevant frames of reference, with less rigid boundaries, rules, and membership requirements. It may also imply shorter and faster cycles of change of what a relevant reference group regards as the appropriate code – but it does not necessarily indicate the abolition of a code. From an empirical viewpoint, there is ample evidence, both experimental and anecdotal to suggest that signification in fashion is far more resilient than some postmodern thinkers would have us believe.[55] Perhaps the best example comes from the professional dress code which signals that even in the 1990s, the ethos of the "dress for success" is still the prevailing code. An in-flight magazine of AirUK, targeted to business people on short commuting flights between UK and Europe, included a handful of tips from a corporate image consultant, such as: "inconsistency in your standard of dress leads others to believe that you are inconsistent in other respects;" "the thinner the briefcase the more status and power the businessman commands . . . a huge suitcase . . . is a real credibility breaker;" "a professional man should not have . . . a tie which is too short . . . socks that do not match the shoes or trousers . . . plastic looking belts;" "women should choose only three or four colours to work into their business wardrobe."[56] Such clichés of the reality of the traditional professions are indeed a far cry from a floating carnival of signs!

2   Another assumption, that of self-referentiality (the fact that fashion is produced from models, and does not represent anything) does not in itself herald the end of meaning either. Point of origin (whether or not fashion corresponds to anything outside of itself) is not the only source that confers meaning. Myth of origin can be invented post-factum. Rationales can be produced and added on, and incorporated into the ethos of a group. Perhaps the best example for this can be seen in the most self-referential ritual of the fashion world: the seasonal fashion show where top designers display their new collections to a carefully chosen and well-connected privileged and limited audience of fashion editors, fashion buyers, and distinguished clients. The cycle of competition, prestige, ingratiation, and glamor that is set in motion by each such event testifies to its ceremonial qualities and signifying function – which are not confined to the fashion world alone.

3   Baudrillard himself points out that even resistance to fashion is still defined within the order of fashion but fails to acknowledge that fashion as a whole (whatever the authority of its signs) is locked into a broader

signification system. In other words, the very participation in the playful carnival of fashion with its floating signs is already inscribed in signification. Paradoxically, the act of subverting signification itself becomes a signifier. It is a status marker of the rich and famous, those powerful enough or distinguished enough to flaunt conventions, those creative enough and confident enough to invent, or those marginalized enough not to care.

4 Finally, on another level, Baudrillard's paradigm of seduction gives away that even loss of meaning is still contained within the sphere of meaning. Postmodern fashion reflects at least one level of meaning: that of countering death. And, almost like the Freudian fetish, the seduction of absence (of meaning) by presence (of artifice) is "the only existing form of immortality" turning even death into "a brilliant and superficial appearance."[57] "This is the despair that nothing lasts, and the complementary enjoyment of knowing that beyond this death, every form has always the chance of a second coming."[58]

Notes

1 Jean Baudrillard, *Symbolic Exchange and Death* (London: Sage, 1993; translation from 1976), p. 133.
2 Jean Baudrillard, *Fatal Strategies* (New York: Semiotext(e), 1990; translation from 1983).
3 Jan 6, 1991, p. 8.
4 Ferdinand de Saussure, *Course in General Linguistics*, trans. W. Baskin, ed. C. Bally, A. Sechehaye, and A. Riedlinger (London: Peter Owen, 1959; originally 1916), p. 67.
5 Cf. Roland Barthes, *The Fashion System*, trans. M. Ward and R. Howard (New York: Hill and Wang, 1983; originally 1967).
6 E.g. James Laver, *Costume and Fashion: A Concise History* (London: Thames and Hudson, 1985; originally 1969); Elizabeth Wilson, *Adorned in Dreams: Fashion and Modernity* (London: Virago, 1985).
7 Erwin Goffman, "Symbols of Class Status," *British Journal of Sociology*, 2 (1951) 294–304.
8 Anderson J. Black and Madge Garland, *A History of Fashion* (London: Orbis, 1975).
9 Elizabeth Ewing, *Fur in Dress* (London: Batsford, 1981).
10 Richard Sennett, *The Fall of Public Man: On the Social Psychology of Capitalism* (New York: Vintage, 1978).
11 René König, *The Restless Image: A Sociology of Fashion* (London: Allen & Unwin, 1973), p. 111.
12 Ibid., pp. 139–45.
13 N. B. Harte, "State Control of Dress and Social Change in Pre-industrial England," in D. D. Coleman and A. H. John, eds., *Trade, Government and Economy in Pre-industrial England* (London: Weidenfeld & Nicolson, 1976).
14 Diane de Marly, *Working Dress: A History of Occupatioal Clothing* (London: Batsford, 1986), p. 44.

15 Ibid., p. 41.

16 Georg Simmel, "Fashion," *American Journal of Sociology*, 62 (1957) 541–58 (originally 1904).

17 Sennett, *Fall of Public Man*, p. 176.

18 Norbert Elias, *The Civilizing Process. Vol. 1: The History of Manners*, trans. Edmund Jephcott (Oxford: Blackwell, 1982; originally 1939).

19 Wilson, *Adorned in Dreams*.

20 Black and Garland, *History of Fashion*.

21 Valerie Steele, *Fashion and Eroticism: Ideals of Feminine Beauty from the Victorian Era to the Jazz Age* (Oxford: Oxford University Press, 1985), p. 139.

22 Valerie Steele, *Paris Fashion: A Cultural History* (New York: Oxford University Press, 1988), p. 93.

23 Kurt W. Back, "Modernism and Fashion: A Social Psychological Interpretation," in Michael R. Solomon, ed., *The Psychology of Fashion* (Lexington, MA: Lexington Books, 1985), pp. 3–14.

24 Charles Jencks, *The Language of Post-Modern Architecture* (London: Academy Editions, 1978).

25 Jean-Francois Lyotard, *The Postmodern Condition: A Report on Knowledge* (Manchester: Manchester University Press, 1984); Craig Owens, "The Discourse of Others: Feminists and Postmodernists," in Hal Foster, ed., *The Anti-Aesthetic: Essays on Postmodern Culture* (Post Townsend: Washington Bay Press, 1983), pp. 57–82.

26 Back, "Modernism and Fashion."

27 Efrat Tseëlon, "Communicating via Clothes," Ph.D. dissertation, University of Oxford.

28 Baudrillard, *Symbolic Exchange*, p. 133.

29 Jean Baudrillard, *For a Critique of the Political Economy of the Sign*, trans. C. Levin (St. Louis: Telos Press, 1981; originally 1972).

30 Thorstein Veblen, *The Theory of the Leisure Class* (New York: Macmillan, 1912; originally 1899).

31 Simmel, "Fashion."

32 Keith Gibbins, "Social Psychological Theories of Fashion," *Journal of Home Economics Association of Australia*, 3 (1971) 3–18; George B. Sproles, "Behavioral Science Theories," in Michael R. Solomon, ed., *The Psychology of Fashion* (Lexington, MA: Lexington Books, 1985), pp. 55–69.

33 Charles W. King, "Fashion Adoption: A Rebuttal to the 'Trickle-Down' Theory," in Stephen A. Greyse, ed., *Toward Scientific Marketing* (Chicago: American Marketing Association, 1963), pp. 108–25.

34 Herbert Blumer, "Fashion: From Class Differentiation to Collective Selection," *Sociological Quarterly*, 10 (1969) 275–91.

35 George A. Field, "The Status Float Phenomenon. The Upward Diffusion of Innovation," *Business Horizons*, 13 (1970) 45–52.

36 Dick Hebdige, *Subculture: The Meaning of Style* (London: Methuen, 1979).

37 Baudrillard, *Critique*, p. 32.

38 Douglas Kellner, *Jean Baudrillard: From Marxism to Postmodernism and Beyond* (Stanford: Stanford University Press, 1989).

39 Baudrillard, *Symbolic Exchange*.

40 Jean Baudrillard, *Seduction*, trans. B. Singer (New York: Saint Martin's Press, 1990; originally 1979); *Fatal Strategies*, trans. P. Beitchman and W. G. J. Niesluchowski (New York: Semiotext(e), 1990; originally 1983).

41 Baudrillard, *Critique*, p. 78.

42 Baudrillard, *Seduction*, p. 103.

43 Baudrillard, *Fatal Strategies*, p. 103.

44 See, e.g., Alison Lurie, *The Language of Clothes* (London: Bloomsbury, 1992; originally 1981).

45 See, e.g., Susan B. Kaiser, Richard H. Nagasawa, and Sandra S. Hutton "Fashion, Postmodernity and Personal Appearance – A Symbolic Interactionist Formulation," *Symbolic Interaction*, 14, 2 (1991) 165–85.

46 Foster, "Postmodernism: A Preface", in *The Anti-Aesthetic*, pp. ix-xvi.

47 Dec 23, 1990, p. 32 (emphasis added).

48 E.g., Fredric Jameson, "The Cultural Logic of Late Capitalism," *New Left Review*, 146 (1984) 53–92; Michael Newman, "Revising Modernism, Representing Postmodernism," in Lisa Appignanesi, ed., *Postmodernism: ICA Documents* (London: ICA, 1986), pp. 95–154.

49 Baudrillard, *Critique*.

50 Angela McRobbie, "Second-hand Dresses and the Role of the Ragmarket," in Angela McRobbie, ed., *Zoot Suits and Second-hand Dresses: An Anthology of Fashion and Music* (London: Macmillan, 1989), pp. 23–49.

51 Jean Baudrillard, *Simulations*, trans. P. Foss, P. Patton, and P. Beitchman (New York: Semiotext(e), 1983; originally 1981).

52 Most of the discussion is based on Jean Baudrillard, "Fashion or the Enchanting Spectacle of the Code," in *Symbolic Exchange and Death*.

53 Ibid., p. 125.

54 Ibid., p. 122.

55 For a review and critique see Tseëlon, *Communicating via Clothes*.

56 *Flagship*, June/July 1993.

57 Baudrillard, *Seduction*, p. 97.

58 Baudrillard, *Symbolic Exchange*, p. 119.

6

FATAL FORMS: TOWARD A (NEO) FORMAL SOCIOLOGICAL THEORY OF MEDIA CULTURE[1]

Jonathon S. Epstein and Margarete J. Epstein

The purpose of this chapter is to offer the beginnings of a formal sociological theory of the mass media. It will be our contention throughout this paper that two of the most frequently debated theories of the media, that of Marshall McLuhan and that of Jean Baudrillard, can be understood as operating within the framework of Simmel's formal sociology. In order to make this argument, we will first outline Simmel's formal sociology, demonstrate its presence in the work of McLuhan, and then present its extension, through McLuhan, into the work of Baudrillard. When understood in the light of formal sociology, both McLuhan and Baudrillard have significant contributions to make to the sociology of culture. Baudrillard, in particular, offers a radical formal sociology that defines the shift into the postmodern at the *fin de siècle*.

SIMMEL: FORMAL SOCIOLOGY

They come to play freely in themselves and for their own sake; they produce or make use of materials that exclusively serve their own operation or realization.[2]

Simmel proposed that sociology be categorized into three types; general sociology, philosophical sociology, and formal sociology. It is his formal sociology that has had the largest impact on the discipline of sociology. The principles of formal sociology rest on the distinction between the "form," or grammar, of the social and the specific "content" of interaction.[3] It was Simmel's assertion that sociology properly done ignored the content of the social world in favor of uncovering the specific forms which guide interaction. In this paper, following Simmel's lead, we will focus on a discussion of social, and more specifically cultural, forms, leaving aside the examination of interactional content.

The Simmelian concepts of "form" and "content" are among the most widely misunderstood terms within current sociological discourse. Simmel's sociology is strongly flavored by the aestheticism of Kant, whose influence on Simmel's conceptualization of "form" and "content" is widely acknowledged.[4] Nietzsche's philosophy, which distinguishes between the "human" and the "social" (and the struggle that results between the two), is also a critical feature of Simmel's sociology.[5] Simmel reads this struggle as a conflict over "vantage points" from which the "individual" can be examined. The "human" consists of those qualities (e.g., "beauty, strength, nobility of character") that mark the individual as part of "Mankind," while culture, or in Simmel's words the "social," develops from these qualities.[6] For example, our individual need for spiritual expression manifests itself in the dogma of formal religion, which at the same time constrains the individual's unsatisfied spiritual needs. Once developed, modern culture tends toward a homogenization that counters the elements of human expression from which the culture in question initially arose. The social manifests itself in multiple forms, that ultimately can place itself in "violent conflict" between the "individual" human and the "social" human, as the continuing conflict between "artistic freedom" and "community standards" demonstrates. For Simmel, this homogenization, or leveling, of the masses always tends toward the lowest common denominator.

While most sociologists accept sociology's kinship to philosophy, many find Simmel's enthusiastic and unapologetic incorporation of Kantian and Nietzschean thought into his social theory as heretical at worst, and unsavory at best. Not surprisingly, one of Simmel's most outspoken critics was Emile Durkheim who criticized Simmel's use of the opposing abstract concepts, form and content, which were explicated by Simmel "with a shorthand approach, materials hastily gathered and not rigorously handled."[7] Simmel's philosophical orientation, for Durkheim, did nothing to promote "the realm of sociology as a science." This is a criticism which was also shared by Max Weber, who nevertheless found Simmel's sociology to be of the highest intellectual order, and based his criticism on the usage of the word "interaction" as a primitive term.[8]

Simmel conceived of social forms as being the general overarching way in which the specific patterns of social interaction unify and create social structure. Forms arise out of teleological necessity and thus are rooted in the assumption that sociological phenomena move toward specific goals, for specific purposes.[9] These forms provide the necessary framework for the "social" to occur. These goals and purposes organize themselves into "grammatical" categories, or forms, which allow for the inherent singularity of social phenomena to come together into a unified whole called "society," and are expressed through culture.[10] Culture, as an expression of the social, by definition, also follows a formal logic.

Culture, for Simmel, was the collection of forms through which life expresses and realizes itself. Among these expressive forms were: art, religion, science, law, and technology. Cultural forms always express the central idealization of being within an epoch and the struggle that results from the particular idealization as such. For the Greeks, during the classical period, this central idea was *being* itself, for the eighteenth-century romantic it was *nature* and *natural law*, followed in the nineteenth century by *life*, *ego*, and finally at the turn of the century *society*. Simmel, however, was ambivalent regarding the efficacy of the latter, since society, as a central concept, demanded submergence of the "individual" into the social as such. Consequently, this concept was not effective in offering a unifying position since it neglected the "metaphysical, psychological, moral and aesthetic values" of experience.[11] In this framework, for example, sociology can be seen as one of many contents of the cultural form *science*, which specifically arose as an expression of the idealization of society in the late nineteenth century.

As expressions, forms are reflections of lived experience. As a grammar, forms are in one sense causal in that they both dictate and guide the content of culture; form reflects, through content, the expression of idealizations of life that are specified by the form. This seemingly contradictory relationship between cause and effect is integral to the logic of formal sociology. Cultural forms, while arising out of life, do not share what Simmel refers to as "the restless rhythm of life."[12] Life opposes form in its fluidity. Forms are, for however briefly, fixed in their own logical space. Life contradicts and forces new forms to struggle against and eventually replace older forms. History, Simmel notes, as a science, is primarily concerned with the changes brought about by the struggle between forms.[13]

The conflicting nature of form, for Simmel, became most clearly visible in the modern era in which a struggle between cultural forms themselves was replaced with a struggle between life and the principle of form, between the need for life to find expression and the form *as such*. This change in orientation was a result of the increasing speed and efficiency of the transmission of both the content and the form across social space, and made possible only by the belief that cultural forms have been exhausted, leaving only remnants in their place. This logic has been noted by Weinstein and Weinstein[14] who hold that Simmel is the modern sociologist who most clearly anticipated the postmodern shift. As Simmel stated,

Moralists, reactionaries, and people with strict feelings for style are perfectly correct when they complain about the increasing 'lack of form' in modern life. They fail to understand however, that what is happening is not only a negative, passive dying out of traditional forms, but simultaneously a fully positive drive towards life which is actively repressing these forms. This is probably since this struggle, in extent and intensity, does not permit concentration on the creation of new forms, it makes a virtue of necessity and insists on a fight against forms simply because they are forms. This is probably only possible in an epoch where cultural forms are conceived of as an exhausted soil, which has yielded all that it can grow, which, however, is still completely covered by products of its own fertility.[15]

The notion that cultural forms have given way to vestiges leads to the assumption that Simmel was a cultural fatalist. Indeed, when read in a certain way, Simmel's culture is a culture in ruins, in which all that is left is the struggle to establish the form of "no form," the cultural equivalent of sociability.[16] Within this framework, cultural contents extract themselves from their cultural forms and "come to play freely in themselves and for their own sake."[17] The idea that expressionist art was an art without form is guided by this logic.[18]

It is also possible, however, to read Simmel not as a fatalist but as a Nietzschean optimist. The exhaustion of form, for Simmel, was, in fact, viewed as the beginnings of triumph of life over form, and expression of the will toward life. No longer would the form's repression of the will toward life be dominant. In modernity, Simmel held that life would be free to express itself in all its cultural manifestations without the constraints of a *total* formal structure.[19] It is important to note, however, that Simmel held that the absence of form was *not* possible for two reasons. First, Simmel felt that the social was a closed system abstracted from "the mere sum total of living men"[20] which is represented "as the most extreme culmination of the formal principle: perfection of form as the ultimate criterion of truth."[21] Secondly, forms are necessary conditions for the possibility of the social. Form always replaces form, there can be no other way within the Simmelian framework. It is more likely that the events to which Simmel was responding represented a struggle between forms in which no clear dominant form had yet emerged. Simmel, though anticipating the postmodern shift, would not have perceived this shift, since he analyzed the pre-technological boom of modern life. He would have had to have been a seer in order to fully understand the tremendous changes in everyday life that technology and the media would bring. As such, his optimistic attitude was based on the *possibility* of a different reality from that to which he was responding. With the emergence of technology as the primary cultural form in the mid-twentieth century, form now constrains life, a reversal of Simmel's conception of modernity. It is with this in mind that we turn to a discussion of Marshall McLuhan.

MCLUHAN: FORM BECOMES CONTENT

... accelerated media change as a kind of massacre of the innocents.[22]

During his lifetime Canadian media theorist Marshall McLuhan was a cultural sensation – a media star. Now, two decades after his death, his cliche "the medium is the message" is no longer well-known and few students know his name; fewer his central concepts of "media" and "message."

McLuhan's theory of culture can be described as a formal theory of media culture. Any medium, according to McLuhan, is an "extension of man,"[23] an extension of the human animal's physical being in the world. For McLuhan these extensions corresponded to stages in history, so that print technologies correspond to modernity, and, it can be argued, the current electronic media technologies corresponds to postmodernity. McLuhan emphasizes that "in our present electric age the imploding or contracting energies of our world now clash with the old expansionist and traditional patterns of organization."[24] It is this clash that delineates the modernist and postmodernist position. As Kroker points out, McLuhan held that: "technologies of communication in the electronic age overthrow the privileged position of the 'contents' of the media, substituting a new sign-language of rhetorical and symbolic effects. This is the age of the enclosure of whole societies within designed environments, of metaphor, and of MEDIA [sic]."[25] As "extensions of man" each medium extends logically from its corresponding bodily counterpart. In this manner a super highway becomes an extension of the foot, the radio becomes an extension of the ear, books and the print media are an extension of the eye[26] and the recent television and computer technologies become, for McLuhan, an extension of the central nervous system.[27] It is through these extensions that cultural forms are realized.[28]

In his most well-known work, *Understanding Media*, McLuhan presents the argument that all media have as their content another medium. (This echoes the Simmelian assertion that all forms have as their content another form.) In this manner the content of the novel is primarily language, and the content of the movie is primarily a novel, story, or play regardless of what the screenplay is *about*. For McLuhan, the actual narrative content of a movie is at best a distraction from the message that the motion picture medium itself conveys, the message that linear, print-oriented culture has reached the point of perfect mechanization.[29] It can be argued in this fashion that the content of information technologies and computer technologies is technology. Technology becomes the mediator of experience, or, as Arthur Kroker would have it, the experience itself; technology is reality. As Kroker points out "[w]e are the first citizens of a society that has been eaten by a technology, a culture that has actually vanished into the dark vortex of the electronic frontier."[30]

McLuhan shared Simmel's notion that cultural forms and media exist in constant struggle; one form is always in a confrontational stance vis-à-vis an opposing form. In the developmental stage of a new form, for McLuhan, the new form will appear as the content of the form which is the opposite of that which the new form will ultimately present.[31] Early television, for example, was dominated by a character very similar to that of motion pictures and radio. At present, motion pictures have frequently come to resemble television, and radio has become a mere tool of distraction for the bored motorist who cannot afford an in-dash compact disk player.

By almost any intellectual standards McLuhan would have to be considered a technological optimist. His writings strongly endorse the position that the world, through the new (circa the mid-1960s) information and communication technologies, is fast on its way to becoming, or has already become, a "global village." The "global village" is made possible, for McLuhan, through the implosion of time and space brought on by the dramatic increase in the speed of information transmission allowed by these new technologies. As McLuhan argues: "the creative process of knowing will be collectively and corporately extended to the whole of human society, much as we have already extended our senses and our nerves by the various other media."[32]

McLuhan, however, did see the downside to this implosion. His concern for the effects that these new technologies may have on humanity was a central concern of his career and was strongly informed by his Catholicism.[33] While the world may indeed be a "global village," the negative effects of the rapidity of information transmission has brought with it the "never explained numbness that each extension brings about in both the individual and society."[34] In perhaps what was the most sociological of McLuhan's discourses[35] he warns that the speed at which information is now transmitted creates "mental breakdown of varying degrees." Further, he argues that as the media become the primary commodity, a view shared by many social critics in the later part of the twentieth century,[36] it is likely that these media will become accepted as the "social bond" causing "subliminal and docile acceptance of media impact" creating "prisons without walls for their human users."[37] It is with the notion of the implosive force of technology and the speed of information that we now turn to McLuhan's most influential and controversial disciple – Jean Baudrillard.

BAUDRILLARD: SPEED AND REVERSAL

... starting from McLuhan's formula the medium is the message, the consequences of which are far from being exhausted.[38]

French sociologist Jean Baudrillard is among the most influential social theorists of the current era.[39] Baudrillard's theoretical orientation rests on several key assumptions regarding the relationship between people and the media which engulf them, what Baudrillard refers to as the "mediascape." His focus is strongly oriented toward McLuhan's central concept that "the media is the message." However, unlike McLuhan, Baudrillard views the implosion of the social through the media to be complete, no longer a process of reorganization into the global village, but now a furious implosion into the "shadows of the silent majority," the "death of the social" and the seductive and superficial depth of meaning in the media.

For Baudrillard, the social comes into being through its expression in cultural forms. These forms are extended through the media and each form has a "code" specific to it. Like both Simmel and McLuhan before him, Baudrillard holds that it is the specific form, and the uncovering of its code, that is of importance to sociology. As an example, it can be shown that in what was to be Baudrillard's final in-depth critique of Marxist theory, his argument rests on the assumption that Marxist methodology examines only the contents of the form "production," "leaving production as a form intact."[40] Baudrillard's early essays initially discussed the present moment under the form "production" from which the conceptualizations of communication and its corresponding technology arose. As his theorizing evolved, it became clear to Baudrillard that the reversal of this formulation, based on the primacy of production, was actually the case. "Communication" in the form of media technologies eclipsed "production" to become the dominant cultural form.[41] Baudrillard's conception of the implosion of content into form has been noted by Kellner who points out that Baudrillard utilizes: ". . . a model of the media as a black hole of signs and information that absorbs all contents into cybernetic noise which no longer communicates meaningful messages in a process in which all contents implode into form. We thus see how Baudrillard eventually adopts McLuhan's media theory as his own . . ."[42]

The (mass) media, for Baudrillard, have become the dominant cultural form in the late twentieth century. In agreement with McLuhan, Baudrillard holds that the content of a particular medium is always another medium. In the Baudrillardian argument, however, the media implosion discussed by McLuhan absorbed the whole of the social world in its vortex. The media have "evolved into a total system of mythological interpretation, a closed system of models of signification from which no event escapes."[43] The fact that the mass media form has created a total, closed system coupled with the speed (a critical variable in Baudrillard's theorizing) of information transmission has led to a blurring of the relationship between cause and effect, between the subject and its object. The relationship between the "extensions of man" and the media becomes obscured.[44] Baudrillard asks the reader to consider the possibility that the relationship between humans and the media is reversing; the media are no longer an extension of man, à la McLuhan; the media now extends into the social, into the domain of the human,[45] in the dramatic reversal caused by speed. It is at this point of reversal that Baudrillard would like to focus his analysis because it is at this precise point that form exists as pure form, or, as Baudrillard would have it, as pure object without referent. It is at this point that the form exists as pure object, in its pure state, and does not refer back to any other form other than itself. It becomes form without content, a fatal form, which, according to the logic of formal sociology, can have no opposing form. They become fatal forms precisely because there is no opposing form. This fatality of form is the stuff of Baudrillard's "postmodern shift." As Kellner points out:

> The escalating role of the media in contemporary society is for Baudrillard equivalent to THE FALL into the postmodern society of simulations from the modern universe of production. Whereas modernity centered on the production of things, commodities and products, postmodernity is characterized by radical semiurgy, by a proliferation of signs. Furthermore, following McLuhan, Baudrillard interprets modernity as a process of explosion of commodification, mechanization, technology and market relations, in contrast to postmodern society, which is the site of an implosion of all boundaries, regions, and distinctions between high and low culture, appearance and reality and just about every other binary operation maintained by traditional philosophy and social theory.[46]

Baudrillard's prognosis for the state of the social, for the reasons stated above, is grim. The global village, which Baudrillard refers to as "the mass" exists, sociologically speaking, only in the public opinion polls and statistics that flash by each day on the evening news. The masses have become the content of the media technology form. As Baudrillard would have it, individuals watch the news in order to discover their opinion, to find the causes to "believe" in, and, most importantly, to uncover an identity. Of course, within his logic, all of this is quite beside the point since all the mass can ultimately do is absorb information in silence. Acting on that information, in the absence of any form to oppose the media form, is not possible.

DISCUSSION: FATAL FORMS

In Simmel's words, 'Negation is the simplest thing possible.'[47]

The American novelist Tom Wolfe once asked of Marshall McLuhan, "what if he is right."[48] The same question becomes an important one regarding Baudrillard's formal sociology. What if it is right? Has the social imploded into the mass, now existing only as a response to statistics and opinion polls, and, if so, where does this leave culture? Indeed, where does it leave sociology? Can there be a formal sociology of media culture that does not destroy the sociological enterprise in its analysis?

By and large the majority of cultural sociological studies are studies of content. As such, following the logic of formal sociology, these studies are of very little use within the formal sociological framework, precisely because cultural forms cannot be understood by an analysis of their content alone. For example, television absorbs the viewer to the point of nonresponsiveness, regardless of the potency of the information transmitted via the medium. As such, the debates of "positive versus negative" influence, while possibly important in and of themselves, fail to grasp that the essential effect of this medium is to negate the possibility of response. Within the framework of formal sociology, this is not good news for the traditional sociologist, due to the fact that most sociology, as it currently exists, is comprised of the analysis of content. In fact, by definition, all statistically driven analyses are oriented toward content over form. As sociology has striven to become a "science," it may have, in a remarkably Baudrillardian sense, thrown the baby out with the bath water and in this manner negated any chance of its own effectiveness in the formal sense. Sociology becomes a shadowplay in which the players remain unaware that the shadows are mere representations and proceed as if they were "real."

A formal sociology of culture, whether Simmelian, McLuhanian, or Baudrillardian in nature, is concerned primarily with the uncovering of the grammatical framework, the code, through which social structure becomes possible and expresses itself. Presently, this formal framework appears to be dictated by technological media. While this particular form is not problematic in and of itself (forms never are) the speed at which technologies are transmitted and generated has caused this cultural form to approach critical mass.

According to Newton's third law, for every implosion/explosion there must be a corresponding and equivalent explosion/implosion. Consequently, Baudrillard's metaphor of the "implosion of meaning in the media" implies that there must have been an explosion following the "implosion." This explosion, for Baudrillard (although he does not use the term), can best be understood with reference to what he has termed the "precession of simulacra," the simulation models which replace "the real" in terms of function in the mediascape. This function, for Baudrillard, is manifested in the "substituting signs of the real for the real itself, that is, an operation to deter every real process by its operational double ...."[49] This is the territory of "hyperreality" with simulation as its form.

Baudrillard offers four forms, analyzed historically, that stretch from the Renaissance period to the present. It can be argued that Baudrillard offered this framework in response to his statement, discussed previously, that Marxist methodology only examined the content of the form "production," "leaving production as a form intact."[50] Baudrillard describes his scheme as such:

> Once, out of some obscure need to classify, I proposed a tripartite account of value: a natural stage (use value), a commodity stage (exchange value), and a structural stage (sign value) .... These distinctions are *formal* [italics added] ones, of course – reminiscent of the distinctions between the particles physicists are always coming up with. A new particle does not replace those discovered earlier, it simply joins their ranks, takes it place in a hypothetical series. So let me introduce a new particle into the microphysics of simulacra. For after the natural, commodity, and structural stages of value comes the fractal stage. The first of these stages had a natural referent and value developed on the basis of the natural use of the world. The second was founded on a general equivalence, and value developed by reference to a logic of the commodity. The third is governed by a code, and value develops here by reference to a set of models. At the fourth, the fractal (or viral, or radiant) stage of value, there is no point of reference at all, and value radiates in all directions, occupying all interstices, without reference to anything whatsoever, by virtue of pure contiguity ... This is the pattern of the fractal – and hence the current pattern of our culture.[51]

It is here, in Baudrillard's discussion of the simulacra, that his theoretical orientation clearly corresponds to Simmel's formal sociology.[52] For example, Simmel held that

> ... all historical developments passed through three phases. The first is the undifferentiated unity of manifold elements. The second is the differentiated articulation of these elements, that have become alienated from one another. The third is a new unity, the harmonious interpenetration of the elements that have been preserved, however, in their specific characters.[53]

Baudrillard's first three stages of appearance reflect Simmel's three stages of historical development: Baudrillard's "natural" stage and Simmel's "undifferentiated unity of manifold elements;" Baudrillard's "commodity" stage and Simmel's "differentiated articulation of these elements, that have become alienated from one another;" Baudrillard's "structural" stage and Simmel's "harmonious interpenetration of the elements that have been preserved, however, in their specific characters" (i.e., in the form of a code).

While Simmel's third stage of development provided an accurate description of the formal structure of the social world that he was attempting to comprehend, nearly a century's worth of technological transformations and the ensuing implosion of the mass in the media culture have rendered this scheme inadequate. This inadequacy stems from the triumph of form over life, in which forms no longer correspond to the life from which they arise, and come to exist independently and for their own sake. It is this inability to account for the detachment of form from life that compels Baudrillard to add the fourth stage, the fractal stage.

In this fractal stage, the boundaries between forms collapse, allowing for the free play among the forms as such. For example, Baudrillard points out that the form "sex" is no longer located in sex, but can be found almost everywhere else, the form "politics" invades all other forms, such as economics, science and art.[54] This free play is the detachment of form from life. No longer do the distinctive human qualities discussed by Simmel contribute, let alone direct, the creation of form. These have become fatal forms under the sign of technology. Fatal forms are possible according to Baudrillard:

> When things, signs or actions, are freed from their respective ideas, concepts, essences, values, points of reference, origins and aims, they embark upon an endless process of self-reproduction. Yet things continue to function long after their ideas have disappeared, and they do so in total indifference to their own content. The paradoxical fact is that they function even better under these circumstances.[55]

At the level of content, one of the most dramatic results of the fatality of form is the curtailing of personal social interaction. The "issues of the day" that we all watch on television do not pertain to us as individuals. We are entertained by the news and absorb it (and are absorbed by it), but there is often no impact. The fatal form is divorced from life and we are held in abeyance as a result. All methods of human interaction, including sexuality, are mediated by, or replaced with, machines. Commerce is largely electronic, as witnessed by the proliferation of bank machines and automated teller machines; our grammar is checked by a software package. It is not uncommon to speak with a machine in the absence of the party you are trying to reach by phone. In an ironic twist on this relatively new phenomenon machines frequently call you, generally during dinner. For the most part we do not find this particularly alarming. Our basic modes of interaction are steadily being replaced with technological substitutes, all in the name of progress.

When forms become fatal, technologies become obsolete before they become a physical reality both in terms of invention and mass production. For instance, the 80486 computer coprocessor, which was mass marketed in 1992, was rendered obsolete before it went into mass production by the announcement of the Pentium coprocessor which has, at the time of writing, just become available.

At the level of form, what is important about these examples is the code by which they proceed. Culture is becoming more impersonal, more anonymous, all encompassing and interconnected, constituting a closed system. It is no longer possible to distinguish between high and low culture except in the minds of those who believe they respond to only one or the other. Culture is no longer plural; it is singular, despite the variation in content. The global village is homogenized; individuality is expected, conformity guaranteed.

The traditional sociological study of culture can be understood as providing an inventory of effects caused by living within a specific formal framework. In this manner it provides a valuable service, not only to the discipline of sociology, but to the culture with which it is concerned as well. Despite formal sociology's insistence on the primacy of form, we all must live with the cultural contents on a continual basis. The typical individual who embarrasses him/herself by actually talking to the computer that has called them on the phone is generally not interested in the cultural code that led to the phone call in the first place. Nor are they generally concerned with the form in which the possibility of the phone call arose. They will be quite concerned, however momentarily, with how to deal with their blunder and the resulting embarrassment. Most of us are content oriented, being quite unaware of form.

Placing Baudrillard within a formal sociological framework allows for a more complete analysis of his work. When viewed in this manner, his conceptualization of (post) modern culture becomes more easily understood. He has elaborated the formal theoretical orientation within which a postmodern sociology can proceed. His terminology can be viewed as providing a framework in much the same way as Marxist terminology provided a framework for earlier sociological analysis. However, Baudrillard's formal sociology is plagued with many of the same shortcomings that are present in Simmel's formal sociological work. Neither Simmel, nor McLuhan, nor Baudrillard elaborate a methodology that can be utilized for concrete analysis of cultural forms and as such, at this point, formal sociology remains strictly descriptive.

Yet, formal sociology provides a strategy for grasping the complexity of human *being*. It allows for the explication of the cultural forms and codes that guide and shape both human interaction and social structure. From Baudrillard's perspective this undertaking is further necessitated by the perfection of forms to the point of fatality in the postmodern scene. In this paper we have outlined the formal orientation of three social theorists, Georg Simmel, Marshall McLuhan, and Jean Baudrillard, in an attempt to show how all three thinkers were primarily concerned with the uncovering of cultural forms and that there is a direct Simmelian influence in the writings of Baudrillard. Formal sociology can be understood as the search for the grammatical framework that makes the social possible. In this manner it stands as the necessary complement to the sociology of culture proper. Future studies in the sociology of culture could benefit greatly by an awareness of the formal framework which guides cultural content as outlined most appropriately for the current sociological moment by Jean Baudrillard.

Notes

1 The authors would like to thank Jerry M. Lewis and Douglas Kellner for comments an earlier drafts of this paper.
2 Georg Simmel, *The Sociology of Georg Simmel*, trans. Kurt H. Wolff (New York: Free Press, 1950), pp. 21–4.
3 Ibid.
4 See David Frisby, "The Aesthetics of Modern Life: Simmels Interpretation," *Theory, Culture, and Society*, 8, 3 (1991) 73–94.
5 *Sociology of Georg Simmel*, pp. 61–84.
6 Ibid.
7 Emile Durkheim, "The Realm of Sociology as a Science," *Social Forces*, 59, 4 (1981) 1054–70.
8 Max Weber, "Georg Simmel as Sociologist," *Social Research*, 39, 2 (1972) 155–163.
9 See Rudolph H. Weingartner, *Experience and Culture: The Philosophy of Georg Simmel* (Middleton, Connecticut: Wesleyan University Press, 1962).
10 *Sociology of Georg Simmel*, pp. 21–5.
11 Georg Simmel, *The Conflict in Modern Culture and Other Essays*, trans. K. Peter Etzkorn (New York: Teachers College Press, 1968), pp. 11–15.
12 Ibid.
13 Ibid., pp. 11–12.
14 Deena and Michael Weinstein, *Postmodernizing Simmel* (London: Routledge, 1993).
15 Simmel, *Conflict in Modern Culture*, pp. 12–13.
16 Simmel, *Sociology of Georg Simmel*, pp. 40–57.
17 Ibid., p. 41.
18 Simmel, *Conflict in Modern Culture*, pp. 16–19.
19 Ibid., p. 15.
20 Simmel, *Sociology of Georg Simmel*, pp. 3–11.
21 Simmel, *Conflict in Modern Culture*, p. 21.
22 Marshall McLuhan, *Understanding Media: The Extensions of Man* (New York: Signet Books, 1964).
23 Ibid.
24 Ibid., p. 47.
25 Arthur Kroker, *Technology and the Canadian Mind*, (New York: Saint Martin's Press, 1984), p. 54.
26 For an extended discussion of the effects of print on human development see Herbert Marshall McLuhan, *The Gutenberg Galaxy: The Making of Typographic Man*, (Toronto: University of Toronto Press, 1962). In this text, McLuhan outlines the logic from which his analysis of modern electronic media proceeds.
27 McLuhan, *Understanding Media*. See also Marshall McLuhan with Quinton Fiore, *From Cliche to Archetype* (New York: Pocket Books, 1970).

28 This point has led some sociologists to argue that in this manner media become determinants of social structure. For one of the earliest discussions see Jerry M. Lewis, "McLuhan: A Sociological Interpretation," in *The Humanities as Sociology* (New York: Charles A. Merrill, 1974), pp. 195–213.

29 McLuhan, *Understanding Media*, pp. 248–59.

30 Arthur Kroker, *Spasm: Virtual Reality, Android Music and Electric Flesh*, (New York, Saint Martin Press, 1993) p. 15.

31 Ibid., pp. 23–35.

32 Ibid., p. 19.

33 For a detailed discussion on the relationship between McLuhan and his Catholicism see Arthur Kroker, *Technology and the Canadian Mind: Innis\McLuhan\Grant*, (New York: Saint Martin's Press, 1984), pp. 52–86.

34 McLuhan, *Understanding Media*, p. 20.

35 Ibid., pp. 36–56.

36 For a critical and in-depth discussion of this position see Mark Poster, *The Mode of Information: Poststructuralism and Social Context*, (Chicago: Chicago University Press, 1990).

37 McLuhan, *Understanding Media*, pp. 23–44.

38 Jean Baudrillard, *Simulations* (New York: Semiotext(e), 1983).

39 For conflicting analyses of Baudrillard's contribution to social theory see Douglas Kellner, *Jean Baudrillard: From Marxism to Postmodernism and Beyond* (Stanford: Stanford University Press, 1989) and Mike Gane, *Baudrillard: Critical and Fatal Theory* (New York: Routledge, 1991).

40 Jean Baudrillard, *The Mirror of Production*, trans. Mark Poster, (St. Louis: Telos Press, 1975), pp. 17ff.

41 For an elaboration on this reversal, see Chapter 2 by Steven Best in this volume.

42 Kellner, *Baudrillard*, p. 68.

43 Jean Baudrillard, *For a Critique of the Political Economy of the Sign*, trans. Charles Levin (St. Louis: Telos Press, 1981), p. 175.

44 Jean Baudrillard, *The Evil Demon of Images*, trans. Paul Patton and Paul Foss (Sydney: Power Institute Publications, 1987).

45 It is here that Kroker has focussed his most recent explorations of the farthest spaces of the "Baudrillardian Scene" which is described in Arthur Kroker, *Spasm*.

46 Kellner, *Baudrillard*, pp. 67–8.

47 Jean Baudrillard, *The Transparency of Evil*, trans. James Benedict, (New York: Verso, 1993), p. 72.

48 Tom Wolfe, "what if he is right? what if he is the most important thinker since newton, darwin, freud, einstein, and pavlov-what if he is right?" [sic] ed., Gerald E. Stern *McLuhan Hot and Cool* (New York: Dial Press, 1967).

49 Baudrillard, *Simulations*.

50 Baudrillard, *Mirror of Production*, p. 17.

51 Baudrillard, *Transparency of Evil*.

52 It should be noted that McLuhan offers a similar, although less clearly delineated, discussion of historical stages of development based on people's relationship to technology in *Understanding Media*, p. 19, when he states:

After three thousand years of explosion, by means of fragmentary and mechanical technologies, the western world is imploding. During the mechanical ages we had extended our bodies in space. Today, after more than a century of electric technology, we extended our central nervous system itself in a global embrace, abolishing both space and time as far as our planet is concerned. Rapidly, we approach the final phase of the extensions of man – the technological simulation of consciousness, when the creative process of knowing will be collectively and corporately extended to the whole of human society, much as we have already extended our senses and our nerves by the various media.

53 *Sociology of Georg Simmel,* p. 19.
54 Baudrillard, *Transparency of Evil.*
55 Ibid., p. 6.

7

SYMBOLIC EXCHANGE IN HYPERREALITY[1]

—

Deborah Cook

As the end of the millennium approaches, Jean Baudrillard continues to play the role of the prophet of doom with his analyses of the ubiquitous reign of the simulacrum. Television, in particular, has served him as a kind of rebus, the deciphering of which has led to his often-bleak view of the hyperreality of our millenary experience. But, although one could easily portray Baudrillard as the Darth Vader of postmodernism, his work on media reception should be scrutinized more closely because in some of it he puts forward the view, similar in some respects to John Fiske's, that consumers do resist the media. Thus, far from claiming that media reception is passive and alienated, Baudrillard sees in some reception a resistive response to the media.

Baudrillard believes that resistance is located in forms of symbolic exchange; among other things, symbolic exchange involves reciprocity between transmitter and receiver which is not subject to the law of exchange or equivalence. Even the more catastrophic forms of symbolic exchange, which Baudrillard praises for their political efficacy, challenge the status quo by sending back to it its own logic, thus effectively reciprocating with it. In "The Masses,"[2] for example, Baudrillard makes the claim that at least one form of response (or non-response) constitutes a resistive and efficacious symbolic exchange with the media. Moreover, in *Pour une critique de l'économie politique du signe*,[3] Baudrillard also implies that, when they are formally restructured, the media themselves will foster forms of exchange which are symbolic and which therefore exhibit reciprocity between transmitter and receiver. I shall first examine Baudrillard's views about a resistive form of symbolic exchange and evaluate its political efficacy. After a brief comparison with Fiske's account of resistive reception, I shall proceed to evaluate the prospects for a formal restructuring of the media. To begin, however, I shall contextualize Baudrillard's contribution to the analysis of media reception by considering its historical background.

Like Baudrillard, critical theorists are widely believed to have held that media reception is overwhelmingly passive and alienated. It is generally supposed that critical theory claims the masses are incapable of resistance to media manipulation. This view can be challenged, however. Citing Marcuse's *One-Dimensional Man*, Curran, Gurevitch, and Woollacott explain that critical theorists attribute not total manipulation but a "reinforcement 'effect' "[4] to the media. The media reinforce behaviour and beliefs which have already been shaped by one-dimensional society. Furthermore, even in this more limited task of reinforcement, Adorno and Horkheimer claim that the media are not entirely successful: "Ideology is split into the photograph of stubborn life and the naked lie about its meaning – which is not expressed but suggested and yet drummed in."[5] Consumers of mass culture are not taken-in entirely by the *naked* lie: "The double mistrust of traditional culture as ideology is combined with mistrust of industrialized culture as a swindle."[6] In other essays, Adorno focuses even more explicitly on the duplicitous nature of the reception of cultural commodities.[7]

In direct response to the alleged pessimism of critical theory, a number of theorists attempted to show how consumers retain a certain degree of autonomy with respect to the media. Elihu Katz has traced back a "limited effects" view of the media "to the pioneer communication research of Paul Lazersfeld and his group." This view stresses "processes of individual selectivity, perception, and recall." Quoting Katz, Herbert Schiller agrees that the limited effects view is the "predecessor of subsequent studies that concentrated on what the receiver (the audience) either brought to or how it utilized the message."[8] In the 1960s, however, new theorists such as "Lerner, Schramm, Pool, and other American communication scholars . . . had no doubt that the modern media and the new information technologies were means of great potential influence."[9] The "limited effects" view was challenged by these later theories. Today, however, it is the "limited effects" view which predominates again in theories of media reception.

Critical theory still serves as the foil for the latest versions of the "limited effects" view.[10] Among other places, these versions appear in contemporary semiological (or semiotic) accounts of mass media reception. The alleged pessimism of critical theory finds its counterpart in the somewhat more positive assessments of Jean Baudrillard and John Fiske. Although Fiske claims he is working within the same parameters as those of the critical theorists – that is, within "a model of power" – he still believes that people are capable of evading or resisting "the forces of dominance"[11] of the mass media. Contrary to the idea that the media oppress and repress, Baudrillard believes media consumers actually exhibit "a kind of refusal and non-reception" which serves as a strategy for "sending back to the system its own logic by reproducing it."[12]

By showing how consumers counter the blandishments of mass culture, Fiske and Baudrillard unwittingly supplement critical theory even as they claim to supersede it. Their work is important because in it they describe what they believe are the strategies and tactics which people employ in their alleged resistance to the bureaucratic society of controlled consumption. In the following two sections of the paper I shall contrast Baudrillard's view of symbolic exchange in media reception with Fiske's analysis of the resistive meanings consumers give to cultural commodities. I shall focus on the weaknesses of these theories rather than on their strengths. The strength of both lies in their analysis of media reception as something duplicitous; consumers are never entirely taken in by the media.

THE SILENT MAJORITY

In *Critique*, Baudrillard denied that symbolic exchange with the mass media is possible because the code of the media is univocal[13] and the structure of the media permits no reciprocity.[14] Possibilities for symbolic exchange lie elsewhere – in graffiti, for example. In *L'Echange symbolique et la mort*, published four years after the *Critique*, symbolic exchange appears in a catastrophic form as death (a more or less symbolic death) because "only death is an act without an equivalent return, an exchange of values."[15] Three years later in *Simulacres et simulation*, Baudrillard again modifies his position slightly. Symbolic exchange can be found in the silence of the masses to the demands of the media. Baudrillard defines the media as "an irreversible model of communication *without response*," and by mirroring the media's irreversibility, the silence of the masses actually serves to reciprocate with the media by sending back to them their own logic. "This absence of response may be understood, no longer in the least as the strategy of power, but as a counterstrategy of the masses themselves in confrontation with power" (pp. 128–9). Such reciprocation is characteristic of symbolic exchange. Baudrillard further elaborates this view in his essay, "The Masses," to which I shall now turn.

Symbolic exchange is Baudrillard's answer to Heidegger's idle talk or chatter. It involves more than the reversibility of transmitter and receiver – Enzensberger's Marxist solution to the problems posed by the mass media[16] – and it constitutes an effective and allegedly resistive (non)response to the media. The model for symbolic exchange is the gift which is "unique, specified by people and by the unique moment of exchange". The gift "is arbitrary and nevertheless absolutely singular" (*Critique*, p. 61). Communication modeled after this form of exchange cannot be assimilated to the instrumentality which characterizes capitalist forms of exchange and it has, in fact, largely been vitiated in capitalist societies. Quoting Douglas Kellner: for Baudrillard, "precapitalist societies are governed by forms of symbolic exchange similar to Bataille's notion of a general economy, supplemented by Mauss's theory of the gift and countergift, rather than by production and utility." Nonetheless, there is "a fundamental dividing line in history between symbolic societies – that is societies fundamentally organized around symbolic exchange – and productive societies."[17]

In capitalist or "productive" societies, it is the formal structure of the mass media which tends to preclude symbolic exchange. Even so, in "The Masses," Baudrillard claims to have discovered in the silence of people in these societies a resistive and symbolic response to the codes which the media deploy.[18] According to Baudrillard, the masses adopt silence as a strategy in order to challenge the social and political status quo. In silence, they reflect the media's demand "like a mirror," and "it is hard to imagine what powers of deception, of absorption, of deviation – in a word, of subtle revenge – there is in this type of response."[19] In silence, the masses disappear; their failure to respond makes it impossible to locate them, to analyze them, and to manipulate them. The media "maximize speech, . . . maximize the production of meaning, of participation"[20] through opinion polls and voting procedures, for example. They want to know what we want; they even demand to know. They treat us like subjects with desires, a will, free choice, in order to negate us as subjects. We respond by objectifying ourselves, by "the *refusal of the will*."[21] To the demand to "constitute ourselves as subjects, to liberate, to express ourselves at any price, to vote, to produce, to decide, to speak, to participate, to play the game,"[22] we respond by delegating "the faculty of choice to someone else by a sort of game of irresponsibility, of ironic challenge, of sovereign lack of will, of secret ruse."[23]

Motivated by his rejection of the pessimistic view of the masses as passive and alienated, Baudrillard attributes to them a wiliness, even deviousness, which gives them the upper hand. He attempts to support his view by citing Hegel's immanent critique of the Enlightenment: it is not possible to deceive a people about itself.[24] Hence, ideology critique is not applicable here. Instead, "[t]he mass knows that it knows nothing, and it does not want to know. The mass knows that it can do nothing, and it does not want to achieve anything."[25] Silence is a clever ruse of the people against the system which attempts to make them impotent and stupid.

This "refusal of the will" is not, according to Baudrillard, an entirely conscious strategy on the part of the masses. Here, he refers to our deepest desires, to a non-Freudian unconscious. To the traditional philosophies of the subject, he opposes another consciousness, or unconscious, which lies "in this ironic power of nonparticipation of nondesire, of nonknowledge, of silence, of absorption of all powers, of *expulsion* of all powers of all wills, of all knowledge, of all meaning onto representatives surrounded by a halo of derision."[26] But, what is this if not Freud's death wish? It is at this point that Baudrillard's analysis in "The Masses" links up with the one in *L'échange symbolique*. Silence represents the symbolic death of the masses.[27] In "The Masses," Baudrillard celebrates their disappearance: the masses no longer will themselves to be subjects but rather to be lifeless objects; they abandon all responsibility and make a mockery of whatever autonomy they may have preserved.

Baudrillard's appeal to the deepest desires of a non-Freudian unconscious – which suspiciously resembles Freud's – is certainly as anthropological as anything he has criticized in Marx. It is also, once again, open to a variety of interpretations. Why, after all, do the masses will not to will, will to disappear? It would appear as if Baudrillard believes that consumers will to disappear in order to resurface in a world where symbolic exchange prevails. Their sacrifice will be vindicated. But there are alternative interpretations; the death wish could just as easily be interpreted as motivated by a sense of despair or defeat. There is no point to willing anything because nothing can be accomplished anyway; the powers that be will win out in the end. And by delegating the responsibility of decision-making to politicians and technocrats, the system which dominates all forms of communication will continue to function; it will not be overturned as Baudrillard believes. Playing dead may be a ruse, but it is not one which subverts the status quo – the masses are ultimately the ones who get caught in the snare of their own lack of desire to will. They effectively hand power over to those who exploit and dominate them.

Another problem with Baudrillard's theory lies in his treatment of "the masses" as an undifferentiated group. Although, in "The Masses," he cannot be accused of exhibiting an "aristocratic, anti-populace prejudice *and* a general disappointment with the promises of progressive thinking."[28] his ideas do fall prey to some of the criticism directed against mass society theses. The "masses" is comprised of socially and economically differentiated groups of individuals. To speak of a single response from an allegedly homogeneous group called "the masses" is therefore highly questionable. Different social groups respond differently to the "hyperreality" of the media. Baudrillard ought to have taken a closer look at the variety of responses to the media.

Silence is not the only response of the disempowered, and it is also not the only effective one. Other responses, such as boycotting, sabotage, pirating, and the like, are probably even more effective. Instead of dismissing everything but the death-mask of silence as ineffective, Baudrillard needs to reassess what constitutes an effective response. Even the use of something as simple as a remote control device constitutes a response to the media. The media themselves view channel-hopping, muting, and editing as threats. These activities are widely practised by television viewers in North America. Although they offer only an indirect response to the media and are less "subversive" than pirating, or than Baudrillard's example of graffiti perhaps, they do permit a kind of interaction with the media which is not solely based on the logic of exchange value. Dead silence – the response which is not a response – is probably less effective than such interaction, and its 'revolutionary' character can too easily be disputed.

Baudrillard is, however, right to insist that media reception is not completely passive and alienating, even though his discussion of the strategy of silence leaves a great deal to be desired. He echoes Adorno[29] when he says of our response to the media that it is duplicitous: "*One believes in them and one does not believe in them.*"[30] Unlike Baudrillard, however, I believe that one reason for this duplicity lies in the survival of other forms of (lateral) communication and exchange. Our everyday conversations with "significant others" pose a direct challenge to the unidirectionality and univocity of the media even though the latter have made important incursions into everyday conversation as, for example, the cliché-ridden *Wild at Heart* shows. Baudrillard's often hyperbolic statements do not allow one to make the fine distinctions necessary for an analysis of everyday speech and behavior, and of the effects which the media have had on them.

THE SILENT MINORITIES

John Fiske's view of media reception may be instructively compared to Baudrillard's. Fiske's description of the allegedly resistive tactics of the disempowered is largely an extension and further application of Michel de Certeau's *Arts de Faire*.[31] According to Fiske, consumers who create popular culture "transform the cultural commodity into a cultural resource, pluralize the meanings and pleasures it offers, evade or resist its disciplinary efforts, fracture its homogeneity and coherence, raid or poach upon its terrain."[32] Consumption is an act of production. Popular productive consumption is primarily directed toward creating meanings and practices which are relevant to everyday life; they do not necessarily square with the "dominant ideology." These meanings and practices are either progressive or reactionary. Although they are not radical, Fiske makes the further claim that most of the meanings and practices of popular culture are progressive in terms of their tactical opposition to the prevailing forces of domination in society. Sometimes, however, "the oppositionality is sporadic, sometimes sleeping, sometimes aroused into guerrilla raids, but never fully anaesthetized."

Fiske tries to find support for his view concerning the tactical character of the production of resistive meanings in de Certeau's idea of guerrilla tactics and in Umberto Eco's "semiotic guerrilla warfare." For his part, Eco believes that "the mass communication universe is full of . . . discordant interpretations," or of oppositional meanings. However, "until now this variability of interpretation has been random."[34] To correct this randomness, Eco proposes semiotic guerrilla warfare – a form of consciousness-raising. Warfare will be waged by "groups of communications guerrillas, who would restore a critical dimension to passive reception."[35] The tactics of these groups would be explicitly political.[36]

As compared to semiotic guerilla warfare, however, the production of resistive meanings is largely reactive; it is unfocussed, unconscious, and sporadic. By characterizing it as tactical, Fiske lends it a political dimension which, in its randomness, passivity, and reactive character, this production only possesses potentially, if at all. He begs the question of the political dimension of popular culture. (As Eco recognized in the above passage, despite its "discordant" meanings, media reception needs to be made self-conscious and critical.) Similarly, to speak of popular culture production as oppositional ideology: they may diverge slightly or substantially from it. This divergence may be explained in a number of ways but, as Fiske himself notes, popular culture is only potentially political, so it can only assume an "oppositional" character if it becomes explicitly political.

Furthermore, Fiske does not explain what the prevailing socio-political meanings and practices of the dominant ideology, challenged by largely unfocussed and sporadic meanings, actually are. He paints the "dominant ideology" in very broad and unelaborated strokes – patriarchal, pluralistic, disciplinary, capitalist, etc. It is therefore not at all clear what it is that those who resist are resisting. Here, as elsewhere, Fiske plays fast and loose with theory; he makes use of a wide variety of often-incompatible theories (Eco, de Certeau, Foucault, Laclau) whose premises concerning the dominant ideology he neither states nor examines critically. To evaluate the political potential of the allegedly tactical oppositionality of popular culture, one needs to know precisely what meanings and practices are being opposed. Is there really a dominant ideology; is it "centralizing, disciplinary, hegemonic, massifying, commodifying" (the adjectives proliferate almost endlessly)?[37]

The incorporation of popular culture by the system is a distinct possibility. While admitting this, Fiske goes on to criticize the view that popular culture might be incorporated because it could lead to "pessimistic reductionism."[38] In "Falsification and Consensus," which Fiske quotes with approval, Eco points out that in the case of many resistive practices, the system has a great capacity to heal its wounds. "And that, indeed, big systems and subversive groups are often twins, and one produces the other."[39] However, it could certainly be argued that, in comparison with the explicitly and self-consciously political action of subversive groups, which Eco is discussing in this passage, the meanings and practices of popular culture are even more susceptible to incorporation. Furthermore, since these meanings and practices are unfocussed and sporadic, they probably pose little or no threat to the system. In fact, on Fiske's account, popular culture often seems to have the effect of making life within the system more tolerable; it serves only to sustain the system rather than to challenge it.

In order to acquire a political potential, meanings must first acquire a social dimension. And, since "politics is social"[40] – another unsupported theoretical claim – the socialization of private meanings is ipso facto politically relevant. Fiske nowhere discusses the differences between private and social meanings nor does he discuss how private meanings, if such there be, can be socialized. And, if private meanings are not necessarily social, what possible impact might they have on political practice? In themselves, private meanings do not even enter the socio-political arena, so their political potential is questionable. As for popular *practices*, these are generally social but, because they are random and sporadic, and not explicitly conscious, their political potential is equally problematic. Furthermore, Fiske has no empirical evidence to support the view that popular culture has political potential. How many women will become feminists as a direct result of having given resistive meanings to "Cagney and Lacey," for example?

Fiske not only leaves to left-wing theorists the task of finding the links between the "micropolitics" of popular meanings and practices and the "macropolitics" of direct political engagement – links which he neither demonstrates empirically nor grounds theoretically – he also hands over to them the role of instructing people about the social dimension of their private meanings. The problems with this delegation of responsibility are legion; they need not be rehearsed here. Even more controversial is Fiske's idea that popular, progressive cultural production is a necessary precondition, if not a necessary cause, of populist radical movements because popular culture "not only maintains social differences, it maintains their oppositionality, and people's awareness of it."[41] Since, however, the relation between popular culture and populist politics is moot, Fiske leaves left-wing theorists holding a leaky bag.

Tania Modleski has pointed out that theories like Fiske's are simply versions of capitalist ideology in which the claim is made that capitalist economies offer something for everyone – that there is a pluralism of choice in consumer societies. If I am a black, unemployed woman in Tennessee, television still has something for me. She also characterizes positions like Fiske's by contrasting them with critical theory:

> If the problem with some of the work of the Frankfurt School was that its members were far too outside the culture they examined, critics today seem to have the opposite problem: immersed in their culture, half in love with their subject, they sometimes seem unable to achieve the proper critical distance from it. As a result, they may unwittingly wind up writing apologias for mass culture and embracing its ideology. Thus, the examples of "resistance" that these critics cite are in fact often anticipated and even prescribed by the culture industry.[42]

By attempting to counter a view of mass culture which sees it as manipulating and controlling consciousness, Fiske goes too far in the opposite direction.

Baudrillard himself implicitly criticizes Fiske's position in his *Critique*. Kellner believes that Baudrillard ignores the fact that "individuals may use . . . [mass communication] to circulate subversive messages, thereby giving rise to new values and visions of life which may be antithetical to existing capitalist societies."[43] But Baudrillard does not simply ignore this possibility, he considers it when he discusses Eco's idea of subversive or resistive reading in *La Struttura Assente*. According to Baudrillard, Eco believes: "codes of reading must be changed, other codes must be imposed. The receiver . . . opposes his own code to that of the transmitter, he invents a real response by avoiding the trap of directed communication."[44] But Baudrillard insists that unless one changes "the structural grid of communication, one is prohibited from any fundamental changes, and condemned to fragile, manipulative practices which it would be dangerous to take as a 'revolutionary strategy.' "[45] Little or nothing changes when the media's messages are opposed with alternative meanings – however "resistive" these may be. Indeed, in his later *Travels in Hyperreality*, Eco seems to have modified his own optimism with respect to allegedly resistive or subversive meanings when he insists on the importance of semiotic guerrilla warfare.

Unfortunately, Baudrillard himself attempts to locate resistance in largely unconscious, unfocussed, and apolitical activity. In the end, he seems to hope that total resignation will somehow manage to subvert the media's communicative structures. Whereas Fiske reads resistance into our every meaning, our every thought, Baudrillard reads resistance into the silence of despair. These views are just as erroneous as the one which reads manipulation and alienation into every action and thought.[46] If one is to speak meaningfully of resistance – as do Eco and Foucault, for example – it must have an explicitly political dimension and not simply a political potential.

What Baudrillard and Fiske have essentially "discovered" is what Adorno already knew: people are not entirely duped by the media. To say that people are not entirely duped is not to say that they resist, however. If people were to resist the media, their resistance would have to combine with attempts to radically restructure the media. In the next part of this paper, I shall consider the idea of a radical restructuring of the media as it arises in Baudrillard's critique of Enzensberger.

BEYOND SILENCE

Both Baudrillard and Enzensberger agree that the one-directional communication flow which characterizes most media "does not serve communication but prevents it. It allows no reciprocal action between transmitter and receiver." From one or two centers, a very small and privileged group in capitalist societies produces and transmits information and entertainment to the majority of the population which receives or consumes them. Despite the prevalence of one-directional communication, however, Enzensberger points out that: "Electronic techniques recognize no contradiction in principle between transmitter and receiver. Every transistor radio is, by the nature of its construction, at the same time, a potential transmitter; it can interact with other receivers by circuit reversal."[47]

With circuit reversal, the "masses' would be involved in producing information; everyone would become a media manipulator.

Before turning to Baudrillard's objections to Enzensberger's idea of circuit reversal, I would like to raise a few of my own. Enzensberger implies that two-directional communication would affect the content of programs without, however, spelling out what the programs would look like. In the absence of such a description, what Enzensberger proposes might, in fact, resemble what the telephone, and two-directional television or computer communication, already provide. In other words, two-directional radio communication is rendered superfluous by the already existing (or soon to exist) two-directional communication of other media.

Of course, for Enzensberger, the point is to establish a dialogue between those who produce and those who consume information. But such dialogue itself presupposes radical changes in the social, political, and economic spheres since the one-directional structure of the media merely reflects the structures of domination which shape the relations between producers and consumers in these other spheres. Furthermore, it is simply unrealistic or naive to assume, as Enzensberger seems to do, that those who have been granted the power to produce information (or disinformation) will give up some of that power voluntarily. The precondition for circuit reversal is the reversal of class structures of domination. And, if class structures are reversed, the entire system may be deconstructed, rendering two-directional radio communication unnecessary or anachronistic.

Baudrillard rejects Enzensberger's proposal of circuit reversal because in it "transmitter and receiver are simultaneously on both sides: manipulation has become reciprocal (hermaphrodite combination)."[48] But, while circuit reversal is not a satisfactory solution, Baudrillard, like Enzensberger, also believes that changing the structure of the media will allow reciprocal communication to take place. Contemporary media "give, and make it impossible for one to respond." If they were to permit an authentic response, it would "break this relationship of power, and institute (or reinstitute), on the basis of antagonistic reciprocity, the circuit of symbolic exchange."[49]

Kellner objects to Baudrillard's idea of symbolic exchange. He accuses

Baudrillard of "both technophobia and a nostalgia for face-to-face communication." Baudrillard contrasts "good" with "bad" communication and "thus occludes the fact that interpersonal communication may be just as manipulative, distorted, reified and the rest as media communication."[50] Part of Kellner's argument here is fallacious (*tu quoque*) because to claim that interpersonal communication may be just as distorted and manipulative as media communication evades the issue Baudrillard wants to discuss concerning the univocity and lack of reciprocity of the latter. None the less, Kellner's view that Baudrillard essentializes communication by making one form of communication the paradigm for all, is worthy of note. Although Baudrillard gives reasons for his choice, his arguments are contentious to say the least. While I agree with Baudrillard that forms of communication which do not permit a response are fundamentally flawed, Baudrillard's definition of communication needs to be spelled out explicitly.

For the Baudrillard of *Critique*, the restitution of symbolic exchange presupposes "the overturning of the entire current structure of the media."[51] In point of fact, however, as is the case with circuit reversal, what is presupposed is radical change in the social, political, and economic spheres. But even when, in *L'échange symbolique*, Baudrillard asserts that symbolic exchange (as death) is not only possible today but also revolutionary, he never adequately justifies his claim that this form of exchange will naturally lead to the radical overthrow of the system. And, in the absence of such radical change, only small enclaves of resistance to the dominant forms of communication are possible. So, while both Baudrillard and Enzensberger agree that the structures of media must be changed, neither recognizes what is required for such a change to occur.

Both Enzensberger and Baudrillard agree that *communication* must involve some degree of reciprocity. Nevertheless, like Enzensberger, Baudrillard fails to take into account media which do appear to allow for such reciprocity: the telephone, two-directional television, computer communication, and the like. Baudrillard's is a conspiracy theory based almost entirely on an analysis of television which is supposed to completely invade consciousness, rendering it helpless. Television effectively subverts all but the most extreme forms of symbolic exchange. It imposes a univocal code which excludes reciprocity. As one of the principal "effectors of ideology" – where ideology is "the operation itself of exchange value"[52] television has turned us all into worshipers at the temple of consumption. For Baudrillard, the media's power is virtually limitless. He indulges in hyperbole which borders on the paranoic. As Mark Poster points out, Baudrillard "writes about particular experiences, television images, as if nothing else in society mattered, extrapolating a bleak view of the world from that limited base."[53]

Just as he rejects circuit reversal, Baudrillard also rejects amateur production which, he claims, Enzensberger also proposes as a solution to the

problem of nonreciprocity. "Enzensberger presents as a revolutionary solution that *everyone should become a manipulator,* in the sense of an active
operator, director, etc.; in short, that everyone should rise from the level
of a receiver to that of a producer/transmitter." Baudrillard rightly points
out that this more active role still occupies a place in the same one-
directional cybernetic structure. The only difference is that the person
holding the position of transmitter has changed. Furthermore: "Whether
or not everyone possesses his or her own walkie-talkie or Kodak, and
makes his or her own films, one knows what the result will be: personal-
ised amateurism, the equivalent of the Sunday hobby, on the margins of
the system."[54]

Enzensberger does not, in fact, propose amateur production as a solution. Instead, he criticizes it, and does so in the same terms Baudrillard
uses. With a video recorder, "the individual, so long as he remains isolated
can become . . . at best an amateur but not a producer." Furthermore, in
tones reminiscent of the critical theorists, Enzensberger writes: "[t]he
programs which the isolated amateur mounts are always only bad, outdated
copies of what he in any case receives."[55] Writers, like Craig McGregor in
Pop Goes the Culture, who claim that video cameras, tape recorders, and
photocopiers "have radically expanded the way in which art is created"[56]
would do well to take heed.

While rejecting circuit reversal as well as amateur production, Baudrillard
does find interesting the examples of politicized uses of the media which
Enzensberger puts forward. These examples, Baudrillard claims, "go beyond a 'dialectic' of transmitter and receiver."[57] According to Enzensberger,
a socialist strategy must "strive to end the isolation of the individual
participants from the social learning and production process."[58] Enzensberger proposes "a collective, organized effort". The result of such effort could take the form of "a mass newspaper written and distributed by
its readers," for example, or "a video network of politically active groups."[59]
Baudrillard praises these examples since "[o]ne effectively finds in them a
process of immediate communication, unfiltered by bureaucratic models,
an original form of exchange because, in fact, there are *no more trans-
mitters and receivers* but people who *respond to each other.*"[60]

With his idea of collective enterprises, Baudrillard believes Enzensberger
has found a more effective solution to the problem of nonreciprocity. In
a collectively organized medium, an effective, symbolic response is possible
because the distinction between producers and consumers has supposedly
been eliminated. People work together to exchange among themselves the
information they need. Collectives require lateral communication – a more
democratic and egalitarian form of exchange. As John Downing points
out: "if we are thinking of organizing democratic media, we cannot imagine them as liberating forces unless they are open to lateral communication
between social beings, with their *multiple* experiences and concerns."[61]

It is interesting that Baudrillard should commend Enzensberger's examples since, in the *Critique*, he already rejected the liberating potential of the media on the grounds that it forbids symbolic exchange by virtue of its structure. In fact, he claimed that "it is in their structure and their operation itself that the media induce a social relation, and this relation is not one of exploitation, but of abstraction, of separation, of the abolition of exchange."[62] Douglas Kellner criticizes Baudrillard on this point. Baudrillard's "theorizing has nothing concerning alternative media practices, for instance; indeed, he seems to rule them out in advance, because on his view *all* media are mere producers of noise, noncommunication, the extermination of meaning, implosion and so on."[63] In fact, there is a contradiction in Baudrillard's thinking about the media here. When properly organized and formally restructured, Baudrillard implies that some media would allow for symbolic exchange on his own terms. The structure the media (or at least certain media) take in capitalist societies does not preclude *eo ipso* the emergence of other, more radically democratic and egalitarian, structures.

For the past few years, Kellner has been involved in an experiment in alternative broadcasting on a public access system located in Austin, Texas. The programs his group produces include interviews with nationally and internationally known figures who present radical or alternative points of view as well as with "various feminists, gays, union activists, and representatives of local progressive groups."[64] According to Kellner, "the alternatives to commercial broadcasting are: (1) an enlarged, strengthened, and revitalized system of public access television and radio; (2) an expanded system of public access television; and (3) development of a people's satellite network, complemented by people's communication centers and a people's information network that would use new technologies to broaden and diversify information sources and services."[65]

Given their views about collective production, Baudrillard and Enzensberger would have to consider Kellner's practices satisfactory. However, it is not clear that such practices actually foster the reciprocal communication between transmitter and receiver which both Baudrillard and Enzensberger propose as a goal. Even in the more collective structures Kellner describes, an effective response to the messages of the media is only possible among producers, not from those who merely consume the messages. By using television, Kellner's group of producers is still talking *at* viewers, not *to* them. Baudrillard's and Enzensberger's acceptance of collective forms of production ignores the reception of the non-producing viewer which their goal of reciprocity specifically targets; the structure of the medium remains unchanged, and the medium itself continues to be owned by capitalists.

In the end, it may be impossible to achieve full reciprocity in media like television and radio (especially if one rejects circuit reversal). Still, the benefits and problems inherent in the more egalitarian and democratic forms of lateral communication as they arise in collective forms of media production deserve some scrutiny. On the one hand, as Kellner points out, alternative broadcasting can provide viewers with the information necessary to make informed decisions, thus strengthening the democratic process. On the other, what it offers is generally a venue for a different kind of media content which appeals only to small groups of people. Herbert Schiller remarks: "The messages of the independents and the alternative-media producers in the United States ... do not generate great popular appeal. The American audience remains encapsulated in a corporate-message cocoon. It is very unlikely that this cocoon will be removed by the efforts of a still-minuscule noncommercial media community, admirable as it is."[66] Furthermore, when they do find an audience, the programs produced by collectives generally preach to the converted; the media continue to serve purely didactic or propagandistic purposes which reflect their authoritarian transmitter-receiver structure, and viewers are generally already predisposed to accept the messages conveyed in these programs.

None the less, a great many writers have insisted on the importance of the lateral communication fostered by alternative media practices. The example of the role the media played in the revolutions in Eastern Europe will perhaps serve to underline their significance. In countries like Romania, political action combined with media which were organized laterally. Broadcasts were organized by the people and for the people and they facilitated the seizure of power. This "revolutionary" use of the media is what is required today if the various social and political movements worldwide are to communicate with each other and form linkages. As the revolutions in Eastern Europe also proved, however, lateral communication in and of itself is not sufficient. Lateral linkages are at once the result and the precondition for revolutionary praxis. They are the result because the solidarity lateral communications encourage is only possible in the context of political and social action. They are the precondition because the move toward greater equality and participatory democracy presupposes that people have already agreed among themselves that this should be the goal of their struggles. In the global move toward the increasing democratization of institutions, and the expansion of personal rights and freedoms, the practices which foster lateral communication will continue to play a central, if subordinate, role.

Notes

1   Parts of this paper were originally published under the title "Ruses de Guerre: Baudrillard and Fiske on Media reception," *Journal for the Theory of Social Behavior*, 22, 2 (June, 1992) 227–38. The author gratefully acknowledges permission from the editor, Charles Smith, to reprint the previously published parts.

2   Jean Baudrillard, "The Masses," trans. Marie Maclean, *Jean Baudrillard: Selected Writings*, trans., Jacques Mourrain, et al. (Stanford: Stanford University Press, 1988).

3   Jean Baudrillard, *Pour une critique de l'économie politique du signe* (Paris: Gallimard, 1972). All translations are my own.

4   James Curran, Michael Gurevitch, and Janet Woollacott, "The Study of the Media: Theoretical Approaches," in *Culture, Society and the Media*, eds., Michael Gurevitch, Tony Bennett, James Curran, and Janet Woollacott (New York and London: Methuen, 1982), p. 14.

5   Theodor W. Adorno and Max Horkheimer, *Dialectic of Enlightenment*, trans. John Cumming (New York: Seabury Press, 1972), p. 147.

6   Adorno and Horkheimer, *Enlightenment*, p. 161.

7   As Martin Jay points out on p. 128 of his *Adorno* (London: Fontana, 1984), in his later works, such as "Freizeit," (see below) or "Transparencies on Film," trans., Thomas Y. Levin, (*New German Critique*, 24–25 (Fall-Winter, 1981–2) 199–205, Adorno speculated "on the limitations of the culture industry's power to manipulate mass consciousness." But Adorno's comments on the limitations of this power may be found in his early (1941) essay "On Popular Music" as well as in *Enlightenment*. Because the products of the culture industry are characterized by their irrationality, Adorno always believed doubt and mistrust were possible.

8   Herbert I. Schiller, *Culture Inc.: The Corporate Takeover of Public Expression* (New York and Oxford: Oxford University Press, 1989), p. 136.

9   Ibid., p. 141.

10 Fredric Jameson considers the role of pessimistic foil to be of great value for "postmodern" theories. What Adorno and Horkheimer do is "to restore the sense of something grim and impending within the polluted sunshine of the shopping mall." (*Late Capitalism: Adorno, or, the Persistence of the Dialectic* (New York and London: Verso, 1990) p. 248.) Although I disagree with Jameson's undialectical interpretation of Adorno's theory of media reception, it is clear that, for theories such as those of Baudrillard and Fiske, it is precisely the pessimistic aspect of Adorno's theory which is stressed.

11 John Fiske, *Understanding Popular Culture* (Boston: Unwin Hyman, 1989), p. 20.

12 Jean Baudrillard, *Simulacres et simulation* (Paris: Gallimard, 1981), p. 131. All translations are my own.

13 "Il n'y a pas de relation réciproque ni de présence l'un à l'autre des deux termes [transmitter and receiver], puisque l'un et l'autre se déterminent isolément dans leur rapport au message et au code, 'intermedium' qui maintient les deux dans une situation *respective* (c'est le code qui tient les deux en 'respect'), à distance l'un de l'autre . . . . Ce qui circule en effet c'est de l'information, contenu de sens supposé lisible et univoque. C'est l'instance du code qui garantit cette univocité . . . . Mais qu'on suppose une relation ambivalente, tout s'écroule. Car il n'y a pas de code de l'ambivalence." (*Critique*, p. 221.)

14 "Donner et faire en sorte qu'on ne puisse pas vous rendre, c'est briser l'échange à son profit [to the benefit of power] et instituer un monopole: le procès social est ainsi déséquilibré. Rendre, au contraire, c'est briser cette relation et instituer (ou restituer), sur la base d'une réciprocité antagoniste, le circuit de l'échange

symbolique . . . . C'est pourquoi la seule révolution dans ce domaine [of the media] – et partout ailleurs, la révolution tout court – est dans la restitution de cette possibilité de réponse. Cette simple possibilité suppose le bouleversement de toute la structure actuelle des media." (*Critique*, p. 209).

15 Mark Poster, ed., "Introduction," in *Jean Baudrillard: Selected Writings*, p. 5.

16 Hans Magnus Enzensberger, "Constituents of a Theory of the Media," in *The Consciousness Industry: On Literature, Politics and the Media*, trans. various (New York: Seabury Press, 1974) pp. 95–128. It should be noted that in his later work, Baudrillard uses the term "reversibility" instead of the term "reciprocity" such that reversibility does become a solution to the problems posed by the media. But, in the later work, reversibility applies to the content of the messages; it is still not a solution when it is content of the messages; it is still not a solution when it is applied to the unidirectional structure of the media.

17 Douglas Kellner, *Jean Baudrillard: From Marxism to Postmodernism and Beyond* (Stanford: Stanford University Press, 1989), p. 44.

18 It should be emphasized that I am interested here in the more "optimistic" dimension of Baudrillard's theory. This is a dimension which is often over-looked or ignored in the extant literature on Baudrillard.

19 Baudrillard, "The Masses," p. 213.

20 Ibid., p. 219.

21 Ibid., p. 215.

22 Ibid., pp. 218–19.

23 Ibid., p. 216.

24 Baudrillard does not give the page reference for this citation, nor does he quote the exact passage. The reference can be found in G. W. F. Hegel, *Phenomenology of Spirit*, trans. A. V. Miller (Oxford: Oxford University Press, 1977), pp. 335–6.

25 Baudrillard, "The Masses," p. 216.

26 Ibid., p. 217.

27 ". . . la seule solution est de retourner contre le système le principe même de son pouvoir: l'impossibilité de réponse et de rétorsion. *Défier le système par un don auquel il ne puisse pas répondre, sinon par sa propre mort et son propre effondrement.*" Jean Baudrillard, *L'échange symbolique et la mort* (Paris: Gallimard, 1976), pp. 63–4.

28 Salvador Giner, *Mass Society* (London: Martin Robertson, 1976), p. 205.

29 T. W. Adorno, "Freizeit," *Gesammelte Schriften* X Band II (Frankfurt: Suhrkamp, 1977), p. 655: "[W]hat the culture industry offers to people in their free time will therefore certainly be consumed and accepted, but with a kind of reservation . . . . [N]ot everything in it will be believed. Apparently the integration of consciousness and free time has still not succeeded completely . . . . [A] society whose pregnant contradictions persist undiminished cannot be integrated totally into consciousness." Translation mine.

30 Baudrillard, *Simulacres et simulation*, p. 124.

31 See Michel de Certeau, *The Practice of Everyday Life*, trans. Steven F. Rendall (Berkeley: University of California Press, 1984), p. xviii: "In the technocratically constructed, written, and functionalized space in which consumers move about, their trajectories form unforeseeable sentences, partly unreadable paths across

a space. Although they are composed with the vocabularies of established languages ... , and although they remain subordinated to the prescribed syntactical forms ... , the trajectories trace out the ruses of other interests and desires that are neither determined nor captured by the systems in which they develop."

32 Fiske, *Understanding Popular Culture*, p. 28.

33 Ibid., p. 169.

34 Umberto Eco, *Travels in Hyperreality: Essays*, trans. William Weaver (New York: Harcourt Brace Jovanovich, 1986), p. 141.

35 Ibid., p. 144.

36 When Foucault, whom Fiske also quotes in support of his idea of popular tactics, spoke of resistance, he was also speaking primarily of the deliberate and focussed tactics of certain disempowered groups.

37 Fiske, *Understanding Popular Culture*, p. 28.

38 Ibid., p. 192.

39 Eco, *Travels*, p. 178.

40 Fiske, *Understanding Popular Culture*.

41 Ibid., p. 161.

42 Tania Modleski, ed., *Studies in Entertainment: Critical Approaches to Mass Culture* (Bloomington: Indiana University Press, 1986), pp. xi-xii.

43 Kellner, *Baudrillard*, p. 37.

44 Baudrillard, *Critique*, p. 227.

45 Ibid., p. 228.

46 In an excellent article which attacks Fiske on much the same grounds that I do (but which often makes its points more succinctly), David Sholle criticizes the notion of resistance as it appears in texts likes Fiske's and Baudrillard's: "Unless 'resistance' has an effectivity it is an empty category. It is not enough to simply recognize that the masses do things with the media, one must also describe where these 'doings' go, how they circulate, what they influence. One must recognize a number of levels of resistance: there is a difference between using the media and doing something with it, between reading and speaking out, between defending and offending. If these distinctions are ignored, the analysis of resistance can end in hollow statements such as Janice Radway's that 'romance reading "temporarily transforms" patriarchal social relations.' " See David Sholle, "Resistance," *Journal of Urban and Cultural Studies* I, 1 (1990) 102.

47 Enzensberger, "Constituents of a Theory of the Media," p. 97.

48 Baudrillard, *Critique*, p. 227.

49 Ibid., p. 209.

50 Kellner, *Baudrillard*, p. 67.

51 Baudrillard, *Critique*, p. 209.

52 Ibid., p. 207.

53 Baudrillard, "The Masses," p. 7.

54 Baudrillard, *Critique*, p. 225.

55 Enzensberger, "Constituents of a Theory of the Media," p. 107.

56 Craig McGregor, *Pop Goes the Culture* (London: Pluto Press, 1983), p. 71.

57 Baudrillard, *Critique*, p. 226.

58 Enzensberger, "Constituents of a Theory of the Media," p. 109.

59 Ibid., p. 110.
60 Baudrillard, *Critique*, p. 226.
61 John Downing, *Radical Media: The Political Experience of Alternative Communication* (Boston: South End Press, 1984), p. 19.
62 Baudrillard, *Critique*, p. 207.
63 Kellner, *Baudrillard*, p. 75.
64 Douglas Kellner, *Television and the Crisis of Democracy* (Boulder, Cal.: Westview, 1990), p. 210.
65 Ibid., p. 182.
66 Schiller, *Culture Inc.*, p. 168.

8

CAPITALISM AND THE CODE: A CRITIQUE OF BAUDRILLARD'S THIRD ORDER SIMULACRUM

―

Sara Schoonmaker

A revolution has occurred in the capitalist world without our Marxists having wanted to comprehend it . . . . This mutation concerns the passage from the form-commodity to the form-sign, from the abstraction of the exchange of material products under the law of general equivalence to the operationalization of all exchanges under the law of the code.[1]

For Jean Baudrillard, there has been a revolutionary transformation in the structure of social control and power. The contemporary social order is so radically different from previous forms that an entirely new social theory is required to understand it. With Foucault, Lyotard, and other postmodern theorists, Baudrillard questions the ability of political economy, and particularly Marxism, to comprehend these new developments. Because of its focus upon the process of economic production, Marxism is rejected as unable to conceptualize the fundamental changes that have transformed contemporary society. Baudrillard's work has become a central part of the broader wave of postmodernism, that has challenged established paradigms in the humanities and the social sciences.[2]

In *Simulations*, Baudrillard highlights his break with Marxism by analyzing stages of societal development as orders of simulacra, or forms in which objects are reproduced. In the current stage of simulation, the digital code provides the basis for radical social transformation. It is the catalyst for changes so extreme that the nature of reality itself is transformed. Objects become simulated, or conceived in terms of their reproducibility according to a binary model. It becomes increasingly difficult to distinguish between objects and the model designed to reproduce them, or between reality and its representation.[3]

Baudrillard raises important questions about the nature of contemporary society, and the role of the digital code in current processes of social transformation. His work challenges Marxists to formulate an alternative understanding of the current conjuncture of advanced capitalism. I develop such an alternative in this chapter, by analyzing how the use of the digital code is shaped by capitalist relations of production and exchange. These relations are fundamental structural features of contemporary society. They constitute a central part of the broader material conditions that influence the production of software and other forms of the digital code.

This chapter is divided into five parts. First, Baudrillard's orders of simulacra are described, to provide an understanding of his conception of the nature of contemporary society and the revolutionary effects of the digital code. I then critique his argument by analyzing the use of transborder data flows and software as examples of the digital code. Transborder data flows are transmitted between computers in different countries through telecommunications links, in an electromagnetic stream of digital signals. Their digital form makes it possible to transcend barriers of space and time in the processes of capitalist production and exchange. I will argue that, rather than ushering in a new social order, these flows are structured, organized, and disseminated within a logic of capital accumulation. The analysis of their use reveals that capitalism remains the organizing principle and structure of contemporary societies.

Using a Marxian framework, I analyze the use of transborder data flows and software to identify three key tendencies of the current conjuncture of advanced capitalism. Each tendency is discussed in a separate section of the paper, and used to evaluate the relative merits of Baudrillardian and Marxian theory. In the second section, I argue that transborder data flows facilitate the expansion of trade and production on a global scale. Third, I analyze how the flows contribute to centralized control of international business operations. Fourth, disputes over software laws in Brazil illustrate the effort to establish political control over new possibilities for production introduced by the digital code. In the last section, these tendencies are analyzed as spatial and temporal responses to broader systemic pressures of capital accumulation to shrink space and reduce turnover time.

BAUDRILLARD'S ORDERS OF SIMULACRA

Baudrillard views the contemporary social order as more subtle and totalitarian, more illegible and radical, than has been conceived either by Marxism or political economy. Baudrillard's theoretical break with Marxism is rooted in his conception of stages of societal development as orders of simulacra, or forms in which objects are reproduced. To highlight the conceptual primacy of both form and reproduction in Baudrillard's work, I refer to the orders of simulacra as "forms of reproduction."

These forms of reproduction correspond to particular assumptions about the relationship between objects and signs, about the nature of reality and the signifiers that represent it. Each order of simulacrum is based upon a medium, or technique, of reproduction. Building upon McLuhan's view that "the medium is the message," Baudrillard conceives each medium as a principle that shapes the meaning of social reality in a particular era.[4]

The first order of the simulacrum is that of the counterfeit. This form was dominant during the classical period from the Renaissance to the industrial revolution. Any objects that were reproduced were viewed as counterfeit copies of a unique original. This form of reproduction corresponded to an assumption that there was a detectable difference between semblance and reality, and between objects and their signifiers.[5]

The second order is that of production, which dominated during the industrial era. It is important to note that Baudrillard conceives of production as a particular form of reproducing objects. Following Walter Benjamin, he views the technique of mechanical reproduction as a medium, form, and principle of this new era of production. This principle transforms the status of the product. Instead of being viewed as a copy of an original, products are conceived as equivalent elements in a series of two or more identical objects. Objects become undefined simulacra, or reproductions, of each other. The relation between objects and signs is no longer that of an original to its counterfeit, but of equivalence.

Baudrillard's break from Marxism is exemplified by the above analysis. The key theoretical difference is the conception of societal change that leads to the era of mass industrial production. For Baudrillard, the major change involves the development of a new principle or form of mechanical reproduction. Baudrillard's conception of societal change is based on developments of new forms of reproduction, rather than modes of production. Mass production techniques are not viewed as part of the forces of production, or linked systematically with changes in class relations, as they would be in a Marxian approach.[6] This position disregards class relations and production activities as key forces that shape the implementation of new technologies, as well as the possibilities to reproduce products on a mass scale. It thus fails to place new technological developments within a social context where they are organized as part of a broader process of capitalist production and exchange. By contrast, Baudrillard argues that the principle of mechanical reproduction introduces a new stage of societal development, because the form of reproduction of equivalent objects in a series replaces the reproduction of a counterfeit from its original. Mass industrial production is made possible by this transformation in the form of reproducing objects.[7]

Simulation is the current order of the simulacrum. Simulation is based upon the reproducibility of objects according to a binary model. The epitome of such a model is the digital code read by computers, that translates all questions and answers, all of reality, into a binary opposition between zero and one. In the stage of simulation, objects are not merely reproduced through mechanical techniques. They are originally conceived in terms of their reproducibility, using a binary code.[8]

Baudrillard views the binary form as the basis for the revolutionary transformation of the social order. McLuhan's notion of the medium as the message is taken to the extreme, as the medium of the code controls the entire process of meaning. Every discourse is rendered inarticulate by the third order simulacrum, "the sign that is also the end of signification."[9] It becomes impossible to distinguish between the object and the sign, between the signified and the signifier, between objective reality and the result of technical intervention. There is no possibility for "interrogation," for a communicative process where questions and answers have meanings that are not predetermined by the digital form of the code. We can no longer really answer, or not answer, because questions and responses have become indistinguishable. Answers are simulated: they reproduce the question. Answers are inscribed in the question by the code.[10]

The nature of material reality is thus transformed as simulation alters the relationship between objects and signs. When a binary model is used to conceptualize an object in terms of its reproducibility, there is an almost imperceptible separation between reality and its representation. A binary code involves "the minimal separation, the least amount of inflection between the two terms . . . the 'very smallest common paradigm' that the fiction of sense could possibly support."[11] Reality becomes defined as "that of which it is possible to give an equivalent reproduction."[12] This definition corresponds to a science based on the premise that under a particular set of scientific conditions, a process can be perfectly reproduced. It also fits with industrial rationality based on a universal system of equivalency, where products are reproduced as equivalent elements in a series.

When objects are reproduced according to a binary model, they become virtually indistinguishable not only from each other, but from the model that generated them. Reality disappears as the process of reproducibility is pushed to its limit. The real becomes not simply what can be reproduced, but "that which is always already reproduced. The Hyperreal."[13] There is no longer a perceptible difference between reality and its representation, between the object and the sign. Hyperreality is completely simulated, reproduced according to a model, instead of existing in an objective sense as separate from the model. "Reality itself, entirely impregnated by an aesthetic which is inseparable from its own structure, has been confused with its own image."[14]

Baudrillard's theory of the orders of simulacra poses a conception of societal development rooted in changes in the forms of reproducing objects. In the current stage of simulation, these changes become so radical that they alter the nature of reality. The form of reproduction through binary models eradicates the difference between the object and the sign, between reality and the model designed to reproduce it.

Contesting semiological determinism

Baudrillard raises important questions about the relationship between the digital code and contemporary processes of social change. However, two aspects of his work make it difficult to evaluate his argument about the nature of that relationship.

First, as Kellner notes, Baudrillard does not clearly define what he means by the code; it is a central concept whose meaning shifts in different parts of his work.[15] In *Simulations*, he uses the terms "code" and "model," "digital" and "binary," interchangeably, without explicitly defining them.[16] Second, Baudrillard does not engage in systematic empirical analysis. He incorporates various examples to support his points, but does not analyze the classes, groups, or individuals that control the code or the process of signification.

These problems led Baudrillard to develop what Kellner calls a "semiological imaginary," a conceptual vision of society as being controlled by the process of signification, which is divorced from the process of economic production. To counteract what he viewed as Marx's subordination of social life to economic factors, Baudrillard developed his own form of "semiological determinism."[17]

Any form of determinism makes it difficult for a theory to analyze the complexities of social reality. For Antonio, determinism can be counteracted by historical holism, a key narrative in Marx's work which involves a non-linear and non-deterministic view of history. As a historical method of analyzing and critiquing capitalism, historical holism allowed Marx to identify the particular forms of production, property, and political organization that existed in a specific period of capitalism's historical development. He could thus analyze "the current tendencies, major sources of conflict, normative aspirations, and objective possibilities for change."[18]

I adopt such a holistic approach in this paper, to analyze how the digital code contributes to a new historical conjuncture in advanced capitalism, by shaping current forms of production, as well as political debates. This analysis is compared to a Baudrillardian view of the code as the basis for a new social order, based upon the reproduction of objects using binary models. For conceptual clarity, the digital code will be defined as a binary sequence of zero or one that can be read by computers. Although Baudrillard never explicitly defines the code in any of his works, his references in *Simulations* to the digital form, binary models, and sequences of zero and one would be consistent with such a definition.[19] As stated above, transborder data flows and software will be analyzed as examples of the digital code, to assess the relative merits of Baudrillardian and Marxian theory.

The digital form of transborder data flows makes them an ideal test case for Baudrillardian analysis. These international flows of computerized data are transmitted in a stream of digital signals. In Baudrillard's terms, the flows are hyperreal objects, completely indistinguishable from each other and from the model that generated them because of their common digital form. There is no distinction between the model and the objects it reproduced, or between reality and its representation. The digital form of the code effaces all differences between the real and the unreal, so that the unreal becomes a "hallucinatory resemblance of the real with itself."[20]

A Marxian analysis of the social nature of transborder data flows provides a basis to critique Baudrillard's concept of the third order simulacrum. Instead of conceiving of the flows as objects reproduced in digital form, a Marxian approach examines the role of the flows in the processes of trade and production in advanced capitalism. They are part of a new historical conjuncture, where the implementation of telecommunications and microelectronics technologies is facilitating both the geographical dispersal and centralized control of production processes. Contrary to Baudrillard's position, the role of the digital code in this conjuncture can best be understood by analyzing specific examples of its use within processes of economic production.

A Marxian analysis of the role of transborder data flows and software in trade and production illuminates three key tendencies of this new conjuncture of advanced capitalism. Each of these tendencies suggests a critique of Baudrillard's concept of the third order simulacrum. First, transborder data flows facilitate global trade and production, and allow the process of commodification to be extended into new areas like trade in services. Secondly, although the flows allow corporate operations to become geographically dispersed, the organization of the telecommunications infrastructure used to transmit them reinforces centralized control of those operations from core cities where that infrastructure is concentrated. Finally, these expanded possibilities for trade and production have become the object of political debates over world trade and development. Conflicts over the development of a software law in Brazil exemplify these new political arguments.

EXPANDING GLOBAL TRADE AND PRODUCTION

In Baudrillardian terms, transborder data flows are simulated objects, reproduced in the form of a digital code. However, analyzing examples of their use reveals that the flows are integrally connected to processes of economic production. In the past decades, transborder data flows have become increasingly central to the international business operations of transnational corporations, which are their major users. The ability to transmit the flows in the form of digital signals allows them to be exchanged in real time. Data can be sent and received virtually instantaneously, transcending traditional barriers of distance for corporate operations. Corporate executives can communicate from different sides of the globe almost as easily as if they were in the same room.

Flows exchanged between branches of the same firm allow corporations to facilitate existing business activities. Detailed information concerning accounts, personnel, and other routine business activities can be transmitted in seconds. International business operations can be conducted more efficiently when firms have almost immediate access to data about activities of corporate branches in different parts of the world.[21]

The availability of information about production operations has also supported the restructuring of production on a global scale. In the last decades, low-skilled manufacturing activities have increasingly been relocated to the Third World. US electronics and automobile companies have shifted production of components and parts to Third World countries with low wages. These parts are then imported at low tariff rates to the USA, where they are assembled and marketed.[22]

As production has become a global assembly line, transborder data flows have made it possible to coordinate the different phases of transnational corporate operations. Each step in the operation can be monitored, without being present at production facilities themselves. For example, manufacturing firms use the flows to schedule production of product components in different parts of the world, as well as integrating their assembly and delivery to global markets. Through this international management process, corporate branches become simultaneously more specialized and more interdependent. Instant global communication enables them to carry out more specialized tasks and coordinate them more efficiently.[23]

Baudrillard's emphasis on the form of reproduction of objects highlights the importance of digitality in creating advantages for corporate users of transborder data flows. However, defining the flows completely in terms of their digital form makes it impossible to understand the value of the data as arising from their content, or from the social interests involved with their use. Such a definition is unable to conceptualize the particular roles played by different kinds of transborder data flows in this new conjuncture of advanced capitalism.

A Marxian analysis allows two different types of flow to be identified, based upon the meaning of the data they carry in the context of capitalist relations of production and exchange. The flows discussed above can be defined as corporate flows, which are exchanged between branches of the same firm to facilitate its global business operations. There is a second type of commercial flow that offers a different kind of advantage to its transnational corporate users. These flows are sold from one firm to another on the market. Because they are produced and traded in the form of digital signals, I refer to commercial flows as "digital commodities."

Digital commodities represent the extension of the process of commodification into new markets for services, like telecommunications, data processing, software, and computer services. Such services do not require direct physical contact between buyers and sellers, and thus represent a form of invisible international trade. For example, financial services like electronic cash management provide corporate treasurers with detailed information about account balances, individual transactions, and money market investments for all of a corporation's accounts scattered in countries around the world. These services give treasurers control over the transfer of funds among the firm's accounts, enabling them to invest their unused cash flow to take maximum advantage of changes in interest, inflation, and exchange rates. They are one example of a growing array of financial services that facilitate greater spreading of risk for corporate operations.[24]

Both corporate and commercial transborder data flows have particular social meanings that arise from their use within the context of capitalist production and exchange. Baudrillard's focus on their common digital form cannot conceptualize the distinct advantages these different types of flows provide for firms operating in the global economy. Although their digital form is important in allowing all flows to be exchanged in real time, the content of the data they carry determines the particular activities that firms will use the flows to engage in. A Marxian definition of commercial flows as digital commodities highlights their distinct role within the processes of production and exchange.

The above analysis contradicts Baudrillard's claim that Marxism is unable to theorize the revolutionary changes occurring in contemporary society with the implementation of the digital code. By examining specific examples of how transborder data flows are used, it becomes clear that this form of the code is integrally linked to production and exchange in advanced capitalism. The flows are not homogeneous codes characterized primarily by their reproduction in the form of digital signals. By shifting the focus of analysis from reproduction to production, the flows can be understood as an electronic neural network for a highly internationalized corporate structure.

In addition to supporting the general expansion of trade and production on a global scale, transborder data flows contribute to a second characteristic of the current conjuncture of advanced capitalism: centralized control of geographically dispersed operations. This tendency toward centralization occurs largely because of the organization of the telecommunications infrastructure used to transmit the flows. This infrastructure both reflects and reinforces historical patterns of concentration of production in the older industrialized countries of the global economy.

CENTRALIZED CONTROL OF PRODUCTION OPERATIONS

The process of globalization of production is characterized by what Castells calls dual tendencies toward centralization and decentralization.[25] The above discussion reveals that transborder data flows have facilitated decentralization by allowing firms to coordinate production activities in different locations. However, centralized control over the work done at corporate headquarters has increased at the same time. Headquarter functions are increasingly complex, as firms seek to manage a global production system with increasingly complex, as firms seek to manage a global production system with plants, offices, and service branches in a wide range of domestic and foreign locations. The decentralization of a firm's production system and labor force has created a countervailing tendency toward central control and planning. Firms with dispersed locational structures have tended to provide top-level management, planning, specialized business services, research, and technical functions from national headquarters.[26]

Centralization of corporate control over national and international economic operations has largely been made possible by the development of a telecommunications infrastructure, concentrated in core cities where corporate headquarters are located. The organization of this infrastructure reinforces the tendency toward centralized coordination of production, for three major reasons.

First, telecommunications facilities involve massive investments in fixed capital and continuous innovations to provide state-of-the-art capabilities. Established telecommunications centers thus have an almost absolute advantage in offering the infrastructure for transborder data flows and other telecommunications services. The expense and complexity of these facilities have led them to become quite concentrated, developed primarily in conjunction with major users that depend upon communications to conduct their global operations.[27]

Secondly, the organization of the telecommunications infrastructure has reinforced the tendency toward centralization because investment in that infrastructure has become more sensitive to demand. This occurred as a result of deregulation, and particularly the divestiture of American Telephone and Telegraph. The main source of demand is in information-intensive industries concentrated in the central business districts of the largest metropolitan locations. Large networks of customers make economies of scale possible in those areas, due to their extensive use of telecommunications facilities. Concentration of industries in core cities thus attracts telecommunications investment, and contributes to existing patterns of centralization of business activities.[28]

Finally, the development of the telecommunications infrastructure is shaped by political considerations. The existing legal framework in the

USA requires new communications lines to follow established rights of way. Intercity rights of way usually correspond to the lines of railroads built during the nineteenth century. Previous transportation nodes have become centers for telecommunications, and new fiber optic networks are expected to continue this pattern.[29]

Baudrillard's concept of the third order simulacrum ignores these economic, political, and historical factors that shaped the development of the telecommunications infrastructure. If transborder data flows are defined purely in terms of their digital form and their ability to be reproduced according to a binary model, it is not possible to understand how their use is shaped by the organization of the infrastructure required for their transmission. The flows do not exist separately from that infrastructure, whose development has depended upon concrete material conditions that are completely independent of the existence of a digital code.

Although centralized control has become a major characteristic of the current period of capitalist development, new forms of production of digital commodities have also challenged that pattern. Political debates have arisen over the legal terms for the production of digital commodities, as the US government has led the effort to secure access to new markets for transnational corporations. Debates between the US and Brazilian governments over the content of Brazil's software law are an example of these discussions. Political conflicts over the new opportunities for production and exchange made possible by the digital code characterize a third tendency of the current conjuncture of advanced capitalism. They also reveal additional problems with Baudrillard's concept of the third order simulacrum.

POLITICAL DEBATES OVER DIGITAL COMMODITIES: CONFLICTS OVER SOFTWARE IN BRAZIL

Software is the quintessential example of a digital commodity, that is produced, traded, stored, and consumed in the form of digital signals. The digital form of software also makes it extremely easy to reproduce. Anyone who has the facilities to *use* a software program is also equipped to make multiple copies of it.

The highly reproducible nature of software has made its theft a common practice, and created the basis for political debates over how to control its production and sale. In the USA, the Software Publishers Association estimated that between three and seven illegal copies are made and distributed for each copy of a software program sold through legitimate channels. Software companies appear to be losing tens of millions of dollars each year to people who make illegal copies of their programs.[30]

Piracy became the subject of concern in the Brazilian software market in the mid-1980s. The International Intellectual Property Alliance estimated that US software companies were losing about $35 million per year from unauthorized duplication and distribution of software in Brazil. These losses were particularly disturbing because US software companies viewed the Brazilian market as a great potential investment. The US Department of Commerce estimated its size to be between $350 and $700 million. Since US companies were estimated to hold a 70 percent share of the world software market, they were expected to be capable of attaining a comparable position in Brazil.[31]

However, Brazil's regulatory environment posed a major deterrent to potential investors. Since the mid-1970s, the Brazilian government had formulated a range of policies to protect the development of local computer manufacturing and software industries, or informatics. At the core of these policies were two major principles. The market reserve prohibited foreign firms from investing in the mini and personal computer markets, and the Law of Similars precluded imports of products already manufactured in Brazil. In 1984, the National Informatics Law extended the market reserve for eight more years. It also provided for the development of a law to cover software, which became a major focus for debate in the following period.

In September 1985, President Reagan initiated an investigation of Brazil for potential violations of Section 301 of the US Trade Act. The informatics law was viewed as damaging to US firms, which were estimated to lose between $340 and $450 million in annual sales because of restrictions on investments and imports. These losses were projected to reach $13 billion by the time the law expired in 1992.[32]

Brazil's lack of copyright protection for intellectual property was a key source of concern raised by the 301 investigation. It was viewed as the major cause of piracy in Brazil, which deterred US software firms from investing in the country. The fear of having their software stolen, and competing in the Brazilian market against pirated versions of their own programs, led these firms to forgo the potential profits of this large and growing market. Computer manufacturers were also affected by the lack of software protection in Brazil. The Computer and Business Equipment Manufacturers Association (CBEMA) estimated that its members earned about 40 percent of their revenues from software and services; a figure that was expected to rise to 60 percent by the year 2000. Copyright laws were viewed as the only way to protect the successful and profitable operation of these firms. Without such measures, costly investments in software development became vulnerable to piracy because of the ease of copying software programs.[33]

The lower house in the Brazilian legislature passed a software law that included an author's copyright in late June of 1987. The legislation was viewed as a major breakthrough by the US government and representatives of the software industry. This success was largely attributed to pressures exerted by the 301 investigation.

In the wake of the passage of Brazilian software legislation, the US government suspended the intellectual property rights portion of the section 301 investigation. The progress of the software law would be monitored; final acceptance of that portion of the case was contingent upon the passage of copyright legislation by the Brazilian Senate.[34]

The above events suggest the importance of Baudrillard's emphasis on the digital form of the code. Software's digital form makes it so easy to reproduce that it becomes virtually impossible for firms to guard themselves against piracy. Furthermore, the theft of software occurs through the process of reproduction itself, precisely because each copy of a program is completely identical to the original. Baudrillard's concept of simulation, or the third order simulacrum, might thus appear to describe the form of reproduction of software according to a model. The digital form of the model would then be viewed as erasing all distinctions between the original object and its representation, which exist only as simulations of each other.

The reproducibility of the digital form does help to explain the reluctance of US software firms to invest in Brazil. These firms treated their software programs as though they were hyperreal, or always already reproduced. They viewed investments in the Brazilian market as tantamount to giving products away to their competitors. Reproduction of their programs was assumed to be the result of such an investment decision.

Baudrillard's concept of the third order simulacrum can be applied to understand why software firms and the US government would be concerned about theft through digital reproduction. However, it cannot explain why they would view these concerns as amenable to a political solution. The digital form was important in creating technical possibilities for piracy, but this was only problematic because Brazil did not have a copyright law to protect software. The political regime governing software was thus the major threat to the interests of US software firms. The threat of US trade sanctions was used to pressure the Brazilian government to formulate software legislation that was acceptable to US corporate and government interests. Defining software purely in terms of its form, as a simulated object, decontextualizes it from political as well as economic conditions that shape its development and use. If software is conceived as a third order simulacrum, the effects of political action are not considered in the analysis.

Baudrillard is mistaken to argue that the digital form of reproduction is a principle of a new type of society. Software's digital form made it technically possible to disrupt corporate control over its production and distribution. However, this form was important because it was implemented as part of a process of *production* within the context of global capitalism. The author's copyright provided a political mechanism to reestablish corporate control over software production. Foreign capital could thus enter the Brazilian software market with the assurance of legal protection for its investments in software development.

Baudrillard's analytical focus on the form of reproduction makes it impossible to identify control over commodity production as the basis for conflicts over software in Brazil, or the underlying class relations that shaped those conflicts. These tensions arose not because software is a hyperreal object reproduced according to a model, but because software is a digital commodity produced for profit on the market. Pressure by the US government and software firms for passage of a copyright law reveal the interests of foreign capital in the Brazilian software case.

Equally important, the Brazilian software case highlights the problem with Baudrillard's main argument against Marxism, that societies can best be characterized as forms of reproduction rather than modes of production. Although the facility of reproducing software was a key reason that the US government became concerned about software in Brazil, this concern was rooted in the importance of software as a potential market for economic production. Software is not merely an object; it is a commodity whose production requires extensive scientific and technological capacities. Debates over the software law arose because of software's status as a digital commodity, whose production and distribution in Brazil could contribute to the overall process of informatics development. They reveal the divergent economic and political interests in such development, that arose in the context of international capitalism. Baudrillard's theory cannot conceptualize these interests, or understand them as part of a global system of production where Brazil's economy has historically been dominated by foreign capital.

The influence of this global system upon the use of the digital code highlights the question posed at the beginning of the paper, about the code's role in broader processes of social transformation. The three tendencies discussed above may be understood as part of larger systemic changes in contemporary capitalism, that Harvey has described as a transition from Fordism to flexible accumulation.[35] Harvey's analysis of these changes provides a framework within which to understand the significance of the digital code for the process of capital accumulation, and illuminates a key contribution of Baudrillardian theory for such an inquiry.

TIME-SPACE COMPRESSION AND THE DIGITAL CODE

Following Lipietz and others in the regulation school, Harvey views the broad pattern of changes in contemporary capitalism as a shift in the regime of accumulation and mode of social and political regulation. A regime of accumulation involves a set of arrangements for allocating the net product between accumulation and consumption that becomes stabilized over a long period of time. It is based upon the view that conditions of production are linked to conditions of reproducing wage workers, so that a change in one set of conditions would correspond to changes in the other. Accumulation and consumption are thus interconnected processes, and the arrangements for allocating the net product between them are developed through political struggle.[36]

A particular regime of accumulation becomes stabilized because it is able to ensure some regularity and permanence for the process of social reproduction. Such stability is facilitated by the development of norms, habits, laws, and regulating networks to encourage individual behavior to conform with the larger patterns of accumulation and consumption. This "mode of regulation" provides a "body of interiorized rules and social processes" that integrates the behavior of capitalists, workers, state employees, financiers, and other social actors in a way that allows the regime of accumulation to function.[37]

The regulation school provides a framework to understand the whole range of relationships and arrangements that facilitates a particular historical pattern of linking output growth to the aggregate distribution of income and consumption. Harvey argues that a new regime of flexible accumulation has emerged since 1973, as a response to the rigid qualities of the old Fordist regime that had been in place since 1945. It involved a transformation in the forms of labor control, technology, consumption habits, and configurations of economic and political power. Under flexible accumulation, labor processes and markets became more flexible, and consumption practices shifted rapidly. Firms were able to reorganize production due to increased geographical mobility, the availability of digital technologies to automate production processes, and the implementation of new organizational practices that allowed for greater pressures of labor control. Completely new sectors of production emerged, along with new ways of offering financial services, new markets, and rapid commercial, technological, and organizational innovations.[38]

The transition to a flexible regime of accumulation was a response to the underlying logic of capital accumulation, that created pressures to accelerate the turnover time of capital in both production and consumption. Innovations involving the automation of production, the use of robots, and new organizational forms like "just-in-time" inventory systems allowed turnover time to be reduced in production. Consumption turnover time was lessened through a shift to rapidly changing fashions; the growth of an advertising industry that fostered the production of "needs" to consume particular products; and the rise of new cultural commodities like film and videos, as well as services like restaurants and tourism. The consumption of these commodities approximated Marx's "twinkling of an eye" as the ideal amount of turnover time for the capitalist.[39]

The logic of capital accumulation also gave rise to pressures to reduce spatial barriers. Capital engages in an ongoing search to reduce turnover time by overcoming spatial and temporal barriers to the accumulation process. Flexible accumulation is characterized by heightened geographical mobility of capital, leading to capital flight and de-industrialization in traditional industrial centers, and changing patterns of industrial development in the newly and older industrialized countries. A central paradox emerges, where the transcendence of spatial barriers through capital mobility leads the choice of location to become paramount. The search for spatial fixes to the problem of overaccumulation becomes an underlying logic for the flexible accumulation regime, as capital searches for the most conducive investment sites by developing highly flexible and mobile accumulation systems.[40]

These responses to the logic of accumulation can help stave off the tendency toward capitalist crisis. Crises of overaccumulation arise periodically in capitalism, due to the inability to reconcile three necessary features of the capitalist mode of production: an orientation toward growth, a need to control labor to maintain satisfactory profits, and the technological and organizational dynamism arising from the competitive search for profit. Overaccumulation occurs when idle supplies of capital and labor develop, without opportunities to bring them together in the process of production. Such conditions were prominent in the 1930s, and have reoccurred periodically since 1973. Marxists view overaccumulation as a perpetual problem for capitalism, whose effects need to be managed and absorbed to avoid threatening the social order.[41]

For Harvey, crises of overaccumulation generally spark the search for temporal and spatial "fixes," leading to periodic waves of "time-space compression." Time-space compression involves revolutionary changes in the objective qualities of space and time that lead people to transform the ways they experience and represent the world. For example, innovations in transportation systems now allow people to travel at up to 700 miles per hour on jet aircraft, compared to 10 miles per hour on the sailing ships and horse-drawn coaches of the sixteenth and seventeenth centuries. This has radically altered conceptions of space and time, and reduced barriers of distance to relationships among people in different parts of the world.

The transition to a regime of flexible accumulation involved a new round of time-space compression, and a new combination of spatial and temporal responses to the problem of overaccumulation. It allowed decision-making time to be condensed in both the private and public sectors, and made it possible to communicate those decisions virtually instantaneously across increasing distances.[42]

Harvey's emphasis on the pressures of capital accumulation to shrink space and reduce turnover time helps explain the role of transborder data flows in contemporary capitalism. It places the three tendencies discussed above in the context of an underlying logic of capitalism, to resolve problems of overaccumulation through spatial and temporal fixes. The first tendency toward the global expansion of trade and production is a spatial response to the rigidities of Fordism, reflected in the increased geographical mobility in the flexible accumulation regime. The use of transborder data flows to coordinate business activities in different parts of the world contributes to the new wave of time-space compression, by allowing instant communication between spatially dispersed operations. This wave is further supported by the second tendency toward centralized control over geographically dispersed production operations. Finally, the ability to trade commodities in digital form also compresses space and time, by allowing trade and production to occur virtually instantaneously. Conflicts over the Brazilian software law may thus be viewed as struggles to define a new mode of regulation that addresses these spatial and temporal changes in the accumulation process; they form part of the larger transition to a flexible accumulation regime.

Harvey provides a theoretical framework to understand these three tendencies as part of a broader set of changes in contemporary capitalism. His work also suggests a different interpretation of Baudrillard's analysis of the importance of the digital code for current processes of social transformation. In positing the code as the basis for a new form of reproduction where objects are always already reproduced, Baudrillard describes a process of radical temporal compression. Baudrillard's concept of hyperreality suggests the ability to eradicate barriers of time in the process of reproduction. Since third order simulacra are always already reproduced, the temporal dimension is collapsed into a perpetual present. This concept thus offers a valuable insight into the temporal effects of the digital code.

If we place this Baudrillardian insight within the context of capitalist production and exchange, it indicates the most radical instance of time-space compression. Temporal and spatial barriers to capital accumulation are totally collapsed, to create a process I call "hyperaccumulation." Hyperaccumulation occurs whenever aspects of the processes of production or exchange occur instantaneously, speeding up the overall accumulation process by collapsing time and space during one of its distinct parts. Digital forms of production and exchange make such an acceleration possible. For example, once software programs are developed, the programs themselves can be mass produced almost instantaneously because of their digital form. Similarly, the programs could be traded in milliseconds in the form of transborder data flows. Other parts of the software production process are slower, such as the production of manuals and packaging to accompany the programs. Trade that included these non-digital elements would require more time to deliver the products to particular markets. Only the digital aspects of these production and exchange processes would thus comprise instances of hyperaccumulation.

By collapsing temporal and spatial barriers in certain parts of the accumulation process, hyperaccumulation contributes to the broader process of
time-space compression under the flexible accumulation regime. Although
Baudrillard frames his theory in terms of reproduction, his concept of
hyperreality helps to theorize this aspect of the temporal and spatial shift
that characterizes the current process of social transformation. A Marxian
analysis allows this concept to be reconceptualized as a process of
hyperaccumulation, that provides a radical temporal and spatial response
to the pressures of capital accumulation to shrink space and reduce turnover
time. The need for this reconceptualization reintroduces problems with
Baudrillard's focus on the reproduction of objects, and suggests some more
general theoretical critiques of the concept of the third order simulacrum.

CONCLUSION

Four main critiques of Baudrillard's concept of the third order simulacrum
emerge from the above analysis. They provide the basis on which to evaluate his arguments about the revolutionary effects of the digital code on the
nature of contemporary society, and about the inability of Marxism to
conceptualize current processes of social transformation.

First, capitalist relations of production and exchange are fundamental
structural features of contemporary society. They are part of a concrete set
of material conditions that affect the implementation of the digital code,
as well as the social meaning of particular uses of that code. Corporate
executives, state policy makers, and a range of other social actors engage
in relationships shaped by their participation in market activities. Decisions
about the use of transborder data flows and software are made within a
social context affected by market relationships. By rejecting economic
production as irrelevant to understanding contemporary society, Baudrillard
eviscerates his theory's ability to analyze how particular forms of the
digital code are integrated into processes of capitalist production and
exchange.

Baudrillard's rejection of Marxism for its focus on economic production
is largely due to a second problem of determinism. Baudrillard engages in
a deterministic reading of Marx, assuming that Marxism reduces all of
social reality to epiphenomena of economic production. In response, he
develops an equally deterministic theory of society as characterized by
forms of reproducing objects. The shift of conceptual focus from production
to reproduction is thus combined with a new kind of technological determinism, where the reproduction of objects in the form of digital signals
defines the nature of contemporary society, as well as reality itself.
Baudrillard's technological determinism enervates his theory's capacity to
conceptualize the complex range of social relations and activities that comprise contemporary society.

Baudrillard's deterministic focus on reproduction is linked to a particular kind of formalism, which constitutes a third problem with the concept of the third order simulacrum. This concept is defined in formalist terms, as the reproduction of objects in the form of the digital code. However, the code itself is never clearly defined. Baudrillard refers to the code, the binary form, digitality, and the model without explicitly theorizing these terms. Nor does he engage in systematic empirical analysis to examine how the code is implemented, or how it is involved in the reproduction of objects. A disparate range of examples is given, without sustained consideration of the material conditions that shape the code's development and use. Baudrillard's view of the current social order is based upon an assertion about the transformative power of the digital form, instead of an analysis of how that form is affected by social actors, institutions, and organizations, operating within an economic, political, and historical context.

Kellner found similar problems with formalism in Baudrillard's analysis of the media. He critiqued Baudrillard's "formalist subordination," which led him to focus on the form of media technology rather than its content, meaning, and use. The form and effects of the media were not placed within a social or historical context. There was a lack of consideration of material conditions and social institutions, of the classes, groups, and individuals that controlled the code and the process of signification. This problem was linked to Baudrillard's "semiological determinism," which led him to view signs and signification as the controlling forces in social life, operating without the intervention of social actors.[43]

Baudrillard's rigid emphasis on the importance of the digital form raises a final critique of the concept of the third order simulacrum, involving the ability to make truth claims about the nature of social reality. In making his case for the revolutionary effects of the digital form, Baudrillard contends that the code both creates the basis for a new kind of society and alters the nature of reality itself. As objects are reproduced in the form of digital signals, it becomes virtually impossible to distinguish between reality and its representation, between the object and the sign. Hyperreality emerges as reality becomes equivalent to its reproduction; it is always already reproduced. There is no objective reality distinct from the model or the code.[44]

This argument about the transformation of the nature of social reality is marked by epistemological confusion. By discussing the nature of reality, Baudrillard assumes that he can know what that reality is, and that he can describe it to others. This assumption contradicts the substance of his argument that it has become impossible to distinguish between reality and its representation. His epistemology thus conflicts directly with the content of his position. The argument that reality has been effaced by the code is based upon a contradictory epistemological supposition that the writer can understand and describe that reality. In other words, by writing a book about the process of simulation, Baudrillard presupposes that there is something real to write about and undermines his own analysis in the process.

The conflict between Baudrillard's epistemology and his substantive argument is a further indication of his broader lack of conceptual clarity and systematic theoretical or empirical analysis. His theory of the orders of simulacra is schematic; it consists of brief assertions about the distinctions between different types of societies characterized by particular forms of reproducing objects. There is no sustained analysis of the basis for social transformation from one order of simulacra to another, and no extensive theoretical or empirical discussion of the systemic connections between the code and social reality in the contemporary social order.

Baudrillard's work is useful in identifying the digital code as a key part of current processes of social transformation. By placing the code at the center of his analysis, he highlights its importance within the present trajectory of change. The concept of hyperreality is particularly important in identifying the ability of the digital code to collapse temporal barriers under certain conditions. These temporal effects of the digital code contribute to broader changes in the construction of space and time that mark a distinct characteristic of the contemporary social order.

Despite these merits, the benefits of Baudrillard's theoretical contribution are undermined by problems of technological determinism, formalism, and epistemological confusion. Equally important, understanding the effects of the digital code on the nature of contemporary society requires an analysis of the role of the code within capitalist production and exchange, rather than a strict focus upon the forms in which objects are reproduced.

Addressing the above problems would challenge three major assumptions made in Baudrillard's work, and entail a radical reconstruction of his theory of the orders of the simulacra. First, capitalist relations of production and exchange are central structural features that characterize contemporary society, which includes the reproduction of digitized software, media, information, and other new technologies. Secondly, the digital code and other information technologies are always implemented within a social and political context that shapes the nature and implications of their use; they do not by themselves constitute the basis for a new social order. Thirdly, understanding the effects of the code requires an analysis of specific examples of its use by social actors within a particular historical context governed by specific political regimes. The above analysis revealed particular ways that the code has contributed to the emergence of key tendencies in the contemporary conjuncture of advanced capitalism. A Marxian approach makes it possible to identify the changing forms of production, exchange, and political struggle that characterize this current conjuncture.

Notes

1 Jean Baudrillard, *The Mirror of Production* (St. Louis: Telos Press, 1975), p. 121.

2 Steven Best and Douglas Kellner, *Postmodern Theory: Critical Interrogations* (New York: Guilford Press, 1991); Barry Smart, *Modern Conditions, Postmodern Controversies* (London: Routledge, 1992); Jean-François Lyotard, *The Postmodern Condition: A Report on Knowledge* (Minneapolis: University of Minnesota Press, 1984); Michel Foucault, *The Order of Things: An Archeology of the Human Sciences* (New York: Vintage Books, 1970); Michel Foucault, *Power/Knowledge: Selected Interviews and Other Writings 1972–1977* (New York: Pantheon, 1980); Baudrillard, *Mirror of Production*; Jean Baudrillard, *Simulations* (New York: Semiotext(e), 1983).

3 Baudrillard *Simulations*.

4 Ibid., pp. 96–100.

5 Ibid., pp. 83–5.

6 Baudrillard alludes to changes in the status of the "producers" in his discussion of the development of mass industrial production, noting that they become undefined simulacra of each other, as do the products they produce. However, these changes are not discussed in detail, and appear to be of secondary importance to the major transformation in the form of reproduction. See ibid., pp. 96–100.

7 Ibid., pp. 96–100.

8 Ibid., pp. 100–1, 103–7.

9 Ibid., p. 106.

10 Ibid., pp. 115–17, 122–3.

11 Ibid., p. 145.

12 Ibid., p. 146.

13 Ibid., p. 146.

14 Ibid., p. 152.

15 Douglas Kellner, *Jean Baudrillard: From Marxism to Postmodernism and Beyond* (Stanford: Stanford University Press, 1989).

16 Baudrillard, *Simulations*.

17 Kellner, *Baudrillard*, pp. 29, 50–2.

18 Robert Antonio, "The Decline of the Grand Narrative of Emancipatory Modernity: Crisis or Renewal in Neo-Marxian Theory?" pp. 88–116 in *Frontiers of Social Theory: The New Syntheses*, ed. George Ritzer, (New York: Columbia University Press, 1990), p. 107.

19 Baudrillard, *Simulations*.

20 Baudrillard, *Simulations*, p. 142.

21 Karl P. Sauvant, "Transborder Data Flows: Importance, Impact, Policies," *Information Services and Use*, 4 (1984) 3–30; United Nations Center on Transnational Corporations, *Transnational Corporations in World Development: Trends and Prospects* (New York: United Nations, 1988).

22 Alejandro Portes and A. Douglas Kincaid, "Sociology and Development in the 1990s: Critical Challenges and Empirical Trends," *Sociological Forum* 4, 4 (1989) 479–504; Aihwa Ong, *Spirits of Resistance and Capitalist Discipline: Factory Women in Malaysia* (Albany: State University of New York Press,

1987); Maria Patricia Fernández-Kelly, *For We Are Sold, I and My People: Women and Industry in Mexico's Frontier* (Albany: State University of New York Press, 1983).

23 George Hickmott, "Data Restrictions: Users' Concerns," *Transnational Data and Communications Report* (Dec 1986, 25–7; United Nations Commission on transnational Corporations, "The Role of Transnational Corporations in Transborder Data Flows: Report of the Secretariat" (New York: United Nations, 1984); Walter O'Connor, "Information – (The Next Trade Problem?" *Data Communication* (April 1986a) 185–9; Walter O'Connor, "Highlights of a Study of the Impact of Restrictions on Transborder Data Flow on U.S. Based Multinational Companies," paper presented at Intelevent, Munich, 1986; Walter O'Connor and Stephen Moser, "Trade Barriers to Information," *CFO* (July 1987) 2–3.

24 Peter Dicken, *Global Shift: The Internationalization of Economic Activity* (New York: Guilford Press, 1992), pp. 362–3.

25 Manuel Castells, *The Informational City: Information Technology, Economic Restructuring, and the Urban-Regional Process* (Oxford: Basil Blackwell, 1989).

26 Saskia Sassen, *The Global City: New York, London, Tokyo* (Princeton: Princeton University Press, 1991), pp. 28–9, 106–8.

27 Sassen, *Global City*, pp. 108–9.

28 Castells, *Informational City*, p. 146.

29 Castells, *Informational City*, p. 146; Sassen, *Global City*, p. 109.

30 Peter Lewis, "Cracking Down on Software Pirates," *The New York Times* (July 9, 1989), D10.

31 House Subcommittee on Commerce, Consumer Protection, and Competitiveness, *Informatics Trade Problems with Brazil*, 100th Cong., 1st sess. (July 15, 1987), pp. 20–1, 93, 102; *Latin America Regional Reports Brazil*, "Mixed Reaction to New Software Law," (March 17, 1988), p. 4; United Nations Centre on Transnational Corporations, *Transborder Data Flows and Brazil* (New York: United Nations, 1983), p. 89.

32 House Subcommittee, *Informatics Trade Problems with Brazil*, pp. 2–3.

33 House Subcommittee, *Informatics Trade Problems with Brazil*, pp. 7, 60.

34 House Subcommittee, *Informatics Trade Problems with Brazil*, pp. 5, 8.

35 David Harvey, *The Condition of Postmodernity: An Enquiry into the Origins of Cultural Change* (Oxford: Basil Blackwell, 1989).

36 Harvey, *Condition of Postmodernity*; Alain Lipietz, "New Tendencies in the International Division of Labor: Regimes of Accumulation and Modes of Regulation," in *Production, Work, Territory: The Geographical Anatomy of Industrial Capitalism*, eds., A. Scott and M. Storper (Boston: Allen and Unwin, 1986), pp. 16–40.

37 Lipietz, "New Tendencies," p. 19.

38 Harvey, *Condition of Postmodernity*, pp. 121–4, 147–56.

39 Harvey, *Condition of Postmodernity*, pp. 156, 288.

40 Harvey, *Condition of Postmodernity*, pp. 147, 196, 296, 306–7.

41 Harvey, *Condition of Postmodernity*, pp. 180–1.

42 Harvey, *Condition of Postmodernity*, pp. 147, 240, 327.

43 Kellner, *Baudrillard*, pp. 29, 51–3, 73–4.

44 Baudrillard, *Simulations*, pp. 145–6, 152.

9

SIMULATION: THE HIGHEST STAGE OF CAPITALISM?

—

James Der Derian

For thirty years, Encore Computer Corporation has envisioned the needs of the most demanding, time-critical flight simulation and training programs in the world. We've understood the pressures for ever-increasing real-time performance; solved complex technical challenges sometimes before our customers knew they had a problem. We've made a business of turning illusion into reality.[1]

The New World Order is messy.[2]

During the last years of the Cold War, as the glacier of political repression receded in the Soviet Union, pressing questions about the future of international politics went not only unanswered but unasked. Years of an ideological stupefaction seemed to have left the West in a state of intellectual lockjaw. The evidence lies, as it were, in the images. When the Berlin Wall fell, George Bush and James Baker appeared on television with a map of Germany in front of them, seeking in cartography what they could no longer locate in reality, the fixity of former borders and former times.[3] When Gorbachev faced a coup d'etat, Henry Kissinger resurfaced to warn us in gravelly tones that, as surely as he was back in the pundit's seat, we were back in the thick of the Cold War.

When these highly tentative efforts by cold warriors on both sides failed to recapture the past, a shop-worn tactic was adopted. This was comprehension by proclamation. The Cold War was over and victory was ours – discounting of course the human costs on the marginal battlefields of the Third World as well as the domestic price of a permanent war economy. Confirmation came when a coalition of states took on Saddam Hussein, a minor-league tyrant whose defeat was to usher in a new world order – ignoring, of course, past and present support by the USA of oppressive regimes and the unipolar, highly selective, and antidiplomatic nature of the interventions against them.

But as the decade turned, as novel images looped on prime time – of Lenin toppling from his pedestal, smart bombs homing in on Baghdad, LA cops whaling away on Rodney King, dead US Rangers being dragged through the streets of Mogadishu – something began to crack in the unselfconscious complacency and sometime complicity of those who had heavily invested in the status quo advantages of late capitalism and a moribund communism. These images spoke of new times, and only reluctantly and with much confusion did the written world respond. One reason is obvious and understandable: we are in the midst of a change that is traumatically disruptive. The initial reaction, one of panic shock, is making its way through the system, striking those nation-states and peoples least buffered by economic security with the greatest severity.

In the USA, commentary has been for the most part monopolized by those who have the luxury and/or inclination to deal with this disruptive change as a matter of philosophy rather than everyday survival. For the politically neutered, nostalgic despair is the favored nostrum; for the bureaucratically dependent, there is inertial denial; and for the momentarily powerful, there is the well-stocked podium for triumphalist gloatings. In the search for wisdom some went back to the future, to engage in neo-Hegelian ruminations on the end to history and the coming of an universal liberalism. Others, pre-Sarajevo, emerged from think-tanks with neo-Kantian schemes for an ethico-rational cosmopolitanism. And the media many, having heard that the Owl of Minerva had been sighted somewhere, asked distracting questions: Is it spotted and endangered? Does it fly at dusk or at dawn? Can we get it live on the evening news? Eventually, inevitably, the distractions overwhelmed the event. Navy SEALS on the beaches of Somalia, the Palestinians wandering in limbo between Lebanon and Israel, Socks the cat lured out from Governor Clinton's mansion with catnip – all were simultaneously illuminated and blinded by the glare of what stands in for a critical consciousness of the world: the regressive reflexivity of a global media, making images of itself making images of . . . ad infinitum. The most important question, what is to come next, was reduced to a matter of programming, requiring no deeper consultation than the *TV Guide*.

One must ask, then, not in spite of but because of the pervasive light and sound show, whether a historic opportunity is being pixillated into just one of a multitude of other reproducible events. This question, from its earliest phrasing by Walter Benjamin to its hyperbolic explosion by Jean Baudrillard, informs this essay. But it is the rise of a new technostrategic force, the global power of *simulation*, which takes this inquiry into the more complex and more troubling international politics of representation that confounds all questions about the future. In short, this is a preliminary report inspired by, but going beyond, Baudrillard, on how simulations of the future – in particular war gaming, war planning, and war media – have forestalled and in some cases foreordained the answer to the question of what is to come next.

For many years the question has been framed by enmity. Perhaps Russia and the remnants of its former empire will manage with one icon and one enemy less. But can "we" – the West, the USA, the autonomous self, and all other categories of identity so easily reduced to the first person plural – survive without an ideological, cultural, religious other? In the absence of a "real" other, in the void left by the end of the Cold War, does the reality principle of international relations, of sovereign states locked in a struggle for power, dictate the construction of simulated others? In his final speech on foreign policy, President Bush assured his audience of West Point graduates that the end of the Cold War would not leave them without a mission. If the USA were to disengage from its global commitments, the results could be disastrous:

> [A]lready we see disturbing signs of what this new world could become if we are passive and aloof. We would risk the emergence of a world characterized by violence, characterized by chaos, one in which dictators and tyrants threaten their neighbors, build arsenals brimming with weapons of mass destruction, and ignore the welfare of their own men, women and children. And we could see a horrible increase in international terrorism, with American citizens more at risk than ever before ... Two hundred years ago, another departing President warned of the dangers of what he described as "entangling alliances." His was the right course for a new nation at that point in history, But what was entangling in Washington's day is now essential.[4]

The question of enmity must be reframed, rephrased: just how "real" is this threat of violence, chaos, and tyrants? Moreover, how are we to judge the authenticity of such claims? After five years of research on the growing role of simulation in the formulation, execution, and representation of US foreign policy, I have come to doubt the ability of those inside the simulation loop of the Washington Beltway to answer such questions. And President Clinton's mantra of the "essential continuity" of his foreign policy with that of Bush is – as the military strategist is wont to say – a "force multiplier" of that doubt.

THE SIMULATION SYNDROME

Before one can begin to understand how simulations have come to fill the void left by the end of a certain enemy and fixed boundaries, it is necessary to review the history of simulations and their increased significance in US military and foreign policy.[5]

The search for significant moments becomes suspect if not tiresome in times of rapid change, but one does stand out for the synchronicity of end and beginning, of the prospect for monumental change and a media-brokered response to it. It happened the first week of February in 1989, when President Mikhail Gorbachev announced the unthinkable, proposing an end to the Soviet Communist Party's monopoly on power. President George Bush responded by calling a five-minute time-out during a war game at Fort Irwin to tell the soldiers the good news. Kitted out in a photo-opportunistic ensemble of camouflage jacket, pin-stripe trousers, and wing-tip shoes, Bush used a radio link to let the 2,689 players, spread out over the Mojave Desert, know that "we are pleased to see Chairman Gorbachev's proposal to expand steps toward pluralism in the Soviet Union." Inspired, the "Soviet" 197th Krasnovian Motorized Rifle Regiment made *borscht* out of the US Third Brigade of the Ninth Infantry Division, and headed for the ridge from which Bush had pledged not "to let down our guard against a worldwide threat." But Bush – clearly impressed by the power of fictitious forces over real ones – had already left for a briefing tour of the Livermore Labs, birthplace and incubator of the most hyperreal form of warfare yet – Star Wars.

Was it a historical irony, a centennial coincidence, or just the dumbness of imperial decline that should suddenly make war games such an attractive diplomatico-strategic tool during the swan song of the Cold War? At first glance, the historical evidence seems to argue more for a parodic repetition in this case than a rational continuity of foreign policy. In 1889 Major William Livermore of the Army Corp of Engineers joined William McCarty Little and Rear Admiral Alfred Thayer Mahan at the Naval War College to set up the nation's first modern system of war gaming. Spurred by the success of the expansionist Prussians who had used *Kriegsspiel* ("war play") before their victories over the Austrians at Sadowa in 1866 and the French in 1870, these early advocates of American war gaming found their positions strengthened when Japan achieved a stunning victory over the Russians in 1904 – a victory plotted out beforehand with newly created war games.

Long before Bush made his trip to the Mojave, war gaming had sallied from the battlefield, emerged from the basements of the war colleges, leaked out of the high-security rooms of research centers like RAND and BDM International, and entered, if not seized, the public imagination. One reason for the shift is the computerization of war gaming. Just as the art of warfare has undergone radical changes, so too has the art of gaming. At the micro-level, the slow, spatial movement of toy soldiers and cardboard ships, the contoured sand tables, and expansive game rooms have largely been replaced by the high-speed electronic calculations and high-resolution screens of computer simulations. And, from their inception thirty years ago, computer war games have undergone radical changes. When the Naval War college finally closed down its old tiled war gaming room in 1958, it was replaced with the Navy Electronic Warfare System (NEWS) which cost more than $10 million dollars and filled a three-storey building. Today those very NEWS games could be played on the home computer.

And, by 1989, they were being played at home, as well as at the movies and in the classrooms. For those nostalgic for the Cold War, there was *Balance of Power*, requiring only 256K memory and the introduction of Syria into any scenario to trigger World War III (personal best: two minutes to reach Armageddon). In almost every mall, video arcades filled up with remarkably sophisticated war games: one could fly as *Top Gun*, rescue hostages (*successfully*), or win historical (and some not so historical) military conflicts. Many of the widly popular *Nintendo* games were based on military simulations. To be sure, not all of the simulations took a positive form. Clearly cautionary in its telling, *War Games* stood out as a warning of what can happen when a hacker who taps into an Air Force computer and nearly triggers a nuclear war between the superpowers has too much fun and too little political consciousness. And on television, we were treated to Ted Koppel's assembling in 1989 – "for the first time ever" – a group of high-ranking military and government officials from the Soviet Union and the USA to play out a war game for, and put the fear of the apocalypse into, an ABC prime-time audience.

We all have some notion of the reality of war, but just what is its simulation? It could be broadly defined as the *continuation of war by means of verisimilitude*. Conventionally, a 'war game' uses broad descriptive strokes and a minimum of mathematical abstraction to make generalizations about the behavior of actors, while the "simulation" uses algorithms and computer power to analyze the amount of technical detail considered necessary to predict events and the behavior of actors. Judging by the gradual shift by the military and think-tanks from games to mainly computerized simulations – reflected in the shift of the Joint Chiefs of Staff gaming organization from SAGA (Studies, Analysis, and Gaming Agency) to JAD (Joint Analysis Directorate) – it would seem that simulation is becoming the preferred, "sponge" term. "Simulation" also has the obvious advantage of sounding more serious than "gaming," and of carrying more of a high-tech, scientific connotation than modeling.

Meanwhile, the war *at* home was increasingly being gamed. Before the 1984 Los Angeles Olympics, the various law-enforcement agencies responsible for security got together to train for possible terrorist attacks. They took advantage of a new "Tactical Mapping System" created by the United States Agency for Advanced Research Projects that had put over 54,000 moving images of Aspen, Colorado on instantly accessible videodiscs (a veritable mink farm for animal rights counter-terrorists?). In Los Angeles, likely building targets were similarly video-taped, down to the detail of door locks and ventilation systems. Anti-terrorist specialists then trained by "walking through" computer simulations, their eyes becoming the camera's eye.

My purpose, however, is not simply to give notice of the computer diffusion of war games. Nor is it to claim that a pervasive militarization of society is likely to result. That might be a possibility, but there is a more complex, if less obvious, danger that Jean Baudrillard, more so than any other social critic, has identified as central to the late modern condition. The proliferation of simulations into all walks of life has weakened, in some cases displaced, and in others completely redrawn, the representational boundary between the simulation and the "real thing."

Driven by the goal of total authenticity and rendered by new scientific methods of reproduction, the war simulation is leading us into a brave new world. The writer J. L. Borges anticipated this realm in his fable about the cartographers who, when ordered by the emperor to draw the perfect map of the empire, created one that exactly and entirely covered the territory. Baudrillard recounts this story to make a telling point: we now have the technical means to make maps and models that seem as real as the reality that they simulate. "Virtual" or "artificial" reality is what the computer scientists – and now the cyber-pundits – have come to call it. Baudrillard first referred to it as the realm of hyperreality, where origins are forgotten, referents lost, and simulations begin to precede and engender reality. This is the world of Mutual Assured Destruction, Star Wars, and Stealth Technology, all of them deterrence machines that most persuasively "work" in the hyperreal world of strategic simulation.

Although Baudrillard prefers abstract hyperbole to empirical detail, it is possible to find examples of hyperreal simulation leading the way in military policy. For the radar operator and the tactical information coordinator of the USS *Vincennes* on July 3, 1988 the blip on their screen looked like an attacking Iranian F-14, even though their highly sophisticated Aegis radar system registered an unidentified airplane flying level at 12,000 feet. Did nine months of simulation training with computer tapes that preceded the encounter engender a hyperreality which absorbed the reality of the moment? Did the Iranian Airbus, in effect, disappear before the surface-to-air missile struck, fading from a plane with 290 civilians to an electronic representation on a radar screen to a simulated target? Can a simulation overpower a reality which does not conform to it? A later military investigation laid the blame on stress: the *Vincennes* and its crew had never been in combat, they were engaged with Iranian speedboats at the time, and surely the memory of the USS *Stark* – which did not fire at an Iraqi warplane and was nearly sunk by an Exocet missile – was on everyone's mind. Yet stress has many origins, and the military shows signs of ignoring the most serious one: the tension that can develop when the simulation becomes too real.

Symptoms have appeared elsewhere in the armed services. Although the Air Force has thrown a veil of secrecy over it, the Army, Navy, and Marine Corps have become alarmed by the sharp increase in cases of "simulator sickness." This is a condition in which users of flight simulators – especially those that make use of powerful computers to create the most "realistic" motions and graphic representations of flight – experience flash-backs, visual distortions, and physical disorientation. Experts are unsure of the cause, but many of them attribute the disorder to "cue conflict," which happens when one's expectations based on experience run up against contrary sensory information.

Should we be on the alert against a similar effect taking hold in the ranks of military and diplomatic officials, as well as with the international relations specialists, who create, play, and promote war games? Is there sufficient evidence of a *simulation syndrome* creeping into our infinite preparations for war as well as war-fighting itself?

Certainly there is not sufficient proof to wean the Navy from its "Global Game" or the Army from its "Janus" game as their preferred training method. Or to deter the Foreign Service Institute from using simulations like the "Crisis in Al Jazira" to educate junior-level diplomats in the art of crisis management and counterterrorism. Or to prevent the ubiquitous think-tanks from modeling everything from domestic crime and narcoterrorism to low-intensity conflict and nuclear war, and selling them to the highest bidder. In turn, we – the inhabitants of advanced mediacracies – have become seduced by the technical reproduction of reality, especially its highest stage of development, the computer simulation. What will happen when the computer representation of reality moves into even more spec-tacular realms, where with the aid of holograms, interactive media, sensor helmets, data gloves, and other technologies of virtual reality we can fully inhabit the cyberspace of a three-dimensional, computer-generated hyperreality?

To answer these questions I believe we must turn, as does Baudrillard, to popular culture and science fiction – to *Bladerunner* and *Robocop*, William Gibson and other cyberpunk writers, Tom Clancy and other techno-thrillists – to compensate for the lagging social sciences. Indeed, the movie *Aliens* provides an eerie foreshadowing to the *Vincennes'* incident. When the Colonial Marines are being buffeted as they enter the atmosphere of the planet where the Alien awaits them, Ripley (Sigourney Weaver) asks the obviously anxious lieutenant how many combat drops this is for him. He replies "thirty-eight," pauses, and then adds – "simulated." He quickly proves incapable of responding to situations that do not follow his simu-lation training.

Simulations have given rise to important intertexts of strategic power and popular culture. Take Tom Clancy and his intertextual relationship to war games. For instance, the best non-fiction book on the subject, *War Games: the Secret World of the Creators, Players, and Policy Makers Rehearsing World War III Today* written by Thomas Allen,[6] sports a cover blurb by Tom Clancy who writes that it "will be the standard work on the subject for the next ten years." And Clancy's second novel, *Red Storm Rising*, a thinly fictionalized mosaic of NATO war games, was authoritatively cited by Vice President Quayle in a foreign policy speech to prove that the USA needs an anti-satellite capability.

At a more mundane level, simulations have acquired a very important budgetary function. After interviews with fast-track colonels from the various war colleges and with modelers from the RAND Corporation, I discovered that there is a very high demand for the best modelers, not just, as one would expect, to provide the best possible preparation for battle, but to convince the essential sub-committees of the Congress where funds should best be allocated. The different services compete to present the most detailed and technically ornate simulation – down to the number of rolls of toilet paper needed in the now-highly-unlikely event of a Russian invasion of Europe – to get a heftier chunk of the budgetary pie. As the arms race shows signs of winding down, the simulation race is speeding up. It would seem that war gaming has been joined, if not supplanted, by gaming wars.

Can we imagine a hundred years from now, when the time for a bicentenary celebration approaches, that strategists will be so far *inside* the simulation of war that they will neither feel a nostalgia for "real" war nor be able to distinguish it from some "original" model? Should we be horrified by the thought? Or just game on?

LENIN'S WARS, BAUDRILLARD'S GAMES

In search of answers, I listened to military officers strut their hi-tech stuff and corporate shills parade their wares at joint conferences on simulations; I followed George Bush's steps and chased after the "Krasnovian Brigade" in a Humvee during war games at the Army National Training Center in the East Mojave desert; and I learned at the Central Command in Tampa how computer gamers were already programming the lessons of the Gulf War for the next war. All the while I kept thinking of those empty pedestals in the former Soviet Union. I began to realize that flesh and blood, concrete and steel would not fill the space nor provide the answers. The debate has already moved, as has the era, to temporal, immaterial, *hologrammatic* icons and enemies, questions and answers.

After the joint defeat of the Cold War (how else can we describe the waste of resources and lives that took place?), defense consultants, thinktank wonks, and military experts made ready the next enemy with the latest computer technology in the most secret of planning offices. Paraphrasing the ancient Roman caveat: if we are to keep the peace, we must simulate for every *conceivable* war. The result: the imaginative resources of simulation are narrowly channeled into war productions, and alternative forms of peace-making are never conceived or realized.

This raises a second, less-obvious but just as important question: has simulation come to play the fin-de-siècle ideological role once monopolized by imperialism? Does it deserve top billing as the "highest (if not last) stage of capitalism?" In search of a provocative if not wholly plausible response I think we must pair the two men who stand out as the most powerful critics of what each perceived to be capitalism's endgame: Valdimir Lenin and Jean Baudrillard. The question, for convenience sake, will be simply put: are we entering an era in which the Marxist, concrete and steel Lenin is to be replaced by the hyperrealist, laser, and microchip Baudrillard? In their own times and in their own ways, they do embody a peculiar combination of critical virtues and practical vices, of offering the most incisive indictments of capitalist society and the crudest legacy of alternatives. In particular, I wish to question whether the simulation practices of the media and the military now represent – as imperialism did at the turn of the century – the gravest dangers and paradoxically (rather than dialectically) the greatest deterrent for change in the so-called new world order. To frame the question, I resort to a brief biography, a joint historiography of imperialism and simulation, and a videography of simulations for sale and simulations at war.

In this effort, two parallel memories of terror converge, as tracks do in the distance. The memories are of my grandfathers' wars and their work. One grandfather fought a three-year guerilla campaign against the Turks; the other was a machine-gunner in World War I. Neither spoke much of their foreign wars, and I learned not to ask. Their work radically differed: one was a straw boss of the coke ovens at the Ford Motor Company in Dearborn, Michigan; the other a beekeeper in up-state New York. The first memory is of my first and last visit to the coke ovens, going into a catatonic terror on the catwalk above the din and heat, resisting the efforts of my father to pry my fingers from the railing. The second memory is of a Civil War battle, watching my other grandfather dressed in the uniform of a Union soldier charge halfway up a hill, discharge a muzzleloader, and die much too convincingly for a credulous, yet again terrified grandson.

The coke ovens moved further and further South, in a perpetual search for others more fearless and hungrier than emigré progeny to keep them fired. I grew up, intent on keeping my distance from industry and war, real or imaginary. That is, until this year when the repressed, in the guise of a research trip, returned with a vengeance. Watching from a desert hill-top while Apache helicopters laser-tagged tanks and soldiers in mock battles, I realized that the message remains the same: the endgame of simulation in work and war is to make the terror of others fun for us. Is it no longer the case that it is needless to say, there is something wrong with that?

A historiography of imperialism and simulation hints at an answer.

In *Imperialism: The Highest Stage of Capitalism* (1916) Lenin explains why social revolution had not, as predicted by Marx, taken place in Europe but most certainly would in Russia. Drawing on Hobson's idea of underconsumption, Kautsky's work on the aggressive nature of finance capitalism, and Baukharin's view that trade wars lead to real wars, Lenin assembled a theory of imperialism that would mobilize millions in the belief that their plight was the necessary and final stage of a better world to come. Imperialism, born of the need to keep the working class happy at home, would create a miserable one abroad. Lenin cites Cecil Rhodes, arch-imperialist and financier for the education of Bill Clinton (among others) for his honest appraisal of this fact: "In order to save the 40,000,000 inhabitants of the United Kingdom from a bloody civil war, we colonial statesmen must acquire new land to settle the surplus population, to provide new markets for the goods produced in the factories and mines. The Empire, as I have always said, is a bread and butter question. If you want to avoid civil war, you must become imperialists."[7] But as the contradictions of capitalism spread, so too would the formation and solidarity of an oppressed class; world revolution would begin at the periphery and work its way back to the center of capitalist power.

A fine allegory, Baudrillard would say. Lenin's effort to chart the causes and consequences of imperialism, to pierce the veil of false consciousness that has postponed revolution, to scientifically represent the world-to-be, is just a mirroring, a doubling of the empire's own cartography of the world-as-it-is. "For it is with the same Imperialism," says Baudrillard, "that present-day simulators try to make the real, all the real coincide with their simulation models."[8] Baudrillard goes beyond Nietzsche in his interpretation of the death of God and the inability of rational man or the proletariat to fill the resulting value-void with stable distinctions between the real and the apparent, idea and referent, good and evil. In the hyperbolic, often nihilistic vision of Baudrillard, the task of modernity is no longer to demystify or disenchant illusion – for *"with the real world we have also abolished the apparent world"*[9] – but to save the reality principle, to refloat the last signifier, to leave the sinking ship of modernism. In this case this means, above all else, to save the sovereign state acting in an anarchical order to maintain and, if possible, expand its security and power in the face of penetrating, de-centering forces, like the ICBM, military (and now civilian) surveillance satellites, the international terrorist, the telecommunications web, environmental movements, transnational human rights conventions, to name a few of the more obvious forces. In his now familiar words: "It is no longer a question of a false representation of reality (ideology), but of concealing the fact that the real is no longer real."[10]

The idea that reality is blurring or has disappeared into its representational form has a long lineage. It can be traced from Siegfried Kracauer's chronicling of the emergence of a "cult of distraction" in the

Weimar Republic,[11] to Walter Benjamin's incisive warning of the loss of authenticity, aura, and uniqueness in the technical reproduction of reality,[12] to Guy Debord's claim that in modern conditions spectacles accumulate and representations proliferate,[13] and finally, to Jean Baudrillard's own notification that the simulated now precedes and engenders a hyperreality where origins are forgotten and historical references lost.[14] In his post-Marxist work, Baudrillard describes how the class struggle and the commodity form dissolved into a universal play of signs, simulacra, and the inertia of mass culture – and the revolution went missing along with the rest of reality. We are at end-times: but where Lenin saw a relentless, dialectical linearity in capitalism leading to social revolution, Baudrillard sees only a passive "silent majority," expecting the virtuality of technology to save them as the reality principle slips under the waves of mass media.

War serves as the ultimate test for the ideology of technology of Lenin's imperialism and Baudrillard's simulation. In Lenin's time, trade wars, nationalism, an arms race, the clash and decline of empires, and the inertia of military planning led to a world war so irreal in its level of lethality that, in the end, its only justification was to end all wars. A divide grew between those on the one side who saw the best hope for a world order without war in the Communist International, and, on the other, in the League of Nations. Lenin's mechanistic, almost messianic faith is evident in his address to the Third Congress of the Comintern, in which he declared that "The imperialist war of 1914–18 and the Soviet power in Russia are completing the process of converting [the] masses into an active factor in world politics and in the revolutionary destruction of imperialism."[15] Upon the signing of the Treaty of Versailles which ended World War I, President Wilson delivered an equally aspirational message, in the novel form of a telegram to the American people, describing the treaty as "the charter for a new order of affairs in the world" based on the practice of international law and a promise for international cooperation that would "cleanse the life of the world and facilitate its common action in beneficent service of every kind."[16] Neither institution survived the world war that followed.

PREPARING FOR CYBERWAR

The Gulf War and the post-war attempt to set up a "new world order" provide rich material for Baudrillard's thesis. Back in 1983 he had already spotted the dark side to a possible end of the ultimate simulation of the cold war, nuclear deterrence: "Like the real, warfare will no longer have any place – except precisely if the nuclear powers are successful in de-escalation and manage to define new spaces for warfare. If military power, at the cost of de-escalating this marvelously practical madness to the second power, reestablishes a setting for warfare, a confined space that is in fact human, then weapons will regain their use value and their exchange value: it will again be possible *to exchange warfare.*[17] And if ever a war was "engendered and preceded by simulation," it was the Gulf War.[18] We had already been prime-timed for this war. From the suburban mall to the classroom to the living room, simulations had proven their seductive appeal. News (re)creations of Felix Bloch handing over state secrets to the Soviets; video games based on tank warfare training; flight simulators just like the real thing; police interrogation techniques that became the model for nuclear deterrence; crime re-enactments on *America's Most Wanted* that made cops of all of us; and, of course, media war games.[19] Two that preceded the actual war involved Tom Brokaw on NBC *News* staging a war game with former US officials standing in for Hussein and Bush; and Ted Koppel on ABC *Nightline* directing an "Ides of November" war game.[20]

Long before Desert Shield became Desert Storm, a sand storm of simulations buried the boundary between truth and fiction. War continued by means of simulation in its media representation as well as through its military preparation. Before Desert Storm the US conducted a series of highly publicized war exercises, the largest being an amphibious Marine landing called "Imminent Thunder." In fact, no landing crafts were used because the seas were running too high. None the less, the simulation "worked." When the allied troops reached Kuwait City they found in a school house used by the Iraqi military as a headquarters a room-sized model of the city. On a sand tableau there were, to scale, wooden ships, buildings, roads, barbed wire – and all the Iraqi guns pointing toward the sea attack that never came.

The nature of the technical reproduction of the war enhanced its hyperreal quality. From the first to the last *shot* of the Six Weeks and One Hundred Hours War, from the night bombing of Baghdad to the night liberation of Kuwait City, reality was reproduced by television cameras equipped with night-vision technology and transmitted in real time by portable satellite link-ups. The grainy, ghostly green images of the beginning and the end of the war took on a representational power of their own. They were more real, more authentic, more appealing than innumerable talking heads – as proven by their reappearance in the opening hours of the Somalia beach landing by US Marines. This new *video verte* powerfully if paradoxically used the latest visual technology to produce the highest representation of reality in the lowest quality image. Abetted by simulated battles, photocentrism won out over logocentrism in the representation of warfare.

The Gulf War was an object lesson in the joint operations of warring and gaming in the age of video. From the initial deployment of troops to the daily order of battle, from the highest reaches of policy-making to the lowest levels of field tactics and supply, a series of simulations made the killing more efficient, more unreal, more acceptable.[21] Computer-simulated by private contractors, flight-tested at the Nellis Air Force Base, field-exercised at Fort Irwin in the Mojave Desert, and re-played and fine-tuned everyday in the Persian Gulf, real-time war games took on a life of their own as the real war took the lives of over 100,000 Iraqis.

But there is also evidence that simulations played a critical role in the decision to go to war. In an interview, Schwarzkopf revealed that two years before the war US intelligence discovered, in his words, that Iraq "had run computer simulations and war games for the invasion of Kuwait."[22] In my own research I have learned that Iraq had previously purchased a war game from the Washington military-consulting firm BDM International to use in its war against Iran; and almost as an aside it was reported in September 1990 on ABC *Nightline* that the software for the Kuwait invasion simulation was also purchased from a US firm.[23] Moreover, Schwarzkopf stated that he programmed "possible conflicts with Iraq on computers almost daily." Having previously served in Tampa, Florida as head of the US Central Command – at the time a "paper" army without troops, tanks, or aircraft of its own – his affinity for simulations is unsurprising.

In fact, Schwarzkopf sponsored a highly significant computer-simulated command-post exercise which was played in July 1990 under the code-name of Exercise Internal Look '90. According to a Central Command news release issued at the time, "command and control elements from all branches of the military will be responding to real-world scenarios similar to those they might be expected to confront within the Central Command AOR consisting of the Horn of Africa, the Middle East and Southwest Asia." The war-game specialist who put Exercise Internal Look together, Lt. General Yeosock, moved from fighting "real-world scenarios" in Florida to command all ground troops – except for the special forces under Schwarzkopf – in Saudi Arabia.

Perhaps it is too absurd to believe that the Gulf War is the product of a US war game designed to fight a war game bought by Iraq from a US company. Perhaps not. My purpose in this study is not to conduct an internal critique of the simulation industry, nor to claim some privileged grounds for ascertaining the causes of the war.[24] Rather, my intent is to ask if, in the construction of a realm of meaning that had minimal contact with historically specific events or actors, simulations demonstrated the power to construct the reality they purport to represent. The question is whether simulations can create a new world order where actors act, things happen, and the consequences have no origins except the artificial cyberspace of the simulations themselves.

Over the last decade there has been a profusion of signs that a simulation syndrome has taken hold in international politics. According to Oleg Gordievsky, former KGB station chief in London, the Soviet leadership became convinced in November 1983 that a NATO command-post simulation called Able Archer 83 was in fact the first step towards a nuclear surprise attack.[25] Relations were already tense after the September shootdown of the KAL 007 – a flight that the Soviets considered part of an intelligence-gathering mission – and since the Warsaw Pact had their own war game which used a training exercise as cover for a surprise attack, the Soviets assumed the West to have one as well. No NATO nuclear forces went on actual alert, yet the KGB reported the opposite to Moscow. On November 8 or 9, flash messages were sent to all Soviet embassies in Europe, warning them of NATO preparations for a nuclear first strike. Things calmed down when the Able Archer exercise ended without the feared nuclear strike, but Gordievsky still maintains that only the Cuban missile crisis brought the world closer to the brink of nuclear war.

The Gulf War is the pre-eminent, but probably not the last, case of a simulation syndrome manifesting itself in the military and the media. Baudrillard was right, in the sense that simulations would rule not only in the war without warring of nuclear deterrence, but also in the post-war warring of the present.[26] The Gulf War was not a war in the conventional sense of a series of battles between reciprocating opponents. It was, rather, a cyberwar of simulations: of the simulation Operation Internal Look 90 against the made in America Iraqi simulation for the invasion of Kuwait; of the NATO war game of Air Land Battle against an Iraqi army that bore no resemblance to the Warsaw Pact; of a war of spectacle against the spectacle of war on the media battlefield; and, finally, of a simulation of victory, the Gulf War Syndrome, against the reality of defeat, the Vietnam Syndrome.

To be sure, the deaths of this war were not simulated: that they were so one-sided and under-represented testifies to the power of cyberwar to obscure the horrors of war.[27] Critics of postmodernist analysis of war noted only the former, and seemed blinded to the latter by their fetishization of the material – oil, territory, the body bag – to the point of making them appear to be the ideological *doppelgangers* of the think-tank geopoliticians who were trundled out nightly on the news. Typical of this positional materialism is a remark made by Todd Gitlin during the war: "It will not suffice to do extended textual readings of Pentagon briefings or Hussein's speeches. One must also know something about American culture, Iraqi history, etc. The whole deconstructive line of solipsism is obviously worthless or worse in this case. Are we talking about a discourse or are we talking about a war?"[28] Of course it will *suffice*, as will not the either/or logic of Gitlin; but it is, to preserve the Marxist rhetoric of the old New Left, *necessary*. Even Edward Said, who was critical of the inability of the American Left (or what was left of it) to understand a "television war," was quick to distance himself from his interviewer's likening of his commentary to Baudrillard's claim that "it was a hyper-real non-event." Said's response cut to the bone: "Good old Baudrillard! For that I think he should be sent there, With a toothbrush and a can of Evian, or whatever it is he drinks."[29]

But Gitlin's citation of interpretive misdemeanors and Said's disparaging remarks pale in comparison with the British philosopher Christopher Norris's book-length indictment of Baudrillard's Gulf War crimes, *Uncritical Theory: Postmodernism, Intellectuals, and the Gulf War*.[30] Before the start of the Gulf War, Baudrillard published an article in the London *Guardian*, "The Reality Gulf," in which he argued that the Gulf War (as paraphrased by Norris) "would never happen, existing as it did only as a figment of mass-media simulation, war-games rhetoric or imaginary scenarios which exceeded all the limits of real-world, factual possibility."[31] At the end of the Gulf War, he reiterated and defended his position in a provocatively entitled article in *Liberation*, "The Gulf War Has Not Taken Place."[32] This was to be understood as a "virtual" engagement, unlike any prior war. According to Baudrillard: "The true belligerents are those who thrive on the ideology of the truth of this war, despite the fact that the war itself exerts its ravages on another level, through faking, through hyperreality, the simulacrum, through all those strategies of psychological deterrence that make play with facts and images, with the precession of the virtual over the real, of virtual time over real time, and the inexorable confusion between the two."[33] Christopher Norris took severe umbrage from these articles, and dashed off a polemic that draws from Derrida, Foucault, Lyotard, and others to refute what he takes to be the excessive, flip, and, indeed, callous attitude of Baudrillard. Norris displays some eccentric interpretations and peculiar habits – not least a deaf ear to irony – but my intent is not to rebut Norris or defend Baudrillard. It is rather to challenge the lines of incommensurability that are drawn by these "materialist" critics between their "real" world and the hyperreal world of Baudrillard. Norris channels the ghost of Thucydides (or at least his "potentialist realism" as expounded in J. Fisher Solomon's 1988 book, *Discourse and Reference in the Nuclear Ages*) to exorcise the "bad philosophy" of postmodernism which gives rise to an "anti-realism" and a "thoroughgoing nihilism."[34] My response to Norris returns to the sub-thesis of this essay, to ask whether the reproductive technologies, globalized contingency, and deracinations of identity in late capitalism have turned realism on its head, rendering the materialists into nostalgic idealists. Perhaps the best criticism of Norris and his ilk comes from the doctor of reality who would never settle on one philosophy, one method, one cure for the multiple ills of an unequally developing society:

My recreation, my preference, my *cure* from all Platonism has always been *Thucydides*. Thucydides and, perhaps, Machiavelli's *Principe* are most closely related to myself by the unconditional will not to gull oneself and to see reason in *reality* – not in "reason", still less in "morality' .... One must turn him over line by line and read his hidden thoughts. *Sophist culture*, by which I mean *realist culture*, attains in him its perfect expression . . . . *Courage* in face of reality ultimately distinguishes such natures as Thucydides and Plato: Plato is a coward in face of reality – consequently he flees into the ideal; Thucydides has himself under control – consequently he retains control over things . . . .[35]

HISTORY ENDS, SIMULATIONS BEGIN?

In the immediate aftermath of the Gulf War, it did seem that Lenin's *and* Baudrillard's worst scenarios had come true: the post-Cold War security state now had the technological edge of simulation as well as the ideological advantage of unipolarity to regenerate, at relatively low cost to itself, an ailing national prestige through foreign adventures. Strategic simulation could then be seen as the first step to chart the unknown territory left by a legacy of imperialism *and* the communist-nationalist reaction, of coming cold wars, trade wars, drug wars, that is, all the endo- as well as exo-colonial wars that threaten to refigure national identities and to undermine the international order. In a sense, Iraq served this purpose well, as the arch-foe which helped to redefine the West. But the effect proved strangely illusory and short-lived, for both the target and the weaponry aimed at it were third-order simulacra, model-based media constructions with lessons which seemed to disappear in the channel-surf of the next crisis. Since then, with the recalcitrance of Baghdad, Mogadishu, Sarajevo, and Port-au-Prince, to real *or* hyperreal solutions, it has become clear that neither imperialism nor simulation is as all-powerful or all-pervasive as Lenin and Baudrillard would have it. If, as Nietzsche divined, history is that which cannot be defined, the contingencies of late modernity by definition will continue to defy such global theories and meta-models.

Equally, the difficulties and maladies posed by the de-territorialization of state power and the disintegration of a bipolar order are likely to elude less radical, more traditional diagnosis, let alone cure. Peering into a future optimistically limned by Lenin and nihilistically disappeared by Baudrillard, I prefer to paraphrase the poets than face the double-vision prompted by these theorists:

Should every post-imperial state reach beyond its sovereign grasp
Or what's a hyperreality for?

Notes

1 Encore Computer Corporation, advertisement for the 13th Interservice/Industry Training Systems Conference.

2   Robert Murray, Head of the Center for Naval Analyses, "President" of the United States for the Naval War College Global War Game.

3   The problems generated by ephemeral post-Cold War borders have since passed on to the map-makers themselves: for the first time Rand McNally's *Today's World* atlas comes with a sticker that entitles the buyer to a free updated map should the atlas become outdated before Dec 31, 1993.

4   "Bush's Talk to Cadets: When 'Force Makes Sense' ", *The New York Times* (Jan 6, 1993), p. A6.

5   For a more complete account, see James Der Derian, "The Simulation Syndrome: From War Games to Game Wars," *Social Text*, 24 (1989) 187–92, from which this is drawn.

6   Published by McGraw Hill, 1987.

7   V. Lenin, *Selected Writings* (Moscow: Progress Publishers, 1977), p. 225.

8   Jean Baudrillard, *Simulations* (New York: Semiotext(e), 1983), p. 2.

9   See F. Nietzsche, *Twilight of the Idols*, pp. 40–1: and James Der Derian, "Techno-diplomacy," in *On Diplomacy: A Genealogy of Western Estrangement* (Oxford: Basil Blackwell, 1987), pp. 199–200.

10   Baudrillard, *Simulations*, p. 48.

11   See F. Kracauer, "Cult of Distraction: On Berlin's Picture Palaces," trans. T. Y. Levin, *New German Critique*, 40 (Winter 1987) 95; and Kracauer's *Das Ornament der Masse* (Frankfurt: Suhrkamp, 1963), forthcoming as *The Mass Ornament*, trans. and ed. T. Y. Levin (Cambridge: Harvard University Press).

12   See W. Benjamin, "The Work of Art in the Age of Mechanical Reproduction," in H. Arendt, ed., *Illuminations* (New York: Schocken, 1969), pp. 241–2.

13   See Guy Debord, *Society of the Spectacle* (Detroit: Black and Red Press, 1983), no. 1, pp. 1 and 23. In a more recent work, Debord persuasively – and somewhat despairingly – argues that the society of the spectacle retains its representational power in current times: see *Commentaires sur la societe du spectacle* (Paris: Editions Gerard Lebovici, 1988).

14   See Baudrillard, *Simulations*, p. 2. The original French version, *Simulacres et Simulation* (Paris: Galilée, 1981), has more on the simulacral nature of violence in cinema. See in particular his readings of *China Syndrome*, *Barry Lyndon*, *Chinatown*, and *Apocalypse Now*, pp. 69–91.

15   Lenin, *Selected Writings*, p. 632.

16   E. D. Cronon, *The Political Thought of Woodrow Wilson* (Indianapolis: Bobbs-Merril, 1965), pp. 482–4.

17   See *Fatal Strategies*, in *Jean Baudrillard: Selected Writings*, ed., Mark Poster (Stanford: Stanford University Press, 1988), p. 191.

18   A first take on the simulacral nature of the Gulf War can be found in my "Cyberwar, Videogames, and the Gulf War Syndrome," *Antidiplomacy* (Oxford: Blackwell, 1992), pp. 173–91.

19   I refer here to the form of representing criminality on *America's Most Wanted* where alleged crimes are re-enacted for the public benefit, and the docu-dramatizing of espionage on ABC primetime news with a stand-in for the alleged spy Felix Bloch handing over a briefcase to a KGB stand-in, both examples of a growing genre of truthful media simulations. There are as well the many commercially available war simulations. To name a few: from Navy simulations there is *Harpoon*, *Das Boot Submarine*, *Wolf Pack*, and *Silent*

Service II; from the Air Force, *Secret Weapons of the Luftwaffe*, *F-19 Stealth Fighter*, *A-10 Tank Killer*, and *F-15 Strike Eagle*; and for those seeking more serious global simulations, *Populous*, *Balance of Power*, *SimCity*, and *Global Dilemma*. On the heels of the Gulf War, war games like *Arabian Nightmare* (in which the player has the option to kill American reporters like Ted Koppel) and the *Butcher of Baghdad* were added to the list.

20   This war game differed from previous ones presented by Koppel (two on terrorism and one on nuclear war): there was not a pasha from Kissinger Associates in sight, and the talking heads barely had equal time with the video simulations. Constructed and narrated by the authors of the book *A Quick and Dirty Guide to War* and the war game *Arabian Nightmare*, the program featured stock clips of war exercises, computer simulations of bombing runs, many maps, and a day-by-day pull-down menu of escalating events. The post-game commentary (known in the ranks as a "hot wash-up") was conducted by two military analysts armed with pointers, James Blackwell and Harry Summers, Jr. They ended with a split decision – and a final cautionary note that "no plan survives contact with the enemy."

21   Simulations in this context could be broadly defined here as the continuation of war by means of verisimilitude, which range from analytical games that use broad descriptions and a minimum of mathematical abstraction to make generalizations about the behavior of actors, to computerized models that use algorithms and high resolution graphics to analyze and represent the amount of technical detail considered necessary to predict events and the behavior of actors.

22   See J. Albright, "Army Mastermind Stays Ahead of the 'Game,' " *Atlantic Constitution* (Oct 25, 1990), p. 1.

23   See T. Allen, *War Games* (New York: McGraw Hill, 1987), p. 4; and ABC *Nightline* transcript (Sept 26, 1990), p. 3.

24   Two excellent criticisms of the internal assumptions of gaming can be found in a review of the literature by R. Ashley, "The Eye of Power: The Politics of World Modeling," *International Organization*, 37, 3 (Summer 1983); and R. Hurwitz, "Strategic and Social Fictions in the Prisoner's Dilemma," in *International/Intertextual Relations*, pp. 113–34.

25   C. Andrews and O. Gordievsky, *KGB: The Inside Story* (New York: Harper Collins, 1991), pp. 583–605; and conversation with Gordievsky, Nov 7–9, 1991, Toronto, Canada.

26   The art of deterrence, prohibiting political war, favors the upsurge, not of conflicts, but of acts of war without war. See Paul Virilio, *Pure War* (New York: Semiotext(e), 1983), p. 27.

27   If we subtract the number of Allied soldiers (the Iraqi dead never "figured") killed by "friendly fire," there were more casualties in the war exercises leading up to "G-Day" (the beginning of the ground war) than during the war itself.

28   Todd Gitlin, "Theory in Wartime: An Interview with Todd Gitlin," *Linguafranca* (Feb 1991), p. 26. For more on the failure of radical critics to get the war right, see Der Derian, "Cyberwar, Videogames, and the Gulf War Syndrome," pp. 173–91.

29　"Orientalism and After: An Interview with Edward Said," *Radical Philosophy*, 63 (Spring 1993) 32.

30　Christopher Norris, *Uncritical Theory: Postmodernism, Intellectuals, and the Gulf War* (London: Lawrence and Wishart, 1992).

31　Ibid., p. 11.

32　Jean Baudrillard, "The Gulf War Has Not Taken Place," *The Guardian* (March 29, 1991).

33　Ibid., p. 193.

34　See Norris, *Uncritical Theory*, pp. 190–1; and J. Fisher Solomon, *Discourse and Reference in the Nuclear Age* (Norman and London: University of Oklahoma Press, 1988).

35　Nietzsche, *Twilight of the Idols*, pp. 106–7.

10

AESTHETIC PRODUCTION AND CULTURAL POLITICS: BAUDRILLARD AND CONTEMPORARY ART

—

Timothy W. Luke

Jean Baudrillard has exerted unusual influence in the fields of art, aesthetics, and cultural production during the 1980s and 1990s. The breadth of his acceptance is unusual given how Baudrillard, in a sense, not only replays Hegel's notion of "the end of art," but also foretells, in another sense, "the end of culture" in the realm of the transaesthetic, the transpolitical and the transeconomic. None the less, Baudrillard's work on simulation, seduction, and hyperreality in the 1980s reverberated strongly among various artist communities, while it also enjoyed an enthusiastic reception in the art criticism network. On one level, some of this can be attributed to Baudrillard's personal celebrity, but, on another level, these influences also can be chalked up to a growing awareness of how the highly charged televisual and cybernetic imagery now driving the processes of informationalization is affecting aesthetic awareness. This study will discuss Baudrillard's analysis of these developments at the end of art as well as how and why his views on these trends became influential in the sphere of artistic production and presentation. In addition, I examine the value of Baudrillard's notions of simulation and hyperreality for theory and practice.

BAUDRILLARD AND THE ART WORLD

In the 1980s, Baudrillard was embraced as an icon in the artistic community as performance, mass media, and studio artists all worked the themes of simulation, hyperreality, and implosion into their works.[1] Even though Baudrillard explicitly disassociated himself from these somewhat mechanical invocations of his ideas by movements like neo-geo simulationist art, a number of painters, appropriation artists, sculptors, and performance artists, ranging from Peter Halley, Sherrie Levine, Jenny Holzer, Ashley Bickerton, and Allan McCollum to Jeff Koons, Haim Steinbach, Simon Linke, Robert Longo, and Barbara Kruger, explicitly or implicitly were seen as expressing aspects of Baudrillard's critical reading of contemporary society. Peter Halley, for instance, declared that his bright, neo-formalist abstractions of cells, flow, and circuits, like *Blue Cell with Triple Conduit* (1986) or *Two Cells with Organizing Conduit* (1986), were significant artistic summations of Baudrillard's simulationist philosophies, while Jeff Koons parodic duplicates of kitsch objects, like *Jim Beam J. B. Turner Train* (1986) or *Bear and Policeman* (1988), have been assessed as complicitous nods toward Baudrillard's notions of the obscene and fatal strategy.[2] Similarly, the insidious play of signs, which many artists saw Baudrillard revealing in his work, can be witnessed in Jenny Holzer's, David Salle's, or Barbara Kruger's aestheticization of slogans, words, or advertisements.

Even though Baudrillard himself openly disavowed any responsibility for these aesthetic initiatives, the rediscovery of Baudrillardian qualities in the art production and consumption of the 1980s and 1990s has not ended. Whether he accepts responsibility or not, Baudrillard's rhetoric of simulation, hyperreality, and seduction enchanted artists in the 1980s, as they began experimenting widely with appropriated images, simulated poses, and materialized hyperrealities. Art critic Suzi Gablik, for example, tracks Baudrillard's influence into the art of the 1980s by bracketing its ironies and solipsisms. She notes, for example,

> with Simon Linke's paintings of commercial gallery advertisements copied straight from the pages of *Artforum*, we cannot really know if this is radical criticism or inspired clowning. . . . Declaring its pointlessness openly, his art baits us with its indifference; the artist openly adopts the posture of a chariation, a sort of trickster who is not going to get us out of the mess we're in, but who will engage in the only legitimate cultural practice possible for our time, which is, in the words of Baudrillard, "the chance, the labyrinthine, manipulatory play of signs without meaning."[3]

Here, Baudrillard's sense of the liquidation of referentiality is keyed directly into the vocabularies of contemporary art criticism.

In his own way, Baudrillard was on to something in the 1980s and 1990s that artists recognized in their own apprehensions about art. His writings echo the questions raised by artists and art critics in the 1980s and 1990s about finding any sort of meaning in contemporary artistic representations. Baudrillard's vision of the political economy of the sign, as many contemporary artists realize, also defines the political economy of the contemporary art world. As Carrier observes, "in the modern art market nothing matters about an art work except that it can be such-and-such a sign . . . in the art market, all works are signs, objects which refer to their exchange value in that market."[4] The impact of mass media on individuals, art audiences, and artistic creation itself are addressed in many artists' minds by Baudrillard's vision of the hyperreal and simulation; hence, appropriating the tropes of simulation and/or aggravating everyone's unease about hyperreality became salient strategies in the art world. Given the prominence of aesthetic observations in his social theorizing as well as the significance attached to his writings by artists, let us review Baudrillard's views of the role played by art in today's cultural politics.

INFORMATIONALIZATION: SIMULATION AND HYPERREALITY

In many ways, Baudrillard's analysis of contemporary cultural politics through art is both complex and confusing. Yet, in a sense, he simply toys, over and over again, with a familiar banal paradox: does art imitate life or does life imitate art? The kicker, of course, is how does he decode the qualities of the art and/or life being imitated as well as what art-forms and life-forms can be re-read to reveal whatever insights this paradox might hold? Baudrillard provides a schematic overview of life, and how it has been changed by the workings of hyperreality that, in turn, affords him the opportunity to inventively reinterpret various aesthetic formations – the World Trade Center, the Beaubourg Museum, Andy Warhol's Campbell's soup can duplicates, or Disneyland – as definitive registers of the implosive transformations he sees at play in today's advanced capitalist societies.

After an epoch of explosive growth, Baudrillard holds that advanced capitalist society now is experiencing an implosive reversal in the circulation of power between the masses and organized institutions. Traditionally, Baudrillard argues "capital only had to produce goods; consumption ran by itself. Today it is necessary to produce consumers, to produce demand, and this production is infinitely more costly than that of goods."[5] As individual desires are autonomized abstractly into pre-packaged needs that serve as productive forces, the social lifeworld devolves into fluid aggregates of atomized individuals, whose roles are to mediate the packaged meaning of their desires in the corporate marketplace. The traditional forms of attaining both individuality and the social, collapse under these conditions. Baudrillard concludes that individual subjects "are only episodic conductors of meaning, for in the main, and profoundly, we *form a mass*, living most of the time in panic or haphazardly, above and beyond any meaning."[6]

Today's posthistorical social mass, at the same time, is neither a subject nor an object. It bears no relation to any historical social referent – a class, a nation, a folk, or the proletariat. Instead, it is often no more than a statistical entity whose only traces appear in the social survey or opinion poll. The silent majorities of the masses perhaps are no longer representable in realist political terms or concretely identifiable in realistic social terms.

The ordinarily assumed "ontological givens" taken for granted by epistemic realism essentially evaporate, according to Baudrillard, in the blackholes of this cyberspace. The complex coding of the media all across the global marketplace set the outer boundaries of the social mass in that "it only exists at the point of convergence of all the media waves which depict it."[7] As a result, every dimension of contemporary social existence essentially becomes a complex simulation of reality, designed specifically to sustain the fragile cycles of political, economic, and cultural reproduction, in which signs of the real take the place of reality itself.

Obviously, modernity itself changes along with the development of this type of advanced capitalist exchange as it becomes more entwined within the informational modes of production.[8] A new reality logic based upon simulation rather than representation constitutes the dominant organizing principle of this new era. Therefore, in Baudrillard's vision of today's new world order, "McLuhan's formula, *the medium is the message*," appropriately is "the key formula of the era of simulation (the medium is the message – the sender is the receiver – the circularity of all polls – the end of panoptic and perspectival space – such is the alpha and omega of *our* modernity."[9] Yet, if the masses no longer act as traditional historical subjects in their new posthistorical habitat, then what happens to their accustomed cultural context, namely, the modern nation-state, industrial economy, liberal democracy, and enlightenment culture?

In the final analysis, Baudrillard claims that what is taken as society by what are regarded as individuals now runs on "a logic of simulation which has nothing to do with a logic of facts and an order of reasons."[10] How can this be? To answer, maybe one needs to look, as Jameson asserts, at the rare, the unusual, and interesting, "for shifts and irrevocable changes in the *representation* of things and of the way they change."[11] Given these criteria, Baudrillard asks, why not look at Disneyland for answers? The power of Disneyland, as its self-defined "imagineers" proclaim, rests in the fusion of its symbolic imaginaries with sophisticated material design and complex process engineering. As Baudrillard notes, "simulation is characterized by a *precession of the model*, of all models around the merest fact – models come first, and the orbital (like the bomb) circulation constitutes the genuine magnetic field of events."[12] The model is the medium, and it becomes the message. So, as Baudrillard suggests, the continuously felt effects of Disney imagineering arise from "concealing that reality no more exists outside than inside the bounds of the artificial perimeter."[13] In his account, Disneyland "the fantasy" exists to induce belief that America, which is, in fact, "the hyperreality," is *real*.

Disneyland is there to conceal the fact that it is the "real" country, all of "real" America, which *is* Disneyland (just as prisons are there to conceal the fact that it is the social in its entirety, in its banal omnipresence, which is carceral). Disneyland is presented as imaginary in order to make us believe that the rest is real, when in fact all of Los Angeles and the America surrounding it are no longer real, but of the order of the hyperreal and of simulation. It is no longer a question of a false representation of reality (ideology), but of concealing the fact that the real is no longer real, and thus of saving the reality principle.[14]

Thus, Disneyland orbitally enforces the prevailing models of international cultural simulation where the *cultural* and the *economic* "collapse back into each other and say the same thing."[15] When all is said and done in contemporary culture, "the Disneyland imaginary is neither true nor false; it is a deterrence machine set up in order to rejuvenate in reverse the fiction of the real."[16]

Baudrillard also suggests that the means of information in today's global transnational economy unhinge traditional metaphorical relations, because the operative semiotic principles of this informational order are those of simulation rather than pre-industrial counterfeit or industrial mechanical reproduction.[17] Abstractions can no longer be seen as "the maps," "the doubles," "the mirrors," or "the concepts" of any terrain metaphorically regarded as "the real." On the contrary, all abstract frames of the real effectively function only as simulations. For Baudrillard, "simulation is no longer that of a territory, a referential being or a substance. It is the generation by models of a real without origin or a reality: a hyperreal. The territory no longer precedes the map, nor survives it. Henceforth, it is the map that precedes the territory – PRECESSION OF SIMULACRA – it is the map that engenders the territory . . . ."[18] In this hyperspace, something very important has disappeared, namely, what always was the ineluctable non-identity of map and terrain. Therefore, a provisional hyperontology of sorts, which Baudrillard is more than willing to provide, must somehow define and describe what now "is" beyond epistemic realism's perspectival space and neutral time.[19]

To understand hyperreality, Baudrillard argues, one must see everything anew:

> No more mirror of being and appearances, of the real and its concept. No more imaginary coextensity: rather, genetic miniaturization is the dimension of simulation. The real is produced from miniaturized units, from matrices, memory banks and command models – and with these it can be reproduced an infinite numbers of times. It no longer has to be rational, since it is no longer measured against some ideal or negative instance. It is nothing more than operational. In fact, since it is no longer enveloped by an imaginary, it is no longer real at all. It is a hyperreal, the product of an irradiating synthesis of combinatory models in a hyperspace without atmosphere.[20]

The simulation system of hyperreality, in the last analysis, rises from this elimination of the representational differences between true and false, concept and object, real and representation, much like the unrelenting flow of 24-hour television headline news which creates unstable stylized narratives to report "what is true" by merging videotaped reality and cable feed representation in an electron haze.

Simulation rests upon absence and negation, eliminating "the real" or "the true" by emulating their appearances as ontological givens. Actually, as Baudrillard suggests,

> ... [the] age of simulation thus begins with a liquidation of all referentials
> – worse: by their artificial resurrection in systems of signs, a more ductile
> material than meaning in that it lends itself to all systems of equivalence, all
> binary oppositions, and all combinatory algebra. It is no longer a question
> of imitation, nor of reduplication, nor even of parody. It is rather a question
> of substituting signs of the real for the real itself, that is, an operation to
> deter every real process by its operational double, a metastable, program-
> matic, perfect descriptive machine which provides all the signs of the real
> and short-circuits all its vicissitudes .... A hyperreal therefore is sheltered
> from the real and the imaginary, leaving room only for the orbital recurrent
> of models and the simulated generation of difference.[21]

The system of simulation destroys the ontological bases "realist" or "modern" representation as the equivalence of the object and concept, real and abstract, referent and sign. While systems of representation may endeavor to appropriate simulation as false representation, the dynamics of simulation turn any and all representations into simulacra, reducing the sign to a free radical capable of bonding anywhere in any exchange. These shifts in the sign constitute the critical juncture in maintaining the "hyperreal" collective order that transnational capitalism has brought to its many customers and clients today. Basically, Baudrillard now claims,

> When the real is no longer what it used to be, nostalgia assumes it full
> meaning. There is a proliferation of myths of origin and signs of reality; of
> second-hand truth, objectivity and authenticity. There is an escalation of the
> true, of the lived experience; a resurrection of the figurative when the object
> and substance have disappeared and there is a panic-stricken production of
> the real and the referential, above and parallel to the panic of material
> production: this is how simulation appears in the phase that concerns us –
> a strategy of the real, neo-real and hyperreal whose universal double is a
> strategy of deterrence.[22]

The practical mediations of generating hyperreality, as Baudrillard appraises it, are the electronic media knitting together the posthistorical flows of informational societies.

Likewise, for art and artists, the coherence of aesthetic representations boils away in these cultural implosions. Traditional notions of causality, perspective, and reasoning are undercut completely by the electronic means of information, which efface the difference between cause and effect, ends and means, subject and object, active and passive. Yet, without these differences, the rationality of epistemic realism is left adrift. Baudrillard observes, "we must think of the media as if they were, in outer orbit, a sort of genetic code which controls the mutation of the real into the hyperreal, just as the other, micro-molecular code controls the passage of the signal from a representative sphere of meaning to the genetic sphere of the programmed signal."[23] Simulation goes beyond the distinctions of space and time, sender and receiver, medium and message, expression and content as the world's complex webs of electronic media generate unbound(ed)-aries of new hyperspaces with "no sense of place."

MAKING ART AND ART OBJECTS TESTIFY

Baudrillard's willingness to see power, art, and sexuality in play every-where and anywhere gives his aesthetic thinking both an unusual range and a frustrating limit. Like Levi-Strauss, Debord, Barthes, Bataille, Kristeva, and Lefebvre before him, Baudrillard in his early work approaches the symbolic and mythic dimensions of society as a realm constructed and maintained by the play of capital and power. This disposition to cite artistic objects or aesthetic productions as indicators of larger social ten-sions or political agendas is foreshadowed in his early works on the soci-ology of objects and the systems of mass consumption, *Le système des objects* and *La société de consummation*.[24] As he asserts in *For a Criti-que of the Political Economy of the Sign*, consumer goods with all of their objective shapes, semiotic syntax, and collective rhetoric "refer to social objectives and to a social logic. They speak to us not so much of the user and of technical practices, as of social pretension and resignation, of social mobility and inertia, of acculturation and enculturation, of strati-fication and of social classification."[25] Thus, art works, art markets, and art consumers, especially as they interact in social, political, and economic terms, provide suggestive sites for him to articulate his claims about the political economy of the sign or the culture of consumption. Their testimo-ny, in turn, becomes one of the few bodies of evidence used by Baudrillard to advance his theoretical critiques.

There are two essays devoted explicitly to art and art world practices in *Critique* that indicate this side of Baudrillard's engagement with art. The first, "Gesture and Signature: The Semiurgy of Contemporary Art" exam-ines how signed art works as well as unique stylistic gestures conduct sign-value that translates into art submitting to both commercial and semiotic integration with the existing world. While modern art aspires to be nega-tive, challenging, radical, "one must surrender to the evidence: art no longer contests anything, if it ever did. Revolt is isolated, malediction

'consumed.' "[26] Art, then, is not the free creation of autonomous producers who express criticism or liberation in creative works. Instead, all art
works simply become another iteration in an individual diachronic series
of variations, differentiated in style, gesture, theme, that gets meaning,
value, and identity from the seriality of their production.

In the second essay, "The Art Auction: Sign Exchange and Sumptuary
Value," Baudrillard examines how expediture and agonistic competition
for art works recharges the existing political economy of value by creating
an economy of sumptuary values. Mastery of the process of signification
in closed rituals, like the art auction, allows the hegemonic class to produce
the surplus value of domination by defining the relative dearness of sign
values. Thus, "the essential function of the auction is the institution of a
community of the privileged who define themselves as such by agonistic
speculation upon a restricted corpus of signs."[27] Within the workings of
art auctions, Baudrillard thought he found a fulcrum needed to move the
world toward cultural revolution by advocating the development of "a
political economy of the sign." "Only such a critique," he claims, "can
analyze how at the very heart of the economic the mode of domination
reinvents (or reproduces) the logic and the strategy of signs, of castes, of
segregation, and of discrimination; how it reinstates the feudal logic of
personal relations or even that of the gift exchange and of reciprocity, or
of agonistic exchange – in order simultaneously to thwart and crown the
'modern' socio-economic logic of class."[28]

After these forays, Baudrillard continually returns to art or aesthetic
themes to comment upon revealing manifestations of larger social crises or
political conflicts. Art often serves as his most compelling "evidence," cited
in his peculiar readings of art works as supports for this or that claim, or
definitive "text," sited in his interpretive visions as the cultural resources
that social theorists must scan for new understandings of what must be
done. Yet, this use of art often proves dissatisfying inasmuch as he often
presents little more than an idiosyncratic description of an event, object,
or practice, leaving his peculiar re-readings as an "explanation" for some
major social transformation. This mirroring, however, is only a mirroring.
Its testimony immerses itself in appearance to the point of simulating or
hyperrealizing what must be represented or realized to be compelling.
While he claims all theory must do this to shake the effects of living under
today's extreme circumstances, it ultimately fails.

THE BEAUBOURG EFFECT

Baudrillard's interpretations of the ultra-modernist Pompidou Center in
Paris typify his metaphysical turn toward cooking up a conceptual gumbo
as critique. The text itself centers upon decoding the object; yet, the decoding

reads out through multiple genres of commentary. Part sociology, part art criticism, part literature, part personal musings, part politics, part architectural review, "The Beauborg Effect" displays the Pompidou Center as a contradictory cultural site that embodies the exposed pipes, ducts, and circuits of high industrial modernism as it ironically generates hyperreal effects.[29] Thus, on one level, the Beaubourg might be regarded as a corpse of an already sublated mode of industrial production, while, on another level, the figuration of the carcass suggests the flux and flow of informational modes of communication.

Baudrillard captures this indeterminacy in his initial framing of the object:

> Beaubourg-Effect ... Beaubourg Machine ... Beaubourg-*Thing* – how can we name it? The puzzle of this carcass of signs and flux, of networks and circuits ... the ultimate gesture toward translation of an unnamable structure: that of social relations consigned to a system of surface ventilation (animation, self-regulation, information, media) and an in-depth, irreversible implosion. A monument to mass simulation effects, the Center functions like an incinerator, absorbing and devouring all cultural energy, rather like the black monolith of *2001* – a mad convection current for the materialization, absorption, and destruction of all the contents within it.[30]

Baudrillard frequently claims metonymy is obsolete, and his reading of art objects or aesthetic formations, like the Pompidou Center, underscores these assertions with an example of radical implosion – neutralizing the social, art, the masses, and meaning in one architecturalized aesthetic negation. The Beaubourg's presence constitutes "a monument to total disconnection, to hyper-reality, and the cultural implosion actually created by transistor networks continually threatened by a huge short-circuit."[31]

Thus, if one reinterprets such aesthetic formations accurately, some sense of the current crisis is revealed, albeit in an increasingly metaphysical manner. In the twin towers of the World Trade Center, for example, Baudrillard uncovers the fact that "signifies the end of all competition, the end of all original reference ... they signify only that the strategy of models and commutations wins out in the very heart of the system itself – and New York really is the heart of it – over the traditional strategy of competition."[32] Whereas the edifice of Rockefeller Center or the Chase Manhattan Bank building still pretend to suggest a competitive stance, the World Trade Center is the penultimate binary sign, opening and closing "on the number two, just as if architecture, in the image of the system, proceeded only from an unchangeable genetic code, a definitive model."[33]

Again, for Baudrillard, art imitates life. The nub of this banal insight is that it is neither life as we have known it nor art as it may have been formed by its creators. The gestalt of the Beaubourg is not modernity rendered museumological, but rather the hieroglyphic summation of what lies beyond the modern. Hence, "this space of deterrence, linked to the ideology of visibility, transparency, polyvalence, consensus, contact, and sanctioned by the threat of security, is virtually that of all social relations today. The whole of social discourse is there, and on both this level and that of cultural manipulation."[34]

The deterrent design of existence, as it is crystallized in the Beaubourg, anticipates and reacts to any possible threat to these hyperrealities. Every effort is made to assure, through continual simulations of all possible eventualities, that nothing will ever be left to chance. Therefore, one sees a purposeful substitution of the signs of the real for reality itself; and, as a result, "reality no longer has the time to take on the appearance of reality. It no longer even surpasses faction: it captures every dream even before it takes on the appearance of a dream. The cool universe of digitality has absorbed the world of metaphor and metonymy."[35] These tendencies on the global level also recapitulate their efforts on the individual level inasmuch as "the same model of planned infallibility, of maximal security and deterrence, now governs the spread of the social,"[36] throughout the networks of social control enforced by this deterrent engineering of existence.

Therefore, an aesthetic site or artistic formation often becomes Baudrillard's instantiation of the elective affinities, binding what passes for "society" together by imploding traditional social relations. In the Beaubourg, he sees "the model of all future forms of controlled 'socialization;' the retotalization of all the dispersed functions of the body and of social life (work, leisure, media, culture) within a single, homogeneous space-time; it is the retranscription of all contradictory movements in terms of integrated circuits. It is the space-time of the whole operational simulation of social life."[37] As an apparatus to impulsively circulate the masses within, among, through stockpiles of aesthetic objects, the Beaubourg produces masses in *"that space of ever greater density into which everything societal is imploded and ground up in an uninterrupted process of simulation."*[38]

Yet, this implosive mass also can become a critical mass. Not content to see the masses merely circulating continuously forever, Baudrillard foresees the masses bearing a potential for violent change simply in being numerous, dense, and chaotic. Since the Beaubourg has been engineered to hold only 30,000 people, the more massive its "mass production" becomes, then one can argue a "production of the masses," from simply having individuals show up *en masse*, becomes a disruptive radical event. The fragile presence of the building suggests disaster waiting to happen, and the masses stampede to it and through it, hoping to make it happen.

The only act, as such, that the mass(es) can produce is the stampede – a projective mass, defying the edifice of mass culture, defiantly responds to the culturalism promoted by Beaubourg by means of its own weight, its most meaningless, stupid, least cultural aspect. In defiance of a mass indoctrination into a sterile culture, the crowd replies with a burst of destruction extended as brute physical manipulation. Thus to mental deterrence the crowd responds with physical deterrence. This is the mass's own form of defiance. Its tactic is to reply in the same terms in which it is solicited, but beyond that, to respond to the simulation within which it is confined by a social enthusiasm which outstrips its objects and functions as a destructive hypersimulation.[39]

In this disposition, then, the Beaubourg also provides a site for producing the mass(es) while it devotes it internal spaces to the eternal values used to promote a traditional culture of an aesthetically-sensitive individual(ity) subject(ivity).

THE TRANSAESTHETIC

More recently, however, Baudrillard has bracketed the entire possibility of aesthetics, conflating politics, sexuality, and art in the broadbands of the transpolitical, the transsexual, and the transaesthetic that marks today's "state of utter confusion."[40] While there continues to be aesthetic production, spinning on virally, radiantly, fractally in the continually recycling of past and present styles, there are no grounds for articulating anything like traditional aesthetics. Art circulates continually at top speed, but a bizarre mix of contradictory styles – neo-geometrism, neo-abstraction, neo-expressionism, neo-representationalism, neo-primitivism, neo-modernism – coexist amidst nearly complete indifference. Everything has an aesthetic dimension, everyone is transfigured by aestheticizing processes, everywhere is beset by the aesthetic orgy of all representational and anti-representational possibilities. Hence, Baudrillard asserts "art is gone . . . there are no fundamental rules, no more criteria of judgement or of pleasure . . . or, to use a different metaphor, there is no gold standard of aesthetic judgement or pleasure."[41]

At this juncture, Baudrillard posits that the revolution once dreamed about by all of the movements of the 1960s has happened, but it did not turn out as expected. Instead, everything everywhere is being liberated "so that it can enter a state of pure circulation, so that it can go into orbit. With the benefit of a little hindsight, we may say that the unavoidable goal of all liberation is to foster and provision circulatory networks."[42] With this general liberation, however, there is a general proliferation of everything that overwhelms traditional logics of value, once described by Baudrillard as the natural, commodity, and structural stages, within the fractal stage. Here and now, "there is no point of reference at all, and value radiates in all directions, occupying all interstices, without reference to anything whatsoever, by virtue of sure contiguity. At the fractal stage, there is no longer any equivalence, whether natural or general. Properly speaking there is now no law of value, merely a sort of *epidemic of value*, a sort of general metastasis of value, a haphazard proliferation and dispersion of value."[43]

Caught in these webs of excess signification, one also sees the eclipse of appearances in realist scenes by disappearances, obscenity, hyperrealism. When plenitude brings forth the void, for Baudrillard, "that's the obscene."[44] In the realm of the transaesthetic, the transpolitical, the transeconomic, the totality of reality washes out as a pornographic hyperreality that boils down to "the obscenity of everything tirelessly filmed, filtered, revised and corrected under the wide angle of the social, morality, and information."[45] Although Baudrillard gets carried away with his paradoxes, often claiming obscenity is more visible than the visible without exactly explaining how this might work, he also sees obscenity deriving from too much meaning, overexposure, or too much saturation.

For culture and politics, the obscene marks the exhausted end of anything once recognizable as culture or politics. When weighted in against his metaphysical reading of the present, very little survives intact. Baudrillard, in fact, becomes quite succinct about this side of the transpolitics or transaesthetics. First, "when everything is political, it is the end of politics as destiny, and the beginning of politics as culture, and the immediate destitution of this political culture."[46] Secondly, "when everything becomes cultural, it is the end of culture as destiny, and the beginning of culture as politics, and the immediate destitution of this cultural politics."[47] Finally, he contends, "and so it goes for the social, history, the economy, and sex."[48]

This alleged fractalization of everything elicits a new microphysics to Baudrillard, but, in fact, it trumps ordinary existence and consciousness with a new metaphysics of disappearance. Now, as Baudrillard surveys the world,

> it is as impossible to make estimations between beautiful and ugly, true and false, or good and evil, as it is simultaneously to calculate a particle's speed and position. Good is no longer the opposite of evil, nothing can now be plotted on a graph or analysed in terms of abscissas and ordinates. Just as each particle follows its own trajectory, each value or fragment of value shines for a moment in the heavens of simulation, then disappears into the void along a crooked path that only rarely happens to intersect with other such paths. This is the pattern of the fractal – and hence the current pattern of our culture.[49]

Given this position, it is tough to believe in aesthetics any longer as an emancipatory or moralistic discourse of interpreting good and evil, beauty and ugliness, truth or falsity, virtue and vice. Still, Baudrillard sees a strange inertia enveloping everything, even as everything can no longer be either understood or judged. Somehow, in this purported vacuum of calculation, he asserts that fractalization is both stable and efficient. That is, "when things, signs or actions are freed from their respective ideas, concepts, essences, values, points of reference, origins and aims, they embark upon an endless process of self-reproduction. Yet things continue to function long after their ideas have disappeared, and they do so in total indifference to their own content. The paradoxical fact is that they function even better under these circumstances."[50]

THE END OF ART

Art provides, however, no exception to this strange rule. Since it failed to realize the utopian aspiration of modernity and become a realized ideal lifeworld, "art has been dissolved within a general aesthetization of everyday life, giving way to a pure circulation of images, a transaesthetics of banality."[51] Entering the transaesthetic realm, we actually are immersed in a general operationalization of art that has materialized aesthetics as an intense, nonstop semiurgic frenzy. Thanks to the accessible artistic possibilities of computers, video technology, electronic instruments, everyone is, or potentially can be, "a creator." Under these conditions, we do not destroy images. Instead, "we manufacture a profusion of images *in which there is nothing to see* .... They leave no trace, cast no shadow, and have no consequences."[52] Because they conceal nothing and reveal nothing, their negative intensity simply underscores how we have been released "from the need to decide between beautiful and ugly, between real and unreal, between transcendence and immanence."[53]

Of course, this sounds impossible. But, Baudrillard does not let his philosophical critique come to a completely dead stop this far out in cold indifference. Even though we may well become diffident beyond our loss of once stable codes of beauty, goodness, and truth, there are supposedly new pleasures of hyperrealist excitement lying beyond realist systems of artistic judgment. So, another kind of fascination displaces aesthetic pleasures in the transaesthetic realm:

> For, once liberated from their respective constraints, the beautiful and the ugly, in a sense, multiply: they become more beautiful than beautiful, more ugly than ugly. Thus painting currently cultivates, if not ugliness exactly – which remains an aesthetic value – then the uglier-than-ugly (the "bad", the "worse", kitsch), an ugliness raised to the second power because it is liberated from any relationship with its opposite. Once freed from the "true" Mondrian, we are at liberty to "out-Mondrian Mondrian"; freed from the true *naifs*, we can paint in a way that is "more *naif* than *naif*", and so on. And once freed from reality, we can produce the "realer than real" – hyperrealism.[54]

In turn, prices on the art markets escalate to hyperreal levels, but, as Baudrillard cautions us, there is nothing immoral going on here. Instead, a fascination beyond good and evil with unconstrained speculation follows from watching the buying and selling of art works that are beyond beautiful and ugly.

In his early works, Baudrillard maintained his stance as a revolutionary critic intent upon directing theory against society in some project of radical resistance. After his *L'échange symbolique et la mort*, however, he plainly adopts a new persona devoted to divining the mysteries of the provocative new metaphysics he discovers in ecstatic communication.[55] Seeing that his previous attempts "to grasp objects as a system already went a little way towards disrupting the traditional view of things," his most recent work looks at "object-passions" or "object-situations" which "is ultimately a question of metaphysics."[56] This essentialist turn, however, is extremely problematic inasmuch as his metaphysics becomes bogged down in his ritually reading reality through a panoply of binary oppositions that end up favoring image over substance, seduction against production, obscene before scene.

On the one hand, Baudrillard actually sees himself appraising object-passions in terms of their "purity," "passions," and "possibilities." Hence, he denies being "a philosopher, in the sense of being interested in arguments or terminology"[57] in order to be a medium of/for the object. In this mode, Baudrillard devotes himself to "the object, the pure object, the pure event, something no longer with an preuse origin or end, to which the subject would like to attribute an origin and an end even though it has none, and which today perhaps begins to give account of itself. Perhaps there is now the possibility that the object will say something to us, but above all the possibility that it will avenge itself."[58] By moving to this new stance, Baudrillard forsakes any prospect of revolutionary critique and embraces the mission of a metaphysician disclosing the mysteries of what he sees as truly "what is" the substance of reality.

Regrettably, however, as Kellner notes, these readings seem to be projections of his own subjective vision over objective situations. The impasse that Baudrillard works himself into here is indeed a fatal turn for his stance as a social theorist:

> Desiring to seduce and to be seduced, he projects seduction onto the being of objects. Desiring sovereignty, he projects sovereignty onto objects. Desiring revenge, he projects revenge onto objects. Supremely ironic, Baudrillard projects objective irony onto objects. Desiring to become a destiny and fatality himself – recall Nietzsche for the psychological roots of this peculiar lust – he ascribes destiny and fatality to objects, and conjures up a fatal universe. Increasingly indifferent to the fate of society and his fellow human beings, Baudrillard ascribes indifference to that supreme object of objects, the masses. Himself impatient, he ascribes impatience to the masses and to

the object world. Losing critical energy and growing apathetic himself, he ascribes apathy and inertia to the universe.[59]

The seductions of the transaesthetic, transsexual, transpolitical, trans-economic, (ob)scene, then, are mostly metaphysic. Unable to illustrate how such tendencies operate in reality, Baudrillard goes one better in hyperreality by ontologizing them into metaphysical fatality that marks the end of culture.

At the end of the day, however, the metaphysical posture that Baudrillard adopts leaves one, ironically, with the straight choice of either taking or leaving his insights. Yet, in doing so, one often also is left feeling taken or lost. By substituting jarring pronunciamentoes for engaging analysis, Baudrillard consciously shifts away from re-evaluating the texture of reality with a morally outraged engagement of critical negativity. Although this was the "pious vow" of the Enlightenment, still embraced by too many contemporary intellectuals in Baudrillard's view, he sees himself going beyond this commitment, forging a new kind of theory in which the theorizing evaluator essentially is, or becomes, the event. That is:

> It is not enough for theory to describe and analyse, it must itself be an event in the universe it describes. In order to do this theory must partake of and become the acceleration of this logic. It must tear itself from all referents and take pride only in the future. Theory must operate on time at the cost of a deliberate distortion of present reality.[60]

For Baudrillard, social theorizing turns into Baudrillard's diaries, Baudrillard driving across America, Baudrillard's interviews, or Baudrillard cruising academic conferences to discover the right kind of theoretical event venues.[61] And, at these new venues, Baudrillard presents theory with new goals:

> . . . the function of theory is certainly not to reconcile it, but on the contrary, to seduce, to wrest things from their condition, to force them into an over-existence which is incompatible with that of the real . . . it must become simulation if it speaks about simulation, and deploy the same strategy as its object. If it speaks about seduction, theory must become seducer, and deploy the same stratagems. If it no longer aspires to a discourse of truth, theory must assume the form of a world from which truth has withdrawn.[62]

Baudrillard takes this stance, because he believes that theory always is "destined to be diverted, deviated, and manipulated."[63]

Since he believes it would be better for theory to divert itself, than be diverted from itself, he calls upon all theory producers and consumers to: "Let us be Stoics." That is, "If the world is fatal, let us be more fatal than it. If it is indifferent, let us be more indifferent. We must conquer the world and seduce it through an indifference that is at least equal to the world's."[64] Unfortunately, by refusing to ground his arguments in sustained social analysis, as he once did in his early works on the anthropology of consumption or the political economy of the sign, Baudrillard diminishes the overall credibility of this style of social theorizing. Yet, he also will not reconcile himself to continuing the naive epistemic realism deployed in conventional social science analysis. Baudrillard recoils from such genres of social theorizing, because "it is here that language and theory alter their meaning. Instead of acting as a mode of production, they act as a mode of disappearance . . . . This enigmatic game is no longer that of analysis; it seeks to preserve this enigma of the object through the enigma of discourse."[65]

If one accepts Baudrillard's pronouncements, there is little that can be said for or about art. In a strange way, Baudrillard, like Hegel, sees an ending of art. Art as a utopian moment or an instance of potential liberation, in Baudrillard's vision, completely dissolves away in the diverting, alluring flux of sign flows. Thus, art galleries, museums, critics, consumers, and finally the artists themselves either are duped entirely by the processes of aesthetic production or are caught up as duplicitous conspirators in the frenzy of overcharged art markets still hyped-up on the rhetoric of avant garde engagement. Perhaps, in the end, as Stearns and Chaloupka argue, "Baudrillard can never be confirmed. This is his seduction."[66] While this quirk is part of his seductive attractions, it also promotes some seriously confounding distractions. If one accepts his notions of representation in hyperreality, there is little to do but become indifferent as a fatal strategy on the obscene. Yet, if one strategizes in these ways, what can be said critically, reliably, or effectively – which are, of course, terms Baudrillard would dispute – about the present situation? Instead of discovering a timeless masterpiece in his *oeuvre*, then, most discussions of his work can only continue advancing their various projects of confirmation and/or disconfirmation, mainly by salvaging this or that suggestive aspect of his work or jettisoning this or that catastrophic remainder which does not work in acts of minor bricolage.

Notes

1   For additional discussion, see Kate Linker, "From Imitation, to the Copy, to Just Effect: On Reading Jean Baudrillard," *Artforum*, 22, 8 (1984) 44–8; Hal Foster, "Signs Taken for Wonders," *Art in America*, 74, 6 (1986) 80–91; Timothy W. Luke, "Jean Baudrillard's Political Economy of the Sign," *Art Papers*, 10, 1 (1986) 22–5; David Carrier, "Baudrillard as Philosopher, or, the End of Abstract Painting," *Arts Magazine*, 63, 1 (1988) 52–60; Suzi Gablik, "Dancing with Baudrillard," *Art in America*, 76, 6 (1988) 27–9; Arthur C. Danto, "Review of Jean Baudrillard's *America* and *Selected Writings*," *The New Republic*, 203, 11–12 (Sept. 10, 1990), 44–5; and, Timothy W. Luke, *Shows*

of Force: Power, Politics, and Ideology in Art Exhibitions (Durham: Duke University Press, 1992).

2 See, for example, Carrier, "Baudrillard as Philosopher," pp. 52–60; Gablik, "Dancing with Baudrillard," pp. 27–9; Grant Kester, "The Rise and Fall of Baudrillard," *New Art Examiner*, 19, 4 (1984) 20–3; and John Miller, "Baudrillard and his Discontents," *Artscribe International*, 63 (May, 1987) 48–51.

3 Gablik, "Dancing with Baudrillard," p. 27.

4 Carrier, "Baudrillard as Philosopher," p. 55.

5 Jean Baudrillard, *In the Shadow of the Silent Majorities* (New York: Semiotext(e), 1983), p. 27.

6 Ibid., p. 11.

7 Ibid., p. 30.

8 See Timothy W. Luke, *Screens of Power: Ideology, Domination, and Resistance in Informational Society* (Urbana: University of Illinois Press, 1989), pp. 2–16.

9 Baudrillard, *Silent Majorities*, p. 101.

10 Jean Baudrillard, *Jean Baudrillard: Selected Writings*, ed. Mark Poster (Stanford: Stanford University Press, 1988), p. 175.

11 Fredric Jameson, *Postmodernism, or the Cultural Logic of Late Capitalism* (Durham: Duke University Press, 1991), p. ix.

12 Jean Baudrillard, *Simulations* (New York: Semiotext(e), 1983), p. 32.

13 Ibid., p. 26.

14 Ibid., p. 25.

15 Jameson, *Postmodernism*, p. xxi.

16 Baudrillard, *Simulations*, p. 25.

17 Ibid., pp. 83–115.

18 Ibid., p. 2.

19 For additional discussion, see Douglas Kellner, *Jean Baudrillard: From Marxism to Postmodernism and Beyond* (Oxford: Polity Press, 1989); and Mike Gane, *Baudrillard: Critical and Fatal Theory* (Routledge: London, 1991).

20 Baudrillard, *Simulations*, p. 3.

21 Ibid., p. 4.

22 Ibid., pp. 12–13.

23 Ibid., p. 55.

24 See Jean Baudrillard, *Le système des objets* (Paris: Denoel-Gonthier, 1968); and Jean Baudrillard, *La société de consommation* (Paris: Gallimard, 1970).

25 Jean Baudrillard, *For a Critique of the Political Economy of the Sign* (St. Louis: Telos Press, 1981), p. 38.

26 Ibid., p. 110.

27 Ibid., p. 117.

28 Ibid., p. 120.

29 Jean Baudrillard, "The Beaubourg Effect: Implosion and Deterrence," *October*, 20 (Spring 1982) 3–13.

30 Ibid., p. 3.

31 Ibid., p. 4.

32 Baudrillard, *Simulations*, pp. 136–7.

33 Ibid., p. 138.

34 Baudrillard, "Beaubourg Effect," p. 4.
35 Baudrillard, *Simulations*, p. 152.
36 Ibid., p. 63.
37 Baudrillard, "Beauborg Effect," p. 8.
38 Ibid., p. 9.
39 Ibid., pp. 9–10.
40 Jean Baudrillard, *The Transparency of Evil* (London: Verso, 1993), pp. 3–13.
41 Ibid., p. 41.
42 Ibid., p. 4.
43 Ibid., p. 5.
44 Jean Baudrillard, *Revenge of the Crystal: Selected Writings on the Modern Object and Its Destiny, 1968–1983* (London: Pluto Press, 1990), p. 185.
45 Ibid., p. 189.
46 Ibid., p. 188.
47 Ibid.
48 Ibid.
49 Baudrillard, *Transparency of Evil*, pp. 6–7.
50 Ibid.
51 Ibid., p. 11
52 Ibid., p. 17.
53 Ibid.
54 Ibid., p. 18.
55 See Jean Baudrillard, *L'échange symbolique et la mort* (Paris: Gallimard, 1976).
56 Baudrillard, *Revenge of the Crystal*, pp. 18, 20.
57 Ibid., p. 20.
58 Ibid., p. 18.
59 Kellner, *Baudrillard*, p. 180.
60 Jean Baudrillard, *The Ecstasy of Communication* (New York: Semiotext(e), 1988), p. 99.
61 For some sense of this tendency, see Jean Baudrillard, *America* (London: Verso, 1988); and Jean Baudrillard, *Cool Memories* (London: Verso, 1990).
62 Baudrillard, *Ecstasy of Communication*, p. 98.
63 Ibid., p. 100.
64 Ibid., p. 101.
65 Ibid., p. 97.
66 William Stearns and William Chaloupka, *Jean Baudrillard: The Disappearance of Art and Politics* (New York: Saint Martin's Press, 1992), p. 4.

11

BAUDRILLARD, MODERNISM, AND POSTMODERNISM

—

Nicholas Zurbrugg

Jean Baudrillard's disclaimer "I have nothing to do with postmodernism" is rich with irony.[1] Considered in terms of his general arguments and assertions, Baudrillard has *everything* to do with postmodernism. For Arthur Kroker, for example, Baudrillard is "the very first of the *postmodern primitives*."[2] For Steven Best and Douglas Kellner, "He has achieved guru status throughout the English-speaking world . . . as *the* supertheorist of a new postmodernity."[3] For Marshall Berman, he is "the most recent postmodern pretender and object of cultic adoration in art scenes and universities all over America today," and the very Anti-Christ of those who consider that "modernism still matters."[4]

At the same time though, Baudrillard's concurrent appeal to "art scenes and universities" hints perhaps at the way in which his impact is both aesthetic and academic, rhetorical and theoretical. In Baudrillard's own terms, his kind of theory is "in many respects indefinable."[5]

> It's not really an aesthetic, it's not a philosophy, it's not a sociology, it's a little volatile. Perhaps this corresponds to a certain kind of floating instability with more in common with the contemporary imagination than with any real philosophy. Possibly that explains why it is not someone like Derrida – who has had great academic success throughout American universities – why it is not so much his references to deconstruction and so forth that have been taken up by artists, as notions of simulation.

What is it that makes Baudrillard's ideas so appealing? Conversely, why do so many of Baudrillard's opponents find his popularity so disturbing? As these pages will suggest, most favorable and unfavorable responses to his work focus predominantly upon its rhetorical play rather than upon its specific accuracy and applicability. While Baudrillard's writing obviously displays a curious mixture of analytical acuity and fictional fantasy, and invites investigation in terms of its slippage from sociological to symbolist rhetoric, it is perhaps most compelling in terms of its visionary – if frequently flawed – sensitivity to many of those mutant values now most at stake within the late postmodern condition.

Like Lenny Bruce, Baudrillard commands attention in terms of his rhetorical excess – in terms of the register, rather than the substance, of his patter. Indeed, Baudrillard happily asserts that "The form of my language is almost more important than what I have to say within it ... It's not a question of ideas – there are already too many ideas!"[7] On the contrary, it seems extremely important to consider the substance of Baudrillard's ideas. To the rather general question. "What analytical and fictional strategies does Baudrillard deploy in his accounts of the postmodern condition?" one must surely add the far more demanding question *"With what accuracy does Baudrillard write about the postmodern condition?"*

More often than not, Baudrillard's critics seem happy to trounce him for philosophical or theoretical misdemeanors, while holding fire regarding the factual accuracy of his observations. In consequence, Baudrillard is more or less granted poetic license to fictionize to his heart's content regarding the present and the future, so long as he makes no serious philosophical or theoretical claims. While this response effectively lets Baudrillard off the hook by declining to evaluate the specificity of his claims, it concurrently releases his critics from any obligation to suggest just what an accurate assessment of postmodern existence might address. Having established the madness of Baudrillard's methods, his contemporaries frequently seem quite happy to add that, all things considered, Baudrillard is still an okay kind of guy, generally or fictionally speaking.

Christopher Norris, for example, stipulates that Baudrillard is "thoroughly inconsequent and muddled when it comes to philosophising on the basis of his own observations," but also freely concedes that "Baudrillard is a first-rate diagnostician of the postmodern scene."[8] Writing with almost unbridled enthusiasm for Baudrillard's evocations of the rhetorical and the conceptual muddle "between delerium and anxiety, between the triumph of cyberpunk and the political reality of cultural exhaustion," the Kroker-Kroker-Cook *Panic Encyclopedia* concludes that *"Jean Baudrillard ... is* the postmodern commotion."[9]

Fredric Jameson similarly locates the postmodern sensibility somewhere between the poles of cultural exhaustion and the energy of cyberpunk fiction, "henceforth, for many of us, the supreme *literary* expression ... of postmodernism."[10] Placing Baudrillard's relevance within a similar cosmos, Best and Kellner deplore the ways in which Baudrillard's theory "tends to degenerate into sloganeering and rhetoric without any systematic or comprehensive theoretical position," but suggest nevertheless that "Baudrillard's best work can ... be read along with the novels of ...

cyberpunk fiction as projecting visions of futuristic worlds which illuminate the present high tech society."[11]

At its best, in works such as David Blair's remarkable film *WAX or the discovery of television among the bees* (1991),[12] cyberpunk culture evokes many of the most challenging issues raised by postmodern technology. In this respect, the cyberpunk movement is but the most recent manifestation of the frequently neglected lineage of postmodern high tech creativity, and, as such, a further reminder that the alleged "reality" of *cultural exhaustion* is perhaps more symptomatic of academic myopia, than of the high tech cultural climate as a whole.

In other words, if Baudrillard's writings may well reflect the "commotion" within academia – or within sections of academia preoccupied with symptoms of 'cultural exhaustion, such commotion may itself be merely a footnote to the more understated but more substantial positive cultural energies of the postmodern condition. Put another way, much of the postmodern cultural theory detecting cultural exhaustion seems likely to prove to be a kind of *flat-culture mythology* with as much conviction as earlier flat-earth theories.

As I have argued elsewhere,[13] postmodern culture is repeatedly misrepresented as an era of cultural and theoretical confusion neutralizing the more positive energies of cultural modernism, and best characterized by the supposed 'deaths' of aura, authoriality, avant-garde integrity, and referential reality. Predicated upon the more extreme assertions of Benjamin, Barthes, Bürger, and Baudrillard, this misreading of the potential of postmodern culture culminates in the mythology that I would term the *B-effect*. While this emphasis upon cultural exhaustion and entropy obviously constitutes *one* impulse within mass culture and within what one might think of as "B-grade" mass-misreadings of the postmodern condition, other more rewarding forms of postmodern creativity – particularly postmodern multimedia creativity – are frequently exemplary of the positive energy that I would associate with the *C-effect*, or the technological confidence and flair of pioneer American postmoderns such as John Cage, and of younger contemporaries such as Laurie Anderson, Robert Ashley, David Blair, Philip Glass, Meredith Monk, Yvonne Rainer, and Robert Wilson.

In this respect, the postmodern condition, viewed as an increasingly distinct cultural era emerging from the mid-1930s and becoming most evident across the arts from the mid-1950s, might best be conceived of as a plurality of successive cultural impulses. At times these impulses negate those of modernism; at times these impulses extend and mutate modernist aspirations across the new media. At worst, such impulses culminate in commercial dross and theoretical cynicism; at best such impulses provoke highly challenging conceptual and creative initiatives.

As the twentieth century draws to an end, it seems increasingly urgent that the cultural practices of the postmodern era be evaluated both in terms of their mediocrities and in terms of their more mature and masterly precipitates. While there is obviously every reason to reconsider potential-ly repressive concepts of mature and masterly creativity, it seems equally evident that repressive politically correct resistance toward the qualitative analysis of our culture, and repressive theoretically correct subscription to accounts of the "deaths" of assorted modernist and pre-modernist values, compound the counterproductive intellectual indifference that the late Félix Guattari denounced as "the virtual ethical and aesthetic abdication of postmodern thought."[14]

The American multimedia artist Dick Higgins diagnoses much the same malaise when he detects "a sort of failure of nerve" among artists and academics over the last two or three decades, although, as Higgins also points out, "there are some individuals who have kept the nerve, kept the vision and kept the energy together."[15] The history of the postmodern mentality is in many respects the chronology of variously maintained, variously lost, and variously regained kinds of "nerve" during five or more decades of increasingly complex social, political, cultural, and theoretical transition. Within the rather restrained parameters of the cultural and theoretical contexts addressed by these pages, the most significant "com-motion" within the postmodern cosmos appears to have been generated by those who have kept or recovered their ethical and aesthetic nerve, and who have nurtured and negotiated the potential of old and new kinds of creative and conceptual energy.

Baudrillard's writings fit very uneasily within this spectrum, in the sense that his emphasis upon "delusional" reality and upon mass-culture leads at best to what one might think of as a first-rate analysis of second-rate "extreme phenomena." More specifically, Baudrillard proposes that "the world is on a delusional course" and that it therefore makes best sense to "adopt a delusional standpoint towards the world."[16] Taken literally, such studiedly apocalyptic assertions rapidly lead to what Gene Youngblood defines as the "numbing powerlessness" resulting from overexposure to Baudrillard's hypotheses.[17] Yet, as Youngblood remarks, while it may at first sight appear that Baudrillard "laments the loss of the original, the authentic, and with them the possibility of Reality and Truth," it also frequently seems to be the case that "Although he doesn't actually say so, it is clear that Baudrillard longs for the recovery of Walter Benjamin's 'aura.' "[18]

To carp about the underly-philosophical, underly-theoretical, and overly-fictional registers of Baudrillard's rhetoric is to miss the still more signifi-cant tension between his writing's explicit denial of reality and truth and its almost unerring emphasis upon what one might think of as prime sites of new – or mutant – cultural realities and truths. More often than not, Baudrillard is not entirely a first-rate diagnostician of the postmodern scene, because he consistently – and perhaps self-consciously – gets things wrong by converting evidence of illumination into confirmation of delusion. Likewise, his theoretical fictions command partial rather than total respect, insofar as they seem programmed to project "panic" paradigms upon high tech society, deflecting critical attention from the subtleties of emergent practices. Yet, on occasion, when Baudrillard preaches from practice (as in his recent comments upon photography) rather than from prose, his insights offer unambiguously required reading.

Commenting upon the curious way in which "the best Dadas ... seem least Dada," the veteran Dadaist Marcel Janco discussed the way in which the Data movement is usually caricatured in terms of its initial "negative speed," rather than viewed more panoramically in terms both of this initial momentum and its subsequent impulse "beyond negation."[19] Like Dada, Baudrillard's work seems characterized by two speeds, the one self-evidently and seductively destructive, the other unexpectedly perceptive and affirmative and, as such, a sporadic source of marvelous exceptions to his more mundane general rules. In turn, postmodern culture and the post-modern condition as a whole require consideration not simply in terms of mass-culture's negative speed, but also in terms of those less obvious practices reaching at once both beyond modernist conventions and "beyond negation."

˘ Considered very generally, Baudrillard appears to be an exemplary post-modern, or anti-modern – or *past-modern* – thinker, in terms of his avowed opposition to the Enlightenment-inspired "communicative rationality" that Jürgen Habermas associates with the modernist project.[20] Yet, as Baudrillard himself remarks, the act of opposition is a relatively indolent gesture, and offers no particular guarantee of any more pragmatic alternative. If most intellectuals "feel very, very comfortable when they are in opposition," they usually "do not know how to define themselves when they are no longer in opposition and have to participate."[21] At his most pessimistic, Baudrillard tends to remark that the 1980s and 1990s leave him in precisely this kind of dilemma, insofar as he cannot identify "a new position, one that is original and credible."[22]

Discussing his work in a more confident register, Baudrillard repeatedly emphasizes, firstly, that his writings are not modernist, and secondly, that they aspire toward some kind of catalytic initiative reaching beyond the "total eclecticism" of a postmodern culture "acquainted with neither hard ideologies nor radical philosophies."[23] Baudrillard's apparent indifference to postmodern culture seems surprising, to say the least, when one considers that his own writings have obviously made major contributions to the analysis of the chronologically postmodern condition. What seems most revealing here is Baudrillard's impatience toward the dead-ends of postmodern mass culture: in this instance, what he convincingly identifies as its "banal energies" impulse toward "total eclecticism." Put another way, Baudrillard's most valid writings point away from indiscriminate eclecticism toward those more substantial problems and practices that one might think of as the *live-ends* of postmodern culture; the exceptions, as it were, to Baudrillard's seductively apocalyptic general rules.

Considered in terms of his most substantial insights, and in terms of his sensitivity toward the most challenging developments of the 1980s and the 1990s, Baudrillard is without doubt a major cultural cartographer of the postmodern cosmos. Thematically, Baudrillard's subject matter is frequently thrilling. Rhetorically and conceptually, however, Baudrillard's accounts of this subject matter frequently appear slightly antiquated. Paradoxically, Baudrillard's rhetorical and conceptual tropes seem predicated upon a curiously *modernist* cultural logic (or poetics). To read Baudrillard's writings on contemporary culture is to confront the new and the déjà vu, as one is both guided toward emergent problems and yet, at the same time, distracted from the specificity of their implications by curiously anachronistic commentary.

More specifically, Baudrillard's arguments successively repudiate the logic of Enlightenment modernism, consciously or unconsciously invoke the poetic logic of cultural modernism, direct attention to key developments in the chronological postmodern social and cultural condition, and then – like other theorists such as Jameson and Huyssen – misguidedly overemphasize the negative impact of mass-culture, and misguidingly underestimate the positive potential of the postmodern era's new mainstream and avantgarde practices.[24] Significantly, Baudrillard himself now acknowledges such shortcomings in his writings and suggests that he is increasingly concerned to identify alternatives to the predictable apocalyptic register of most accounts of postmodern techno-culture: "Up to now I think that technology has been analysed in too realistic a way ... it has been typecast as a medium of alienation and depersonalisation ... it's possible to continue forever in this sort of direction. But I sense now that a sort of reversal of focus is taking place ... I'll always continue to offer a radically critical analysis of media and technology ... But it's also necessary to identify another form of analysis – a more subtle form of analysis than that one."[25]

Ironically, the terms of Baudrillard's emergent positive focus frequently seem as nostalgic as his initial negative focus. Just as Baudrillard's preceding analyses of mass culture – like those of Jameson and Huyssen, moreover – frequently remind one of the rhetoric of Max Nordau's "panic" reading of late-nineteenth-century cultural transitions in *Degeneration*,[26] Baudrillard's recent positive appraisals of technology seem similarly *fin de siècle* in register. In the same way as Mallarmé's notes on "Music and Literature," for example, associate the creative process with the transition from states in which artists "elicit emptiness," to "celebrations" in which "sublime" forces "lovingly ... shed glittering lights ... through empty space,"[27] Baudrillard describes his practice as a photographer as one in which "I isolate something in an empty space and then it irradiates this emptiness – there's the irradiation of the object within this emptiness." Qualifying this seemingly symbolist process in self-consciously surrealist terms, Baudrillard adds that it is a kind of "automatic writing." "I enter into this second state – this kind of rapid ecstasy – much more often in my photography than in my writing. The ecstasy of photography . . . is much stronger, much more spontaneous and automatic. For me photography is a kind of automatic writing . . . I've experienced what I'd have to call my greatest sense of pleasure – and indeed, my strongest sense of passion – in the realm of images, rather than in the realm of texts."[28]

Perhaps, after all, modernist cultural rhetoric *is* the most effective discourse for describing the kind of "ecstatic" technological creativity that Baudrillard has in mind. My point here is that Baudrillard often appears at a loss to describe postmodern culture in anything other than the prior discourse of the modernist arts: a paradox which perhaps points to two dilemmas which still await adequate resolution. On the one hand, it may well be the case that the notorious ruptures widely perceived between modern and postmodern mentalities are neither as terminal nor as topical as many have imagined. Perhaps the 1980s and the 1990s signal not so much the supposed *disappearance* or *termination* of modernist values, as their *reappearance* or *transmutation* through new eyes and new technologies. Theories of the great "divide" between modernism and postmodernism require more careful delineation.

On the other hand, definitions of the postmodern theoretical temper also now require reconsideration. Too often, the "postmodern" is equated with the early, somewhat impatient and intemperate avowals of Parisian theoreticians. Significantly, both Barthes and Baudrillard have gradually acknowledged that postmodern technological practices may well be surprisingly compatible with the very notions of singularity, originality, subjectivity, and creativity which their earlier writings – like those of their followers – dismissed, displaced or deconstructed beyond recognition. In this respect, Baudrillard's recent emphasis upon what he terms the "ecstasy" and the "singularity" of photography offers a welcome alternative to his earlier rather tiresome insistence upon the notionally neutralizing effect of the media. Like Barthes, Baudrillard now comments: "I'm considerably in favour of '*punctum*' in the sense of the singularity of the object at a given moment."[29]

Were this the whole story, Baudrillard's present writings might well appear to adumbrate an unexpected happy ending to his earlier accounts of the postmodern misadventure. Ironically, and somewhat perversely, Baudrillard not only invariably qualifies his own most affirmative ideas, but also almost always compulsively *disqualifies* such insights, indulging in a kind of conceptual infanticide, for fear, perhaps, of manifesting overly explicit commitment to aesthetic, poetic, or ethical ideals. Whereas Proust, for example, elegiacally invoked Ruskin's genius in terms of "one of those extinguished stars whose light still reaches us,"[30] Baudrillard insists that his seemingly romantic allusion to "the scintillation of being" in *The Transparency of Evil* has no such transcendental overtones. Rather, it seems to denote detached uncertainly, not unlike the whimsical reference to "the star whose ray / announces the disappearance / of its master by the presence of itself," in the American poet Ed Dorn's magic realist epic *Gunslinger*.[31] Like Dorn, Baudrillard seems to have an eye for the cool, slightly surreal paradox.[32] "I use the term "scintillation" in terms of the way that it's used with reference to stars – for very distant stars which perhaps have died, but which still seem to shine ... there are two alternatives here, there seems to be light, but perhaps there isn't any light, and perhaps it's just an apparition."

At his most positive, Baudrillard suggests that his most credible position is that of the conceptual *agent provocateur* – the master of "this art of appearance, this art of making things appear."[33] Acknowledging that this "art" has something in common with science fiction, but little in common with either postmodernist or modernist mentalities, Baudrillard typically explains:

> It's not postmodern. I don't know what one means by that. But I'm no longer part of modernity, not in the sense where modernity implies a kind of critical distance of judgement and argumentation. There is a sense of positive and negative, a kind of dialectic in modernity. My way of reflecting on things is not dialectic. Rather it's provocative, reversible, it's a way of raising things to their 'N'th power, rather than a way of dialectizing them. It's a way of following through the extremes to see what happens. It's a bit like a theory-fiction. There's a little theoretical science fiction in it.[34]

Considered in terms of a modernity based upon critical distance, judgment and argumentation, nothing could be less modern than Baudrillard's commitment to "following through the extremes to see what happens." If the Baudrillardian project pivots upon the fatal strategy of "raising things to their Nth power," the Habermasian project of modernity emphasizes instead the Enlightenment ideal of furthering "rationalized everyday life" by cultivating "objective science, universal morality and law, and autonomous art according to their inner logic."[35]

As Stjepan G. Mestrovic suggests, debates regarding the respective absolute merits of rationalized inner logic and accelerated Nth power hyperlogic seem surprisingly dated if one considers the way in which the majority of contemporaries cheerfully accommodate and reconcile both forces. Arguing that "the Enlightenment 'project' is an illusion" which "died long ago," and which was fully "discredited ... during the previous turn of the century," Mestrovic concludes:

> All the concern expressed by postmodern theorists with this 'project' constitutes an anomic aberration, a long-standing collective neurosis that stems

from repression of the irrational. The proof is that while intellectuals write about completing the Enlightenment project, the rest of humanity turns to irrationalities of every sort to satisfy its collectively hungry heart – religion, nationalism, cults . . . and all kinds of sentiment thrive in postmodern culture.[36]

Whether one likes it or not, it seems evident that a major – and doubt-less enduring – dimension of postmodern culture consists of *irrationalized* or *extrarationalized* everyday life – the consoling fictions that Don DeLillo's novel *White Noise* associates with "The tales of the supernatural and the extraterrestial. The miracle vitamins, the cures for cancer, the remedies for obesity. The cults of the famous and the dead."[37] Mestrovic's central argument is that the rational cult of the Enlightenment project is more likely to do harm than good in present circumstances, in which "the West needs a new faith," rather than "the collective repression of the heart in favour of excessive intellectualism, the mind."[38] Accordingly, it appears redundant to engage in obsolete debates regarding the merits of the En-lightenment project, irrelevant to waste time pondering the ambiguities of the term postmodernity, but essential "to confront and tame the irrational, and reach the goal of a cosmopolitan society of humankind."[39]

To be fair to Baudrillard, his own arguments frequently express contempt for the "self-verification," "tautology", and "permanent recurrence" that he associates with irrelevant debates in which "nothing will ever put itself into question."[40] Nevertheless, his enthusiasm for projecting his attention "somewhere else, to see what is going on elsewhere,"[41] by peering "through the extremes,"[42] beyond "the end of linearity, the end of finality, of the final perspective,"[43] is itself something of a conceptual trap.

Despite his undoubted distaste for fixed rhetoric and for inflexible ref-erences, and despite his reluctance to promote "complacent catastrophism,"[44] Baudrillard's fundamental conviction that he inhabits "a world that has lost all sense of perspective, where sight, distance and judgement have been lost,"[45] repeatedly culminates in complacent indifference toward notions of theoretical, social, or cultural progress. While he often refers to his "serious" concern for various issues "at stake," his aversion to referential and judgmental categories usually leaves him more or less literally at a loss for any words save those of disbelief and dissociation.

What is at issue here, then, is the question of whether the so-called postmodern critique of modernist formulations of particular values and categories necessarily negates them. Baudrillard consistently takes this to be the case. But as others such as Mestrovic, Lyotard, Berman, and Nicholson all suggest, it has become increasingly evident that the postmodern condition does not so much negate the legitimacy of modernist values as *reinstate* these values by offering them more flexibility with regard to contemporary "differences."[46] This conciliatory impulse is frequently an-ticipated by the more progressive forces of cultural modernism. In this respect, the priorities of mainstream postmodern theory often appear to offer belated confirmation to the ideals of the modernist cultural avant-garde.

Consider, for example, the following extracts from the Dadaist poet Tristan Tzara's "Lecture on Dada." Initially questioning the legitimacy of those "intelligent movements that have stretched beyond measure our credulity in the benefits of science," Tzara commends "the point where the yes and the no and all the opposites meet, not solemnly in the castles of human philosophies, but very simply at street corners, like dogs and grasshoppers."[47] Subsequently claiming that "Only the elasticity of our conventions creates a bond between disparate acts," Tzara concludes:

> The Beautiful and the True in art do not exist; what interests me is the intensity of a personality transposed directly, clearly into the work; the man and his vitality; the angle from which he regards the elements and in what manner he knows how to gather sensation, emotion, into a lacework of words and sentiment.[48]

Significantly, Tzara not only rejects monolithic categories such as "The Beautiful" and "The True." At the same time he calls for the coexistence of "all the opposites" and proposes alternative, more elastic "conventions," placing considerable value upon concepts of creative "intensity" and "vitality."

At his most positive extreme – or, one might say, at his most *Dadaist* extreme – Baudrillard similarly expresses commitment to "singularities, exceptional events."[49] While many of Baudrillard's writings mechanically reiterate that "it is impossible to distinguish between good and bad excess,"[50] it seems significant that he frequently acknowledges the aesthetic value of contemporaries such as the film-maker Jean-Luc Godard: "You can *live* in a Godard film. It is at the same time a different dimension and a way of handling images, which is the only one worth calling modern to my mind."[51]

Baudrillard's nihilism, like Tzara's nihilism, is clearly tempered by aesthetic insights; by his unexpected discovery that in a world which should logically lack value, new – or unfamiliar – modes of handling images, words, and sentiment suggest that certain kinds of aesthetic value still survive as they transmute and multiply against all odds. Discussing the novelist Elias Canetti, Baudrillard, again rather hesitantly, acknowledges that all is not quite so grim as he usually intimates. Cautiously prefacing his comments with the stipulation that "it is not the ensemble of his work but fragments of it that have excited me," Baudrillard continues: "The fragment is like a nucleus of an ephemeral destiny of language, a fatal particle that shines an instant and then disappears. At the same time, it allows an instantaneous conversion of points of view, of humours and passions."[52]

Parisian postmodern theory would doubtless relate this kind of emphasis upon the ways in which language's "fatal particles" afford an "instantaneous conversion" of points of view: to Barthes's notion of the text as "the *stereographic plurality* of its weave of signifiers;" to Derrida's focus upon "the traces of differences . . . the *spacing* by means of which elements are related to each other;" to Foucault's attention to the ways in which texts generate "discontinuity . . . rupture, break, mutation, transformation;" or to Deleuze and Guattari's ideal of "a book made of plateaus, each communicating with the others through tiny fissures, as in the brain."[53] Considered in such contexts, Baudrillard's admiration for Canetti's fragments seems both predictable and respectable, and altogether typical of the Parisian postmodern intellectual temper.

Yet, at the same time, this sensibility is itself still more typical of the modernist poetic sensibility, which is perhaps simply another way of suggesting that far from representing the cutting edge of the postmodern mind, the Parisian intellectual temper is best understood as a manifestation of academia's embarrassingly belated assimilation of the dominant insights of modernist poetics. Writing a whole century before the rhizomic rhetoric of May 1968, the aesthetician Walter Pater contrasted the multiplicity of "impressions, unstable, flickering, inconsistent" with the apparent "solidity with which language invests them" concluding that "our one chance lies in expanding" the "interval" of existence, "in getting as many pulsations as possible into the given time."[54]

Stéphane Mallarmé's writings in "Crisis in Poetry" similarly adumbrate an aesthetics of "hesitation, disposition of parts, their alternations and relationships – all this contributing to . . . rhythmic totality."[55] In turn, Virginia Woolf's essay "Modern Fiction" concludes that the modernist novelist's task is to "trace the pattern, however disconnected and incoherent in appearance, which each sight or incident scores upon the consciousness," irrespective of "whatever aberration or complexity it may display."[56]

Not surprisingly, perhaps, both modernist novelists such as Joris-Karl Huysmans, and postmodern Parisian theorists, such as Baudrillard, share particular enthusiasm for the traces of intertextual plurality, difference, discontinuity, and interconnected fissure within the prose poem and the condensed literary fragment. Recounting the poetic aspirations of Des Esseintes, the hero of *Against Nature*, Huysmans relates: "Of all forms of literature, the prose poem was Des Esseintes' favourite. Handled by an alchemist of genius it should, he maintained, contain within its small compass and in concentrated form the substance of a novel, while dispensing with the latter's long-winded analyses and superfluous descriptions . . . every adjective . . . would open up such wide vistas that the reader could muse on its meaning, at once precise and multiple, for weeks on end."[57]

For his part, Baudrillard has almost exactly the same to say regarding his exploration of partially precise, partially multiple, discourse in *Fatal Strategies*.[58] Discussing this volume in the year of its publication, almost exactly a century after the publication of Huysmans's *Against Nature*,

Baudrillard comments: "You could almost make each paragraph into a book ... I want to slim things down ... to get rid of things ... to create voids between spaces so that there can be collisions and short circuits. For the traditional imagination that is not acceptable. It's a sacrilege."[59]

Both the traditional realist imagination and the "purposive" mindset of the Habermasian modernist project would undoubtedly judge such discourse "sacrilege." Dismissively alluding to what he terms the "nonsense experiments" of the "hopeless surrealist revolts," Habermas, for example, insists that "destructured form" is "altogether incompatible with the moral basis of a purposive, rational conduct of life."[60] Yet, as Mestrovic remarks, such "repression of the irrational"[61] appears puzzlingly anachronistic. To all intents and purposes, irrational or destructured forms of thought became assimilated into the twentieth-century mentality decades ago. As the novelist William Burroughs puts it, "It must be remembered that the unconscious was much more unconscious in Freud's day than in ours."[62]

Baudrillard makes much the same point in *America*, where he emphasizes that "everyday" aspects of American culture "simply are extraordinary." "They have that extravagance which makes up odd, everyday America. This oddness is not surrealistic (surrealism is an extravagance that is still aesthetic in nature and as such very European in inspiration): here, the extravagance has passed into things."[63]

In much of his writings there is something seductively contemporary in Baudrillard's conscious attention to the semiotics and semantics of everyday life in the 1980s and 1990s.[64] Yet, at the same time, Baudrillard's arguments frequently appear limited in terms of the ways in which their subversive project pivots upon such substantially passé, cultural modernist categories as the surreal, or upon such latterday Dadaistic or semi-situationist anti-aesthetic gestures as his avowal: 'I don't want culture; I spit on it."[65]

As the veteran Dadaist pioneer Raoul Hausmann remarked with regard to the various "neo-Dada" movements of the 1960s, "Renaissances are, for the most part, sad and without issue."[66] Viewed with hindsight, much of the momentum of Parisian postmodern theory seems informed by this kind of oddly nostalgic, and ultimately unproductive register, characterized as it is – as Foucault observed – by the afterglow of the surrealist dream, "the dream that cast its spell, between the First World War and fascism."[67] What one senses here is the retrospective illumination of the cultural *archeologist*, as opposed, say, to any special sensitivity to the cultural potential of the present work-in-progress that writers such as Burroughs have associated with "*astronauts* of inner space."[68]

To be sure, the surrealist dream may well have appeared a very revolutionary vista to the mandarins of the French academy when compared with the academic "ethics" that Foucault associates with the three decades preceding May 1968.[69] But to those already versed in the poetics and politics of cultural modernism, and to those alert to the positive potential of early postmodern technological culture, a revival of the surrealist temper, with its cult of destructured textuality, appeared something of a mixed blessing.

On the one hand, the poetics of surrealism already seem a little dated, when compared with subsequent poetics born of the electronic media: the domain of techno-poetics. On the other hand, as the multimedia sound poet Henri Chopin points out, the cultural politics of surrealism were still more restrictive than the parameters of surrealist poetics, in the sense that surrealism monopolized the attention of Parisian intellectuals and decelerated recognition of concurrent developments in modernist culture, such as the Dadaist and futurist artists' exploration of emergent modes of mechanical *production* which only became readily available with the advent of new recording and printing technologies in the late 1950s and early 1960s.

Reflecting upon the "ethics" of the Parisian avant-garde in the 1950s, Chopin revealingly emphasizes the extent to which the creative community ignored the technological modernist experiments and aspirations of surrealism's "other" – the futurist and Dadaist movements of Italy, Russia, Switzerland, and Germany.

> In 1949, Dada was completely unknown and completely eclipsed by Surrealism ... It was all very vague – nobody knew what Dada was, and nobody knew very much about Italian Futurism or Russian Futurism ... When Surrealism appeared, artists like ... Raoul Hausmann were completely forgotten and neglected ... I had to visit the artists themselves before I finally learned that their world was much more creative than Surrealism, and discovered the true art of the twentieth century.[70]

Chopin's fellow sound poet, Bernard Heidsieck, hints at the same kind of general problem, when remarking that the recent Musées de Marseilles exhibition, "Poésure et Peintrie" – the first-ever major French survey of modernist and postmodernist developments in visual poetry, may finally "clarify the situation" and "present forty years of a different history" by examining the present in terms of "the vanguards of the early twentieth century, futurism and dada."[71] The prevalence of surrealist references and rhetoric within post-structuralist theory, and the failure of this theory to offer any informed analysis of multimedia elaborations of the Dadaist and futurist vanguards, tell their own story.

Like many French intellectuals of his generation, Baudrillard frequently appears trapped behind conceptual and rhetorical blinkers. Refreshingly, though, he cheerfully claims to be "a very bad analyst" of art's "foreign domain,"[72] while writing many of the most provocative general accounts of this domain, and indeed, while attaining increasing recognition as a photographic artist in his own right.[73] Clearly, Baudrillard's relationship with his subject matter is far more complex than one might initially suppose.

On the one hand, Baudrillard seems neither willing nor able to address the positive potential of the innovative postmodern technological practices that Chopin emphatically identifies as the "true art" of the last four decades. But, on the other hand, Baudrillard appears compelled to confront the present as best he may. As the lines below from his essay "Xerox and Infinity" indicate, Baudrillard's "best" culminates in marvelous discursive bravado – not unlike that of the gentle giants of the World Wrestling Foundation. Both defusing and diffusing defiance within deftly formulaic generalization, Baudrillard seems to steer his way to the heart of the problem – in this instance, the exact quality of electronic communication – by a process of energetic exaggeration and elimination. Catching his argument in mid-stride, one reads:

> . . . just as the sudden and fabulous expansion of communication and information techniques is connected to the undecidability which circulates in them – the undecidability of knowing whether there is knowledge in there – so the undecidability in communication is of knowing whether or not it is a genuine form of exchange . . . . I defy anyone to decide this – rather, to go on to believe that all these techniques finally lead to a real use of the world, to real encounters, etc.[74]

At this point, Baudrillard's argument dramatically changes gear from what one might think of as Nth power analytical exaggeration and defiance, to registers of Nth power fabulation and affirmation. Having asserted the implausibility of yet another aspect of contemporary culture (a hypothesis, moreover, quite at odds with the confidence with which artists such as Diamanda Galas claim that they "dominate" their technology),[75] Baudrillard's pessimistic description transmutes into optimistic emphasis upon the "crucial" dilemma that he now perceives in terms of the spectacular "race-chase" between "man and his virtual clones on the reversible track of the Moebius Strip."[76]

Against all odds, perhaps, the paradoxical impact of Baudrillard's fusion of calculated incredulity and enthusiastic theoretical fantasy appears strikingly relevant. Even if Baudrillard's accelerating antitheses seem both to misunderstand and misrepresent their subject, they compel the reader to reconsider some of the most "fascinating" facets of contemporary culture. Claiming that "No one understands the stake of these techniques any longer," Baudrillard challengingly concludes:

> No, the crucial stake, and the actual one, is the game of uncertainty. Nowhere can we escape it. But we are not ready to accept it, and worse still, we expect some sort of homeopathic flight of fancy by reducing this uncertainty with yet more information and yet more communication, thereby aggravating the relationship with uncertainty. Again, this is fascinating: the race-chase of techniques and their perverted effects, has started, the race-chase of man and his virtual clones on the reversible track of the Moebius Strip.[77]

The disadvantages and the advantages of such Nth power speculation and fabulation become still clearer in the context of another of Baudrillard's contemporaries, the late multimedia composer, John Cage. Resisting Baudrillard's assumption that postmodern technology axiomatically generates uncertainty, Cage posits that "our souls are conveniently electronic,"[78] and are well able to work with contemporary media. If Cage's balanced optimism points to the perils of Baudrillardian oversimplification, Cage's defense elsewhere of forms of "purposeful purposelessness,"[79] as opposed, for example, to Habermas's commitment to "purposive, rational conduct,"[80] highlights the heuristic value of Baudrillard's ludic provocations, as texts initiating further debate and disrupting rationalist discursive stagnation.

As Baudrillard observes, his Nth power rhetoric tends to prompt both celebration and denegration. "Everything I write is deemed brilliant, intelligent, but not serious."[81] As becomes increasingly apparent, Baudrillard's calculated defiance toward available concepts of the serious coexists with his frequent claim that his work is "serious just the same."[82] In Linda Nicholson's terms, Baudrillard appears overly dependent upon the elements of "human ingenuity or luck" which seem to prevail when all conventional models of communication break down.[83] Bypassing referential analysis, Baudrillard gambles with "little stories ... little things which start and which have often been the sites of emergence: situations, wit, dreams."[84]

While Baudrillard prefers to present his writings as intimations of extinction charting "the curvature of things, the mode in which things try to disappear,"[85] his work seems most interesting as what he would term "a 'wager' "[86] intent upon identifying – and in a sense predicting – significant "sites of emergence." Pondering upon the quality of that which has not yet been referenced, and resisting the rhetoric of present references, Baudrillard's writings offer a series of theory-fictions calculated to evince their subject matter's most compelling contradictions and challenges.

With luck or with ingenuity, Baudrillard seems to imply, a certain kind of consciously non-referential theory-fiction, rigorously at odds with conventional truth-claims, and inclined to examine the evidence of "things" as opposed to subjectivities, may possibly hit the mark in terms of its contemporaneity. Such, at least, is Baudrillard's avowed strategy for attaining – and perhaps communicating – some sense of "the scale" of contemporary reality.

> In reality, things happen in such a way that they are always absolutely ahead of us, as Rilke said ... things are always much further along than theory simply by virtue of the fact that the use of discourse is in the domain of metaphor. We can't escape it. In language we are condemned to using ambiguous extrapolations. If we claim a truth, we push effects of meaning to the extreme within a model. All that theory can do is be rigorous enough to cut itself off from any system of reference, so that it will at least be current, on the scale of what it wishes to describe.[87]

As Baudrillard remarks, his attempt to work to one side of referential analysis, "on the scale" of his subject matter, places him "on the margin" of mainstream intellectual writing; a position that he feels he shares with "the artists of the nineteenth century."[88] Like the American novelist Kathy Acker, Baudrillard seems to locate himself within something very close to the "*poète maudite* lineage" of those who "posit themselves as being *against* the ongoing society and culture."[89]

If it is the case, as Linda Nicholson argues, that many of the transitions between mainstream modernist and postmodernist thought involve "only . . . a shift in how we understand and use . . . categories,"[90] Baudrillard can best be understood as an impatient thinker unwilling merely "to watch the extension, the adaption, generalized reconversion of all those things."[91] Dismissing the banality of "people in the sociological sense;"[92] dissociating himself from academia – "as soon as I see three intellectuals together I run away;"[93] deploring notions of social progress – "I detest buoyant activism in fellow citizens, initiatives, social responsibility;"[94] and at the same time declaring himself a voluntary exile on the main street of art – "I want to remain a foreigner there;"[95] Baudrillard appears to oscillate between the aristocratic and plebian poses that Poggioli associates with the antagonistic impulse in the modernist *fin de siècle* mentality.

In other words, somewhat as Nicholson defines the transition between modernism and postmodernism in terms of shifts between different deployments of "common values" and "big categories,"[96] Baudrillard's subversive tactics ultimately appear little more than updated and slightly modified variants of the two heroic attitudes that Baudelaire associated with modern life – what Poggioli calls "the dandy and the criminal . . . aristocratic secession and plebian transgression."[97] Neither of these attitudes really places Baudrillard's work among the great discursive innovators of cultural postmodernism. Rather, his writings rank among the most brilliant conceptual catalysts of postmodernism, as opposed to those whose work progresses beyond the negativity that Poggioli associates with "*anti-*" discourse, via the radical experiments of "*ante-*" discourse, to "the moment of creation" when substantially new practices come into being.[98]

Discussing the more or less plebian sense of transgression in his "brutal reaction" toward the contemporary arts, Baudrillard characteristically defends his position as a theoretical terrorist on the grounds that he "can't envisage any other," adding: "It's something of an inheritance from the Situationists, from Bataille, and so on. Even though things have changed and the problems are no longer exactly the same, I feel I've inherited something from that position – the savage tone and the subversive mentality. I'm too old to change, so I continue!"[99]

Baudrillard's sense that he is "too old to change" and his reliance upon past cultural models accrue still more poignancy in the context of his suggestion that he would have preferred to live in the era "between Neitzsche and the 1920s–1930s," when "people like . . . Benjamin lived through the high point of a culture and the high point of its decline." Persuaded that "Postmodernism registers the loss of meaning" in a world in which "all that remains is a state of melancholia," or post-1930s sadness, Baudrillard concludes: "Today, we see the result of this process of decline and everyone is wondering how to remake a drama out of that. Personally, the only rebound that I found is America."[100]

As I have argued elsewhere,[101] Baudrillard's account of America drifts between symbolist and surrealist frames of reference, rather than ever coming to terms with the specific contemporaneity of American postmodern culture. The first three pages of *America*, for example, ponder upon such aspects of *l'Amérique sidérale* – "sidereal" or "astral" America – as: "the magic of the freeways;" "the fascination of senseless repetition;" "the timelessness of film;" "the transparency and supernatural otherworldly cleanness of a thing from outer space;" "magic, equal and opposite to that of Las Vegas;" "magical presence, which has nothing to do with nature;" and "the surrealistic qualities of an ocean bed in the open air."[102]

At best, *America* offers a sparkling account of American mass-culture as seen by a postmodern descendant of the surrealist poet Aragon's *Paris Peasant.*[103] At worst, as Kathy Acker observes, "It becomes a celebration of consumerism and of the culture we've got," and "a celebration of . . . the disappearance of value."[104] Considering the impact of video in terms of the ways in which discos like the Roxy emulate "the effects you find on screens," Baudrillard reduces the entire potential of video to this kind of neutralizing illusion, insisting: "Video, everywhere, serves only this end: it is a screen of ecstatic refraction."[105]

While *America* initially charms the reader as a witty travelog, written with imaginative flair by an "Aeronautic missionary" leaping "with cat-like tread from one airport to another,"[106] it finally seems flawed for precisely the same reasons that Baudrillard judges Bourdieu's sociology to be inadequate – as an exercise in "self-verification" with every potential for becoming "a sort of stereotype, an analysis which is going to produce the obvious for us."[107] As Baudrillard observes: "All of the themes that I first examined in my previous books suddenly appeared . . . stretching before me in concrete form . . . all the questions and the enigmas that I had first posited conceptually. Everything there seemed significant to me, but at the same time everything also testified to the disappearance of all meaning." [108]

Not surprisingly, Baudrillard's infatuation with America – or with America's exemplification of his own worst suspicions – was shortlived. Baudrillard now admits: "I have lost my exaltation over America. It's become trivial."[109] Reciprocally, whereas Baudrillard's *America* testified to the pleasures of discovering and effortlessly decoding foreign vistas – "I know the deserts, their deserts, better than they do"[110] – Baudrillard now seems to prefer the kind of armchair travel advocated by Huysmans' Des Esseintes. Somewhat as Huysmans' hero reasons: "After all, what was the good of moving, when a fellow could travel so magnificently sitting in a chair?",[111] Baudrillard defends the fictional register of his book *La guerre du golfe n'a pas eu lieu* (1991), on the grounds that all of the "sentimental ideological pathos"[112] of debates about the Gulf War were themselves little more than a fiction which actual travel would appear unlikely to ameliorate: "*Les Presses de la Cité* invited me to go to the Gulf and cover the war. They were going to give me everything: money, documents, flights, etc. I live in the virtual. Send me into the real, and I don't know what to do. And, anyway, what more would I have seen? Those who went there saw nothing, only odds and ends."[112]

The strengths and weaknesses of such "virtual" hypotheses are, of course, that they accelerate more plodding cultural analysis into both illuminating and deceptive excess. Working rather more cautiously, Marshall Berman, for example, has modified Habermasian notions of modernity into a more flexible concept of "modernism today" which comfortably encapsulates every "attempt to arrive at some sort of universal values" by "struggling to break through to visions of truth and freedom that all men and women can embrace."[113] With this conveniently open-ended definition in mind, Berman pronounces that "1989 was not only a great year, but a great *modernist* year."[114] Considered in terms of the lyrics to the song "Imagine," 1989 might equally well be said to be a great "Lennon year." Alternatively, considered in terms of Lyotard's definition of postmodern thought as the process of struggling "without rules in order to formulate the rules of what *will have been done*,"[115] 1989 might just as well be defined as a great "postmodernist year."

All that now separates Berman's and Lyotard's utopianism is the shift of emphasis between the former's approval of universal values, and the latter's antipathy to "the nostalgia of the whole and the one."[116] Confronted by such pedestrian distinctions, one might well turn with more sympathy to Baudrillard's attempt to look beyond mandarin quibbling over the merits and compatibilities of modernist and postmodernist great years, toward theory "on the scale"[117] of the next millenium. "My wager has been one of anticipation even if it meant making a leap, going forward beyond the year 2000; what I proposed was erasing the 1990s and going straight to the year 2000 to play the game on the other side through excess rather than lack."[118]

Somewhat as William Burroughs defines and defends the postmodern avant-garde as "*not setting out to explore static pre-existing data*," but rather, as "setting out to create new worlds, new modes of consciousness,"[119] the most utopian of Baudrillard's statements similarly contend: "Everything is involved here: to recreate another space which would be without limit (contrary to the former one) with a rule of play, a caprice . . . .

And what is being lost at the moment is this possibility of inventing an enchanted space, but a space at a distance also, and the possibility of playing on that distance."[120]

As both Burroughs and Baudrillard appear to discover, rhetorical "play" and "caprice" may well disrupt restricting intellectual ethics or conventions, but seldom suffice to inaugerate radically new alternatives to dominant practices; that is, alternatives which are not simply "shifts" to and from available discourse, but points of entry or "sites of emergence"[121] into new discursive possibilities. In Barthes's terms, such possibilities may well be "born technically, occasionally even aesthetically," long before they are "born theoretically."[122] To cite but one example, one might refer to Henri Chopin's discussion of "sound poetry, made for and by the tape-recorder," and as such, a practice "more easily codified by machines and electricity ... than any means to writing."[123]

Chopin seems to have no doubt that his research identifies what Burroughs and Baudrillard would term new worlds, new spaces, and new modes of consciousness. While he acknowledges that cultural modernism disrupted nineteenth-century realist conventions "by offering poetic language a certain dynamism (Futurism) ... by resituating discursive thought in more subtle forms (Surrealism)," Chopin defines the specific innovative quality of postmodern sound poetry in terms of its unprecedented exploration of "electronic (recording) technology, which reveals the multiplicity of the voice, of utterances, of semantic values, etc."[124]

Neither Burroughs nor Baudrillard – or indeed the majority of cultural theoreticians and historians presently attempting to define the quality of postmodern culture – seem to share the confident insights common to the pioneers and practitioners of postmodern techno-culture. Nevertheless, as writers who are also involved with other arts (Burroughs, as a painter, Baudrillard as a photographer), and who were both represented in the "Trans-Actions" section of the 1993 Venice Biennale, among other artists "whose work is based on the merging of different disciplines,"[125] Burroughs and Baudrillard frequently evince considerable sensitivity to the multi-disciplinary cultural temper of the 1990s.

Burroughs, for his part, evokes his position as that of someone who has metaphorically "blown a hole in time with a firecracker," but who feels "bound to the past," and who finally resigns himself to "Let others step through."[126] Baudrillard seems to experience a similar dilemma. His most optimistic polemic asserts that one way or another "we must try to jump over the wall"[127] of psychology and sociology, to go "through the wall of glass of the aesthetic"[128] and to "pass through all disciplines."[129] But having proposed such initiatives, Baudrillard often appears unwilling or unable to follow them through. Speculating that "Perhaps the only thing one can do is to destabilize and provoke the world around us," Baudrillard concludes: "We shouldn't presume to *produce* positive solutions. In my opinion this isn't the intellectual's or the thinker's task. It's not our responsibility. It might occur, but it will only come about by reaction.... It needs to be provoked into action."[130]

What seems most significant about Baudrillard's ambiguous writings is the fact that even when compulsively asserting "the disappearance of all meaning"[131] they continue to assert the "crucial," "actual," and "fascinating" nature of the search for meaning.[132] Despite all protests to the contrary, he repeatedly posits that intellectual inquiry should be serious and should have something "at stake." For example, when Baudrillard rejects "ill-digested rationalities, radicalities," it is because they have "no support, no enemies and ... nothing at stake."[133] Elaborating this discrimination in the following unusually assertive avowal, he specifies: "I need a challenge myself, there's got to be something at stake. If that is taken away, then I will stop writing. I'm not mad. At a given moment, however, you cause things to exist, not producing them in the material sense of the term, but by defying them, by confronting them. Then at that moment it's magic."[134]

Here, I think, we see Baudrillard in his true colors, seeking challenges in a world which he contends to be bereft of challenges, asserting that values can be at stake in a world that he associates with the disappearance of values, and aspiring to create magic in a world in which, apparently, "The maximum in intensity lies behind us; the minimum in passion and intellectual inspiration lie before us."[135] Like Des Esseintes, the hero – or anti-hero – of Huysmans' *Against Nature*, Baudrillard offers the spectacle of the hesitant utopian, "the unbeliever who would fain believe ... the galley-slave of life who puts out to sea alone, in the night, beneath a firmament no longer lit by the consoling beacon-fires of the ancient hope!"[136] In Baudrillard's terms, even if utopia "does not exist," and "may even be impossible," it is the intellectual's fate and privilege to continue "raving a little ... going beyond their objective situation and creating utopia." For, in his rather chilling judgment, "This is the only positivity they can have."[137]

Like that of any other significant theorist or artist, Baudrillard's position in the postmodern cosmos is far from simple. Considered in the relatively banal context of what Foucault called "the transformations that have actually been produced" and the systems "according to which certain variables have remained constant while others have been modified,"[138] Baudrillard offers the spectacle of a predominantly *modernist* postmodern; a theoretical revolutionary whose rhetorical variables have not really modified to any great extent.

At first glance, the titles of Baudrillard's essays and books may well seem highly topical and contemporary in their focus and theme. But, as I have suggested, Baudrillard's voluntary stance as a marginal oppositional figure, and his emphases upon the paradoxical, the magical, the surreal, and the hyperreal, are all continuous both with the early postmodern subversive tactics of the situationists,[139] and with the still earlier strategies of a succession of modernist generations ranging from such *fin de siècle* writers as Pater, Mallarmé, and Huysmans, to the subsequent pre-war mainstream modernism of Woolf, and the post-war avant-gardism of the Dadaists and the surrealists.

While Baudrillard's recent photographic work appears to have modified many of his early hypotheses, Baudrillard's overall vision seems to lack the radical audacity of such modernist *"primitives of a completely renovated sensitiveness"* as the Italian futurist Umberto Boccioni and the Berlin Dadaist Raoul Hausmann;[140] those whom Benjamin associates with the prophetic aspiration toward new practices requiring a "changed technological standard,"[141] and whom Chopin regards as "a beginning" as distant from present postmodern multimedia practices as "the plane piloted by Blériot" is distinct from "supersonic planes like the Concorde."[142]

It is precisely this kind of discursive *beginning*, aspiring toward, arising from – and then once again demanding – *changed technological standards*, that reflects postmodern culture's most vital technical and conceptual energies. As Howard Rheingold suggests, such discursive innovation is significant both as an initial avant-garde exception to the general rules of the postmodern condition, and as a subsequent conceptual and technical catalyst serving "to enhance the most creative aspects of human intelligence, for everybody, not just the technocognoscenti."[143] If the work of those whom Burroughs terms the *"astronauts* of inner space" – and those whom Rheingold terms the *"infonauts"* – is of crucial relevance to an understanding of our time, then, as Rheingold concludes, it is because "some of them may provide clues to what (and how) everybody will be thinking in the near future."[144]

Not merely pointers to new ways of *thinking*, new communications technologies also obviously adumbrate new forms of practical *activity* and *interactivity*. In this respect, neither Baudrillard's accounts of vertiginous cycles of technological simulation devoid of "real use," "real encounters," and any "genuine form of exchange,"[145] nor Gene Youngblood's diagnoses of more positive systems of technological simulation which incarnate "freedom in the digital age," but which apparently "refer to nothing outside themselves except the pure, 'ideal' laws of . . . the dematerialised territory of virtual space," seem commensurate with the *"real situations"* which Morris Berman distinguishes from the cybernetic fantasy-world of self-contained "circuits" and "feedback loops."[146]

What postmodern cultural theory needs, in other words – over and beyond the *analytical* rigor demanded by those who see Baudrillard's work as "grossly undertheorized,"[147] and the *speculative* spontaneity that Baudrillard opposes to the grossly overtheorized caution of those incapable of looking toward – and beyond – the year 2000, is *empirical* sensitivity to the specific liberating potential of emergent practices enriching postmodern *real time* in the here and now of the mid-1990s. Put another way, both the analytical and the speculative impulses in postmodern cultural theory and postmodern cultural fiction run the risk of neglecting those positively innovative discourses-in-progress which exceed their respective categories, and which in Barthes's terms exist technically and aesthetically long before obtaining adequate theoretical – or fictional – formulation.[148]

Arguably, the cartography-in-progress of innovative discourses-in-progress – as opposed, say, to the more mundane cataloging of "transformations that have actually been produced" – constitutes one of the most challenging tasks for those confronted by what Foucault terms the "abundance of things to know: essential or terrible, marvelous or droll." As Foucault concludes, there are still ┇too few means to think about all that is happening."[149]

Whatever other reactions his writings and utterances may provoke, Baudrillard continually commands respect in terms of the unusual tenacity and vivacity of his attempts to identify "means to think about all that is happening." Once one acknowledges that cultural and theoretical variants of modernism and postmodernism extend across several generations and advance at differing speeds across several contradictory fronts, it becomes evident that Baudrillard is no more typical of the postmodern mentality as a whole than Habermas is typical of its modernist equivalents. Rather, Baudrillard, like Habermas, has moments of partial lucidity, "on the scale"[150] of what he wishes to describe.

At times, Baudrillard seems altogether reluctant to describe the present in anything other than rather restrictive apocalyptic rhetoric. Nevertheless, even though Baudrillard's discursive and conceptual prejudices frequently deflect his vision away from their unerringly topical targets, toward the nostalgic never-never land of modernist poetics and nineteenth-century agonistic posture, there is frequently something profoundly engaging and inspiring in Baudrillard's idiosyncratic attempts to grapple with those issues which he finds most challenging and most at stake. Compared with the unadventurous ways in which other cartographers of postmodern culture carefully sift elementary shifts within the familiar shallows of twentieth-century discourse, Baudrillard's finest "virtual" descents into uncharted contemporary depths offer models of passionate engagement with the most crucial developments within the postmodern condition.

Notes

1 Jean Baudrillard, quoted by Mike Gane in "Ironies of postmodernism: fate of Baudrillard's fatalism," *Economy and Society*, 19 (1990) 331.
2 Arthur Kroker, *The Possessed Individual: Technology and Postmodernity* (London: Macmillan, 1992), p. 62.
3 Steven Best and Douglas Kellner, *Postmodern Theory: Critical Interrogations* (London: Macmillan, 1991), p. 111.

4 Marshall Berman, "Why modernism still matters," in Scott Lash and Jonathan Friedman, eds., *Modernity and Identity* (Oxford: Blackwell, 1992), p. 45.
5 Jean Baudrillard, quoted in Mike Gane, ed., *Baudrillard Live: Selected Interviews* (London: Routledge, 1993), p. 166.
6 Ibid., p. 166.
7 Ibid., p. 171.
8 Christopher Norris, "Lost in the Funhouse: Baudrillard and the Politics of Postmodernism," in Roy Boyne and Ali Rattansi, eds., *Postmodernism and Society* (London: Macmillan, 1990), p. 140.
9 Arthur Kroker, Marilouise Kroker, David Cook, *Panic Encyclopedia: The Definitive Guide to the Postmodern Scene* (London: Macmillan, 1989), p. 265.
10 Fredric Jameson, *Postmodernism, or, The Cultural Logic of Late Capitalism* (Durham: Duke University Press, 1991), p. 419.
11 Best and Kellner, *Postmodern Theory*, pp. 140 and 143.
12 For further information, contact David Blair, PO Box 174, Cooper Station, New York, NY 10276. Richard Kadrey reviews *WAX* in *MONDO 2000*, 7 (Summer 1992) 104–5, as "a new video-based artform" in which "video cinematography blossoms from new digital image-processing tools" (p. 105), which takes narrative compression to "a whole new level," attaining "the effect of a novel . . . in 85 retina-battering minutes" (p. 104). Discussing the conceptual and compositional *advantages* of current technology, Blair comments: "Fortunately, I discovered a non-linear editing system in New York that had been made available for artist use. The other artists had no idea what the hell they could use it for, but I went to see it, and realized this was exactly what I was trying to do. You could have 2000 pairs of digitised frames available, each pair representing the first and last frames of a shot. These were all lined up, and by pushing buttons, you could rearrange their order, like rearranging a collage on paper. Then you could order the machine to play the shots represented by these virtual stills, in the order they were arranged. Editing became so fast, it really was just like composition. And I could really try out every possible combination before I chose the sequence that I really wanted" (unpublished interview with the author, Sydney, 1992).
13 I discuss my concepts of the *B-effect* and the *C-effect* in more detail in *The Parameters of Postmodernism* (Carbondale: Southern Illinois University Press, 1993).
14 "Postmodernism and Ethical Abdication," Félix Guattari interviewed by Nicholas Zurbrugg, *Photofile* (Sydney), 39 (July 1993) 13.
15 Dick Higgins, unpublished interview with the author, Barrytown, July 5, 1993.
16 The concept of "Extreme Phenomena" appears in the title of Jean Baudrillard's *The Transparency of Evil: Essays on Extreme Phenomena*, trans. James Benedict (London: Verso, 1993). Baudrillard's notes on delusion appear on p. 1.
17 Gene Youngblood, "The New Renaissance: Art, Science and the Universal Machine," in Richard L. Loveless, ed., *The Computer Revolution and the Arts* (Tampa: University of Southern Florida Press, 1989), p. 14.
18 Ibid.

19 Marcel Janco, "Dada at Two Speeds" (1966), trans. Margaret Lippard, in Lucy R. Lippard, ed., *Dadas on Art* (Englewood Cliffs, NJ: Prentice Hall, 1971), pp. 37–8.

20 Jürgen Habermas, "Modernity versus Postmodernity," trans. Seyla Ben-Habib, *New German Critique*, 22 (Winter 1981) 7.

21 Gane, *Baudrillard Live*, p. 74.

22 Ibid., p. 64.

23 Jean Baudrillard, "The Anorexic Ruins," trans. David Antal, in Dietmar Kamper and Christoph Wulf, eds., *Looking Back on the End of the World* (New York: Semiotext(e), 1989), p. 43.

24 I elaborate my reservations regarding Jameson's accounts of postmodern culture in "Jameson's complaint: video-art and the intertextual time-wall," *Screen*, 43, 1 (1991) 16–34, and question Huyssen's interpretation of the impact of mass-media culture in *The Parameters of Postmodernism*, pp. 129–37.

25 Jean Baudrillard, unpublished interview with Nicholas Zurbrugg, Paris, June 4, 1993.

26 See Max Nordau, *Degeneration* (1896; New York: Howard Fertig, 1968). The other prime "panic" cartographers of the postmodern condition are, of course, Arthur Kroker, Marilouise Kroker, and David Cook, authors of the alarming *Panic Encyclopaedia* (London: Macmillan, 1989).

27 See Stéphane Mallarmé, "Music and literature" (1894), in William W. Austin, ed., *Debussy's "Prelude to 'The Afternoon of a Faun' "* (New York: Norton, 1970), p. 113.

28 Baudrillard, interview with Zurbrugg, 1993.

29 Ibid. Barthes discusses "punctum," in *Camera Lucida: Reflections on Photography* (New York: Hill and Wang, 1981).

30 Marcel Proust, "John Ruskin," in *Mélanges (1900–1908)*, collected in *Contre Sainte-Beuve* (Paris: Gallimard, 1971), p. 129.

31 Edward Dorn, *Gunslinger 1 & 2* (London: Fulcrum, 1970), p. 77.

32 Baudrillard, interview with Zurbrugg, 1993. See Baudrillard, *Transparency of Evil*, p. 174.

33 Gane, *Baudrillard Live*, p. 55.

34 Ibid., p. 82.

35 Habermas, "Modernity versus Postmodernity," pp. 11 and 9.

36 Stjepan G. Mestrovic, *The Coming Fin de Siècle: An Application of Durkheim's Sociology to Modernity and Postmodernism* (London: Routledge, 1991), pp. 211–12.

37 Don DeLillo, *White Noise* (London: Picador, 1986), p. 326.

38 Mestrovic, *The Coming Fin de Siècle*, p. 210.

39 Ibid., p. 212.

40 Gane, *Baudrillard Live*, p. 63.

41 Ibid., p. 66.

42 Ibid., p. 82.

43 Ibid., p. 175.

44 Ibid., p. 48.

45 Ibid., p. 44.

46 See Mestrovic, *The Coming Fin de Siècle*, pp. 210–12; Jean-François Lyotard, "Answering the Question: What is Postmodernism?" trans. Régis Durand, in

Lyotard, *The Postmodern Condition: A Report on Knowledge*, trans. Geoff Bennington and Brian Massumi (Manchester: Manchester University Press, 1986), p. 82; Berman, "Why Modernism Still Matters," p. 54; Linda Nicholson, "On the Barricades: Feminism, Politics, and Theory," in Steven Seidman and David G. Wagner, eds. *Postmodernism and Social Theory: The Debate over General Theory* (Oxford: Blackwell, 1992), pp. 87–91.

47   Tristan Tzara, "Lecture on Dada," (1924) in Herschel B. Chipp, ed., *Theories of Modern Art: A Source Book by Artists and Critics* (Berkeley: University of California Press, 1968), pp. 386 and 389.

48   Tzara, "Lecture on Dada," pp. 386–87.

49   Gane, *Baudrillard Live*, p. 68.

50   Ibid., p. 37.

51   Ibid., p. 34.

52   Ibid., p. 159.

53   Roland Barthes, "From Work to Text" (1971), in Barthes, *Image-Music-Text*, trans. Stephen Heath (London: Fontana, 1977), p. 159; Jacques Derrida, *Positions*, trans. Alan Bass (Chicago: Chicago University Press, 1981), p. 27; Michel Foucault, *The Archaeology of Knowledge and The Discourse of Language*, trans. A. M. Sheridan-Smith (New York: Pantheon, 1972), p. 5; Gilles Deleuze and Félix Guattari, "Rhizome," trans. John Johnson, in Deleuze and Guattari, *On the Line* (New York: Semiotext(e), 1983), p. 50.

54   Walter Pater, "Conclusion" (1868), in Pater, *Studies in the History of the Renaissance* (1873), in Richard Ellmann and Charles Feidelson, Jr., eds., *The Modern Tradition: Backgrounds of Modern Literature* (New York: Oxford University Press, 1965), pp. 183–4.

55   Stéphane Mallarmé, "Crisis in Poetry" (1886–95), trans. Bradford Cook, in Ellman and Feidelson, *Modern Tradition*, p. 111.

56   Virginia Woolf, "Modern Fiction" (1919), in Ellmann and Feidelson, *Modern Tradition*, pp. 124 and 123.

57   Joris-Karl Huysmans, *Against Nature* (1884), trans. Robert Baldick (Harmondsworth: Penguin, 1979), pp. 198–99.

58   Jean Baudrillard, *Les Strategies Fatales* (Paris: Bernard Grasset, 1983).

59   Gane, *Baudrillard Live*, p. 38.

60   Habermas, "Modernity versus Postmodernity," pp. 10, 12, 10, and 6.

61   Mestrovic, *The Coming Fin de Siècle*, p. 211.

62   William S. Burroughs, "On Freud and the Unconscious," in Burroughs, *The Adding Machine: Selected Essays* (New York: Seaver Books, 1986), p. 89.

63   Jean Baudrillard, *America*, trans. Chris Turner (London: Verso, 1988), p. 86.

64   See, e.g., Baudrillard's allusions to microphysics, television screens, contact lenses, assorted networks and circuits, and the domain of Telecomputer Man in *Transparency of Evil*.

65   Gane, *Baudrillard Live*, p. 105.

66   Raoul Hausmann, "Dadaism and Today's Avant-garde," *The Times Literary Supplement* (Sept 3, 1964), p. 801.

67   Michel Foucault, "Preface" to Gilles Deleuze and Félix Guattari, *Anti-Oedipus: Capitalism and Schizophrenia*, trans. Robert Hurley, Mark Seem, and Helen, R. Lane (New York: Viking, 1977), p. xii.

68   The term "astronauts of inner space" derives from Alexander Trocchi's

formulation "cosmonaut of inner space," first used at the 1962 Writers' Conference in Edinburgh. William Burroughs refers to this occasion in "Alex Trocchi Cosmonaut of Inner Space," his introduction to Trocchi's *Man at Leisure* (London: Calder and Boyars, 1972), p. 9. Jeff Berner, ed., subsequently titled a collection of avant-garde texts and manifestos *Astronauts of Inner Space* (San Francisco: Stolen Paper Review Editions, 1966).

69 Foucault, "Preface" to *Anti-Oedipus*, p. xii.

70 Henri Chopin, interview with Nicholas Zurbrugg, in Nicholas Zurbrugg and Marlene Hall, eds., *Henri Chopin* (Brisbane: Queensland College of Art Gallery, 1992), p. 41.

71 Bernard Heidsieck, "Poésure et Peintrie," interview with Nathalie de Saint Phalle, *Galeries Magazine*, 53 (Feb–Mar 1993) 54. See the encyclopedic catalog accompanying the exhibition "Poésure et Peintrie" (Marseilles: Musées de Marseilles-Réunion des Musées Nationaux, 1993). Henry M. Sayre's *The Object of Performance: The American Avant-Garde since 1970* (Chicago: University of Chicago Press, 1989) and Jean-Yves Bosseur's *Sound and the Visual Arts: Intersections between Music and Plastic Arts Today*, trans. Brian Holmes and Peter Carrier (Paris: Dis Voir, 1993) both similarly emphasize what Sayre terms "a modernism that might be said to be founded in dada and futurism" (p. xi), and what Bosseur associates with "experiments carried out … by Futurists and Dadaists or, more recently, by John Cage" (p. 5).

72 Gane, *Baudrillard Live*, p. 168.

73 Baudrillard further discusses his photography in "Cover story – Jean Baudrillard," interview with Serge Bramly, *Galeries Magazine*, 53 (Feb–Mar 1993) 78–87, 125. See too Corrina Ferrari, "L'occhio esclusivo," in the catalog *La Biennale di Venezia: XLV Esposizione Internazionale d'Arte – Punti cardinali dell'arte* (Venice: Marsilio, 1993), p. 574.

74 Jean Baudrillard, "Xerox and infinity," trans. Agitac (London: Touchepas, 1988), unpaginated.

75 Diamanda Glass, "I dominate my electronics," interview with Carl Heyward, *Art Com*, 22 (1983) 23. Galas comments: "There is a stupid concept that electronics have us evolving to this unfeeling inhuman state. I dominate my electronics."

76 Baudrillard, "Xerox and infinity."

77 The conclusion to this essay (first published as "Le Xerox et l'Infini," in *Traverses*, 44–5 (Sept 1988) 18–22) is modified in the version in Jean Baudrillard's *La Transparence du Mal: Essai sur les phénomènes extrêmes* (Paris: Galilée, 1990), pp. 58–66 and in the version tanslated as *Transparency of Evil*, pp. 51–9. An abbreviated variant of the essay's original final lines (significantly lacking the affirmation "Again this is interesting"), serves as conclusion to the essay "Supercondictive Events," ibid., pp. 36–43.

78 John Cage, letter to the *Village Voice* (Jan 20, 1966), in Richard Kostelanetz, ed., *John Cage* (London: Allen Lane, 1971), p. 167.

79 John Cage, "Experimental music" (1958), in Cage, *Silence: Lectures and Writings* (Middleton, Conn.: Wesleyan University Press, 1983), p. 12. While Best and Kellner claim that Baudrillard's scientific metaphors are often "not appropriate or particularly illuminating" (*Postmodern Theory*, p. 138), I would argue that the particularly illuminating qualities of Baudrillard's thought is

its *poetic* impetus and its *heuristic* momentum as thought self-consciously looking beyond the precise analysis that Best and Kellner would prefer.

80 Habermas, "Modernity versus Postmodernity," p. 6.
81 Gane, *Baudrillard Live*, p. 189.
82 Ibid., p. 202.
83 Nicholson, "On the Barricades," p. 89.
84 Gane, *Baudrillard Live*, p. 56.
85 Ibid., p. 38.
86 Ibid., p. 39.
87 Ibid., p. 125.
88 Ibid., p. 75.
89 Kathy Acker, interview with Nicholas Zurbrugg, quoted in Zurbrugg, *The Parameters of Postmodernism*, p. 148.
90 Nicholson, "On the Barricades," p. 89.
91 Gane, *Baudrillard Live*, p. 66.
92 Ibid., p. 45.
93 Ibid., p. 24.
94 Ibid., p. 14.
95 Ibid., p. 168.
96 Nicholson, "On the Barricades," p. 89.
97 Renato Poggioli, *The Theory of the Avant-garde*, trans. Gerald Fitzgerald (Cambridge, Mass.: The Belknap Press of Harvard University Press, 1968), p. 32.
98 Ibid., p. 137.
99 Gane, *Baudrillard Live*, p. 168.
100 Jean Baudrillard, interview with Catherine Francblin, *Flash Art*, 130 (Oct–Nov 1986) 55.
101 See Nicholas Zurbrugg, "Baudrillard's *Amérique* and the 'Abyss of Modernity,'" *Art and Text*, 29 (June–Aug 1988) 40–63.
102 Baudrillard, *America*, pp. 5 and 103.
103 See Louis Aragon, *Paris Peasant* (1926), trans. Simon Watson Taylor (London: Picador, 1980).
104 Acker, interview with Zurbrugg, *Parameters of Postmodernism*, p. 146.
105 Baudrillard, *America*, pp. 36–7.
106 Ibid., p. 13.
107 Gane, *Baudrillard Live*, p. 63.
108 Ibid., p. 135.
109 Ibid., p. 187.
110 Baudrillard, *America*, p. 63.
111 Huysmans, *Against Nature*, p. 142.
112 Gane, *Baudrillard Live*, p. 182.
    Ibid., p. 188.
113 Berman, "Why Modernism Still Matters," p. 54.
114 Ibid., p. 55.
115 Lyotard, "Answering the Question: What is Postmodernism?," p. 81.
116 Ibid.
117 Gane, *Baudrillard Live*, p. 125.
118 Ibid., p. 22.

119 Burroughs, "On Coincidence," *The Adding Machine*, p. 102.

120 Gane, *Baudrillard Live*, p. 61.

121 Ibid., p. 56.

122 Barthes, "The Third Meaning," *Image-Music-Text*, p. 67.

123 Henri Chopin, "Open Letter to Aphonic Musicians," trans. Jean Ratcliffe-Chopin, *OU*, 33 (1968) 11.

124 Henri Chopin, Reply of July 17, 1979 to a questionnaire on " 'Advances', and the Contemporary Avant-garde," *Stereo Headphones*, 8–9–10 (1982) 74. See Chopin's more detailed consideration of the specific qualities of sound poetry in his history of the genre, *Poésie Sonore Internationale* (Paris: Jean-Michel Place, 1979). For more recent studies of the genre see Vincent Barras and Nicholas Zurbrugg, eds., *Poésies Sonores* (Geneva: Contrechamps, 1993).

125 Achille Bonito-Oliva, unpaginated *Press Release* for the 45th Venice Biennale, 1993.

126 William S. Burroughs, *Cities of the Red Night* (London: John Calder, 1981), p. 332.

127 Gane, *Baudrillard Live*, p. 39.

128 Ibid., p. 25.

129 Ibid., p. 81.

130 Ibid., p. 170.

131 Ibid., p. 135.

132 Baudrillard, "Xerox and Infinity."

133 Gane, *Baudrillard Live*, p. 37.

134 Ibid., p. 44.

135 Baudrillard, "The Anorexic Ruins," p. 40.

136 Huysmans, *Against Nature*, p. 220.

137 Gane, *Baudrillard Live*, p. 80.

138 Michel Foucault, "The Birth of a World" (1969), interview with Jean-Michel Palmier, in Sylvère Lotringer, ed., *Foucault Live: (Interviews, 1966–84)*, trans. John Johnston (New York: Semiotext(e), 1989), p. 60.

139 For further discussion of situationism as an early postmodern movement, see my article " 'Within a Budding Grove:' Pubescent Postmodernism and the Early *Evergreen Review*," *The Review of Contemporary Fiction*, 3, 10 (Fall 1990), 150–61.

140 Umberto Boccioni, Carlo D. Carrà, Luigi Russolo, Giacomo Balla, and Gino Severini, "The Exhibitors to the Public" (1912), in Chipp, *Theories of Modern Art*, p. 297. Here, as in other futurist manifestos, these artists claim to be "primitives" of the machine age.

141 Walter Benjamin, "The Work of Art in the Age of Mechanical Reproduction" (1936), in Benjamin, *Illuminations*, trans. Harry Zorn (Glasgow: Collins, 1979), p. 239.

142 Chopin, Reply of July 17, 1979, p. 74.

143 Howard Rheingold, "New Tools for Thought: Mind-Extending Technologies and Virtual Communities," in Loveless, *The Computer Revolution and the Arts*, p. 23.

144 Burroughs, *Cities of the Red Night*, footnote 49; Rheingold, "New Tools for Thought."

145 Baudrillard, "Xerox and infinity."

146 Youngblood, "The New Renaissance: Art, Science, and the Universal Ma-
     chine," p. 15; Morris Berman, "The Cybernetic Dream of the Twenty-first
     Century," in Richard L. Loveless, ed., *The Computer Revolution and the
     Arts* (Tampa: University of Southern Florida Press, 1989), p. 94.
147 Best and Kellner, *Postmodern Theory*, p. 128.
148 Roland Barthes, "The Third Meaning," p. 67. I am thinking here of various
     kinds of experimental technological postmodern creativity which overtheorized
     analysis frequently marginalizes out of existence (refusing to recognize that
     which it cannot categorize) and which overfictionalized theory frequently
     exaggerates out of existence (as discourse supposedly beyond all "real" and
     "genuine" exchange). Qualitative recognition seems to offer the first step
     toward subsequent theoretical definition of such innovative practices. Dis-
     cussing the sound poet Henri Chopin's semi-abstract composition "La Peur"
     (collected on Chopin's LP *Audiopoems*, TCS 106 (London: Tangent Records,
     1971)), the composer Sten Hanson emphasizes its thematic validity and its
     technological intensity as a "40-minute poem about how man mobilises all
     his inner resources to analyse and fight his fear – of destruction, of living,
     of dying," in which "The combination of the exactness of literature and the
     time manipulation of music makes it possible to penetrate and influence the
     listener more deeply and more strongly than any other artistic method"
     (Hanson, "Henri Chopin, the sound poet," *Stereo Headphones*, 8–9–10 (1982)
     16). In much the same way, the medievalist Paul Zumthor's discussion of
     "La Peur" concludes: "Chopin's sonic variations on the word 'fear' consti-
     tute, to my mind, one of the most powerful poems of our time" (Zumthor,
     "Une poésie de l'espace," in Barras and Zurbrugg, *Poésies Sonores*, p. 12).
     My point here is that Hanson's and Zumthor's *identification* of qualitatively
     significant postmodern technological creativity both oversteps the reserva-
     tions of cautious orthodox theory, and avoids the apocalyptic overstatement
     of speculative fictional assertion, laying tentative claim – as it were – to new
     discursive fields requiring further analysis. Without such initial sensitivity to
     emergent practices arising within – and making reference to – what Morris
     Berman terms "real situations," the terms of cultural analysis seem fated to
     become indistinguishable from the kind of self-contained simulacra that too
     many critics mistake for the substance of the postmodern condition, and the
     objects of cultural analysis – as Jameson discovers – "all turn out to be 'the
     same' in a peculiarly unhelpful way" (Jameson, "Reading without interpre-
     tation: postmodernism and the video-text," in Nigel Fabb, Derek Attridge,
     Alan Durant, and Colin MacCabe, eds., *The Linguistics of Writing: Argu-
     ments between Language and Literature* (Manchester: Manchester University
     Press, 1987), p. 222).
149 Foucault, "The Masked Philosopher" (1980), interview with Christian
     Delacampagne, in Lotringer, *Foucault Live*, p. 198.
150 Gane, *Baudrillard Live*, p. 125.

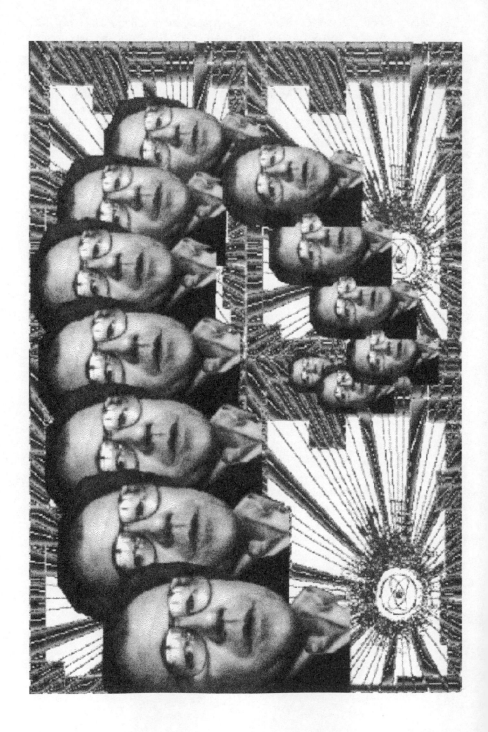

12

VALORIZING 'THE FEMININE' WHILE REJECTING FEMINISM? – BAUDRILLARD'S FEMINIST PROVOCATIONS

A. Keith Goshorn

The initial concern of this essay was to help answer a troubling question which frequently arises in critical studies of Baudrillard's writing: What is his final position toward feminism? Is he a friend or foe? What is the underlying impetus behind the seemingly bold attempts to provoke feminist sensibilities often perceived in Baudrillard's writing? How accurate is Jane Gallop's often cited remark that Baudrillard is "... the French male theorist who most explicitly and most frontally adopts an adversarial relation to feminism?"[1] Is Baudrillard just abysmally ignorant of current feminist theory, or are these provocations merely of a piece with his long-practised intellectual style of presenting a critical challenge by trying suddenly to place in doubt the well-established presumptions of even the most respected thinkers, perhaps ultimately more of a gesture of engagement and honor issued from a self-described theoretical "terrorist?" But does this strategy often only lead to "... arbitrary and gratuitous provocations?"[2] The abundance of inflammatory remarks toward women in his writings leads me to doubt if there could possibly be any credible defense mounted for Baudrillard's case as a potential ally for feminists. Thus, it is somewhat of a surprise to discover the possibility that Baudrillard (the atavistic reclaimer of the "secret" and the "surprise") in his more recent writings may have arrived, almost in spite of himself, at a position on gender and sexuality that at times intersects favorably with the most progressive trends in current feminist thought.

Trying to answer any of the above questions immediately underscores the relatively few passages in Baudrillard's texts where he specifically mentions feminist thinkers (Irigaray, Kristeva) or makes references to what he perceives to be feminist thought and attitudes, as well as the relatively small amount of direct commentary by feminists on his work (Morris, 1984, 1988; Burchill, 1984; Moore, 1988; Jardine, 1985; Gallop, 1985; Hunter, 1989; Braidotti, 1992). This scarcity raises the question of whether Baudrillard's reputation and/or his attitude toward women have interfered with any kind of productive engagement of the one with the other, especially when there are multiple indications that Baudrillard is in fact involved in a common struggle with feminism against the naturalized hegemony of certain patriarchal institutions and the masculinist project of rational mastery in Western culture.

Yet more crucial than the above general considerations should be an examination of Baudrillard's rather careless employment of a category of "the feminine," particularly in constructing one of his central theoretical figures, the notion of *seduction*. His usage of "the feminine" here and elsewhere in his writing surely appears, on the surface, to be risking a narrowly essentialized definition of the term, and one drawn from the social postures of a previous century at that. Worse, he might be said to be participating in a continued "metaphorization" of the feminine,[3] which marks the distancing and objectification of women as Other-ness. Seen in this light, his posture would only be typical of a long history of male philosophers trying to "place into discourse" an idealized or imaginary "feminine" while remaining relatively indifferent to or ignorant of the status of the "real" women around them. Furthermore, can he also fairly be charged with employing an outmoded binary and oppositional sense of masculine/feminine polarity – even though he is obviously trying to exca-vate through the theory of seduction a strategy which, even in the words of his harshest critics, seems to "... subvert ... fixed dualities between masculine and feminine"[4]? The charges of his allegedly essentialized usage of femininity (and masculinity) must be weighed not against any possible ameliorations by elder male generational oversight (if it is indeed only that), but against the possibility that his intention has been rather to deconstruct the historical function of the *category* itself and how it has supposedly been used. From this perspective, his aim is not primarily to create a discourse of female submission, but to develop a counterfactual sub-discourse which set an overt agenda by which masculine prerogatives have only constructed themselves in defensive and insecure postures against a naturally superior female order and its dominant set of "secret" goals.

While any, even preliminary, understanding of his precarious position here will require some defining extrapolations of what a deliberately uncipherable and non-representative theory of seduction represents, a fair-minded critique will require some speculation as to what purpose the author intended by such a theory as well as a judgment of its results. One must then determine what advantages and disadvantages Baudrillard has given himself in trying to counter the tyranny of the rationalist productivist ethic with language drawn from a long-passed epoch rife with sexist and "aristocratic"[5] overtones. And, finally, we can ask whether he may be wisely obliged to abandon an unworkable theory of seduction in his attempt to formulate a subversive counter-weight to the dominating mode of capitalist productivism. And, regardless of our judgment on any of the above, at this point in time, our attention is merited by any theorist who undertakes to question and challenge, even indirectly, the cultural foundations of the religion of "free market economy" which, along with its semiotic viruses of commercial promotionalism and the commodification of discourse, have so thoroughly naturalized themselves into nearly all aspects of contemporary life, especially its discourse of "sexuality." Baudrillard deserves further scrutiny from feminists most particularly here for his attention to the exchange value basis of traditional sexuality and its reflection of capitalist objectification, paradoxically reproduced by its emphasis on individualist "subjectivity" or subjective "individualism." For this sexuality as feminists have known all along, is tainted as a sub-set derivative of what Baudrillard calls "the abjection of free enterprise."

Although it is unavoidably necessary in addressing the issues at stake in this essay to use the conventional distinctions of "male" critics and "female" critics, I do not intend to suggest in any way a grouping of qualities around or inherent to either. Likewise, I do not mean to imply anything necessarily synonymous between "women" and "feminists," even if these two do occasionally get thrown together here. Furthermore, it should be obvious by now that to be a feminist is not to automatically belong to one gender or the other. Indeed, one of the foremost points I hope to establish is that Baudrillard's continuance in identifying women only with certain universalized "feminine" qualities is a severely detrimental limitation to the overall more-radical intentions of his theoretical project.[6] This becomes evident when we begin to see the contradictions that result from his acceptance of the Freudian axiom of a single, masculine libido theory of sexuality implicit in his early writings on seduction, in contrast to his later theorizations of entering a condition of *transsexuality* which begin to resonate with the more progressive feminist notions of gender as a culturally learned performativity. His notion of transsexuality is but an aspect of a greater cultural movement of *transvestism*, which is the term he utilizes to characterize the implosion of previous fixed cultural polarities into what he sees as our current state of *indeterminacy*.[7]

Ultimately, more is at stake here than simply deciding whether Baudrillard has made sexist remarks, held onto essentialized notions of women and "the feminine," or has been a deliberately antagonistic provocateur of feminism and the social movements for women's "liberation." What finally matters in the resolution of such questions is whether significantly new currents of thought have arisen which have possibly erased the need or the basis for past antagonisms. The one thing which I would assert with some certainty at the outset is that both the adherents of the multiple strains of today's feminisms as well as the multiple adherents of Baudrillard's theoretical project will be far better off if they can listen to and learn from each other. For the French theorist is no more a "traditional male" than he is the embodiment of his self-described "supreme femininity." And the most alert of today's feminists no more see themselves as a group of self-liberated "autonomous feminine subjects" than they are a group of "non-seductive female phallocrats" as seen in the eyes of some of their detractors.

In trying to present all sides of the case for and against him, I had planned to adopt a stance in this essay that Baudrillard should be seen as neither friend nor foe of feminism, but someone who has occasionally tried to engage with generally perceived feminist positions (or more accurately with his own perceptions of women and feminism). Such a neutral stance becomes more difficult the more one encounters both his outrageous remarks concerning women and certain unexpected parallels in his theoretical positions with those of an oppositional feminism. While perhaps he cannot be faulted, as certain of his male peers are, for adopting predictable strategies of friendly rapprochement that mask familiar patterns of attempted control and distancing, Baudrillard clearly is lacking an adequate overview of the many strands of feminist thought as shown by the dearth of specific references throughout his commentaries. Also quite apparent is his interest in the broader cultural categories of "woman," the "feminine," and "femininity" rather than in any specific issues of women's social condition or feminist theory.

The reader may judge for herself from the discussions that follow whether Baudrillard does at least, as I contend, share a common opposition to the excesses of phallogocentrism and the extant pathologies of masculinist behaviors and institutions in contemporary Western culture. Looking for traces of his own hidden "gender ideology" is at least somewhat easier with Baudrillard than with other male thinkers who do not wear their biases so openly as to serve as deliberate provocations. Whether Baudrillard is, at heart, truly antagonistic to the concerns of feminism, or is, on the contrary, personally concerned with engaging in a dialogue – to "take feminism against the grain," as Sylvere Lotringer has rather generously described it[8] – remains to be seen. The conclusions to which both I and, hopefully, the reader come should be deferred to the end of the following discussions.

Baudrillard, as a French theorist from a particular intellectual period, has a certain past to overcome which sometimes impedes and interferes with his own direct perception of women and gender relations in contemporary culture. In spite of his numerous and frequent critiques of psychoanalysis and its failure to "inscribe its own necessary death" within its own discourse of 'truth,' Baudrillard himself is ultimately limited and victimized by the lingering power of its truth-effects. He, apparently, like others of his intellectual generation who came of age during the "return to Freud" via Lacan, is far too invested in either disproving or defending psychoanalytic positions to break free from the limits of its universalizing view of sex and sexuality. Thus, even as he sides with feminists against the social results of the primacy of the "one" masculine libido in the construction of gender roles, he nevertheless accepts this theoretical explanation at its face value and tries to find a strategy around its cultural dominance that will be more effective than (what he perceives as) the women's movement:

> Freud was right: there is but one sexuality, one libido – and it is masculine. Sexuality has a strong discriminative structure centered on the phallus, castration, the Name-of-the-Father, and repression. There is none other. There is no use in dreaming of some non-phallic, unlocked, unmarked sexuality. There is no use seeking, from within this structure, to have the feminine pass through to the other side, or to cross terms. Either the structure remains the same, with the female being entirely absorbed by the male, or else it collapses, and there is no longer either female or male the degree zero of the structure. This is very much what is happening today: erotic polyvalence, the infinite potentiality of desire, different connections, diffractions, libidinal intensities – all multiple variants of a liberatory alternative coming from the frontiers of a psychoanalysis free of Freud, or from the frontiers of a desire free of psychoanalysis.
>
> The danger of the sexual revolution for the female is that she will be enclosed within a structure that condemns her to either discrimination when the structure is strong, or a derisory triumph within a weakened structure.[9]

I present this lengthy citation here for several reasons – not only to illustrate Baudrillard's obviously rather entangled relationship with psychoanalytic discourse, but also to show that his relation to feminism is not a simple one of adversarial antagonism. Regardless of the traction of his stance in critical disagreement, it is clear that he is concerned about what is to be the fate of women and the future of a historical form of "sexuality" that is in a state of flux. The critique above is really aimed more at the various theories of libidinal and sexual liberation or revolution which proliferated in the 1960s and 1970s. Yet the recognition in this 1979 text of the accelerating dissolution of traditional sexual structures and gender categories points to the social issues developing from these changes that have polarized into some of the most prominent political struggles of the succeeding decades – from the rights for control over reproductive freedom to the rights of sexual minorities and gender identifications. Whatever one thinks of his rhetoric vis-à-vis feminism, Baudrillard has provided some unique cultural analyses of the unseen changes unfolding around the challenge to the "phallic exchange standard." In trying to theorize his own alternative strategy for its subversion through the figure of *seduction*, I suggest that by the 1990s he may have begun to think himself out of what some had perceived as a conservative turn in his political trajectory.

COMPLICATIONS IN THE RELATION OF FEMINISM TO "POSTMODERNISM"

In evaluating Baudrillard's theoretical relationship to feminism I chose not to count too heavily the numerous passing asides in the form of personal commentaries found throughout the *Cool Memories* volumes and *America*.[10] Yet it is also in these relatively "popular" texts where many of the most provocative, scandalous, or self-condemning statements about women have been made by Baudrillard. These are often the utterances regarding which he has been already indicted for various forms of sexism, usually charges that have been brought, we should note, by other white male scholars. While these comments cannot be ignored, I believe the confessional nature of these "journal entries" should occupy a somewhat differently scrutinized region of textual analysis than his formal theoretical contentions, akin as they are to something closer to the confessions or revelations of personal "process."

I bother to address this point here because of the number of ostensibly scholarly critiques of Baudrillard the postmodern theorist which have drawn almost exclusively on statements made in these popular-audience publications.[11] What is objectionable about this is the often-complete lack of familiarity with the complexities of Baudrillard's ideas in the larger body of quite different theoretical works apparently never read by these critics. One thing is made clear in this situation, however, and that is that Baudrillard continues to grow as a controversial emblem of the multiple sins of "postmodernism." These sins, some his own, some belonging to others mistakenly conflated with his work, are what keep him in the spotlight as a magnet, a scapegoat for all that is wrong with "postmodernist thinking" and its frequently cited political "irresponsibility," its social "indifferences," or its philosophical "nihilism."

In the case of animosities emanating from feminists toward Baudrillard, we must take pains to recognize to what degree the complaints against Baudrillard issue from a broader mistrust, fear, and suspicion of that highly generalizable category known as postmodernism, and the post-structuralist critiques which have accompanied it. Feminists who see themselves and their work as allied with a cause or a socio-political movement have been no less anxious than any other political constituency over such troubling issues as the "death of the subject." Within the broad span of contemporary feminisms there are those who see any acknowledgment of this theoretical contention to be a loss of agency and therefore unacceptable for their political project. Seyla Benhabib's comments in this regard are exemplary of the rather widespread view that feminism and postmodernism are not allies:

A certain version of postmodernism is not only incompatible with but would undermine the very possibility of feminism as the theoretical articulation of the emancipatory aspirations of women. This undermining occurs because in its strong version postmodernism is committed to three theses: "the death of man . . ." the "death of history . . . ," and "the death of metaphysics . . ." Interpreted thus, postmodernism undermines the feminist commitment to women's agency and sense of selfhood, to the reappropriation of women's own history in the name of an emancipated future.[12]

Others recognize that if the alleged death of the humanist subject is a cultural development as well as a political one, it is not escapable by mere denial or contestation. Judith Butler has voiced a forceful counter to such thinking that is worth including here:

To claim that politics requires a stable subject is to claim that there can be no *political* opposition to that claim. Indeed, that claim implies that a critique of the subject cannot be a politically informed critique but, rather, an act which puts into jeopardy politics as such. To require the subject means to forestall the domain of the political, and that foreclosure, installed analytically as an essential feature of the political, enforces the boundaries of the domain of the political in such a way that the enforcement is protected from political scrutiny. The act which unilaterally establishes the domain of the political functions then as an authoritarian ruse by which contest over the status of the subject is summarily silenced.[13]

Butler's mapping out of the contours of this impasse suggests immediately recognizable analogs, from the foreclosure of political debate over a host of issues that never receive media attention in domestic and international politics to, appropriately enough, the way Baudrillard's "metaphysical" discourse is summarily dismissed by some, as no longer legitimate social or political theory.

Some feminists scholars have chosen to concentrate on the challenge of theorizing political action without the requirement of traditional agency, or, as in Butler's argument, that there "need not be a 'doer behind the deed,' but that the 'doer' is invariably constructed in and through the deed."[14] Inasmuch as Baudrillard is associated with a vision of postmodernity in which there remain few decisions in the control of the individual as "agent," a condition at least partially responsible for the "indifference of the mass(es)," he also frequently becomes marked as the purveyor of this condition. The contemporary state of confusion, even among critical intellectuals, is illustrated by the strange fact that the theorist (and especially Baudrillard) is somehow held responsible for, or branded as a champion of, the condition he or she merely describes (i.e., ". . . Baudrillard's soulless world of signs and simulacra"). As elsewhere in the current postmodern situation that exists beyond the former adjudication of verifiable "evidence," the voices of dire warning are met by the voices of stubborn refusal. Wendy Brown has emphasized the political dilemma as it manifests itself within feminist circles:

> From feminists who array themselves "against postmodernism," the rare acknowledgement of a distinction between postmodern conditions and theory, between epoch and politics, is a political move. The conflation of such elements by those steeped in materialist analysis and practiced at attending to fine gradations of *modernist* feminisms speaks a stubborn determination to vanquish evidence of historical developments which its antagonists blame on *thinking* – the latter often portrayed as dangerously relativist, irresponsible, unpolitical, or unfeminist. In other words, the move to blur or collapse these critical distinctions speaks a desire to kill the messenger .... If the "postmodern turn" in political/feminist theory is, at its best, an attempt to articulate and engage the characteristic powers of our age, what frightens feminism about this age and about developing a politics appropriate to it?[15]

We could add that such anxieties apply quite well to responses to the agenda offered by Baudrillard, underlining his emblematic role as the embodied threat of a radical postmodern theory. Brown also reminds us of another factor that is often overlooked in the attacks on postmodern theory and theorists in the name of progressive political activism – the defensive nature of causes, including certain versions of the cause of feminism, which hold on to what might be called an "exceptional identity," elsewhere associated with "identitarian" politics:

> ... reactionary foundationalism is not limited to the political and intellectual Right, but emerges across the political spectrum from what they perceive to be postmodern political decay and intellectual disarray. Like identity politics, it is both a symptom of and act of resistance against the epistemological, political and social terrain postmodernity forces us to inhabit. Reactionary foundationalism ... rarely and barely postures as Truth. More often, it presents and legitimates itself as the indispensable threads preserving some indispensable good, e.g., Western civilization, the American way of life, feminism, or Left politics.[16]

This critique, of course, inhabits the same familiar realm of poststructuralist criticism where Baudrillard has long resided. We see him continually dedicated throughout his writings to combating the ossifications of meaning produced and reproduced by truth constructions which fail to recognize their own inevitable reversibility and cultural limitations. And Baudrillard is obviously not the type to make special exceptions for anyone on this call, not for feminism, the truth of "Desire" ("female" or otherwise), or the campaign for women's rights – any more than for "History" or "Capital." What he argues against is a lack of awareness, failure to recognize the full scope of all the codes and overlays of meaning constructed by the culture in which one lives. Unfortunately for him, what he lacks is awareness of the many specific efforts of feminist scholars on these very issues and of how his own historical construction as a privileged, white, heterosexual male conditions his perceptions of feminism in particular.

At the same time, it is quite appropriate to facilitate a collision between Baudrillard and feminism, heretofore auspiciously avoided by both sides. In the case of the male theorist it will inevitably expose his own reactionary, gender-bound conservatism around certain unexamined issues; and in the case of the political cause of feminism, it may supply a useful challenge toward tactical re-evaluations. I would hope that what is thus displayed might show that Baudrillard is neither the sacrosanct theorist who has superseded all possible challenges, nor the gratuitous theoretical terrorist attacking others solely for the sake of self-publicity – neither as innocent or as guilty as he is alternately made out to be. And finally, it is hard to avoid the truism that Baudrillard, as much as any other contemporary writer, can be and generally is read with wildly divergent interpretations and conclusions. This is about the only safe thing to be said about him without risking a glaring contradiction at some later point. This probably is partly by design in his own work, but it becomes particularly relevant, as we shall see, when examining his contentions about women and feminism.

THE ROLE OF SEDUCTION

When introducing the collection she edited, *Seduction and Theory*, Dianne Hunter describes for us the appropriateness of attention to the term *seduction* in acknowledging how it "... focuses a current debate concerning the status of woman – as the fetishized object of the male gaze on one hand, and, on the other, as a source of metaphor for deconstructive theory and practice."[17] Baudrillard is heavily implicated on both sides of this debate. He obviously has utilized it beyond what anyone might have expected as a privileged metaphor in a complex deconstructive discourse found in *De la séduction*. But his views on the status of women and where he is personally situated in relation to the "male gaze" and fetishized objects, opens up an interminable problematic in his writings which thoroughly complicates his use-value for feminists.

To understand Baudrillard's conception of the role of seduction, and particularly as it applies to feminism and women's "liberation," we must see it in the heavily burdened role in which he has tried to cast it. Seduction in Baudrillard's narrative (sometimes here approaching a *grand récit* or a "master narrative," thus giving a certain kind of justification to Kellner's claims of a literal "metaphysical" turn in Baudrillard's thinking) is conceived as an antidote to the whole reigning discourse of "production" and its naturalized truth. But seduction is still "greater" than this, for he believes it actually can, and does, function in continual daily opposition to not only the cultural hegemony of production, but also the even-more deeply submerged truth claims in the historically oppositional discourse of "revolution" and "liberation." ("For revolutions and liberations are fragile, while seduction is inescapable. It is seduction that lies in wait for them – seduced as they are, despite everything, by the immense setbacks that turn them from their truth – and again it is seduction that awaits them even in their triumph."[18]) This crucial issue will be further discussed later, but it is important to note that Baudrillard's harshly criticized writing "against the left" in *Le P.C. ou les paradis artificiels du politique* (1979) and *La gauche divine* (1985) as well as his critique of "women's liberation" are in some ways a precursor to today's mounting critique of "identity politics."

However, to use this defense of Baudrillard in his remarks against feminism becomes more problematic. While feminists have cautioned against the risks of both identity politics and of universalizing the category of "women,"[19] Baudrillard goes further, or not as far in this case, and blithely accuses a universalized feminism of being anti-seductive, as seen in this rather antagonistic interjection included in a chapter of *Seduction*: "Even the most anti-seductive figures can become figures of seduction. (It has been said of the feminist discourse that, beyond its total absence of seduction, there lies a certain homosexual allure.) These figures need only move beyond their truth into a reversible configuration, a configuration that is also that of their death."[20]

If nothing else, this passage perhaps confirms at least one of Gallop's (1985) charges against Baudrillard that, for all his talk about needing to be seduced in order to be seductive, he remains resolutely unseduced by any form of feminism, holding to his own rigidly irreversible (and sometimes blatantly ill-informed) opinion. His parenthetical remark also reproduces an old patriarchal cliche, that feminists are only women who are not interested in men, yet who imitate men, thereby reducing a political enterprise to a matter of sexual orientation.

A further contradiction arises when we consider that within Baudrillard's numerous writings, seemingly every possible nuance of the term *seduction* and its historical usage has been carefully, subtly attended to and analyzed. In the light of this protracted effort over many years spanning several publications, it is rather odd to realize how apparently little attention has gone into the analysis of (even his own usage of) the terms *feminine*, *female*, *woman*, and *women*. What is at stake here is whether he partakes in the much scorned practice of male thinkers who use ". . . the feminine as a metaphor for all that Western thinking has not been able to represent."[21] This is an issue that of course has received much attention, from the major French feminists of the 1970s to Alice Jardine's treatment in *Gynesis*, and Rosi Braidotti's *Patterns of Dissonance*. While many other male theorists have been taken to task along these lines, Baudrillard's relative neglect or avoidance by feminists has prevented his coming under close scrutiny here. Yet the reader is periodically taken aback to find seemingly archaic opinions voiced by Baudrillard, as for example this interview statement: "I consider women to be the absence of desire. It is of little import whether or not that corresponds to real women. It is my conception of 'femininity.' "[22] To be fair we should add that he has tried at times to qualify what appears as his essentialized usage of femininity in his own provocative fashion: "To be sure, one calls the sovereignty of seduction feminine by convention, the same convention that claims sexuality to be fundamentally masculine. But the important point is that this form of sovereignty has always existed – delineating, from a distance, the feminine as something that is nothing, that is never 'produced,' is never where it is produced (and certainly cannot, therefore, be found in any 'feminist' demand.)"[23]

Alas, certainly for many others, it is of great importance not to reproduce the imaginary conception of women that has so often characterized the role of "the feminine" for male thinkers. Certainly, at times, it does seem he is participating in a continuation of that modern cultural practice where "images of women" become "conventionalized signs producing a category of woman, not woman as a subject."[24] Yet this may be in some ways a premature judgment when we recognize that Baudrillard's long-standing analysis of "simulacra culture" makes him pre-eminently aware of this very process and its analogs, particularly the role of *fashion* and the historical role of women and the female image in the history of promotional signs. In fact, he has often contended that the image of "woman" has become the very emblem of "promotional culture." Thus, for rather complex reasons in his overall cultural analysis and his attempt to counter certain current trends, Baudrillard is *not* interested in woman as subject, but rather is specifically interested in the subversive possibilities of woman precisely *as* object.

It is worth examining the understanding Baudrillard holds about the existing cultural institution of "sexuality" because his position there will determine whether he himself is still broadcasting a perpetuation of the restrictive "one libido and it is masculine" theory of gender construction carried over from psychoanalytic conceptions or, whether he can be judged to be surprisingly in agreement with many feminists about the masculinist construction of what passes as "sexuality." Many of Baudrillard's most direct and revealing statements about his perception of women and the feminine as cultural categories come not in the texts that deal with seduction,[25] but rather in *Forget Foucault*. Here, Baudrillard's previous critique of the tendencies in Marxist rhetoric toward a redemptive or transcendental meta-narrative are matched by an equal criticism of the hidden trope of production immersed in psychoanalytical as well as anti-psychoanalytic models of sexual energy. Illustrating even here the maintenance of some dimension of a political critique, he contends that the problem with these theoretical edifices describing either the repression or the liberation of sexual desire is their derivation from the truly dominant, hegemonic and unseen master discourse of our cultural era, that of *capital*:

> The compulsion toward liquidity, flow, and an accelerated circulation of what is psychic, sexual, or pertaining to the body is the exact replica of the force which rules market value: capital must circulate; gravity and any fixed point must disappear; the chain of investments and reinvestments must never stop; value must radiate endlessly and in every direction. This is the form itself which the current realization of value takes. It is the form of capital, and sexuality as a catchword and a *model* is the way it appears at the level of bodies. . . . to discover the secret of bodies an unbound "libidinal" energy which would be opposed to the bound energy of productive bodies, and to discover a phantasmal and instinctual truth of the body in desire, is still only to unearth the psychic metaphor of capital.[26]

If this is, indeed, the case, then it is difficult to imagine that following such strategies that adhere to this already naturalized, deep-set model could lead to any significantly different direction.

Baudrillard's own theory of seduction has been consciously developed to avoid all of these traps, striving to distinguish its fundamentally subversive and "outlaw" status among both normative and oppositional discourses on this culture's psycho-sexual condition:

> If sex and sexuality, such as the sexual turns them into, are really a mode of exchange and production of sexual relations, seduction on the other hand is contrary to exchange, and close to challenge. Sexuality has precisely become a "sexual relation," it can be talked about in these already rationalized terms of value and exchange, only by ignoring any form of seduction – just as the social only becomes a "social relation" when it has lost any symbolic dimension.[27]

Yet Baudrillard's notion of seduction is constantly accumulating further responsibilities and exceeding its apparent intentions. The question that we must pose is whether, even as a purely figural signifier of oppositional reversibility, it can handle all the heavy roles which he has nominated it to carry? In spite of its noble intentions, there are, nevertheless, abundant risks in his discourse on seduction versus other "productivist" forms of sexuality. Not only are familiar positions reversed and parodied and played off one another, but they are alternately defended and criticized – even some of the most obviously traditional "phallic" stances – all in the name of subverting the exchange economy of productivism and the patriarchal institutions that authorize it. No doubt this is the way Baudrillard would have it; what he is reaching for is a grasp of strategies that supersede any given cultural and social identities or the rational-technological methods of tracking and manipulating them.

In the long run, we can imagine the possibility of Baudrillard's ambitious theory of seduction overcoming even his own bad reputation of potential sexism and gender antagonism with which he personally has allowed it to be associated. And it need not be something of an "embarrassment" to him, as Mike Gane has suggested,[28] even if he sometimes is that. Here again Baudrillard has provided, perhaps inadvertently, another example of "objective irony," when theory itself acts as object and proves itself and its strategies superior to those of the subjects who think they have created it and thus control it.

CRITICISM AND CITATION BY FEMINISTS

After Douglas Kellner's earlier, more severe, indictment of Baudrillard which described him as "attacking and ridiculing" feminism,[29] the characterization of Baudrillard's scattered comments about women and feminism as "violent provocations" has been echoed by a relatively sympathetic male critic, Mike Gane.[30] Yet it has been Jane Gallop's originating remarks in a brief essay published earlier in 1989 which probably have been the most influential in disseminating the notion that Baudrillard is no friend of women or feminism and probably is the origin of much of the antagonism that allegedly exists between the two. It is Gallop who declared not just that Baudrillard has been insultingly critical of feminist sensibilities, but that he was an outright "adversary" who has made a "rather rabid attack ... on feminism."[31] In "French Theory" Gallop made some pointedly insightful criticisms that effectively did put Baudrillard in his place in regard to some insufficiently thought-out comments on women and feminism appearing in *De la séduction*. She was, of course, interested in this particular text because she, herself, had recently published a book called *The Daughter's Seduction* which dealt with feminism and psychoanalytic theory. Although Gallop obviously had read Baudrillard's text she couched her remarks in the role of "introducing" a new French theorist to a feminist audience, explaining that he was "certainly not as well known in Anglo-American circles as other contemporary French theorists" and being uncertain whether the text on seduction had ever been translated into English. Thus, she hardly presumed to be speaking as an authority, nor did she presume her feminist readership to be well-familiar with his work. It should also be noted that Baudrillard is deemed an adversary because "Throughout the book he persists in seeing feminism as stupid, wrong, mistaken .... he cannot imagine – except for the defenses of a triple mediation – finding feminism seductive. Feminism can only be an adversary, forcing him away from seduction's reversibility into the strategy of irreversible truth, the very position he has designated as weaker, stupider, inferior." Yet ultimately, for Gallop "It is his assumption of this position of superiority (that he knows what is best for women), of speaking the truth – more than any content of 'truth' he may utter – which offends me."[32]

There does not seem to be much of a defense available for Baudrillard against these charges, except to recall that what was popularly identified as the "woman's movement" in France in the late 1970s (the period when *De la séduction* was written) had a considerably more beleaguered public-relations image than that which has finally been attained in the 1990s, especially when we consider the fact that it was not until 1981 that women actually gained the right to vote in France. To understand how he could be so openly critical of "the women's movement" and feminism requires an understanding of the French context in which his early work on seduction was written. And, in this case, it is a contextualization that, if it will not let Baudrillard off the hook, it at least makes a great difference in understanding why he has been able to show so little respect for the very idea of feminism. Consider here the testimony of Alice Jardine, who, like Gallop, has also named Baudrillard as taking a negative stance against feminism, but who has tried to explain the context in which he appears no different from many other French theorists of his time, including some taken to be feminists themselves:

> I would even go so far as to say that the major new directions in French theory over the past two-decades – those articulated by both men and women – have, by and large, posited themselves as profoundly, that is to say conceptually and in *praxis*, anti – and/or post-feminist. Feminism as a concept is traditionally about a group of human beings in history whose identity is defined by that history's representation of sexual decidability. And every term of that definition has been put into question by contemporary French thought.[33]

We might also recall that Jacques Derrida's characterization of the angry "feminist" which he opposed to the "affirmative woman" in his controversial text *Spurs*[34] from the same period is much more antagonistic than Baudrillard's. Applying the same criticisms of Derrida to Baudrillard that have been voiced by several feminist writers, from Irigaray to Jardine to de Lauretis, we can ask whether Baudrillard is guilty of the same implicit strategies of "gynesis," of the placing of women and the "feminine" into discourse only to better control them by continuing to "represent" them? While it would seem to be the case that Baudrillard, like Derrida, is critical of feminism because of its perceived continuation of *phallogocentrism*, the former is decidedly not interested in marking out a "safe" discursive space or merely a "textual femininity," as Sally Robinson describes the gestures of Derrida which she sees as ironically disguising another layer of the masculine attempt at further *mastery* by "occupying" the place of the feminine.[35] In fact, Baudrillard wants to "loose" the powers of seduction, which he considers to be feminine, against the overwhelming cultural control in daily life of production and the compulsion to master the object world. On the other hand, when Robinson cites de Lauretis's critique in *Technologies of Gender* where she accuses Derrida and other male theorists by implication of "displacing the question of gender onto an ahistorical, purely textual figure of femininity,"[36] we have the basis for a legitimate interrogation of Baudrillard's figure of *seduction*. Baudrillard may not "deny" the history of women's oppression, nor the subjective difference in women's experience of gender, but he certainly has done no better at recognizing "the epistemological contribution of feminism to the redefinition of subjectivity and sociality" as de Lauretis, Robinson, and many others have further charged of contemporary male philosophers. Indeed, his discourse on the seduction and ambiguity of "the feminine" could benefit immensely from the incorporation of multiple feminist critiques of long-essentialized categories.

Yet, in his apparent taunting of feminism, Baudrillard is not *just* trying to provoke a response from women; and he exhibits familiarity with the issues of the "anatomy is destiny" debate, particularly as it is manifested in psychoanalytic discourse. In a rare gesture, he even quotes a passage from French feminist Luce Irigaray to make his point (albeit to show how she reproduces without realizing it the "anatomy is destiny" position in her own critique of it).[37] Baudrillard recognizes the same problem, identified by feminist theory, of the need to combat the "phallocratic structure," but he clearly thinks his own strategy is a better one than that which he sees as the frontal approach of "the woman's movement."[38] What he is trying to do here is to maintain (or resurrect) a space for *seduction* and the importance of appearances which he contrasts to feminist goals of "autonomy, difference, a specificity of desire and pleasure, a different relation to the female body, a speech, a writing"[39] In other words, if the development of the traditional structures of "sex" and "sexuality" has been based upon the universalized dictates of the masculine libido according to psychoanalytic theory, and if "any theory of the subject is always appropriated by the masculine," as Irigaray has phrased it, then Baudrillard does not think it will do much good to simply reverse the marked term on the "strong" side and try to stand in its place, to create a new form of subjective autonomy in the name of what would be, for him, only a female phallocracy. He also questions what is being missed in the rejection of the historical "advantage" of women and its under-appreciated (by feminists) subversive "virtues":

> There is a strange, fierce complicity between the feminist movement and the order of truth. For seduction is resisted and rejected as a misappropriation

of women's true being, a truth that in the last instance is to be found inscribed in their bodies and desires. In one stroke the immense privilege of the feminine is effaced: the privilege of never having acceded to truth or meaning, and of having remained absolute master of the realm of appearances. The capacity immanent to seduction to deny things their truth and turn it into a game, the pure play of appearances, and thereby foil all systems of power with a mere turn of the hand.[40]

Needless to say, this argument rests on Baudrillard's idealized sense of the "feminine," and he speaks as if he knew exactly how all feminists felt about the subject of seduction. Yet contradictions abound here as Baudrillard claims that seduction is important precisely because it *"alone is radically opposed to anatomy as destiny,"* and because "Seduction alone breaks the distinctive sexualization of bodies and the inevitable phallic economy that results,"[41] in both cases seemingly in allegiance with feminist positions. He even tries to invoke the commentaries of Joan Riviere's 1929 essay "Femininite sans mascarade" to back up his usage of the category of the "feminine" in the services of seduction as something that is indifferent to distinctions of artificial and authentic; in her words "Whether femininity be authentic or superficial, it is fundamentally the same thing."[42] This nuance is utilized in a complex but tenuous argument that continues to be developed throughout *De la séduction*, and its success or failure rests upon a number of further direct provocations which include some startling defenses of the "traditional woman."[43] By giving his definition of femininity the allegedly subversive quality of "reversibility," Baudrillard has been trying to theorize a force that is in some subtle way superior to the power that has always resided with the phallocentric discourse of complementary polarities. Thus, "Masculinity has always been haunted by this sudden reversibility within the feminine. Seduction and femininity are ineluctable as the reverse side of sex, meaning, and power."[44]

Realizing that Baudrillard has aligned himself with feminists against phallocratic masculinity, we may wonder if perhaps he has deliberately issued his provocations as a challenge (*défi*) to see how feminist thinkers will respond to his theorizations. Yet one sometimes gets the impression that Baudrillard has backed himself out on a limb for the sake of a few favored theoretical terms. The fact that he has done little either to update his original writings on seduction and "the feminine" in light of the recent immense amount of relevant feminist scholarship, or to respond to criticisms, fails to recommend him to a feminist readership.

Throughout his work the liberated, self-determining "woman" is posed against Baudrillard's own specific notion of a reversible "femininity." Faced with this situation we can either rush to condemn his apparently limited and archaic notion of femininity and the continued "metaphorization" of the feminine, or we can try to recognize here a critique of what appears to be another version of the self-determining bourgeois subject that

Baudrillard finds evidenced in the feminist crusade for emancipation and autonomy, as well as other movements attempting to recuperate a fading sense of subjective agency. After all, he has long staked his claim on the inevitable superiority of the *object* over the subject, and we soon learn that he is quite serious in contending that women's former (for him, successful, because *artifice*-ial) role as sexual object was far preferable to any subjective strategies they have since devised for their advancement. This is not quite as simplistic or as foolish as it first appears to be, and it leads us to an early consideration of what may be Baudrillard's most telling or crucial statement on women. In *Forget Foucault* Baudrillard has more explicitly stated his seemingly paradoxical stand of upholding the value of the feminine, opposing phallocracy, and yet totally doubting the efficacy or wisdom of the movement for "women's liberation." The following statement, included as a footnote to his explanation of the reversible quality of his motion of *challenge*, may give the reader a further opportunity to assess his "adversary or ally" relationship to feminism:

> This is no doubt the same reversibility the category of the feminine has exerted on the masculine throughout the entire course of our culture's sexual history: thus the challenge the feminine offers the masculine of taking its pleasure (jouissance) alone, and of alone exercising the right to pleasure and sex. Women's right to reserve sex and to deny pleasure, their constant reversals, and their continuous refraction of sexual power into the void have always exerted an incalculable pressure, with no possibility of response from the "strong" masculine side except a headlong flight into phallocracy. Today phallocracy is crumbling under this very challenge, taking with it all forms of traditional sexuality – and not at all due to social pressure from any sort of feminine liberation.[45]

Whatever quaint charm the language and sentiments of this passage may hold, and whether one may agree in any way with his own intentionally "challenging" argument, it is made all too clear that Baudrillard is laboring under his own very archaic conceptions of what women are and do, let alone under his own reified idea of "the feminine."[46] Anyone living today in contemporary Western culture surely knows that any or all of the qualities he or she attributes to women can be, and often are, as easily the prerogatives of men; and one would think that surely he must be aware of the absurdly antiquated essentialism of such notions. Nevertheless, there is the possibility of an underlying historical argument here that should be distilled from its immersion in glib personal opinions.

Although I have chosen not to concentrate on Baudrillard's personal commentaries collected in the *Cool Memories* journals, there are a few passages whose direct relevance demand attention. (The most outrageous and absurd remarks about women here have already been discussed at length by both Kellner and Gane.)[47] An instance where Baudrillard directly speaks of what he thinks his relation to feminism to be, if only as an aside, is cited here to show how Baudrillard consciously places himself on the side of women, but not at all in the camp of feminism:

> Revolution – including the revolution of desire – is even less kind to those who think it has already happened than to those who oppose it. Thus it is not the Revolution which will turn me into a woman. That will come about by my espousing here and now – passionately – the position of femininity itself. Now for feminists this is unpardonable. For this position is more feminine, with all the supreme femininity it implies than that of women will ever be.[48]

It is not too difficult to see why such writing might provoke feminists, enough so to convince one that surely it has been intended to do so, even in this context. Besides presuming he knows what feminists would think, and there is an ironic tone of masculine bravado in this declaration of a male's assuming a state of "supreme femininity," perhaps he is deliberately trying to cast himself in the position of the "worst" ("I'm not a feminist, I'm *worse*!"), following his own theory of outbidding and hyperrealization. Only such a twist could mollify the arrogance of such a passage.

Yet this appears among a section of reflections when Baudrillard reveals, at least, that he has thought often about the difficulties of actual, and not just abstract, relations between men and women – including his own. Other passages are more obstinately opinionated, but still others, which have no doubt been taken as insulting provocations, reveal, upon close reading, a sometimes-surprising degree of complexity in his reflections on gender. These must be weighed against the most criticized, already notorious passages, generously scattered throughout *Cool Memories* and *America*, where women are remarked upon with a careless profusion of cliches and profundity, with that peculiar mix of cruelty and admiration that marks the defiantly "unliberated" male. While it can stand as no excuse for his most tasteless affronts to feminism, Baudrillard obviously stands on the far side of some vague generational dividing line before which men felt some deep-set obligation to resist the claims of a new role for women. In this respect, he deserves to be called a reactionary, perhaps at times even a "Rightist." And perhaps Gallop will continue to be correct in saying that "Baudrillard cannot seduce feminism with his truth, because he protects his truth from being seduced by feminism."[49]

Many feminists have taken Gallop's pronouncements at face-value and have proceeded, from the assumption that he is "hostile" to women, to disregard him altogether, but a few have chosen to expand the critique of the theorist branded as their adversary. A case in point is an interesting essay by Suzanne Moore. Moore puts a different spin on the cultural studies trope of postmodern "tourism," visits by citizens of the colonizing nations to the lands of their formerly colonized subjects now in the voyeuristic guise of the tourist. As she puts it: "What I want to look at here is a new kind of gender tourism, whereby male theorists are able to take package trips into the world of femininity. The glossy tourist brochures of contemporary theory offer cut-price entry into these exotic places."[50]

While the target of Moore's rather aggressive attack runs from the lyrics of the androgynous pop star Prince to Roland Barthes, she does find time to single out Baudrillard for a special indictment. To her credit, she is, nevertheless, able to invoke usefully other aspects of his theory in other contexts of her essay. Moore summarizes the arguments of other feminists in making the case again that an idealized category of the feminine has always, and again with contemporary poststructuralist theory, served as a signifier for all that the masculine subject cannot represent, through its many permutations as *absence*, *lack*, the *unsaid*, the *Other*, *desire*, *indeterminacy*, and all those other correlates that mark the limits of a male-constructed rational discourse. Her complaint is how attention to these limits, and recognition of their relationship to women and femininity, is perhaps now more than ever allowing male thinkers to address "the feminine" without really engaging with actual women and their different social experience. Do these theoretical maneuvers allow them to simulate an *entry* into the feminine while remaining equally indifferent to the status of those real women around them? Although Moore does not deal with it specifically, the most salient question suggested here vis-à-vis Baudrillard is whether or not or to what degree his theorization of the figure of *seduction* parallels this pattern?

Meaghan Morris is one of the few feminists to have published any article of length on Baudrillard, and she remains one of only a few critics who seem to be able to address Baudrillard on his own level. Capable of sometimes mimicking or even mocking his style, she none the less takes up the challenge offered by Baudrillard, and seems more capable than many of his critics of integrating his multiple themes into an intelligible critical synthesis. In the introduction to her book *The Pirate's Fiancée*, Morris already had charged that Baudrillard's discourse was among those "tending to deny *all* critics (. . . feminists in particular for Baudrillard . . .) a place from which to speak, or the possibility of having something to say."[51] She attempts to follow Baudrillard's rhetorical constructions only to pronounce them as a grand endeavor in *hype*, and one that, ironically, ultimately places us back in the "prison house of language" again. For all her incisiveness and insight, Morris also remains among those stiffly unamused critics of Baudrillard who refuse to respond to his humor or acknowledge his parody, those who resolve to remain "unseduced" by his poetically hyperbolic style:

> So Baudrillard's discourse is garrulous about the silence of an object which might somehow speak: so it vaunts the powers of enigma and seductive

senselessness, while creating a most severe and rigorous and predictive alle-
gorical mode of reading and writing: so it summons fictions, not to end but
to double and redouble ever-expanding exposition: and so, in the end does
Theory (not the crystal, the corpse, the beauty, the hostage) come to embrace
itself as work-of-art, dire object, and absolute commodity.[52]

And she is ultimately bothered by that typical stumbling block that
many find in his writings, the familiar presence of *nihilism*, which, once
ascertained, seems to invariably provide, along with a sense of relief, a
cynical and jaundiced view of the author. Morris finds a bleak nihilism
accompanied by a predictable retreat into the well-worn *modernist* refuge,
the old trap of the intellectual speaking only to himself: "We ourselves
have made sure there is no way out: and turning as we confirm on every
page that nightmare absence of Things, we see the sign of our own dear
despair approaching – with the assurance that in this place, whatever the
question, we will know the answer already."[53]

The tone of Morris's indictment thus rests with those readers who can
only approach Baudrillard's writing with a disposition of *resentment*, as
Lucio Privitello has said of another astute but unseducible critic of
Baudrillard.[54] Again, one cannot get around the fact that for all the readers
who are charmed or inspired, there is something about this emblematic
French postmodernist that alternately provokes suspicion, distrust, and
resistance. It would be easy to imagine that these negative impressions are
linked to the perception of underlying retrograde sentiments such as the
alleged sexism with which he had been charged. However, even in this
most thorough analysis available by a feminist, Morris's "Room 101,"
there are no complaints on that account. It is further relevant that Gallop's
better-known critique of Baudrillard's "adversity" to feminism is not based
on a perception of sexism or misogyny, but rather on his audacity in giving
women unsolicited critical advice (potentially, at least, a form of sexism)
and refusing to be "seduced" by the popular rhetoric of feminism. Thus
what we might finally conclude from the feminist readings of Baudrillard,
whether critical or approving, is that the basis of antagonism, when it
exists, derives as much from disagreement with his theoretical positions
and his intellectual personality as it does from any inherent adversality
between the two.

RESPONSES BY MEN TO BAUDRILLARD'S PROVOCATIONS

After reviewing the evidence of Baudrillard's verbal offenses against
feminism, it seems very difficult to mount any kind of convincing defense
or excuses. Without doubt he is often "guilty." As to what degree, and
how this should or should not affect our reading of his overall project are

more difficult questions that will have different conclusions for different readers. But one senses with Baudrillard, and perhaps with his whole generation of males, that simmering beneath the surface is a resentful sense of feminists as "thought police," as enforcers of politically correct positions or of a "new political orthodoxy" marked out by women that push him toward some semblance of an "adversary." And if so, does that identify him as a rightist? Or as a "neo-conservative," remembering that one definition for this category is "a former liberal who's been mugged?" Perhaps those who once openly and without contest enjoyed the multiple privileges of an earlier phallocratic/phallocentric culture are more sensitive and reactive to its "crumbling" erosion than are younger generations of males who have never been fully able to, or have never wanted to, enjoy such inegalitarian privileges? A defensive reaction may also be visible in Baudrillard's attempts to counter-charge that beneath the feminist injunctions for acceptable/non-acceptable behavior between genders is an only slightly veiled attempt to reinstate their own laws in place of the patriarchal laws they have helped to dismantle. (This is similar to the position Derrida took in questioning the feminist project in a 1984 seminar.)[55] In the first collection of his journals from the early 1980s (*Cool Memories I*) Baudrillard wrote that" . . . the feminist imaginary . . . sees no difference between rape and seduction, every advance on the other is an unacceptable infringement of one's space (*une promiscuité unacceptable*). But what is an inviolable and inalienable body? A dream of castration. The feminist dream is also the dream of the law (habeas corpus)."[56]

Nevertheless, there are a few dim signs that Baudrillard is trying to "evolve" in his understanding of women, if not correcting his *provocateur* attitude, as seen in these 1982 remarks:

> Man is a touching sight in his contemplative pornography (peep show, live show, etc.). He confusedly pays homage with his gaze to the perfection of a body which lacks nothing. For men do not believe in this business of the castrated woman. They know woman has a perfect body and that her body will never lack anything. And their gaze reflects this: if the feminine body can offer itself in this way, deliver itself up to the eyes without withholding anything, this is a sign of a great power. The power of prostitution which man will never know, any more than he will know that of parturition.[57]

The above passage is followed by remarks contrasting the behavior of women watching a male striptease. But here he finds the female spectators motivated by their own fantasies of "castration" and "revenge," once again showing the ties that still bind his thinking to the Freudian master-narrative.

Curiously enough, in spite of Baudrillard's undisguised provocations of feminists, it would seem, none the less, that male critics have often been more hostile and scathing than any women on record in their attacks on his perceived anti-humanist 'nihilism" (by conservatives and mainstream liberals) and his politically "incorrect" statements about women, Marxism, and American culture (by left academics). At least three male critics have been so bothered by the perspectives taken in his writings that he was pronounced utterly "lost" (Christopher Norris "Lost In the Funhouse" (1990), Arthur Vidich, "Baudrillard's *America*: Lost in the Ultimate Simulacrum" (1991), and J. Hoberman, "Lost in America: Jean Baudrillard, Extraterrestrial" (1989)). Thomas Dumm goes so far as to say that: "Baudrillard, whose old fashioned Euro-colonial racism and sexism are embarrassingly evident in *America*, uses that racism to connect the savage and the primitive in the United States in ways that astonish and infuriate even the most racist and sexist amongst us."[58] Yet, without diminishing the extent of his verbal affronts, we might wonder if there may be some connection in the serious offense taken by some males to Baudrillard's criticism of US culture and of its women, particularly as found in *America*, to that enduring chivalry that can be so easily provoked into a fight to preserve the sacred honor of "my country" (mother, sweetheart), or "our women", etc. Could this be something akin to the masculine registry of transgression of an unconscious code of identity and its obligatory proprietary protection, the stuff of traditional patriarchal, heterosexual male pride? Indeed, Baudrillard's remarks about American culture brought out the patriotic pride of even radical left critics who were seen in the rare posture of defending all those good qualities of the country that Baudrillard had so outrageously failed to see. Beyond this, there is also, perhaps, a need to consider the full motivations of men who speak from the position of the indignant feminist in condemning the sexism of other males, something that sometimes allows ventilations of frustrations and anxieties built up from fears or previous experiences of reprisals for their own offenses. No doubt on some level Baudrillard knowingly incites such reactions – the other, initiating side of the traditional male ritual of provocation and challenge.

Yet there is another aspect of Baudrillard's personality, of his intellectual character, that cannot be captured by merely calling him a provocateur, or even a "theoretical terrorist." I mentioned in an earlier writing[59] that Baudrillard could aptly be compared in attitude to the hard-core punks of the late 1970s and early 1980s. But not only does he slam-dance with utter disregard on the well-manicured playing fields of formal academic discourse, he engages in a mock parody of the excesses of masculine behavior, just like the early punks, in order to deconstruct and expose its insecurities. In both cases there is an implicit challenge offered, which, if taken literally and missing the comic ritual, results in indignant insults registered by the earnest critic-observers who failed to get the joke. The tendencies of either sincere earnestness or moral attachment to fixed signs of ideological righteousness, whether found on the right or the left side of political identification, inevitably serve as a barrier to the reception and understanding of postmodern art and theory, especially those forms which play with the reversibility of sign-forms as part of their practice.

But there are other dimensions to the hostile opposition Baudrillard seems to stir up that are more interesting than these rather basic provocations, other reactions that transcend political lines. One of these is the fact that Baudrillard has, unlike anyone else in the theoretical arena, seemingly tried to occupy the position of having given up, renounced, let go of, ceased getting support and protection from, and has quit giving fealty to any and all legitimating authority or "Fathers," intellectual, spiritual, or political (allowing for the one unconscious exception discussed perviously of his own entanglement in Freudian conceptual structures). And only those with commitments to the past, with some remaining fealty to a Father, could find "nihilism" here while missing the search for "some ritual more adventurous than the pursuit of meaning." The "Name of the Father" in all versions would seem to have been purged progressively from his thinking, and the "rules of the game" are for Baudrillard always privileged over the Law, any Law. There is no inherent reverence or respect for any apparent "metas-" or "masters" – no gods, no narratives, and not science, not literature, not politics, not history or any implicit humanism, no valorization of the individual or the collective, not rationality or reason or any other submerged guise of patriarchal religions or humanisms. If this absence is the cause of what is for many so disturbing about his writing, it is also the cause of his appeal. So purged of truth-claims is Baudrillard that one need not take seriously any of his own frequent rhetorical ones. His widely perceived nihilism can also be a refreshing, invigorating postmodern achievement. It is also fitting that he disclaim all formal identities: no longer a sociologist or an academic, not presuming the crutch of any other "professional" title nor accepting the critical accolades of "philosophical poet," he can only joke about being a "pataphysician," a "metaphysician," a writer of "science fiction," or perhaps "a moralist." And it is especially because of all of this that his archaic and reactionary positions on women and feminism are so self-defeating and such a disappointment. For a thinker to have gone so far in escaping the influences of the past and its regimes of truth, it is both sad and inexplicable, perhaps inexcusable, that he has not been able to elude the most common blinders of simple gender bias.

Thus, there seems to be a reactionary counter-current evident in Baudrillard's radically acute vision of the way the social world is currently dysfunctioning, one that is most evident in his invocations of the category of the feminine. While in the broader cultural picture firmly contesting the rights of everything else of which patriarchal values are representative or supportive, his atavistic insistence on upholding worn-out gender stereotypes allows masculinist biases and potentially sexist sentiments a back-door re-entry. Baudrillard's sometimes totally retrograde version of "woman" and women is simply out of key with everything else he would appear to uphold. His notion of "femininity," the operative term behind the central figure of seduction, could possibly function just as well under another name. Unlike others, I do not think the philosophical and politically significant theory of seduction is an "embarrassment"; nor do I think it should be abandoned. To be widely heard, however, it will have to be brought out of its eighteenth-century trappings and into the present context of human relations where, by his own account, images and appearances, now more than ever, are paramount. Perhaps what Jean Baudrillard, postmodern media theorist, is in need of more than anything else is simply a "public relations" manager to eliminate his needless and damaging gaffes.

ARTIFICE AND DIFFERENCE

When deciding to valorize the activities of artifice as an aspect of his theory of seduction, it is doubtful that Baudrillard realized that there was already an ongoing debate among feminists about whether this tradition in its personal practice has been detrimental or useful to women. Probably without knowing it he was entering and complicating this debate by casting traditionally "feminine" practices in a new light as potentially, even inherently subversive.[60] Reading the ability of women to play with the given context of their environment and alter their disadvantaged position in a world overtly dominated by the power of men, suggests a certain affinity with such feminist visions as Donna Haraway's celebrated "Manifesto for Cyborgs."[61] Although Baudrillard's thinking in regard to women is neither as supple or as romantic as Deleuze and Guattari's talk of "desiring-machines" and "becoming-woman," he nevertheless stands on the side of these attempts to develop the weaker "minority" position to resist and neutralize the dehumanizing cultural effects of rationalist instrumentalism and productivism – that which Haraway proposes resisting with the rather "homeopathic" tactic of the cyborg, an artifice of human and machine consciousness. It is seduction which in his thought tends to take on the role of a reverse or "soft" instrumentalism to counter the hegemonic masculinist model, while Haraway envisions the cyborg countering the "artifactualization" of the world by science and rationality. What she reads as the resultant "de-vivified" world has recognizable parallels with his vision of disenchanted world of commercial simulacra. None the less, there are feminists who take issue with the "subversive" rehabilitation of artifice, as exemplified by Rita Felski's remarks below after citing the precedent of "female machines" in nineteenth-century novels:

> The representation of femininity as artifice and/or machine is already a well-established trope in modernity existing alongside, and sometimes in conflict

with, the more familiar ideal of women as redemptive, unalienated nature. Such representations, however, seem to function less as subversive challenges to the ideology of humanism than as misogynistic fantasies of gaining final control over an unruly female body. Haraway's assumption that the appeal to artifice is more transgressive than the evocation of nature becomes questionable in the light of such a history.[62]

Yet Baudrillard (and perhaps Haraway as well) is actually pursuing a somewhat different track, one that for him involves another paradoxical invocation of a form of personalized *simulation* and *dissimulation*. This is another gesture toward subjects acting more like objects as a means of countering the debilitating effects of the generalized cultural absorption in commercial or promotional simulation which he equates with an "obscene" attempt at further "mastery of the real." In *Fatal Strategies* he speaks at length on the concomitant "loss of the secret, of distance, and of the mastery of illusion," and offers some subtle but significant distinctions that are rarely noticed:

> We have completely forgotten the form of sovereignty that consists of the operation of simulacra as such. But culture has never been anything but that: the collective sharing of simulacra, as opposed to the compulsory sharing of the real and of meaning today. Sovereignty lies only in the mastery of appearances, and complicity lies only in the collective sharing of illusion and secret.
>   Everything that forgets this scene and this mastery of illusion and veers towards the simple hypothesis and mastery of the real falls into the obscene. The mode of apparition of illusion is that of the scene; the mode of apparition of the real is that of the obscene.[63]

For those who can hold in check the tendency to relegate all of the above to the realm of "metaphysics," there are several interesting issues mentioned which touch upon the practice of artifice and illusion as enchanted forms of simulation and their potential for deployment in the struggle against institutionalized truth, meaning, and control. What is surprising in the argument above is the sense that we are always in some way living in a "culture of simulacra," and thus, perhaps, it is only the extreme degree of total immersion in *commercial* simulacra which characterizes the present postmodern culture and which has brought it to our critical attention as a dystopian development. Needless to say, such an understanding flies in the face of those superficial critics of Baudrillard who have tried to cast his critique of simulation as one of nostalgia railing against the lost authenticity of the past, thereby placing him in the most reactionary mode. But we are reminded again of the distinctions he has always maintained between "enchanted" and "disenchanted" simulations, the latter including those which are produced for the sheer currency of promotional sign-forms (*publicité*). Furthermore, we are reminded here that he has obviously also complicated the notion of complicity beyond its usual simple legal implication in English. What is suggested is also a notion of "communal complicity" in sharing certain illusions and secrets in the sense of a voluntary "game with rules," as opposed to our present immersion in the "compulsory sharing of the real and of meaning today," enforced by the *law*(s).

Of crucial relevance here is his previously mentioned thesis that women's overt subordination to men in the past has been part of a complicit cultural cover-up of men's inferiority and insecurity in the face of the superior power of women and the feminine, something which has been disguised behind the erections of phallic institutions of power and mastery in the limited domain of the "real." It has been on the basis of such thinking that Baudrillard has tried to justify his "advice" to women to not completely abandon this historical advantage by "passing through to the other side" and occupying the site of phallic power in the (ironically) illusory scene of the real. But there is ample room for contradictions and controversy here. For which is worse? A traditional hierarchy of social relations propped up by collective complicity in a ritual which situates overt power with one gender and covert or hidden power with the other. Or a self-identified "progressive" society which replaces a previously ritualized subordination with the overt *signs* of "liberation," that are too often only those of commercial "hype" functioning as the basis and pretext for developing the formerly subjugated group as an expanded market of consumption? This familiar model of "production" of a new market is also, in an important sense, the *re*-production of subjugation, and one which has obvious parallels with racial and ethnic minorities being sold products in the name of their minority *identities*, but which, in fact, are being reprocessed and sold back to them as part of new market development tactics. These models and methods of late capitalist activities, of course, mark that point at which the production of new signs is more important than the production of new "products," but it also amplifies the reasons for Baudrillard's dismissive skepticism toward the motifs of "liberation," "revolution," and other such modernist terms of resistance which, in the present postmodern culture, are so smoothly recuperated into the system of commercial promotion and exchange. Thus, he comments that "It is because femininity secretly prevails that is must be recycled and normalized (in sexual liberation in particular)."[64] It is in this light also that his critique of "the women's movement" should be judged. Because he, like other social critics in France in the 1970s, saw the "second wave" of feminism as one being driven by the successful selling of the *sign* of women by the commercial, promotional apparatus of market capitalism.

Yet, ultimately, the more telling indications of Baudrillard's underlying conservatism or radicalism on the issue of gender is to be measured from his later writings when he becomes more concerned with the effects of the steady erosion and dissolution of the traditional markers of sexual difference. Baudrillard recognizes, just as many feminists have recognized, that one of the most significant features of contemporary culture is the crisis of phallic masculinity and its predominant symbolic institutions. The gradual slide into a state of cultural *indeterminacy* in all domains is made particularly evident through the loss of clear-cut sexual difference previously firmly established by the standards of a traditional phallic heterosexuality. Concern with this has become an increasing preoccupation for Baudrillard that will challenge his own political alignment within the contemporary scene of postmodern theory. Indeed, where anyone goes at this point in responding to such realizations is, in the present context, an unavoidably political decision – ranging from reactionary calls to return to "traditional family values" to the organized demands for equal legal rights for all sexual persuasions and preferences.

How to deal with this has been no less controversial among feminists, as can be seen from Butler recounting the troubling worries arising from debates over the meaning of gender, "as if the indeterminacy of gender might eventually culminate in the failure of feminism."[65] In his writing in the early 1980s, Baudrillard clearly worried that the loss of the traditional social polarity which gave rise to the "masculine prerogative" would be the end of the historical form of seduction between male and female if things were reversed (here not being faithful to his own faith in reversibility):

> The transfer of sexual iniative to the woman has created a new situation. For the masculine prerogative, from the time of the "woman as object," at least gave rise to a whole culture of passion and seduction, to a novelistic culture linked to the game of sexual interdiction. Such a culture is scarcely possible in the opposite direction. One doesn't see the man assuming the modesty and secrecy, provocations and withdrawal, the whole sublime and subliminal strategy of the object, which made for the eternal feminine. There is no eternal masculine because there is no interdiction which protects the man from the sexual demands of the woman. The woman who wants a man has no need to seduce. The man, if the woman so wishes, will still have to seduce her.[66]

We see here how much he is still caught in the perceptions of traditional sexual order and is on the verge of a reactionary, gender-based complaint. Yet by the end of the 1980s he was ready to embrace the slide into sexual indeterminacy as he constructed a new theory of postmodern culture defined by "the law that is imposed upon us by the situation itself and which we can call postmodern: that is, the law of the confusion of genres and genders."[67] In a provocative *geste de bons mots*, he described how the earlier sexual revolution had ironically led to "a new game of sexual *indifference*"[68] as "sexuality loses itself in the theatrical excess of its ambiguity and indifference."[69] The new cultural field he sees, that of indeterminacy and *transsexuality* translating into all spheres of social interaction, has partly been brought about by "the loss of virile mythologies, and also of feminine emblems."[70] Throughout this transitional period, as is typical with Baudrillard, profundity is always intermixed with the utterly banal.

A careful reading of all of these texts – which perhaps began with the publication of "What Are You Doing After the Orgy?" – will find him floating on the edges of what appears to be a near-reactionary conservatism.[71] His stance almost begins to sound like the lament of a staid moralist before coming to declare in "Le mélodrame de la difference" that *difference*, especially of the sexual sort that has preoccupied much contemporary criticism, is at bottom only a "utopia," a product of discourse and therefore a variable construct of culture.

It is only in his travels to America, where Baudrillard begins to warm to the changes in the possibilities opened up by the post-"Orgy" state of total "liberation" of sexual identities. His instinct is to mock this new state of affairs a bit as he circles around it, before he decides that it just might be preferable:

> A new development in the field of sexuality. The orgy is over, liberation is over; it is not sex one is looking for but one's gender, i.e., both one's look and its genetic formula. People no longer oscillate between desire and its fulfillment, but between their genetic formula and their sexual identity (to be discovered). This is a new erotic culture. After a culture based on prohibition ... this is a culture based on the questioning of one's own definition: "Am I sexed? What sex am I? Ultimately, is sex necessary?" ... The more general problem is one of an absence of difference, bound up with a decline in the display of sexual characteristics. The outer signs of masculinity are tending towards zero, but so are the signs of femininity.[72]

After much previous concern and, at times, anxiety over the dissolution of difference in the wake of the sexual revolution, Baudrillard finally begins to grapple with the positive potentialities of the current situation:

> Pushed to its logical conclusions, this would leave neither masculine or feminine, but a dissemination of individual sexes referring only to themselves, each one managed as an independent enterprise. The end of seduction, the end of difference, and a slide towards a different system of values. An astonishing paradox emerges: sexuality might become once again a merely secondary problem, as it was in most earlier societies, and be eclipsed by other stronger symbolic systems (birth, hierarchy, asceticism, glory, death). This would prove that sexuality was after all only one possible model among many.[73]

It is only here we can begin to see the intersection with the work of Judith Butler and other important feminist theorists who have analyzed the cultural construction of gender as a performative identity and the critical stakes involved. A firmly fixed, naturalized, and legalized sense of gender identity is the cornerstone of the entire patriarchal edifice, that which has led to phallocentric vision and phallocratic privileges. If this founding structure can be shown simultaneously by Baudrillard and feminist theorists to be a historical construction, a gradually modulating cultural artifice, a performance that changes over time, then surely he must merit at least the rank of a fellow traveler, however difficult that may be for him, or for feminists, to admit.

CONCLUSIONS

We have earlier noted how the critic being assigned responsibility for what he or she has described and analyzed is nowhere more apparent than in Baudrillard's public reception. Whether in this case he celebrates, laments, or condemns (or does all three simultaneously) what he describes is a separate issue. For all those who refuse even to consider that what they call "Baudrillard's world" is to some degree that also of their world, he becomes indeed the messenger that must be slain, vehemently, and with the most severely effective tactic of public ridicule whenever possible. Rather than thinking of him as a sociologist of a possible dystopian future, I prefer to think of him as "the sacrificial messenger" of the bad news of our times – to adapt a phrase of Arthur Kroker's.

We should also take note of the fact that the same male critics who are most upset over Baudrillard's apparent refusal to take at face-value the "reality" of partisan political affairs, excoriate him for taking an "extreme oppositional stance toward every last truth claim, every form or vestige of enlightened thought."[74] Nevertheless, this situation indicates the particular impasse at which Baudrillard's work as cultural critic and social theorist has arrived. No matter how compelling his work may be for those who respond positively to his uniquely poetic-philosophical-anarchist style, it remains equally resented and ignored by those who resist the play and counterplay of his unorthodox approach. Indeed, it is ultimately because of his *post-post-* methodology – where Baudrillard *performs* the "loss of the center," and demonstrates "a dispersal of power" from the theorist-as-subject – that, for the more conventional-minded academic, he incarnates "... the real scandal, the hologram from hell," as Ron Silliman once phrased it.[75]

While this situation marks the limitations of his current influence, one cannot help but wonder whether Baudrillard's deliberate introjection into his own work of a heavy dose of what he describes as "femininity" (with all the qualifications we might want to give that), does not also work against its broader acceptance in the still very-masculine world of social theory. After all, the orthodox academy still privileges the production of ordered, systematic gestures toward coherence, verifiability and finality – precisely what Baudrillard claims to oppose. And when other male critics fault Baudrillard for being "hyperbolic and declarative, often lacking sustained, systematic analysis when appropriate,"[76] or "a purveyor of some of the silliest ideas yet to gain a hearing,"[77] or "thoroughly inconsequent and muddled when it comes to philosophizing on the basis of his own observations"[78] – it begins to sound suspiciously like the rigidly smug masculinist standards of an earlier era when women were diminished and ruled not fit for participation in the "serious" scholarship of the old boys' club.

Feminists may be justified in being offended and insulted by the deliberate provocations and the "rude-boy" tactics of this self-appointed theoretical gadfly. In the long run, however, we may yet find that Baudrillard will be seen by feminists as far more of an intellectual ally than an adversary. There are good reasons for Baudrillard's contentions, and the style in which they are delivered, continuing to be so defensively resisted and resented in the formal academy. What is at stake is nothing other than the power relations instituted by at least two centuries of cultural roles arising from hegemonic epistemologies and their academic, intellectual, and *gendered* enforcement. Baudrillard stands on both sides of the contestation, as challenger and as one who needs challenging. Within the orthodoxies of academic conventions, Baudrillard frequently finds himself as a widely nominated candidate for a still-existing position as the "hysterical woman." (Whether he qualifies or is the counter-point to what Arthur and Marilouise Kroker describe as "the Hysterical Male" is an entirely different question).[79]

The final criterion for evaluation of Baudrillard or any other theorist who invokes conceptions of "the feminine," or any metaphorization deriving from "woman," is whether they seek to appropriate a sense of femininity in order to "recontain women (and especially feminist women) within Woman in order to maintain male (sic) hegemony over discursive spaces,"[80] – that is, whether it is done with a motivation of avoidance, defensiveness, or control. Braidotti is justified in uttering a warning against all the many quick exploitations and adaptions of "the feminine" in critical/theoretical or philosophical writing for the past few decades which she aptly terms "neo-feminine products" for consumption. She charges that "the celebration of a femininity reduced to metaphors of the void, lack, non-being, the valorization of woman as textual body, rather than a female sexed body, hides one of the most formidable types of discrimination exercised against women in recent years."[81]

But when we re-examine Baudrillard's use of the feminine, it would seem that he, unlike several other well-known French theorists, is not at all interested in a female *textual* body, but precisely with the female sexual body and its repertoire of *seduction* as a model for subverting the cultural reign of the dominant masculine culture of power-sex-meaning (with the *efficacy* of his theory being another matter). Indeed, it is the sense of a crisis in masculine rationality which is seen by feminists such as Braidotti, Jardine, and Robinson as directly responsible for the "inflationary rise" of male discourse employing some form of textual or metaphorical femininity. We could argue over the difference or the relative distance between a metaphor and a *model*, but more pertinent is to remember Jardine has suggested that feminism and this metaphoricizing of the feminine, of putting into discourse the feminine, do not *necessarily* contradict each other; rather it may be in some cases that they "overlap and interact with each other, perhaps even render each other inevitable in some way?"[82] To poise "seduction" against the excesses of power, production, control, mastery, and rational meaning does not seem to contradict the broader agenda of feminism but rather to reinforce it.

Finally, there is an important analogy to be made between Baudrillard's general reception and something David R. Hiley has argued about – the reasons for widespread resistance to Foucault's analyses of power and culture. In a 1984 essay of a similar title, Hiley contended that the positions Foucault takes are disturbing to many, particularly those on the "progressive left," because he offers only "political engagement without liberal hope or comfort." He argued that what many "progressive" intellectuals want is "liberal comfort that the current struggles are the right ones because they are grounded in a critique of repressive and legitimate practices," while others want "liberal hope that the current struggles are guided by a sense of community and a vision of an improved future."[83] Like Foucault, Baudrillard cannot and would not, from his perspective, begin to speak in such tones. Because he is first and foremost a critic of *macro*-conditions, there is little attention to specific strategies or current proprieties of social and academic protocol. Because he concentrates on the very demise of all those institutions of the previous liberal social contract that have been effectively dissolved by postmodern culture and the military/business-class policies of an ultra-conservative late-twentieth century power oligarchy, he can find few signs of community concern and collective redemption in the situation that presently befalls us. The value of a Baudrillard in this context would never be as any kind of proper exemplar of intellectual guidance, but perhaps as a far-more-necessary stiff medicine, as an antidote to the continued refusal to see our collective situation in its most stark and grim contours. With his attitude of irreverence toward all redeemers and discourses of truth, we might at least learn – instead of panic or denial or castigation of others – to laugh back in the face of our common demise.

Notes

1 Jane Gallop, "French Theory and the Seduction of Feminism," *Men in Feminism*, eds., A. Jardine and P. Smith (New York and London: Routledge, 1989), p. 113.

2   Mike Gane, *Baudrillard: Critical and Fatal Theory* (New York and London: Routledge, 1991), p. 60.

3   For a complete discussion of this critique see Rosi Braidotti, *Patterns of Dissonance* (Cambridge: Polity Press, 1991).

4   Douglas Kellner, *Jean Baudrillard: From Marxism to Postmodernism and Beyond* (Stanford: Stanford University Press, 1989), p. 145.

5   This is the label often affixed to Baudrillard in Douglas Kellner's writing, above and elsewhere, drawn from Baudrillard's invocation of the ritualized seduction from eighteenth-century origins.

6   This can be said in spite of his occasional insistence that he himself can espouse a "supreme femininity" more feminine than that of women themselves. See Jean Baudrillard, *Cool Memories* (London and New York: Verso, 1990), p. 7.

7   This position is outlined in a speech given at the University of Montana in 1989 and published as "Transpolitics, Transsexuality, Transaesthetics" in *Jean Baudrillard: The Disappearance of Art and Politics*, eds., William Stearns and William Chaloupka (London and New York: Macmillan/Saint Martins Press, 1992).

8   Sylvere Lotringer, in an interview with Baudrillard "Forget Baudrillard" published in *Forget Foucault* (New York: Semiotext(e), 1987), p. 95.

9   Jean Baudrillard *Seduction* (Montreal: New World Perspectives, 1990), p. 6 (translation of *De la séduction*, (Paris: Galilée, 1979).

10 I cannot see the justification to read these highly personal memoires as on a par with the rest of his serious theoretical essays. Likewise, although one cannot avoid mentioning certain passages, nor do I include the controversial travelog *America/L'Amérique* (London: Verso, 1988; Originally, 1986) among the texts that comprise the legitimate corpus of Baudrillard's scholarly writings. One may gain all sorts of insights into the personal foibles, prejudices, and distorted impressions of Baudrillard, the person, from these writings, and certainly the personal is political, especially in any published form. But does not anyone who has the courage to bare their intimate life and personal opinions, also deserve to be recognized for being in a different writerly mode and addressing a different public audience than when writing for an intended critical readership of professional peers?

11 Notable for their narrow reading of Baudrillard's theory are Christopher Norris in "Lost in the Funhouse: Baudrillard and the Politics of Postmodernism," *Textual Practice*, 3, 3 360–87; Paul Buhle, "*America*: Postmodernity?" *New Left Review*, 180, 163–75, reviews of *America* by Norman Denzin and Arthur Vidich in *Theory, Culture & Society*, 8, 2 (1991); and Alex Callincos, *Against Postmodernism, A Marxist Critique* (Cambridge: Polity Press, 1989).

12 Seyla Benhabib, "Feminism and Postmodernism: An Uneasy Alliance," *Praxis International*, 11, 2 (July 1991) 146.

13 Judith Butler, "Contingent Foundations: Feminism and the Question of 'Postmodernism,'" *Praxis International*, 11, 2 (July 1991) 150–7.

14 Judith Butler, *Gender Trouble: Feminism and the Subversion of Identity* (New York and London: Routledge, 1990), p. 142.

15 Wendy Brown, "Feminist Hesitations, Postmodern Exposures," *Differences*, 3, 1 (1991) 65.

16	Ibid., p. 68.
17	Dianne Hunter, ed., *Seduction and Theory* (Champaign: University of Illinois Press, 1989), p. 1. The general lack of familiarity with Baudrillard's writings among many feminists is indicated by Hunter's virtual omission of any reference to Baudrillard's theoretical writings on seduction beyond her oblique comments an the one essay by Andrew Ross which critiques Baudrillard's "Bad Attitude." Her remarks reveal a rather severe misreading of his key theoretical terms. Although it would seem obligatory when editing a book on the subject of seduction to have read Baudrillard's work on the same subject, this does not seem to be the case.
18	Baudrillard, *Seduction*, p. 92.
19	Brown, "Feminist Hesitations;" Riley *Am I that Name?* (, 1988).
20	Baudrillard, *Seduction*, p. 45.
21	Suzanne Moore, "Getting a Bit of the Other: The Pimps of Postmodernism," in *Male Order: Unwrapping Masculinity*, eds., R. Chapman and J. Rutherford (London: Lawrence and Wishart, 1988), p. 179.
22	Jean Baudrillard, *Forget Foucault/Forget Baudrillard* (New York: Semiotext(e), 1987), p. 95.
23	Baudrillard, *Seduction*, p. 7.
24	Abigail Solomon-Godeau, "Living with Contradictions: Critical Practices in the Age of Supply-Side Aesthetic," *Universal Abandon*, ed., Andrew Ross (Minneapolis: University of Minnesota Press, 1988), p. 204.
25	Baudrillard, *Seduction; Les strategies fatales* (Paris: Bernard Grasset, 1983).
26	Baudrillard, *Forget Foucault*, pp. 25–6.
27	Jean Baudrillard, *In the Shadow of the Silent Majorities, or, The End of the Social* (New York: Semiotext(e), 1983), pp. 90ff.
28	Gane, *Baudrillard*, p. 65.
29	Kellner, *Baudrillard*, p. 123.
30	Gane, *Baudrillard*, p. 225.
31	Gallop, "French Theory." Several of Gallop's remarks have been cited by feminists including the follow paraphrase of Baudrillard by Gallop: "Women, he warns, are in danger of losing their power, but if they would only let themselves be seduced by what he says ... A line if I ever heard one." (p. 114).
32	Gallop, "French Theory" p. 115. There is still another possible reason for the disproportionate feminist fall-out following Gallop's criticism of Baudrillard's appropriation of seduction and his issuing of direct "advice" to women. Her article appeared in the controversial collection *Men In Feminism* edited by Paul Smith and Alice Jardine which stirred up strong reactions against some of the well-intended, but embarrassing, confessional pieces by men. They tended to show, again, the lack of progress men in general have made in understanding feminist issues. Thus its coverage of male scholars' attempts to engage with or "in" feminism has been read with a healthy skepticism and suspicion.
33	Alice Jardine, *Gynesis* (Ithaca and London: Cornell University Press, 1985), p. 20. In a footnote she places Baudrillard at the head of the list of most blatant offenders: "Baudrillard, Deleuze, Derrida, Lacan and Cixous, Kofman, Kristeva, Lemoine-Luccioni, and Macciocchi are among the theorists in France who have adopted the most explicitly negative attitudes toward classical feminism."

Yet later in the book she does not hesitate to cite his work in positive and useful ways.

34 Jacques Derrida, *Spurs* (Chicago: Chicago University Press, 1979).

35 Sally Robinson, "Deconstructive Discourse and Sexual Politics: The 'Feminine' and/in Masculine Self-Representation," *Cultural Critique*, 13 (1989) 211.

36 Ibid., p. 40.

37 Ibid., p. 26.

38 Ibid., p. 8.

39 Ibid., pp. 7–11.

40 Ibid., p. 8.

41 Ibid., p. 10.

42 Ibid.

43 Ibid., p. 19: "The 'traditional' woman's sexuality was neither repressed nor forbidden. Within her role she was entirely herself; she was in no way divested, nor passive, nor did she dream of her future 'liberation.' " It is the occasional careless statement like this which is an embarrassment to Baudrillard, in my opinion.

44 Ibid., p. 2.

45 Baudrillard, *Forget Foucault*, pp. 56–7ff.

46 One could imagine that Baudrillard might be another ivory-tower philosopher lost in dialog with his own imaginary, someone with little or limited contact with actual women, but this conclusion is belied by the inclusion of numerous observations and anecdotes, from his own personal liaisons, liberally scattered throughout his published journals (*Cool Memories* and *America*). Unfortunately for him, such experience should remove even more possible excuses for his harboring of conceptions of women that often resemble the late nineteenth century more than the late twentieth.

47 Kellner, *Baudrillard*; Gane, *Baudrillard*.

48 Baudrillard, *Cool Memories*, p. 7.

49 Gallop, "French Theory," p. 114.

50 Moore, "Getting a Bit of the Other," p. 167.

51 Meaghan Morris, *The Pirate's Fiancée* (London: Verso, 1988), p. 6.

52 Meaghan Morris, "Room 101, Or A Few Worst Things in the World," in André Frankovits, ed., *Seduced and Abandoned* (Glebe, Australia: Stonemoss Services, and New York: Semiotext(e), 1984), p. 114.

53 Ibid.

54 Lucio Privitello, "The Evening's Porcelain," *Canadian Journal of Political and Social Theory*, XIV 1 & 2 (1990) 107.

55 See "Women in the Beehive: A Seminar with Jacques Derrida," reprinted in Alice Jardine and Paul Smith, eds., *Men in Feminism* (Routledge: New York and London, 1984), pp. 189–203.

56 Baudrillard, *Cool Memories*, p. 77.

57 Ibid., p. 51.

58 Thomas Dumm, "The Invisible Skyline," in *Jean Baudrillard: The Disappearance of Art and Politics*, eds., Sterns and Chaloupka (London: Macmillan; New York: Saint Martin's Press, 1992), p. 111.

59 A. K. Goshorn, "Jean Baudrillard's Radical Enigma: The Revenge of the Object Without Regard for the Subject," in *Jean Baudrillard: The Disappearance of Art and Politics*, p. 223.

60 But see Gane, *Baudrillard*, pp. 55–64, who points out that in spite of Baudrillard's attempts to credit the traditional "seductive" role of women with a superior, if non-dominant, power (as mentioned earlier in this essay) there has nevertheless remained "a structural or positional asymmetry" in his vision of the traditional division of the sexes that does not, in spite of what he claims, put women in a position of equality, not even in the all-important attribute of *reversibility* which he so valorizes.

61 Donna Haraway, "Mainifesto for Cyborgs," in Elizabeth Weed, ed., *Coming to Terms: Feminism Theory and Politics* (New York and London: Routledge, 1989), pp. 173–204.

62 Rita Felski, "Feminism, Postmodernism, and the Critique of Modernity," *Cultural Critique* (Fall 1989) 33–56.

63 Baudrillard, *Fatal Strategies*, p. 50.

64 Baudrillard, *Seduction*, p. 16.

65 Butler, *Gender Trouble*, p. vii.

66 Baudrillard, *Fatal Strategies*, p. 122.

67 Stearns and Chaloupka, *Jean Baudrillard*, p. 10.

68 Ibid., p. 19.

69 Ibid., p. 20.

70 Baudrillard, *Cool Memories I*, p. 50.

71 Jean Baudrillard, "What Are You Doing After the Orgy," *Artforum* (Oct. 1983), pp. 42–6.

72 Baudrillard, *America*, pp. 46–7.

73 Ibid., p. 48.

74 Christopher Norris, "Lost in the Funhouse," eds., Boyne & Rattansi in *Postmodernism and Society* (Basingstake: Macmillan, 1990), p. 120.

75 Ron, Silliman, "What Do Cyborgs Want?" In Sterns and Chaloupka, *Jean Baudrillard*, p. 3.

76 Mark Poster, ed., *Jean Baudrillard: Selected Writing*, (Stanford: Stanford University Press, 1988), p. 8.

77 Norris, *Uncritical Theory: Postmodernism, Intellectuals and the Gulf War* (London: Lawrence & Wishart, 1992), p. 11.

78 Ibid., p. 140.

79 Arthur Kroker and Marilouise Kroker, introduction to *The Hysterical Male*, (Basingstoke: Macmillan Education, 1991).

80 Robinson, "Deconstructive Discourse and Sexual Politics," p. 227.

81 Braidotti, *Patterns of Dissonance*, p. 134.

82 Jardine, *Gynesis*, p. 26.

83 David Hiley, "Foucault and the Analysis of Power: political Engagement Without Liberal Hope or Comfort," *Praxis International*, 4, 2 (July 1984) 204.

13

THE DRAMA OF THEORY: VENGEFUL OBJECTS AND WILY PROPS

—

Gary Genosko

Jean Baudrillard began his intellectual career as a Germanist. During the 1960s, before the publication of his first theoretical study *Le système des objets*,[1] he produced a significant number of translations of diverse texts in the arts and social sciences from German into French, many of which remain standard works. The bulk of his work in translation was in the area of theater and, in particular, the revolutionary "documentary theatre" (théâtre-document) of German playwright Peter Weiss. Any critical appreciation of the importance of theatre in Baudrillard's theorizing must take notice of these important beginnings.

In the period from 1964 to 1968, Baudrillard published translations of four plays by Weiss; these translations represent only a fraction of Weiss's substantial output as a playwright and social critic. The first play *Pointe de fuite*[2] was followed by the well-known work which took its cue from the fact that the Marquis de Sade delivered the memorial address at Jean-Paul Marat's funeral after the latter's assassination in 1793. The dramatic elaboration of this event would be realized by a small troupe directed by de Sade consisting of inmates from the very place (Charenton) where he was confined from 1803 until his death in 1814; the play in question is *La persécution et l'assassinat de Jean-Paul Marat représente par le groupe théâtrale de l'hospice de Charenton sous le direction de Monsieur de Sade.*[3]

Baudrillard's translation of Weiss's *L'instruction, oratorio en onze chants*[4] preceded the important text *Vietnam Diskurs* which, in French translation, incorporates its lengthy sub-title, *Discours sur la genèse et le déroulement de la très longue guerre de libération du Vietnam illustrant la nécessité de la lutte armée des opprimés contre leurs oppresseurs ainsi que la volonté des Etats-Unis d'Amérique d'anéantir les fondements de la Révolution.*[5]

In *Notes on the Cultural Life of the Democratic Republic of Vietnam*, Weiss wrote that "behind every cultural activity stands the bombing war, with its devastating consequences. Every cultural expression ...

immediately points to the war."[6] For Weiss, the rigorous deictic uniformity of the wartime economy of Vietnamese cultural signs stands exemplarily over and against the irregular misfiring of imperialist America's war without fronts. The method through which Weiss expressed his support for the people's war of liberation in the *Discours* belongs to the tradition known as "political theater," of which Bertolt Brecht's didacticism is a leading example; one of Baudrillard's first translations in the area of theater was, in fact, Brecht's portrait of the exile as a dialectician, *Dialogues d'exilés*.[7]

Documentary theater attempts to lay bare the dissimulations of power by taking, first of all, select cuts into existing documentary material (radio broadcasts, government documents, photographs, interviews). This theater is not "inventive" in the sense that it creates contexts for the interaction of dramatic personages; it is a matter, on the contrary, of restructuring materials – a work of critical reorganization and insight. The fragments which result from such cuts are edited in the fashion of a collage which serves as a useful example, a "model schema" of how to read current events. Reflection upon this model reveals the latent conflicts and falsehoods of these events as well as bringing the public into this theater's critical inquest on an equal footing with the accuser and the accused. The radically democratic, quasi-legal underpinnings of this process are most evident when Weiss suggests that it may take the form of a tribunal which extends, revises, or even completes debates and inquiries *a posteriori*.

It would be mischievous even to suggest that Baudrillard should have held fast to the politics of Weiss and Brecht. Baudrillard's translations did, however, situate him in the oppositional intellectual culture of the period, although his other activities in the 1960s, especially his engagements with Marxist sociology in the pages of *Utopie, Revue de sociologie de l'urbain*,[8] did a great deal more to define and develop his own positions.

I have shown elsewhere[9] how a theater in a very different vein has exercised an important influence on Baudrillard over the course of his career. The work of French playwright Alfred Jarry, in whose writings one finds the "science" of pataphysics and the sophomoric character of Père Ubu, is much in evidence throughout Baudrillard's writings in both adjectival and substantive forms. In *Cool Memories II*, for example, Baudrillard confesses: "Pataphysician at twenty – situationist at thirty – utopist at forty – transversal at fifty – viral and metaleptic at sixty – that's my story."[10] Baudrillard's formative or pataphysical years have not ended. Pataphysics is for Baudrillard a reservoir of metaphors, a supply of cheap textual pranks and looks awry (at science in particular). It is a learned and obscure French institution that travels well, provides aesthetic atmosphere, and is never above a low blow.

In this paper I continue my exploration of Baudrillard's relationship with several traditions in the theater by examining his controversial concept of the "revenge of the crystal." The crystal's revenge has been treated as an anti-human, cynical "capitulation to reification" by Douglas Kellner.[11] From a different perspective, Mike Gane hints at the broader aesthetic context in which the concept belongs by referring to the Underground man's fear of the rise of the Palace of Crystal in Fyodor Dostoyevski's *Notes From Underground*, in relation to Baudrillard's attempt to recover what cannot be accounted for in any political economy.[12] Gane thinks that no such capitulation has taken place because both Baudrillard and the Underground man claim that there is something which cannot be reduced to the crystal palaces of perfection erected by "progressive humanists." In Dostoyevski's novel this unclassifiable something is a principle of goodness, while for Baudrillard it is a fatal reversal embodied in the genius and cunning of the pure object or crystal.

Although Gane does little to develop his reference to Dostoyevski, he points out that the Palace of Crystal signifies the complete mastery of human beings by means of scientific reason. Nature and society will, then, be played like "a sort of piano keyboard or barrel-organ cylinder," as Dostoyevski put it. But the Underground man insists that human beings do not always act according to the dictates of reason and in their own best interests: "it is indeed possible, and sometimes *positively imperative* (in my view), to act directly contrary to one's own best interests. One's own free and unfettered volition . . . inflated sometimes to the point of madness – that is the one best and greatest good, which is never taken into consideration because it will not ft into any classification."[13] In Baudrillardian terms, the abstract combinatorial possibilities dictated by the code inter human beings in the Palace of Crystal. This palace is dead because "everything which expurgates its *part maudite* [accursed share] signs its own death," Baudrillard states.[14] Every effort is made, Baudrillard adds, to expel evil from paradisiac palaces of crystal. This search for "operational whiteness" equals death. Today power accrues to the one who can re-introduce this devil's share into crystalline systems. Indeed, what frightens the Underground man is that it may not even be possible to stick out one's tongue at the "eternally inviolable" palace. There is, however, something ironic in the very idea of the crystal palace which runs counter to its realization. For the Underground man, the independence of volition is irreducible to the algorithms and mathematical expressions of human desire, whereas for Baudrillard one may say that there is a certain crystal which demonstrates its indifference to the dictates and structures of the palace by pursuing its own interests. Baudrillard does not borrow in any straightforward way the idea of the crystal from Dostoyevski. Gane's turn to literature in order to track the polysemic crystal indicates, however, the aesthetic context which I will explore in this paper.

The story of the object told by Baudrillard may be constructively contextualized and elaborated upon through a reflection on two developments in the theory of drama. In particular, it is Antonin Artaud's theater of cruelty to which I turn for a source of a theoretical and theatrical context for the notion of the object's revenge. In the second instance, I appeal to the semiotics of theater of the Prague School, especially the groundbreaking proto-structuralist work of Otokar Zich in the 1930s and Jiri Veltrusky's dialectical structuralism of the 1940s, in order to explain how a certain energy and oddity may be said to reside in an object. The fundamental theatricality of Baudrillard's theorization of the object, or what one may call the drama of theory, has led me to consider the theory of drama. In this light, Patricia Mellencamp's remark in her essay on Baudrillard and Herbert Blau seems misleading: "Baudrillard's is a grey world without theater."[15] Given Baudrillard's debt to Jarry, for example, such a phrase seems patently false. What Mellencamp alerts her readers to is the end of theater as representation, the end of the ironically named "Baudrillard scene" in the transparency of the obscene. Mellencamp's phrase may be understood in the context of Artaud's turn to objects, gestures, and non-linguistic signs. This is a theater in which the object will have its revenge on Western metaphysics. The relationship between Artaud and Baudrillard may be best understood within the context of the diverse critical positions taken on Artaud's writings by key poststructuralist thinkers.

VENGEFUL OBJECTS

In "De système des objets au destin de l'objet" in L'autre par lui-même, Baudrillard describes a "double spiral" winding forward from his early engagement with objects in Le système des objets toward a switching point at which his subject-based theorizing ultimately moved to the side of the object: "The desire of the subject is no longer at the center of the world. It is the destiny of the object which is at the center."[16]

In what at first appears to be a flight into hyper-anthropomorphism, Baudrillard posits a principle of reversibility which plays a game with, primarily but by no means exclusively, the subject/object distinction at the heart of the Western philosophical tradition. In this reversal, the object "takes revenge." It is the object's destiny to take revenge on the subject through the "passions" of indifference, inertia, ironic silence, conformity, etc. The object, then, leads the subject astray; in this way it avenges its subordination and marginalization.

The fatal strategy of the object consists neither in its de-alienation and liberation, nor in its (re)production of value-giving intentionality on the model of an ego. The object does not mimic the subject's operations. Rather, it has an "Evil Genius" and is fatal inasmuch as it is enigmatic. It is this enigmatic quality which enables the object to challenge the subject's will to know, control, and conquer its universe. In an interview entitled "Le cristal se venge," Baudrillard explained that the crystal is neither passive nor a subject. It is not involved in a process of projection and identification (the mirror stage, desire, etc.). The crystal has a destiny rather than a desire to fulfill. This pure object's passions are of the order of irony, inertia, and the ruse, while the passions of the subject are invigorating and final (expressing and fulfilling desires and claims).[17]

The crystal is fatal in several senses. First, it is irresistible and will be the ruin of the subject; not only is the object seductive, it remains indecipherable, and as such it fulfills its destiny by thwarting the will to power/knowledge of the subject. Secondly, Baudrillard's concept of the object's destiny is buoyed by the crisis of the subject in structuralist and poststructuralist discourses. Baudrillard takes advantage of the "death of the subject" and the critiques of power, knowledge, and history to exploit this moment of weakness by effecting a turnaround on behalf of his special object. He would have his readers believe that the object was only waiting for an opportunity to realize its destiny.

Baudrillard's crystal is a polysemous figure which may be identified with anyone and anything treated, traditionally and otherwise, for better and for worse, as an object. This does not mean the revenge in question is that of the objectified over the objectifiers. Although Baudrillard claims that his pure and fatal object is not a subject, he does admit that it can designate "people and their inhuman strategies."[18] After all, there are no terms in his description of the objective passions of the object that are inapproporiate for some subjects. They, too, can create confusion, surprise, behave like objects, treat one another as objects, cultivate indifference, believe in destiny, etc. But this is surely not Baudrillard's point since the crystal is neither simply an animal nor a vegetable, and not exactly a mineral. Baudrillard's crystal is a precious thing to be sure, itself unlikely to be crystalline; rather, it is like the ball toward and into which one gazes in order to arouse a myriad of sensations. The crystal is a fetish whose potency is tied to its ambivalence, by which I do not mean the sort of attitude one may take toward the power of a crystal ball.

The crystal suggests the undecidable sponge Jacques Derrida found at the work in the poetry of Francis Ponge: a zoophyte such as a sponge has a medusant character, he writes, because it is "neither simply a thing, nor simply vegetal, nor simply animal." The sponge is an animal plant, full of water and air, and a medium which incorporates and expunges.[19] Baudrillard's crystal is just as much a sign of writing as Derrida's sponge. It is precisely the sort of textual operator he needs to effect a writing practice equal to the demands of the symbolic order he has consistently favored in his theorizing. The crystal is Baudrillard's precious hybrid object, a transparent medium ready to be filled with content like Marshall McLuhan's electric light. The crystal is the sort of hybrid in which Baudrillard has always shown interest. An object may be a perfect domesticate, but is a domesticated animal such as a dog a perfect object? For the dog, Baudrillard thinks, is a household "object," often no more than a piece of sentient furniture, bred for the narcissistic interiors of urban dwellings, absolutely dependent upon its owner whom it exalts, and castrated either physically or symbolically. Like other interior animals, Baudrillard maintains, dogs are a species in between beings and objects.[20] In order to be a perfect object, a dog must always exalt its owner, it must never breakdown, as it were, enduring like a prized possession. The perfect domesticate is found in a Disney character: the barking ottoman which regains its full share of caninity when the spell over the castle is lifted at the climax of the film *Beauty and the Beast*. There is, then, a bestiary in Baudrillard, but not in the deliteralized sense Gane would have one believe in his Baudrillardian bestiary without animals!

The identity of the promiscuous crystal fluctuates, drawing the reader of Baudrillard in several directions. Baudrillard's concept of ambivalence (one of the means by which the symbolic moves beyond signification) makes the crystal's identity uncertain, what Derrida would call undecidable. This ambivalence is, most importantly, immanent to the concept of the crystal, and this enables it to function as a lure in Baudrillard's text. Brian Singer, English translator of *De la séduction*, recognized that his own ambivalence about Baudrillard was in the end immanent to the work itself; yet, this is, for Singer, the work's fascination.[21]

The play of uncertainties is part of what I call the drama of Baudrillardian theory. The inexorable rise of the pure object is the drama of theory. The tactical maneuvers of Baudrillard's crystal lead me directly into the theory of drama.

Postmodern theater was born with Artaud's *Le théâtre et son double* in the 1930s.[22] As early as the mid-1920s, Artaud had already conceived of the theater as a challenge to the spectator, as an event which would instill in the spectator the idea of its profound seriousness and demonstrate that one would no longer be able to leave the theater unscathed. His experiments with the Alfred Jarry Theatre were decisive for the emphasis he came to place on the theater as a means for challenging the Western tradition itself, especially the form of a naturalistic theater which sought to imitate reality. The idea of the "masterpiece" also became a target for Artaud. In the brief essay "Sur le théâtre balinais," Artaud – with all the hyperbole of someone who wants to conjure a miracle – highlights the importance of objects and their ineluctable advance against the hegemony of words in a struggle to express themselves in their very concreteness. In this sense the danger, surprise, and astonishment experienced by the spectator would, for Artaud, be provoked by things themselves.[23]

While the importance of Artaud's contributions to contemporary debates on representation in poststructuralism has been recognized by numerous scholars, this recognition has not equalled uncritical acceptance. For Artaud remains a controversial figure whose ideas are still hotly debated.

In "The Theatre of Cruelty and the Closure of Representation," Derrida describes this theater's production of a "nontheological space."[24] This space is neither opened by means of speech nor is it merely an addition to a dramatic work. By challenging the privileged status of the already written, lived, or thought by means of *mise en scène* itself, Artaud exceeded, in Derrida's words "all the limits furrowing classical theatricality (represented/representation, signifier/signifed, author/director/actor/spectators, stage/audience, text/interpretation, etc.) [which] were ethico-metaphysical prohibitions, wrinkles, grimaces, rictuses – the symptoms of fear before the dangers of the festival."[25] This space of festival is opened every time a bar is lifted between the aforementioned paired terms; this bar game may be defined as a *refusal* to re-present a pre-existent text and a *refusion* of hitherto barred terms. The theater of cruelty has no place for "the supreme Logos," the man-God; it is not a "theatrum analyticum," the analytic scene of the return of the repressed.

What Derrida saw in Artaud was his courage in the face of recognizing that no theater could possibly fulfill his desire. Artaud was caught in a struggle to represent what is unrepresentable and to find a space which could be used to demonstrate life to a being whose "only inhabitable place – locus – is language," as Julia Kristeva has affirmed.

"Modern theater does not take (a) place,"[26] Kristeva writes, for the reason that one is always in language, in a space structured by what she calls the symbolic. In dislodging speech from its dominant role in the theater and the tradition, Artaud did not take solace in silence. This is not a speechless theater, even though Kristeva suggests as much in her remarks on Artaud's effort "to do without language" and his turn to "colors, sounds and gestures."[27] But Artaud would, however, agree with Kristeva that there is no escaping from language in the theater, despite one's best efforts. There is only the conscious rigor of a cruelty which is not clouded by the unconscious (a concept for which Artaud had no use), or what Kristeva includes in her concept of the semiotic. Kristeva criticizes various attempts (by Robert Wilson, Yvonne Rainer, Richard Foreman) in the French and American theaters throughout the 1960s and 1970s to realize Artaud's dream of an immediate, communal theater without the remainders of text, readers, and interpreters, and a thrill-seeking bourgeois audience. These efforts could only represent the unrepresentable, remainderless energy of Artaud's conception of such a theater, caught as they were in the trap of failing by succeeding. They heightened the desire for a place to "remake language." or at least to reassemble the semiotic and the symbolic once more. The Artaudian 'festival" is not for subscribers.

The "nontheological space" of Artaud's theater is, in Jean-François Lyotard's short essay "La dent, la paume," thoroughly "theological."[28] Derrida's enthusiasm for Artaud is not contagious. Between A and B (i.e., signifier/signified, work/performance, tooth/palm) there is a gap (*nihil*) which must always be bridged by a connection (*religio*). Mind the gap, Lyotard says, because the bar differentiates and connects the theater with something beyond itself; don't let the bar become a religion of representation, let the bar stand on its own. The bar binds the sign; a Marxist-materialist conception of language is the "religion" of Brecht's epic theater; and, as Hans Bellmer digs his nails into his palm when he has a toothache, Lyotard thinks that the palm represents the tooth for any réflexion, for all réflexologie.[29] Artaud fares no better.

In Lyotard's estimation, what stopped Artaud short of grasping the reversibility of the pure libidinal energy of a debarred A/B, was that he had already found a "religion": "In order to put intensities to work, he manufactured a 'tool' which would serve as a new language, a system of signs, a grammar of gestures, a 'hieroglyphics'. This is what he thought he found in Eastern theatre, particularly in the Balinese and Japanese theatres. He thus remained a European; he repeated the 'invention' of the agreement of the body and the senses, and made the great discovery (at the antipodes) of the unity of the libido as Eros and of the libido as death drive; he repeated his ethnological mise en scène on the Eastern stage."[30] Lyotard surely knows that a theater of energy is a religion too. There is, at the end of his essay, only the following question: "It [an energetic theatre] has to produce the highest intensity (by excess or lack) of what there is, without intention. This is my question: is it possible, how?"[31] Lyotard also asks one to wait for an answer, even though he has already provided the means for only a negative response. Artaud's "orientalism" was marked, according to Baudrillard, by his "often scabrous affinity with magic and exorcism, even orgiastic mysticism."[32] Scripts, masterpieces, and psychology are for Westerners, Artaud believed, while the metaphysics in action of the Eastern theaters constitutes a new poetics of space. Baudrillard has repeatedly denounced various forms of mysticism (including psychoanalysis) which require the liberation of an "original" source of "energy."

At this point one may recall the final paragraph of Michel Foucault's presentation of Gilles Deleuze's "theatrum philosophicum," a passage impressive for its cruel scenography of wild dancing, explosive laughter, reversals, blind gesturing, and disguises all in the service of a thought which plays the history of philosophy as we have known it as mise en scène, as everything that is required in staging a performance.[33] Ultimately, the positions of Foucault and Deleuze will diverge on the question of the relation between Artaud's art and madness.

Baudrillard's contribution to poststructuralist debates concerning Artaud's place in the critique of representation is his emphasis on the object. In "En finir avec les chefs-d'oeuvre," Artaud comes to consider, in the course of answering a hypothetical misreading of his sense of cruelty as 'blood', "the much more terrible and necessary cruelty [more than mutual dismemberment] that things can exercise against us. We are not free. The sky can still fall on our heads. The theater can make us understand this."[34] Artaud was convinced of the *"revelatory aspect of matter*, which seems all of a sudden to scatter into signs in order to teach us the metaphysical identity of the concrete and the abstract."[35] This lesson was well-learned by Baudrillard. For him, the active manifestations of things display an "offensive resistance . . . to [their] investigation."[36] Baudrillard's objects "take revenge" through a profound reticence. Even "science" "underestimates [the object's] vices, the derision, the offhandedness, the false complicity."[37] Artaud's things come forth brillantly, while Baudrillard's objects are rather taciturn. Not all of Artaud's things behaved so well. What he enjoyed in the Marx Brothers' film *Monkey Business* was the degree to which "things get out of hand . . . objects, animals, sounds, master and servants, host and guests, everything comes to a boil, goes mad, and revolts."[38]

There is, however, in Artaud's praise of Vincent van Gogh, a troubling aspect of the theatrical celebration of "things gone mad." Indeed, if Blau is correct that "we have made a ceremony out of what Artaud calls 'the revenge of things',"[39] then Baudrillard may be considered to be the most recent master of cermonies of a universe in which such revenge has tended to carry over into a madness as chilling as receiving an eye or an ear in the mail. No one should confuse Artaud's enjoyment of the Marx Brothers with his praise of van Gogh. Artaud thought of himself and van Gogh as fellow "aliénés authentiques"; they were superior men whose visionary insights into "le mythe des choses" unfortunately brought them into contact with the repressive regime of psychiatry. Not only did Artaud blame "dear brother Theo" (van Gogh's brother) and Dr. Gauchet, under whose care at Auvers-sur-Oise van Gogh spent his last months before he died of a self-inflicted gunshot wound, for precipitating van Gogh's suicide, but he attempts to justify on the basis of his experience as a psychiatric inmate that, in a striking literary confession and anti-psychiatric diatribe, van Gogh was "suicided by society": "I myself spent nine years in an insane asylum and I never had the obsession of suicide, but I know that each conversation with a psychiatrist, every morning at the time of his visit, made me want to hang myself, realizing that I would not be able to cut his throat."[40] The lives of van Gogh and Artaud cannot be deliteralized and assigned to metaphor. Artaud describes throughout his essay on van Gogh how the painter revealed the "passion," "nerve," and the "tidal wave" of things beyond their "neurotic destiny"; that is, van Gogh had insight into their "psychotic destiny." Artaud claimed that it was psychiatry, not these things themselves, which took revenge upon van Gogh and himself.

'Artaud the Schizo," as Deleuze and Félix Guattari have called him, was one of several model "schizorevolutionary" figures upon whose works and lives their reading of schizophrenia as a liberatory, albeit risky, process was based and developed. Artaud's writings, in fact, inspired Deleuze and Guattari's concept of the body-without-organs, an anoedipal body whose potentialities are realized through intense, inventive connections beside the libidinal limits imposed by capitalism, the signifier, genital sexuality, castration, etc. It is not the dysfunctional "hospital" schizo driving this interpretation, but the literary schizo denouncing the holy family of psychoanalysis. Artaud – the anti-psychiatry/psychoanalysis protestor and in his time a "survivor" of many asylums – made what Deleuze and Guattari refer to as a breakthrough, as opposed to breaking down or being broken down into a clinical entity, beyond "a neurotic or perverse recoding"[41] and into a universe of scrambled codes where one circulates or "schizzes" from bit to bit without a goal.

Deleuze and Guattari would eventually write of Artaud in "November 28, 1947: How Do You Make Yourself A Body Without Organs?" that "even if Artaud did not succeed for himself [in lifting the roadblocks on his "intensity map;" in his experiments with drugs; no one, not even Artaud, can experiment in peace], it is certain that through him something has succeeded for us all."[42] (The date in the title refers to the period [November 22–29] during which Artaud was in Paris recording "To Have Done With The Judgment Of God," from which Deleuze and Guattari quote; this is Artaud's "radiophonic" experiment to which Deleuze and Guattari refer in passing.) The schizophrenic process of Artaud's experiments makes his *oeuvre* a privileged reference guide for "how to" achieve a breakthrough. Artaud himself, at times, seemed to recognize where he went wrong or not far enough, the point at which desire became dangerous, having been emptied by too many drugs, for example. Deleuze and Guattari's reading of Artaud is tempered by Foucault's questioning of the uneasy relationship between madness and art.

One need only recall Foucault's closing remarks in *Madness and Civilization* regarding Artaud's madness as the *absence of the work of art* to understand the point at which he precluded Deleuze and Guattari's position on Artaud. Artaud's madness was, even for Foucault, none the less appreciable, infinite in its dimensions, itself reiterating the art work's absence like an insistent signifier: "Madness is the absolute break with the work of art; it forms the constitutive moment of abolition, which dissolves in time the truth of the work of art; it draws the exterior edge, the line of dissolution, the contour against the void. Artaud's oeuvre experiences its own absence in madness, but that experience, the fresh courage of that ordeal, all those words hurled against a fundamental absence of language, all that space of physical suffering and terror which surrounds or rather coincides with the void – that is the work of art itself: the sheer cliff over the abyss of the work's absence."[43]

Deleuze, Guattari, and Foucault agree that any meeting of madness and art is dangerous, a game of life and death and living death in an institution; this meeting can destroy the work of art and the artist since it becomes a place into which the artist escapes without an exit. Foucault's sense of the madness of Artaud's *oeuvre* or, more precisely, the latter's "experience of its own absence in madness," which is evidence at once of Artaud's courage and terror and suffering, is marked by breaks, edges, and an abyss; this is a partitioned landscape. There is no breakthrough for Foucault: madness does not pass through the fissures of the work of art. But for Deleuze and Guattari, these fissures are the kinds of lines of escape, becoming and cleavages that the work of art, understood as a tool which facilitates a flight from the signifer, subjectivity, genitality, the walls of reason described in so much French literature, and a plateau which ends in a sheer cliff, can provide. Artaud's "works of madness," as Foucault called them, were works, but not of art.

In both the work of Artaud and Baudrillard, the object is said to have its revenge on the subject and logocentrism. In a theatrical theory like Baudrillard's, just as in Artaud's sense of theater, the object diverts attention from the actors, speech, and the signifieds of the performance. Baudrillard's pure objects are only "schizorevolutionary" to the extent that his position on them is anti-psychoanalytic.

This is precisely the argument Baudrillard makes in the section "Le cristal se venge" in *Les stratégies fatales*.[44] Seduction is an anti-psychoanalytic concept in Baudrillard's understanding since it is neither accounted for in terms of desire in the psychic economy of the individual, nor in the reduction to symptoms of all appearances in Freudian dream interpretation and the psychopathology of everyday life. Baudrillard had already pointed in *De la séduction* to the fact that Freud abandoned what is called "the seduction theory" (that the infantile experiences of adult analysands of rape and other sexually abusive attacks were compatible with nothing other than real, material events) in the service of the unconscious, non-material phylogenetic fantasies of sexual abuse, and of "seduction" as a screen memory in infantile sexual and psychic development. Baudrillard's notion of seduction bears no relation to "the seduction theory." He is primarily concerned with the theory's status as a "lost object" killed off in the name of "science."[45]

Seduction is, however, an enigma which challenges the "truth" of analytic interpretation. It has nothing to do with the economy of desire, Baudrillard insists, since it originates beyond the individual and subsists "elsewhere." The exteriority or radical objectivity of seductive pure objects is essential to their sovereignty and their "election" of someone/thing to surprise and to lure into a fatal convergence of circumstances and events. Baudrillard's sense of the play of things is far from the heaving and persecutory world of the psychotic.

THE WILY PROP

Patrice Pavis's question "Mise en scène ou mise en signe?"[46] carries me from Artaud's theatricalization of the theater as mise en scène to the Prague

School's semioticization of the object as *mise en signe*. The aesthetics and structuralism of Zich and Veltrusky respectively provide a further means by which to decode the drama of Baudrillard's theory of the object, which becomes in this context a wily prop. The concept of the wily prop is another name, drawn from a different tradition, for Baudrillard's pure object. But this variation allows me to turn the semiotic tables on Baudrillard. By positioning his pure object in the semiotics of theater tradition, I return to Baudrillard the very thing he struggled to transcend: sign theory. This is my countergift to Baudrillard. Despite the sophistication and virulency of his critiques of semiology and structuralism, I resemioticize his vengeful objects because his efforts to make theory dramatic have landed him, quite unwittingly, in a semiotic tradition. Baudrillard understands perfectly well the necessity of a countergift, although perhaps not the one I have in mind.

The object is played by the dramatic forces of the stage which catapult it into a leading role in the performance, among whose many features it stands in a relation equal to or more significant than the actor. It is in terms of a subject-object or actor-prop continuum that Prague School theorists have modeled the force of the sign-vehicles of the stage as they are made to shift along the continuum in a given performance. As Keir Elam has observed in *The Semiotics of Theatre and Drama*, experiments in the modern theater have often involved the object's acquisition of a force "in its own right":

> It is notable that many of the so-called experiments in the twentieth-century theatre have been founded on the promotion of the set to the position of "subject" of semiosis, with a corresponding surrender of "action force" by the actor: Edward Gordon Craig's ideal, for example, was a mode of representation dominated by a highly connotative set in which the actor had the purely determined function of über marionette. Samuel Beckett's two mimes, *Act Without Words 1 & 11*, play with the reversal of subjective-objective roles between actor and prop – the human figure is determined by and victim of, the stage sign-vehicles ("tree" . . . etc.) – while his thirty-second *Breath* has the set as its sole protagonist.[47]

Zich's aesthetic conception of an energetics of dramatic space was an important precursor of the understanding of the dynamism, mobility, and transformability of the sign-vehicle. In Zich's aesthetics, dramatic space consists of lines of force which radiate from certain dramatic centers of a performance (i.e., characters) and, in their turn, in a given dramatic situation, interact in a variety of ways.[48]

Veltrusky's concept of "action force" may be applied all along the continuum from actor to prop. This application furthers Zich's non-hierarchical assignation of forces by breaking the active-passive division between the one who initiates semiosis and the thing that is acted upon.

Veltrusky specifies that "the prop is not always passive. It has a force . . . that attracts a certain action to it."[49] A prop can shape action even in the absence of an actor. Although objects may become "spontaneous subjects equivalent to the figure of the actor," this transformation does not take place through personification. Zich thought that an object such as a wig or hair-piece occupied neither pole of the continuum between the actor's make-up and clothing.[50] Indeed, objects may become subjects, just as subjects may be presented as objects in theatrical configurations.

Baudrillard has sought to "rediscover the aesthetic force of the world" in the object's passion.[51] The theater can assist in this "rediscovery," as Veltrusky himself hoped, by expanding the epistemological horizon of everyday life; that is, by lifting the bar which normally separates subject/things and exercises control over the latter. Baudrillard stretches this idea to its limits through a theatricalization of the world, a re-enchantment of things. He converts the passivity of the object into the seat of its passions (*passions indifférentielles, passions inertielles*). In its most impoverished sense, it is the artist's passion which passes into the work. The passion of the work is, however, not an object of one's passionate inclination, but the object's condition. The object may be animated by its passions, as well as being *passionnant*, fascinating, seductive, and, in this, fatal.

Lyotard, one may recall, accused Artaud of purloining his concept of cruelty from Eastern theatrical traditions and once again reinventing the "East" for the "West." This reimaging of the "East" also applies to Baudrillard, whose concept of ceremony is derived from The Peking Opera, "oriental" ceremonies and cultures in general, the Hindu Book of Manu, etc. The "ceremony of the world" is Baudrillard's theater of cruelty, a minutely defined circulation of pure ceremonial signs heavy with obligations which are exchanged with a formal strictness according to explicit rules. Baudrillard's sense of ceremony is non-representational. It is not a stage or a scene, even though certain experiments in theater have preserved some elements of the symbolic violence of ceremony and ritual. Ceremonial violence is akin to theoretical violence. Both are theatrically cruel since they oppose naturalism and expressionism with a logic immanent to a set of rules. In Lyotard's terms, Baudrillard found the same "religion" as Artaud in the "East" and the chain of non-representational signs arranged and connected non-causally. Connections in this universe are all on the level of appearances. Baudrillard maintains, then, an "empty space" (Lyotard's *nihil*) in the violent brush of weapons in the Peking Opera, the uncrossable darkness of the duel, and the river between lovers. This "gap" is rendered palpable by the efforts to cross it. The gap cannot be occupied because it is the space held open by ceremony itself, a guard against the promiscuity of direct and free contacts.[52]

Baudrillard's crystal is in Naomi Segal's terms a *banal object*.[53] Although I have emphasized the ways in which certain concepts in the theory of theater may be used to explicate Baudrillard's reading of objects, Segal presents an important parallel reading of the power of commonplace objects in literature. Through both positive and negative narrative encounters with it, a banal object forces a crisis and resolves it. Like Baudrillard's objects, it can display a wilful malevolence – a *Tücke des Objekts* – toward the writer. Neither Segal's banal object, Baudrillard's crystal, nor the wily prop may be thought of as completely passive instruments. The crystal is, then, Baudrillard's (Proustian) madeleine as much as the gnarled roots of existential (Sartrean) drama. Segal's insight into the banal object touches upon the matter of Baudrillard's literary (as opposed to strictly theatrical) inspiration for the object's revenge. Baudrillard's essay "Du système des objets" is introduced by a statement from the French essayist, art critic, and Sinologist Victor Segalen. In his *Essai sur l'exotisme*, Segalen wrote: "The essential exoticism is that of the Object for the Subject,"[54] a quotation used by Baudrillard on more than one occasion. Segalen's importance for Baudrillard's theorizing has become increasingly evident in his books of the 1980s and 1990s, even though no mention is made of his influence in the major works of the critical literature.

EXOTICISM

Baudrillard's aesthetic project is firmly grounded by several critical traditions concerning objects in the theater and literary theory. Why, then, did he turn to Segalen? Baudrillard, of course, has always been interested in objects: from the system of object-signs to the object-form, a mutation of the commodity and the Saussurian sign, through the incessant symbolic exchange of gift-objects to, most recently, vengeful pure objects. An object which avenges itself is truly exotic.

Although the relationship between the works of Baudrillard and Segalen is too complex to be fully developed here, I will show that in Segalen's *Essai* there are two concepts which inform Baudrillard's theoretical approach to objects.

First, the object (that is, whatever or whomever occupies this pole in a given context in the theorizing of Baudrillard and Segalen) is exotic for the subject to the extent that this exoticism is essential and radical: the object is irreducibly other and fundamentally foreign to the subject and to itself (for Segalen, the object pole may be occupied by the Other, the Diverse, Difference, etc.).[55] The object withstands interpretation and retains its seductiveness for Baudrillard even though it has been repeatedly probed by eager hermeneuts, scientists, et al., all of whom have made claims on its otherness and leveled the "primordial exoticism" of the object through the homogenizing forces of understanding and the travels of theory.

In spite of all the unfortunate connotations of the word *exotisme* (such as picturesque expressions and touristic impressions of distant lands, peoples, and things), Segalen used it to resuscitate the idea of the irreducibility of objects, cultures, languages, places, etc. Just as Segalen sought to counteract the degradations of tourism and colonialism, Baudrillard suggests that, in spite of research across the disciplines into objects of all kinds, the essential exoticism of objects can be resuscitated in the form of the crystal's revenge. The hypothesis of exoticism upholds the incomprehensibility of the object and guards its beauty against the intrusions of the subject. Indeed, exoticism is dead when the crystal no longer defies – or at least upsets – the subject's will to explain away objective powers as its own fetishism, anthropomorphism, projection, etc.

Secondly, according to Segalen, "Difference can only be sensed by those who possess a strong Individuality."[56] He adds that: "Exoticism is not therefore this kaleidoscopic state of tourism and the mediocre onlooker, but the lively and inquisitive reaction to the collision of a strong individuality with an objectivity whose distance it perceives and savours (the sensations of Exoticism and Individualism are complementary)."[57] Individualism assumes mythic proportions in Segalen's theory of exoticism. A strong individuality is the condition of the possibility of radically exotic experience. Such individuals are called "Exotes", Segalen's neologism for "born travellers" whose strength lies in their ability to savor the "unforgettable rush" of "the moment of Exoticism" in the "acute and immediate perception of an eternal incomprehensibility."[58] "Pseudo-exotes" are, by contrast, mere tourists, for whom "fusion" and "assimilation" are goals. The very idea of "resistance-as-object" has become, as Arthur Kroker has attempted to develop it through Baudrillard's concepts of the "silent majorities" and "fatal strategies,"[59] a dress-up game. The "Exote" doesn't fuse; neither play-acting nor becoming-an-object will suffice. For the "Exote" has Rimbaud's foreignness to his own culture; even better, an authentic "Exote" was Glenn Gould at the piano playing Bach. Baudrillard writes: "Glenn Gould: his bodily trance, completely independent of the perfect technical mastery of his hands which fly over the keys without looking at them, while his head swings with his eyes closed. No pianistic grandstanding. The absolute ear."[60]

In 1964 Gould abandoned live public performances in favor of the studio. Innovative documentary projects for radio ("contrapuntal radio") occupied him for some ten years throughout the 1970s. His now-notorious personal quirks (interviews with himself; reviews of books about himself; his media "personalities") and fascination with sound and recording technologies were in no way diversions. An "Exote" does not abolish himself before the other of the score, the recording technology, his "career," the concert audience; he did not play at becoming-the-great-pianist-performer, etc.

Baudrillard fancies himself an "Exote." He is a superior individual along

Segalen's lines since he can conceive of the object's Difference in terms of its challenge to the subject. Although he is not in Artaud's terms one of the "aliénés authéntiques," Baudrillard has none the less seen the irresolvable strangeness and irrevocable sovereignty of the "revenge of things" and therein manifested a strong individuality. Still, as I have shown, he certainly does not stand alone. The crystal's revenge, however, is an aesthetic revival of the object beyond the confines of the theater, and far from the dictates of psychosis.

CONCLUSION

Baudrillard's re-enchantment of the world is not driven by madness. Artaud might even have scoffed at Baudrillard's neurotic crystals. Today in North America, the crystal's revenge has a specific reference in the context of a New Age sub-culture whose enthusiastic misappropriations of numerous traditions has brought quartz crystals into a marketplace of saleable and portable mysticisms. This is not the revenge of the pet rock, but of healing crystals! All the same, the reasons for Baudrillard's use of the term *cristal* are quite transparent. Crystal is not only a variety of glass (leaded) with a high degree of brillance. It is a hyperreal object of sorts in its own right since it is, by definition, more transparent and heavier than ordinary glass; crystal, then, is glassier than glass.

A new domestic order recently established itself in the United States with an inaugural evening of entertainment. This is not supposed to be just another Pepsi generation, although a new advertising campaign for a Pepsi product (clear and caffeine free) made its debut on television with the Clinton government. The television advertisement for Crystal Pepsi ("Right Now") was created by Phil Dusenberry for the BBDO agency, whose advertisements for Pepsi and Macintosh won numerous industry awards and set commercial stylistic agendas throughout the 1980s. Dusenberry is best known for his soft-sell documentary which resembled a Pepsi commercial for Ronald Reagan's presidential campaign in 1984 (although he also worked for Reagan in 1976 and 1980). The appearance of Dusenberry's new Pepsi advertisement on the eve of the Democrat(ic) takeover of power in Washington is precisely the sort of objective irony at the heart of things which continues to fascinate Baudrillard. The revenge of the Crystal Pepsi reveals a horrible irony: political change is diminished by its symbolic association with a new soft-drink whose last "generation" fit together perfectly with Republican politics (Dusenberry worked for Reagan, Bush, and a variety of conservative groups). The Palace of Crystal Pepsi renders political change irrelevant – and even dangerous. Crystal Pepsi takes its revenge on another generation by dragging its conservative past into the the present. Dusenberry puts the Right in "Right Now."

In addition, the crystal plays a role in Baudrillard's attack on the commodity. He asks his readers of *Les stratégies fatales* to forget Marxian hieroglyphics. How, after all, can one hope "to get behind the secret" of a crystal since it is more transparent than glass? Yet, if the crystal serves Baudrillard's purpose of parodying "opacity" and the interpretive claims which render it transparent, it also serves well as an example of what, for Baudrillard, Marx paradoxically accomplished: Marx made the commodity more transparent than glass – a crystal. This was a great accomplishment, unfortunately crushed, writes Baudrillard, by "Marxian dogma." The crystalline commodity, however, retained for Baudrillard's Marx a "disquieting strangeness" in virtue of "its challenge to the judicious arrangement of things, to the real, morality, utility."[61] In rendering the commodity transparent, Marx momentarily glimpsed the enigma of pure objects. By the same token, too much transparency can itself be opaque and enigmatic since it enables one to see nothing but paradoxes.

As far as Baudrillard's conception of the object is concerned, his exotic individualism was secured less by the adoption of an aristocratic position than by an anti-structuralism as fierce as it was theatrical. Baudrillard eschews the kind of dichotomania associated with semiology, structuralism, cybernetics, linguistics, etc. The metaphysics of the code is in large part due, as Baudrillard has maintained, to binarity, digitality, and the proliferation of two-sided units of minimal separation (0/1; signifiant/signifié; life/death; and the digital logic of the referendum: yes/no).

In aligning Baudrillard with the conceptually relevant precursors of Artaud, the Prague School, and Segalen, I have not re-paired him. My countergift of a semiotics of theater tradition was not, however, an ultimatum. For the wily prop, once received, may and must be passed along to someone else, with gestures as theatrical as those with which it was overcome in the first place. I have regrouped the influences on his concept of the crystal and shown that it bears the mark of the theatrical and literary traditions which have addressed similar concepts but in different contexts and under different circumstances. By reworking for himself the active object and complementing his Segalian individualism, Baudrillard attempts to ensure by definition the object's incomprehensibility, and therefore its exoticism, while at the same time impairing the subject's control over the object(ive) universe. Only a true Exote forsakes such control.

Notes

Unless otherwise indicated, translations are my own.

1 Jean Baudrillard, *Le système des objets* (Paris: Gallimard, 1968).
2 Peter Weiss, *Pointe de fuite* (Paris: Seuil, 1964).
3 Peter Weiss, *La persécution et l'assassinat de Jean-Paul Marat représente par le groupe théâtrale de l'hospice de Charenton sous le direction de Monsieur de Sade* (Paris: Editions de Seuil, 1965).

4 Peter Weiss, *L'instruction, oratorio en onze chants* (Paris: Seuil, 1966).
5 Peter Weiss, *Discours sur la genèse et le déroulement de la très longue guerre de libération du Vietnam illustrant la nécessité de la lutte armée des opprimés contre leurs oppresseurs ainsi que la volonté des Etats-Unis d'Amérique d'anéantir les fondements de la Révolution* (Paris: Seuil, 1968).
6 Peter Weiss, *Notes on the Cultural Life of the Democratic Republic of Vietnam*. trans. Dell Publishing (London: Calder and Boyars, 1970), p. 179.
7 Bertolt Brecht, *Dialogues d'exilés* (Paris: L'Arche, 1965).
8 Baudrillard reflects on his work with the journal, the utopia of everyday life, and the crisis of the urban in the 1960s in his article, "L'Amérique, ou la pensée de l'espace," *Citoyenneté et urbanité* (Paris: Esprit, 1991); see also his remarks in Maria Shevtsova, "Intellectuals, Commitment and Political Power: An Interview with Jean Baudrillard," *Thesis Eleven*, 10, 11 (1984–5) 166–74.
   The first issue of *Utopie* appeared in May 1967. It survived for only seven issues, ending with the August-September issue of 1973. Over the six years of its publication, Hubert Tonka served as managing editor, although this continuity was not reflected in the review's membership, which shifted substantially during the first issues until a core group of four remained: Isabelle Auricoste, Baudrillard, Michel Guillou, and Tonka. Several of the essays which would form the basis of Baudrillard's *Le miroir de la production* and *Pour une critique de l'économie politique du signe* appeared here alongside other uncollected pieces.
   Baudrillard's reflections on his activities with *Utopie* are invariably positive. He still collaborates on urban issues with Tonka and Auricoste (see his "Préface" to their *Parc-ville Villette*, Paris: Editions du semi-cercle, 1989) and recycles utopist conceptions such as *structures gonflables*. In *Cool Memories II*, he wrote: "The rights of Man have an inflatable structure. The [French] Revolution and its commemoration have become inflatable structures" (p. 31). In March 1968, *Utopie* mounted an exposition of *structures gonflables* at the Musée d'art de la ville de Paris. Pneumatic objects expressed well the spectacular ideology of consumer society. Circa 1968, one may recall that in Italian furniture design, Jonathan De Pas, Donato d'Urbino and Paolo Lomazzi's inflatable armchair named "Blow" (1967), as well as their proposals for pneumatic housing units, captured the paradoxical fullness/emptiness of mass culture. The inflatable structure remained a potent concept for Baudrillard since it signified the absence of the revolution, and the impossibility of a revolution like it in the future, in its mediatized commemoration.
   In the early 1970s, Baudrillard was a member of the Centre d'études des communications de masse at the École pratique des hautes études in Paris, where he taught in addition to the seminars he gave at Nanterre, Vincennes, and other centers, experimental or otherwise, such as CELSA (Centre d'études littéraires et scientifiques appliquées) at Université de Paris IV. Baudrillard was the Center's expert on design and, in fact, he served on the jury of the "Compasso d'oro" prize in Italian design in Milan in 1970 and attended the World Congress of Design in Aspen, Colorado, in the same year. He spoke on design at the École des hautes études commerciales (1971) and taught in the Département d'urbanisme at Vincennes (1972–3).
9 Genosko, "Fellow Doctors of Pataphysics: Ubu, Faustroll, and Baudrillard,"

in *Jean Baudrillard: The Disappearance of Art and Politics*, eds., William Stearns and William Chaloupka (New York: Saint Martin's Press, 1992), pp. 146–59.

10   Baudrillard, *Cool Memories II* (Paris: Galilée, 1990), p. 131.

11   Douglas Kellner, *Jean Baudrillard: From Marxism to Postmodernism and Beyond* (Stanford: Stanford University Press, 1989), p. 154ff.

12   Mark Gane, *Baudrillard: Critical and Fatal Theory* (London: Routledge, 1991), pp. 69–70.

13   Fyodor Dostoyevski, *Notes From Underground* [1864] and *The Double*, trans., Jessie Coulson (Harmondsworth: Penguin Books, 1972), pp. 33–4.

14   Baudrillard, "Le théorème de la part maudite," in *La transparence du mal* (Paris: Galilée, 1990), p. 111.

15   Patricia Mellencamp, "Seeing is Believing: Baudrillard and Blau," *Theatre Journal* 37, 2 (1985) 144.

16   Baudrillard, "Du système des objets au destin de l'objet," in *L'autre par lui-même. Habilitation* (Paris: Galilée, 1987), p. 69.

17   Baudrillard with Guy Bellavance, "Le cristal se venge," *Parachute* 31 (June, July, Aug 1983) 27.

18   Baudrillard, *Les stratégies fatales* (Paris: Grasset, 1983), p. 204.

19   Jacques Derrida, *Signéponge/Signsponge*, trans., Richard Rand (New York: Columbia University Press, 1984), p. 68ff.

20   Baudrillard, *Le système des objets*, pp. 107–8; see also *Cool Memories 1980–1985* (Paris: Galilée, 1987), p. 138 and pp. 194–5.

21   Brian Singer, "Baudrillard's Seduction," in *Ideology and Power in the Age of Lenin in Ruins*, eds., Arthur and Marilouise Kroker (Montreal: New World Perspectives, 1991), p. 150.

22   See Fred McGlynn, "Postmodernism and Theatre," in *Postmodernism – Philosophy and the Arts*, ed., Hugh J. Silverman (New York: Routledge, 1990); Antonin Artaud, *Le théâtre et son double* (Paris: Gallimard, 1964).

23   Artaud, "Sur le théâtre balinais," in *Théâtre*, pp. 100–1.

24   Jacques Derrida, "The Theatre of Cruelty and the Closure of Representation," in *Writing and Difference*, trans., A. Bass (Chicago: Chicago University Press, 1978), p. 235ff.

25   Ibid., p. 244.

26   Julia Kristeva, "Modern Theatre Does Not Take (A) Place," trans., Alice Jardine and Thomas Gora. *substance*, 18/19 (1977).

27   Ibid., p. 131.

28   Jean-François Lyotard, "La dent, la paume," in *Des dispositifs pulsionnels* (Paris: Union générale d'editions, Collection 10/18, 1973).

29   Ibid., p. 96.

30   Ibid., pp. 99–100.

31   Ibid., p. 104.

32   Baudrillard, *L'échange symbolique et la mort* (Paris: Gallimard, 1976), pp. 338–9.

33   Michel Foucault, "Theatrum Philosophicum," in *Language, Counter-memory, Practice. Selected Essays and Interviews*, ed., Donald Boucard (Ithaca: Cornell University Press, 1977).

34   Artaud, "En finir avec les chefs-d'oeuvres," in *Théâtre*, p. 123.

35   Artaud, "Théâtre balinais," p. 91.

36 Baudrillard, "Media et information: Stratégie d'objet et ironie objective," in Derrick de Kerckhove and Amilcare A. Iannuci, eds., *McLuhan E La Metamorfosi Dell'Uomo* (Roma: Bulzoni Editore, 1984), p. 149.

37 Ibid.

38 Artaud, "The Marx Brothers," in *Selected Writings* (New York: Farrar, Straus, and Giroux, 1976), p. 240.

39 Herbert Blau, "Counterforce II: Notes From the Underground," in *The Impossible Theater: A Manifesto* (New York: Collier, 1965), p. 247.

40 Artaud, "Van Gogh, the Man Suicided by Society," in *Selected Writings*, p. 496.

41 Gilles Deleuze and Félix Guattari, *Anti-Oedipus. Capitalism and Schizophrenia*, trans., Robert Hurley, Mark Seem, and Helen R. Lane (New York: Viking, 1977), p. 135.

42 Deleuze and Guattari, "November 28, 1947: How Do You Make Yourself A Body Without Organs?" in *A Thousand Plateaus*, trans., Brian Massumi (Minneapolis: University of Minnesota Press, 1987), p. 164.

43 Foucault, *Madness and Civilization: A History of Insanity in the Age of Reason*, trans., Richard Howard (London: Tavistock, 1967), p. 287.

44 Baudrillard, *Les stratégies fatales*, p. 154ff.

45 Baudrillard, *De la séduction* (Paris: Denoel-Gonthier, 1979), p. 80ff. The two "sciences" in question are psychoanalysis and linguistics.

46 Patrice Pavis, *Problèmes de sémiologie théâtrale* (Montreal: Les Presses de l'Universitaire du Québec, 1976), p. 135.

47 Keir Elam, *The Semiotics of Theatre and Drama* (London: Methuen, 1980), p. 16.

48 Otokar Zich, *Esthetics of Dramatic Form*, quoted in Christine Kiebuzinska, *Revolutionaries of the Theater: Meyerhold, Brecht, and Witkiewicz* (Ann Arbor: UMI Research Press, 1988), pp. 34–5.

49 Jirí Veltrusky, "Man and Object in the Theatre," in *A Prague School Reader on Esthetics, Literary Structure and Style*, trans., Paul L. Garvin (Washington, DC: Georgetown University Press, 1964), p. 88.

50 Zich quoted in ibid., p. 86.

51 Baudrillard, "Du système des objets," p. 73.

52 Baudrillard, *Les stratégies fatales*, p. 185ff.

53 Naomi Segal, *The Banal Object: Theme and Thematics in Proust, Hofmannsthal, and Sartre*. Bithell Series of Dissertations, Vol. 10 (Leeds: Institute of Germanic Studies, University of London, 1981), p. 4.

54 Victor Segalen, *Essai sur l'exotisme, une esthétique du divers* (Paris: Fata Morgana, 1978), p. 37; quoted in Baudrillard, "Du système des objets," p. 67 and "L'exotisme radical," in *La transparence du mal*, p. 153.
     Segalen's *Essai* is a series of programmatic announcements, definitions of key terms, journal entries, quotations, and extracts from letters written by the author in Paris from June 1908 to March 1909, during his voyage through China (Nov 1909–Jan 1914), upon his return to China (April 1917 – Oct 1918), and in the course of his hospitalization in Brest in 1919.

55 In a forthcoming article, "Exotes comme nous: Baudrillard et Segalen," *Société* (Montreal, 1993), I develop what I call the "dirty secrets" of exoticism: anti-feminism, anti-egalitarism, and anti-colonialism by default. I trace the identity

of the Other in Baudrillard's work with that of the so-called "savage" in order to show how the hypothesis of exoticism supports a theory of hyperracism which purports to lay bare the hypocrisy of structural-humanitarian ecumenicalism and the slow genocide entailed by the recognition of difference, but whose consequences are equally horrible and unjust.

56 Segalen, *Essai*, p. 24.
57 Ibid., p. 25.
58 Ibid.
59 See Arthur Kroker, "Baudrillard's Marx," *Theory, Culture and Society*, 2, 3 (1985), pp. 73–4.
60 Baudrillard, *Cool Memories II*, p. 36.
61 Baudrillard, *Les stratégies fatales*, p. 135, n. 1.

14

BAUDRILLARD, TIME, AND THE END

—

William Bogard

I

In *Fatal Strategies*, among other places, Baudrillard returns to Elias Canetti's "tormenting" thought on the end of history. It is, Canetti writes, as if at "a certain point, history was no longer real. Without noticing it, all mankind suddenly left reality: everything happening since then was supposedly no longer true; but we supposedly didn't notice. Our task would be to find that point, and as long as we didn't have it, we would be forced to abide in our present destruction."[1]

Baudrillard thinks Canetti's thought is seductive but pious. If history is no longer real or true, then we are simply, once and for all, beyond it. It is the attempt to *return* to history, the task itself rather than the likelihood of its failure, that promises to be destructive. For Baudrillard, our "present destruction" is not nothing, a space of negativity, but a mediascape saturated with simulacra of history. At the end of history, the historical may disappear as a real or true movement of time, but it proliferates as a reference in simulation.[2] Suddenly history is in everything, even more real and true, that is, more *explicit*, than ever, mediated by a vast array of info- and bio-technologies.[3] Via screens, telematic networks, cyborgian recording and projection devices, whole histories are miraculously and ecstatically restored to memory (or rather, to the spectacle of memory, to which we devote ourselves today more than memory itself). Nothing is forgotten, everything is tracked and replayed, captured on tape, preserved in electronic files, stored on disk. Things which once had no history, are now, or soon will be, nothing but history, their past forever destined to precede them (e.g., the body, whose life course the new genetics decodes as a *future* history – of disease, achievement and failure, risk). Thus, in multiple ways, the end of history is deterred or forestalled, at least in appearance; it's granted a reprieve to exist in a twilight zone of disenchanted simulacra, haunting the ruins of time. Today, for Baudrillard, Canetti's pious task has become more like an obsession; retrograde movements and the forces of reversion are everywhere, out to block the exodus from history by coding it into anything whatsoever.[4] But it's too late. The simulation of history is exactly what confirms the irreversibility of history's disappearance and the impossibility of a genuine return. For Baudrillard, it is a matter of abiding a "present destruction" where the sheer repetition of the historical at last and finally absorbs history, where history disappears into the infinity of its reproduction.

After the end of history, the first question is: what now? In Baudrillard's work, there are two images of the future, very close but none the less very different, like distorting mirrors of one another: a *future past*, i.e., the paradoxically *soon-to-be but already-gone present* seen from the sliding vantage point of a phantasmagoric future (or bestiary, to use Mike Gane's term[5]), a world of clones, bubble-boys, cyborgs, sim-sex, and other virtual realities. This is the image of simulation, which insofar as it involves a reference to doubling or repetition, is a form of "looking back" or return. The second image is the future as seduction, the annihilation or immolation of signs and the systems of power they generate, beyond history and what Baudrillard calls the present melancholy of things. Baudrillard does not "look back" from this second future, yet it is also a form of return, in fact, for Baudrillard, what always returns (in Nietzsche's sense of eternal recurrence). Seduction is what Baudrillard opposes to simulation, an eternal return to the serial "return" of simulation (infinite, *modulated* repetition), a breathless intoxication at the limits of time to the drab technical domination of the code; it is the enchanted, magical form of simulation.[6] There is no choice between these two futures, only a duel whose outcome is never certain. But Baudrillard's bets are on seduction, not only to absorb the fantastic, bestial world we are now entering, and which in another sense is already over, but in the same movement, to explode his own (simulated) vantage point in the "hereafter" beyond the end of history, his own "looking back" on that end. One looks back in order to see what's following, to capture the object and possess it; looking back is a form of repetition or retracing, i.e., of simulation. But one who is seduced does not look back. In seduction one becomes the object, loses oneself in the object, only to seduce it better in return.[7]

II

"This is where the rest of life begins," Baudrillard writes, referring to the end of projects. "But the rest is what is given to you as something extra, and there is a charm and a particular freedom about letting just anything come along with the grace – or ennui – of a later destiny."[8] The day after

tomorrow we'll forget about the end of things and be seduced by something else. Even boredom is a release from the contemplation of completed tasks. Today, however, we are all melancholic; a "sadness at leaving"
now pervades everything.[9] This is no longer the nostalgia of dialectics,
Baudrillard says, like that of Adorno or Benjamin, but an *affectation* which
arises from being incurably unhinged from history yet surrounded by the
ghosts of all we have lost. It is significant here that he emphasizes the
element of the false or affected appearance in melancholy, which, like *joie
de vivre*, is a mask, not "in line with the involution of things."[10] This is
what ties melancholy to simulation – both are forms of artifice, both are
responses to the end of projects. In Baudrillard, melancholy is now in the
very state of things; objects and events now project a certain sorrow, in the
sense of being detached at last from their histories, yet destined to repeat
them forever in simulation. In a world stripped of historical finality and
direction, hyper-finalities now multiply with a vengeance, as we begin the
"micro-processing of all desires" in the era of dead capital, dead Marx,
dead language, dead time.[11] Simulation, the order of repetition to infinity,
is now our impoverished compensation for what can never be repeated.
And melancholy is the similarly impoverished but inescapable artifice
through which objects and events call attention to their own disappearance.

I recently heard Martin Jay identify Baudrillard's reflections on the general
melancholy of things with the historically recurring thought of the apocalypse.[12] He cited Baudrillard's preoccupation with the end of history and
the general melancholy which pervades things today as evidence of a profound nihilistic despair which runs through "postmodern" thinking at the
fin-de-millenium. Such remarks, to me, reflect many misunderstandings of
Baudrillard, whose work I find to be neither apocalyptic, nor nihilistic, nor
"postmodern," nor even, despite his own self-characterization in *Cool
Memories*, melancholic. Baudrillard certainly cannot stand outside his own
milieu, which is perhaps all these things, if that is what he is being asked
to do; instead, he traces the ways objects and events pass through that
milieu, redoubling their paths of resistance, retreat, and attack. Follow the
object, he says, study its moves, let it speak for itself. But also, if necessary,
play indifferent, let the object attend to you, be responsible for you (this,
for example, is how Baudrillard conceives the "original" strategy of the
masses in relation to their simulation in the media). For Baudrillard, seduction is a game with the highest stakes, a ritual and a challenge, not a
will to nothing, not a desire for the end or for revelation (truth), not an
affected sadness at the departure of history.[13]

If "apocalyptic" has the sense of the end "to come," then Baudrillard,
like Canetti, begins his reflection from an end already lost. The apocalypse,
if that is what it was, is over, or endlessly deterred in simulation, which
amounts to the same thing. Signs of the apocalypse are everywhere in
popular culture, but that only means that the event itself has somehow

definitively evaded us, like World War III or the second coming. The future has already passed by, and all we saw was its retreating image on an electronic screen.

Many of Baudrillard's texts produce this paradoxical sense of time inversion and reversal, of histories written before their events (but which none the less are not prophesies), of pasts inhering in presents and futures in pasts. This is because Baudrillard adopts in his writing the temporal frame of simulation, which is *repetition in advance*. Baudrillard can and does claim, without contradiction, that the future has already happened, or that the past which we thought occurred in fact never took place, except in simulation, and that that was its dominant "reality" (he makes an argument like this in his recent reflections on the Gulf War, to which I shall return below[14]). The title of his article, "The year 2000 has already happened," for example, looks back on the millenium that, from the simulated, futuristic standpoint he adopts, *precedes* today.[15] That is precisely what a simulated order is, an *order of precession*, the absorption of the real by its model, i.e., by its future past.[16] Similarly, his remarks at a New York conference on the end of the world reflect his belief in the general superfluousness of intellectual discussions about the "coming" millenium, their poverty in the shadow of a *simulacrum of the end* which antedates and overwhelms the event and is superior to it in every sense.[17]

It is in that sense that the order of simulation surpasses even nihilism. To be a nihilist, Baudrillard claims, would be "admirable" if the system could still be challenged by a radical indifference to meaning or value, to limits in general. But the system is not only already indifferent to limits, it reproduces them in simulation, thereby mocking this very indifference. God is not dead, Baudrillard writes, contra Nietzsche, he is hyperreal. Or, we could add, if he is dead, it is a simulated death. Nihilism cannot subvert an order that radicalizes nihilism to the point of its own reversion, its own de-radicalization, that substitutes for the indifference to limits the obscene transparency of everything.[18]

If Baudrillard's thought is nihilistic, it is only in the sense that he is part of the general revenge of things everywhere seeking to escape their servitude, to recover their destiny and sovereignty after the end of history. After the apocalypse, after the revelation to end all revelations (the revelation that today revelation is impossible, that nothing remains secret), we now repeat, with all the irony of a simulated return to history, the events which brought this catastrophe about. Today, the technical assemblages of simulation recover historical time and project it back as a new determination and finality. The contemporary order of simulation is the very sign of our hyper-nihilism, this exhaustive and exhausting redoubling of limits, of ends, the real, of time and history (and, of course, for Baudrillard, of sex and desire, the social and the political, all of which have become excrescent and obscene). This is the important point: simulation points at nothing beyond itself; it is an interior, sealed space, a closed system that cannot be transcended or dialectically negated (negation is powerless before what is "truer-than-true"), a modulated series projected into a dead future. Still, the system is implosive, it cannibalizes or parasites itself, it contains gaps. And if there are no limits to simulation, in Baudrillard there is still the possibility of its seduction, its reenchantment in a space beyond all limits.

III

In Baudrillard's bestiary, the interiority and self-enclosure of simulation erupt in a general terrorism of appearances. We are all hostages of this new order, and all terrorists, too.[19] Suddenly, everything becomes political, everything is sexual, everything must have its history, its identity, and its destination, everything has significance, and interpretations are available, instantly, for anything, anywhere (instant analysis). Simulation absorbs its environment in a pure abstraction. It is an "abstract machine" (Deleuze) that envelops the object in its repetition and launches it into orbit.[20] It is the ultimate *diversion*, a mode of distraction that dissolves any space of negativity or reflection. We become lost in it, aliens. It produces just the opposite effect of despair; rather, an ecstatic experience of instantaneousness and presence (telepresence), or the vertigo generated by a false sense of motion, of standing on the edge of an abyss or void that is in appearance a plenitude. In simulation, there is *no time* for despair, *no space* for nostalgia, because simulation is the cancellation of distance, space, and ultimately (linear, historical) time itself, and the substitution of simulated distances, simulated times, etc., the immediacy or embrasure of a pure, encompassing "experience."[21]

This is what guides, for example, the technical evolution of television, the progressive erasure of distance between viewer and screen, image and event. Television, in the logic of its development, aims not at the *illusion* of presence, but to eliminate that illusion by rendering the artifice – the technical support and staging – of the televisual image invisible or undetectable. To eliminate, that is, through technical means, the distorting, disconcerting effects of the technology itself (here, the screen and the camera), which signals that what is being watched is "only" a reproduction, a "mere appearance." (This project, of course, is not unique to television, but informs the history of all recording and reproduction technologies). To make the image indistinguishable from – no, even better than – the scene. Perfect television would be like the holodeck on "Star Trek:" The Next Generation – a seamless, "noiseless" projection that is fully interactive. In the twenty-fourth century world of the holodeck, one "enters" the televisual apparatus, and the room is transformed by voice command into a perfect simulation of space-time which transcends the material limits of projection.

The "television" (i.e., the room) disappears and is replaced by a new sim-territory, bounded now from the "inside." No more screen, no more camera, no more television or room, a new geography and temporal order spreads out before the gaze. In "Star Trek," the holodeck eliminates the "illusion of being there" by not only making the technology "appear to disappear," but in some sense to *really* disappear, opening onto a hyper-logistics of perceptual control (a perfectly prepared environment for testing, training, instruction, drilling, etc., with none of the attendant risks).[22]

In Baudrillard, the order of simulation is the sign of the end of the media in general (he presides over its final rites in his article "Requiem for the Media").[23] The mass media are not mediatory but actually anti-mediatory, in that they do not allow response, that is, the reciprocity of symbolic communication or exchange. Today we live in the ecstasy of communication precisely because communication is lost in the implosion of the media in the masses (and vice versa). That is, we transfer our disappearing capacity for understanding and sociality, for communication, to the abstraction of an operation, to the precession of codes, polls, indices, profiles which retain no distance from their instantiation and dispersion in social relations and objects. In Baudrillard (whose views on these matters have changed somewhat over the years) the end of the media is the point at which the obscenity of the media begins, its incursion into all forms of communication, into the language and practice of sexuality, politics, and the social, each of which is resurrected in an abstract and abstracting technology – and in an assemblage of power – which itself replays over and again its own irretrievable disappearance.

IV

Simulation corresponds in the first instance to the category of the past, not a specific past, but what we might call the past-in-general. This is because it is first of all a form of repetition, a "return," an abstract "again" (simulations are copies, clones, replicants, decoys, miniatures, models). But simulation also *absorbs* the past (*its* past) in repeating it. Baudrillard, for example, writes about the disappearance of the Holocaust in the mode of its unending reiteration, its *preservation* as a historical event. It is the same with other so-called historical preservation projects (urban renewal, wilderness areas, even modernity itself): what is past is gone, but there it is! That was Bataille's formula for a miracle: something impossible, but there it is neverthless.[24] Simulation is like a miracle, for only a miraculous technology could revive the past in the present (and project it endlessly into the future). Of course, it is an artificial miracle, staged with mirrors; what appears in simulation is a trick, an illusion – something repeated is taken for the original – but its secret aim is real magic, an enchanted world with true miracles. In short, simulation aims for seduction, which is its own disappearance. That would be the real miracle, and sometimes Baudrillard seems to believe in it. Most of the time, however, the endpoint in the technical evolution of simulation would only mean, in the case of electronic communications, for instance, that you become the television and television becomes you, the miracle produces a cyborg time-traveler, a technobody that, for Baudrillard, is fascinating but hardly seductive.[25]

Within the envelope of the repeated past, simulation produces other "miracles"; time in general, any-time-whatever, is reproduced on its screen – future, past, present, all can be repeated or played back, and, moreover, this can be done at variable speeds (fast forward, slow motion, reverse motion, freeze frame, stop time); in simulated time, within the general form of repetition in advance, an old dream is realized – any time is possible, and time flows in any direction. Simulation, we could say, is the disenchanted ecstasy of time. It *kills* time (ask any video game addict); it makes time split off from itself (from the linear time of history, the certain movement of the present into the past and the future). And, again, this is precisely why Baudrillard's thought has nothing to do with melancholy (or anguish or nostalgia). He, like everyone else, is too caught up in this spectacle of time's immolation, its journey into the digital void.

Simulation creates a superficial plenitude. If we feel today that we are flooded with signs and the significance of things, it is because all signs (as well as all interpretations, meanings) today are equivalent in terms of their final destination. The universe of dead signs: mass media images have a brief lifespan before they die and are discarded; today one image is the same as another in terms of its miniscule allotment of time, and that time frame is constantly shrinking as more and more images are compressed within it (the average commercial, for instance, now contains images that last only micro-seconds – if this trend continues, the result will be a completely subliminal advertisement!). For Baudrillard, the end of history is also the end of the hierarchical regime of signs, and the beginning of the "flat," homogeneous regime of signals and codes.[26] In a simulated, informated order, everything is suddenly reversible: sex can be art, art can be sex, and both can be politics, the media can be the masses, the social can disappear into itself, and so forth. Simulation transforms a world of signs into electronic pulses and pours them into a gap in timespace opened up by the end of history. The effect is nothing like overdetermination, in the Marxist sense. It is not that objects can have too many names today, but rather the object *overwhelms* its names like a vortex into which they descend and disappear forever. For Baudrillard, this is the experience of seduction, the immolation and disappearance of names in a space of radical otherness, of being thrown into the depths of an unnameable, unspeakable timelessness.[27]

Into this gap in space and time, simulation inserts a *virtual* timespace, a replication or projection of spatio-temporal dimensionality which envelops the subject completely, that is, makes him an interactive component of the scene. (Virtual reality technology is the most obvious example here. In Baudrillard's terms, we might refer to such technologies as forms of expression of the truer-than-the-true, the more-real-than-the-real, etc., because they substitute doubles of the true or real which can now be replicated to infinity.) Deleuze has given us the best analysis of virtual forms in his analysis of cinematic images, and also the best description of the relation of the virtual image to the general category of the past.[28] Although we cannot recount Deleuze's theory of images here, which draw on Bergson's reflections on time, he draws our attention to forms of images which in actual and virtual images coincide – "crystal images" – in which there is posited an *indiscernible difference* in the image of the present which passes (the actual) and the image as continually preserved (the virtual as the past in general, which splits off from the passing present yet is nothing different from it). This is precisely, in different terms, the operation of simulation, which posits an indiscernible difference in two times (or two spaces) – the time that was there but is now gone (stored, in its entirety, in memory), and the space that has suffered the same fate. The end of history to which Baudrillard's work refers is also the disappearance of territories (a deterritorialization, to use Guattari's term) followed in turn by a reterritorialization, a replication of territories in simulation. All this is becoming more familiar to us, again, in the emerging technologies of virtual reality. If we use these machines today and see so much for their use in the future, it is because we acutely sense the disappearance of real times and spaces. Artificial time and space is, in a sense, our solace. Baudrillard, however, notes the superficiality and transient nature of that solace. For him, otherness, seduction, timelessness, genuine as opposed to artificial distraction, are the essential things. Seduction eventually overwhelms simulation. And, if not, at least this is where Baudrillard sees the real stakes played out today, no longer in the revolutionary strategies and tactics of the past. Revolutions never win us anything, they always reproduce the conditions they set out to destroy; in the last analysis, seduction is the real and best gamble. When one loses in the game of seduction, at least one loses everything.

V

Up to this point, I have avoided what is perhaps the crucial question: why the fascination with this seemingly absurd hypothesis, the end of history, the real, the disappearance of historical time? Beyond the end of history, we could not assign a cause to its disappearance (cause being essentially bound up with the idea of history and sequential time). So what is the point in positing it at all, other than perhaps an exercise in tracing the possible trajectories of a fiction? When Baudrillard claims that the Gulf War never happened, he is not being ironic, at least not in any simple sense. He is drawing our attention, instead, to an irony or paradox in the object or event itself (and, on occasion, is himself seduced by that irony). It is the irony of an event that is an ongoing non-event (or pure event), like the Persian Gulf War which was only the potentiation and intensification of the operations of the global electromagnetic war apparatus, which today never stops. The irony of the Gulf War was its hyperreality. That does not mean it was an unreal war, but a war in which the gap between reality and artifice was barely discernible. Not a television war exactly, but a war where television (and a host of other simulation technologies) was thoroughly and seamlessly integrated into the conflict.[29] A hyperreal war does not mean a war with no effects, that produced no casualties. Quite the contrary, the simulation of war – computer-assisted battle, cyborg soldiers, pilot "associates," expert battlefield systems, vision systems, satellite surveillance, military manipulation of the media – is perhaps the deadliest technology of all. It means only that between the simulated, virtual war and the actual, real war there is only the gap of a disappearing difference, so thoroughly does the telematic technology of war now suffuse its preparation and conduct. In fact, like Virilio's pure war, war now becomes nothing but its continuous preparation.[30] But preparation is also continuous, pure enactment. The Gulf War never happened. That *can* mean: it just *keeps* happening. Or, like the year 2000, it just *keeps* being over, played out again and again in advance *even in its execution*, in endless war games, battlefield scenarios, casualty figures, incinerated bodies, lethal, murderous video, a great simulacrum of death. Maybe, at some point, the real Gulf War took off in another direction, but we'll never know where or when, or if it still runs parallel, *in another lost dimension*, to the implosion of the war in the media and the media in the war. Baudrillard does not mean to say it is *like* the war never happened, which we can immediately understand, the way wars come and go in the news. "Like" is only a convention to describe what has become the coincidence of virtual and actual in our present experience of things, including time itself. Like the Bergsonian image of time splitting into passing present and past preserved, the distinction is still possible and makes some sense, but the difference has contracted to the zero degree. War becomes a pure event, with no "beginning" and no "end"; it doesn't inhabit the space of happenings, bounded events with causes or effects. It only strikes like a nameless, ironic catastrophe, a punctuation or potentiation of energies within a zone of abstraction extending without limits in all directions.[31]

That is why it is impossible, or at any rate soon will be, to produce a critique of telemated wars, like those in the Persian Gulf. They have no fixed geo-temporal limits, no external points of reference, no truth or falsity. Or, they are such perfect falsifications (or fabrications) of events, that in a fantastic reversal, they become simply true, their truth existing precisely in their superbly (and absolutely) rendered falsity. All this, of course, is strictly unintelligible from perspectives like those adapted against Baudrillard by Christopher Norris, who only sees in the claim that the Gulf War never happened a great, absurd, posturing lie manifestly contradicted by the event itself. Norris opens what I think is a fundamentally misguided assault on Baudrillard by citing Adorno (in *Minima Moralia*) on the "confounding of truth and lies" in the modern age, the contemporary attack "at the very heart of the distinction between the true and the false" in which Hitler, of whom no-one can say whether he died or escaped, survives."[32] Baudrillard as Hitler? In fact, Baudrillard begins precisely from Adorno's critical despair over the "absolute lie that now has the freedom to speak the truth" (what else is perfect simulation?) and suggests a way forward. Baudrillard's insight is that critique is inferior to and powerless against simulation (as the strategy of the subject is inferior to that of the object, as negation is inferior to and powerless against objective irony). A critique of simulated, cyborg war can only be a critique of its *production* values, i.e., of its illusions, how ineptly or expertly the war-apparatus secrets its operations (through disinformation, propaganda, etc.). It has no force against that which in its very logic and at its foundations refuses the distinction of truth and falsity (only that which engages in a similar or parallel refusal is effective). Critique is limited to movements in real time and real space, to the material content of events, and its (always possible) misrepresentation in the media; it is overwhelmed by the simulation of events, by the disappearance of those events in the media and – a point which Norris does not fully comprehend – *the disappearance of the media in them*. In the electromagnetic battles of the Persian Gulf the spectacle of war and its conduct merge. At home plugged into our televisions, in the airspace over Baghdad, in the command and communications bunkers of the Saudi desert, together, simultaneously, we experience the ecstasy of pure war, whose absurdly transparent and unlimited horror nullifies even the most finely crafted critique.

To return to my argument, it is simulation, the technologies of simulation, that make the loss of history a genuine hypothesis. It is precisely the loss of history that explains, or offers an explanation for, the contemporary proliferation of those technologies. If the order of historical time had not disappeared, if in a more general sense the past was still present symbolically for us, there would be no simulation panic. Of course, simulation belongs to a set of strategies that are enacted whenever the order of time is left behind, to return to what has disappeared. Simulation can never be a fatal strategy. It is always a serialized, modulated return, an "again" or "once more." For Baudrillard, only seduction is truly fatal. It risks the seducer's existence without the thought of any return. Clearly, for

Baudrillard, who follows Bataille in this sense (while refusing to describe the process in terms of a transgression) this is an affirmative, although admittedly paradoxical, action; not the distanced, backward-looking, and somewhat pathetic attitude of a melancholic. Again, for Baudrillard, if this is the general state of things, then it is the only – and *our only* – point of departure, and a moment that we must explore for its possibilities, however foreclosed they appear. Melancholy is *in* simulation, in an order which cannot be transcended, but which none the less contains gaps, moments of seduction and pure timelessness which break through the regime of repetition and sameness (although we are lucky when we find them). At unpredictable points, we fall back into those gaps, those uncharted zones, residues of the vacuum at the end of history, points of ultimate danger and exhilaration unmapped and uncontrolled by simulation.

VI

We now move in the "time" of the hypertelic, beyond any end, in an alien environment, like "crustacean(s) that leave the sea far behind."[33] The hyper-, the obscene, the excrescent, these super-saturated forms are what "fill in" after the end of everything (information fills in for dead language, cyborgs for dead labor, junk bonds for dead capital, television evangelists for dead God, video games for dead time). Sex spirals into pornography, the body into obesity, and the object takes its revenge by refusing to be an object, a *useful thing*. It is as if in Bataille's sense we had somehow permanently transgressed the sphere of utility, but not to emerge in the sovereign dimension, that is, no longer governed by ends, but in the more-than-useful, or the hyper-utilic.[34] Utility, that is, is simulated. Of course we all know this in a vague way, and it is nothing really new: there are no more needs, because we are told by advertising and publicity that we need everything, and what can need be in the face of an unlimited necessity? Today, needs are absorbed into the same void as everything else; they have no meaning or depth and are all equivalent to each other. I need a brand of shoes like I need a new life, a new body, a new outlook, or a new name, something to show I exist because my identity is as imploded as my desires. The disappearance of real (or true) needs breeds the proliferation of simulated ones (but who's to say what a real need is any longer?).[35] Today we are saturated to death with utility. But it is not enough to try, in a sovereign gesture, like Bataille, to live beyond utility. The problem today is how to live with its simulation, without hope or the illusion of return to the reality of needs.

Baudrillard's stance in relation to all this is not a sovereign one. Transgression is not possible precisely because there is no return to the law – the history – which allows it, other than a cynical return. In fact, in the current situation, it is precisely transgression that is simulated, because it has disappeared once and for all as a real possibility (what are you doing after the orgy? Baudrillard asks). What happens past the end, which we sped past without realizing it, is, for Baudrillard, like an immense *speeding-up of slowing-down*, an accelerating inertia where nothing ever happens despite, or rather because of, the in-your-face intensity of contemporary events. The more things change in appearance, that is, the greater the pace of simulation, the more the metastatic, cancerous dimension of the present reveals itself.

Baudrillard, of course, does not think that everything about simulation is negative (in fact, it is not a negativity at all). The space of nuclear war, for example, is a simulated space (perhaps today the most simulated space, virtually every scenario of exchange having been played out in advance for nearly 50 years). Nuclear weapons only have a use-value in simulation, that is, a hyperutility. Produced to excess, they are not exchangeable – in the same way that hostages are no longer exchangeable – a nuclear war has become, or rather it always was, pure war[36] – wars at the speed of light, wars where the military observation-machine and the military simulation-machine merge together (Virilio). Baudrillard notes the objective irony of the situation, i.e., wars so potentially destructive they can only be fought in another dimension, the purely formal dimension of simulation (simulation is always about missing or lost dimensions, in this case, the timespace of exchange).[37] Baudrillard's comments on nuclear war give us another indication of the non-apocalyptic dimension of his thought. The "apocalyse" of nuclear war is over. If the "real" apocalyse has not happened, the simulated one has, over and over in the war-game rooms of the global military machine. Baudrillard says the simulated war may perhaps save us from destruction. We should applaud the escalation of the nuclear arms race and fear its de-escalation (to the point where the use-value of these weapons is once again redeemed and they become exchangeable). I don't think this logic is inconsistent with his later position that the simulation of war can be deadly. Baudrillard never claims that building more nuclear weapons will stop us from blowing up the planet – we have already blown it up thousands of times in computer scenarios! The last time we blow it up will only be the final absurdity in a chain of absurdities, an anticlimax that will never measure up to the horror already present in its model.

VII

At the end of history, there is no revelation, no moment of truth (hence, nothing like a genuine apocalypse). Like living in Canetti's post-historical time, the world would seem false, but we wouldn't know it. Instead, we would be bombarded from all sides with virtual realities, the truer-than-true, over which the false has no power (only the "falser-than-false," i.e., seduction.) In fact, both truth and falsity are absorbed in the radical but continually retreating uncertainty of virtual realities. Where am I? Who am I? What is this? Is it real? These are the disappearing questions posed in cyberspace, all of which are dissolved, ultimately, into indifference. Truth and falsity have no value in simulation, or rather only a *structural* value, that is, in relation to a preprogrammed, predefined context. That is why truth and falsity can be everywhere and nowhere today, gone forever, yet as references in simulation, as projections of some code, present in everything, every image.

It is sometimes thought that Baudrillard offers us an original analysis of the image, a new way of seeing the visual media. This is not a complete way of looking at things, however. In Baudrillard, images as forms of seduction are virtually absent from our world, or rather they have been absorbed, like everything else, into simulation.[38] The seduction of images, their power of attraction and latent violence, has become affected, disenchanted. (When tennis star Andrew Agassi, for example, can tell us in a commercial that image is everything, we can be absolutely certain that it's dead.) Like truth and the rest, the image, the imaginary, today is everywhere and nowhere, and the sheer excess of images available to us makes them all the same, compressed into equivalent and continuously shrinking frames. What remains is the empty shell of time into which we pack increasingly segmentalized, diminishing images. Compression is an essential feature of excrescent, simulated forms – more information in smaller spaces and lesser times, the goal being pure information which occupies no space and takes no time at all. This means that the informated image, as it turns out, doesn't really die at all; it *vaporizes*, i.e., it implodes, following the revenge of all objects, of everything that has been turned into an object, a use-value, a "thing" (again, recalling Bataille).

Thinking of this kind – compression, miniaturization, implosion – is at the heart of cybernetization, genome research, military intelligence, polling, virtual reality. Ultimately, it is the quest for instantaneity or simultaneity, to be anywhere without having to go anywhere, without having to travel in "real" space, to use "real" time. It is, in fact, to arrive *ahead of time* ... a curious, concentrated mode of immortality and omniscience. Contemporary simulation technology fascinates us with this disenchanted image of the absolute power of perception and motion, absolute control in a fully interactive sense (video games, flight simulators, telepresencers) but within a closed, programmed environment. The household of the future past, with the aid of its integrated infocenter, will also be a workplace, a shopping mall, a school, a church – all business and pleasure mixed together and conducted from the terminal (these images already have the anachronistic, suburban quality of 1950s promotions for the latest kitchen gadgets). Still, Baudrillard does not totalize simulation, or rather, its totalization is only a seductive image projected back from the future. There are still holes in this cyborg world, places where seduction returns, where images once again have stakes (despite how effective, for example, television has been in stripping the image of its power). Again, Baudrillard believes seduction will overcome the current impoverished state of images. But there is no single method or rule that would tell us how to discriminate between what is seductive and what is only simulated. What remains an abstract distinction dissolves for Baudrillard at the level of experience, that is, of discernment. That, again, is why Baudrillard is not a critic in the conventional sense. Critique requires difference and a certain stability of relation, but in his work, critique is always retreating, disappearing, changing location and time, and only by a superhuman effort (and then only temporarily) does it break free from the leveling, homogenizing forces of simulation.

Seduction is the great attractive, dynamic force in Baudrillard. But his "wish" is less pious than Canetti's. What matters is no longer a return to history but what seduces history, no longer a rediscovery of the real but what seduces the real, and ultimately, what seduces seduction (I shall return to this). For Baudrillard, I have suggested, it means turning one's attention to the object, in fact, becoming the object, for example, becoming-woman (I once heard Baudrillard say he *was* a woman, without hint of irony).[39] Baudrillard here is also closer to Deleuze than he himself would admit, in his distaste for all forms of interiority and closed systems (like simulation), in his desire for the exterior, to become the object itself, like a shaman or sorcerer;[40] becoming-animal, becoming-machine, becoming-other. Difference (or rather, *otherness*) over sameness, the multiplicity and strangeness of experience over the isolation and solitude of the subject. Baudrillard is very much like a nomad, only in hyperspace, a primitive in virtual reality.[41] If we return to our original questions, we can once more see how distant this is from melancholy. If he describes himself in such a way, it is only because the end of history is now our common point of departure. One has the sense in reading him, like reading a good piece of science fiction, that anything is possible, that nothing is foreclosed, that the world can be enchanted even in its banal simulation (what else is America?), and that we have to find (that is, to wait for) seduction *here* if we are going to find it anywhere.

Baudrillard's seduction has affinities to Bataille's erotic, the elements of danger, limitless violence and risk to life, the tension between attraction and repulsion. But while the erotic is essentially related to the moral realm and prohibition in Bataille, and from there to death, we have seen that seduction for Baudrillard is a game, an interlude, where disappearance is the rule ("It is not enough to die, one must learn to disappear"). He remarks that one does not transgress the rules of a game like the prohibitions of the law; one either plays or not. Seduction, like a game, is a suspension of time. Or rather, it is timelessness itself, frozen, glacial time. Of course, this can also describe simulation. Video games, television, virtual reality gear suspend time, too. Baudrillard never condemns this technology; at least, his distaste is expressed selectively within the context of a kind of wonderment that seduction could take such strange forms. Revolving restaurants, Disneyland, interactive video are all perhaps indications of the absurdity of modern culture, but they are none the less inspired, if banal, technologies. They seduce, if only in a stuporific way. For Baudrillard, their seduction is, perhaps, inferior to a single timeless glance in which a million signs go up in flame, but they are *our* seduction, and any way forward from here must make do with them. In most cases, they are harmless enough, although, like any technology, there is always the element of danger. Baudrillard tries to play on our ambivalence here, and he oscillates between the attraction and repulsion of these technologies, their risk and their fascination, and, above all, their effect on the experience of time.

Baudrillard ends *Cool Memories* with the entry "This journal is a subtle matrix of idleness." The book, that is, is an exercise in "killing time." Seduction is what captures us in moments of idleness or distraction. Finally, it is the end of melancholy, the end of reflection on ends. It is what takes us away from contemplating loss and propels us forward beyond the end of things. On the other hand, we should be thankful for melancholy (and simulation), because at the very least it opens a space for the possibility of seduction. Here Baudrillard crosses Bataille's path once more. Baudrillard wants to kill the time of work, of production and the project, of servile utility. His preference is for the spaces where time is "electrocuted:" in the endless reversibility of language, fantasy, dream, the monumentality of desert spaces, in eroticism. Empty time, idle time, disappearing time: this is what we have at the end of projects, but we are all too busy today to notice. There is nothing more to do but wait to be seduced, to stand by idly for the silent passion which marks the end of ends and the beginning of a later destiny.

VIII

Mike Gane was right, if only in a negative sense. Baudrillard is not a postmodernist.[42] If modernity was a sustained reflection on Ends (the End of history, philosophy, art) which reached its first concise expression in Hegel, then the postmodern is the simulation of those Ends in a vacuum – the virtual proliferation of finalities in telematic orders. It is here that postmodernity reveals its fundamental complicity with modernity, insofar as it both proclaims the latter's death and stages its miraculous recovery.[43] Baudrillard, to the extent that anyone can these days, refuses both. However, many times Canetti's thought returns to torment Baudrillard; he does not take up Canetti's task, which leads directly (and back!) to the postmodern, to the simulation, the *illusion* of ends – that is, to the recovery of the end of history beyond history, of modernity beyond modernity – which is our present destruction.[44]

To think with Baudrillard, therefore, it is necessary to think not about the end of history, but *through* its simulation, through, in fact, the simulation of ends or finalities in general. Although he is identified with a postmodern preoccupation with ends, for Baudrillard, the question is probably meaningless. I imagine that Baudrillard's own pious wish is to be done once and for all with the question of ends.[45] Still, the constant return to this theme in his own work indicates how difficult it has been for him to break with the sense of historical anticipation and determination which accompanies such reflections.

In a less overt way than some of the writers whose work influenced his own – Nietzsche, Bataille, Debord, Foucault – Baudrillard has been engaged in a long duel with Hegel, who first posed the question of the end of history in its modern form. Baudrillard leaves little doubt of his anti-Hegelianism. The parallels and points of contact with Hegel's thought, however, raise interesting questions. Hegel would have seen simulation as a "bad infinity." As form, simulation is only the sameness of an interminable series – there is no synthesis, no transcendence, only programmed variation and repetition. And Baudrillard would agree. Simulation cannot exceed what it is (its instructions and hardware).[46] If we could imagine the perfect simulation apparatus – think, for instance, of virtual reality brain implants – it would be a mock-up (and hence a mockery) of Hegel's Absolute – an informated, prosthetic god. Without transcending anything, at the same time it would provide the illusion of transcendence, perhaps even succeed, for a time at least, in abolishing that illusion (staging its disappearance). One must analyze simulation pataphysically, that is, as the imaginary solution to the problem of limits.[47] Insert a program, press a button, and you are there, really, instantly, anything you want, everywhere you want to be (like VISA, like the Net) at the touch of a finger. What else is the dream of the computer/bio-information revolution and the coming revolution in virtual reality other than the perverse replication of the subject at the end of history, who, without moving, can do anything, be anywhere, transcend all limits, even that of time itself? "All information in all places at all times. The impossible ideal. But the marriage of computers with existing comunications-links will take us far closer to that goal than we have ever been."[48]

The evolution of simulation technology thus parodies (or replays) the evolution of the historical subject, whose destination is the enclosed, circular space where the rational and the real perfectly coincide. The difference between Hegel and Baudrillard is that Hegel *arrives*, whereas for Baudrillard the destination is always a paradoxical space, to which one arrives only in simulation. Baudrillard, like Hegel, thinks you cannot pass beyond your destination. In simulation, though, you are always already *at* your destination (with virtual reality, you're wearing it!). There is no "End" of simulation, even though its technical development subscribes to an apparently Hegelian logic. At the "End" of simulated history, in the perfection of its technology, stands the Simulated Absolute Subject, the Simulated Sovereign (that is, the Cyborg), a figure beyond the system of expenditure, like pure movement without the conversion of energy. Here, at the dissolving border between life and telematics, limits do not exist, nothing is prohibited, anything is possible. This is simulation's mimickry of the sacred – omnipotence and omnipresence, but in a hyperreal universe, the Absolute in cyberspace, the illusion and the allure of a virtual transcendence.

If the development of simulation parodies the development of the absolute subject in history, what does this mean for seduction, simulation's enchanted twin? Seduction, for Baudrillard, is an eternal return, a "willed recurrence," not a return in time.[49] It is what seduces time. Like simulation, it subverts the linear time of production, clock time, worktime. It is not, however, so much time's limit as, once again like simulation, an ecstasy of time, the ecstasy of its disappearance (with seduction, time flies!). For Hegel, in contrast, time is limited. This is because Hegel equates time with historical time, i.e., with human history. For Hegel, the end of history is, quite simply, the end of time (and not merely its disappearance); the moment of Absolute Knowledge is also the last moment of time. This is Hegel's "eternity," the eternity that is revealed in the final dialectical movement of history, history which consequently is finite and expresses the essential finitude of human being.[50] In Baudrillard, seduction is not a kind of absolute knowledge or wisdom; it does not lie outside time, does not transcend time. It is not time's limit. Instead, like simulation, it arrests it, suspends it, speeds it up, slows it down, reverses it, subverts its power and meaning, in short, seduces it. There is a "time of seduction," but it is not "real time," nor even quite the illusion of time, but rather the indiscernibility of time's reality and artifice. And as for seduction itself? In Baudrillard, *seduction never ends* – it has no limit. In this it is only like simulation; it cannot transcend itself. Nothing seduces seduction, like nothing simulates simulation; nothing is greater than seduction – not even, Baudrillard claims, the order that destroys it (production) – and seduction is never greater than itself.

One, in short, cannot transcend seduction, because seduction has nothing to do with limits, with overcoming (and hence, with negation, the dialectic, and everything Hegelian). It is all-enchanted appearances. For all this, it is hard not to feel that Baudrillard never quite completely uncouples seduction from transcendence and the discourse on limits, and that perhaps, at its basis, this is all part of an elaborate ruse. In Baudrillard, seduction still sounds very much like a final, essential term, in the best Hegelian sense: everything begins with and returns to seduction.[51] Baudrillard, of course, would deny this: he would say nothing is final about seduction; just the opposite, it is always a gamble, a wager, never a sure bet. It is, like simulation, a zone of interiority lacking an outside – or, at best, forming an "outside" that always folds back onto an "inside," obliterating the distinction. This, again, explains Baudrillard's fascination with games, the passion for the rule as means of deliverance from the law. Such a passion could only arise within a system which is perfectly closed in on itself, and which no longer maintains its connection with the "dialectic of the possible and the impossible, there being no accounts to settle with the future."[52] Or, one might add, with the past.

Perhaps in his duel with Hegel, Baudrillard must become Hegel (and not just this, but more-Hegel-than-Hegel). He must allow himself to be seduced by Hegel, to become his destiny by following or repeating him (in simulation).[53] He could then add "Hegelian" to the labels nihilist, melancholic, postmodernist, and all the rest that have come to him via his generally negative reception by contemporary critical theory. It is Baudrillard's indifference to labels, however, that finally makes these exercises in philosophic name-calling seem ridiculous. If Hegel returns over the horizon of Baudrillard's thought, it's Hegel's holographic double, Hegel the cyborg, the sim-Absolute, the ultimate illusion and fantastic game of transcendence at the end of history. After all, that's the fascination of the modern technologies of simulation, which project us, in their cold, relentless logic, from the very beginning, to the end of history, the end of time. Beginning, end, everything already compiled (just pay your quarter). And here Hegel's return would be the supreme irony of the object – transcendence is now the cyborg, not the human, project. Even more: it is the sacrifice of that project and the desire which fuels it to an apparatus which can never surpass itself.

Notes

I would like to thank Philip Turetzky, Keith Goshorn, and Douglas Kellner for their helpful criticisms of this paper.

1   Jean Baudrillard, *Fatal Strategies* (New York: Semiotext(e), 1990), p. 14. The quote is from Elias Canetti, *The Human Province*, trans., Joachim Neugroschel (New York: Seabury, 1978) p. 69. Baudrillard also comments on this passage in "The Year 2000 Has Already Happened" in Arthur and Marilouise Kroker, *Body Invaders: Panic Sex in America* (Montreal: New World Perspectives, 1987), p. 35ff., and in *Forget Foucault* (New York: Semiotext(e), 1987), p. 67ff.

2   Baudrillard, *Forget Foucault*, p. 68.

3   "Technology is explicitness" (Lyman Bryson). Quoted in Sol Yurick, *Behold*

Metatron, the Recording Angel (New York: Semiotext(e), 1985). There could hardly be a better formula for simulation, which in its highest form is pure exposure (ob-scenity), nothing secret, nothing hidden, nothing left to interpretation or the imagination.

4 I don't mean this in a political sense. The effort to recover history is transpolitical. In Baudrillard, it is not only history that succumbs to simulation (but also the political, the social, the sexual, the aesthetic ...). The space of simulation corresponds to the transfinite, the radical dissemination of the *multiplicity* of ends.

5 Mike Gane, *Baudrillard's Bestiary: Baudrillard and Culture* (London: Routledge, 1991).

6 Jean Baudrillard, *Seduction* (New York: Saint Martin's, 1990), esp. p. 147. Simulation for Baudrillard is not simple repetition (or series) but precession, i.e., repetition in advance. Here the governing process is modulation. The model specifies the order of repetition in all its possible different registers and combinatorials. In the order of simulation, what is real is not just reproduced, but what is "always already reproduced." Cf. *Simulations* (New York: Semiotext(e), 1983) pp. 99–101. I will return to this at a later point in the text.

7 Cf. Baudrillard's remarks in Sophie Calle and Jean Baudrillard, *Suite vénitienne/ Please follow me* (Seattle: Bay Press, 1988), p. 76ff.

8 Jean Baudrillard, *Cool Memories*, trans., Chris Turner (New York: Verso, 1990), p. 3.

9 The phrase refers to Erje Ayden's book of the same name (New York: Autonomedia, 1989). In "Forget Baudrillard," Sylvere Lotringer begins his interview of Baudrillard with a question about the end of things, which Baudrillard immediately redirects back to Canetti's hypothesis: "I don't know if it's a question of an end. The word is probably meaningless in any case, because we're no longer sure that there is such a thing as linearity. I would prefer to begin, even if it sounds a little like science fiction, with a quotation from *The Human Province*." (New York: Semiotext(e), 1988), p. 67.

10 Baudrillard, *Cool Memories*, p. 4.

11 Baudrillard, *Seduction*, p. 2; cf. also Baudrillard, *In The Shadow of the Silent Majorities ... or the End of the Social* (New York: Semiotext(e), 1983), pp. 73, 77ff.

12 Plenary speech at 10th anniversary conference of "Theory, Culture, and Society," Pittsburg PA, Aug 1992.

13 Cf. Baudrillard, *Seduction*, p. 131ff.

14 Baudrillard, "The Reality Gulf," *The Guardian* (Jan 11, 1991). Also Baudrillard, "La guerre du Golfe n'a pas eu lieu," *Liberation* (March 29, 1991).

15 Baudrillard, "The Year 2000 Has Already Happened," in *Body Invaders*.

16 Baudrillard, *Simulations*.

17 Cited in Douglas Kellner, *Jean Baudrillard: From Marxism to Postmodernism and Beyond* (Stanford: Stanford University Press, 1989), p. 209.

18 Jean Baudrillard, "On Nihilism," *On the Beach* 6 (Spring 1984), pp. 38–9. Baudrillard develops the themes of transparency and obscenity in *The Transparency of Evil: Essays on Extreme Phenomena* (New York: Verso, 1993).

19 Baudrillard, *Fatal Strategies*, p. 35.

20 Cf. Gilles Deleuze's characterization of an "abstract machine" in *Foucault* (Minneapolis: University of Minnesota Press, 1988), p. 37.

21 Everything today is an experience. Experience this book or film, experience white-water rafting, experience wilderness! It is as if experience was now in the object, which now serves as a stand-in for the radical absence of subjective experience in our society. If we desire to experience everything today, if experience is in everything, that only reflects, like history and the real, its definitive loss and mutation into hyperreal forms.

22 Paul Virilio's work on the logistics of perception in modern war technology, and the relation between seeing and foreseeing (simulation) in military operations, is of seminal importance in this context. Cf. *War and Cinema: The Logistics of Perception* (London: Verso, 1989), p. 3 and the entire last chapter.

23 Jean Baudrillard, In *For a Critique of the Political Economy of the Sign*, trans., Charles Levin (St. Louis: Telos Press, 1981), pp. 164–84.

24 Georges Bataille, *The Accursed Share, Vol. 2* (New York: Zone Books, 1991), p. 206ff.

25 In Baudrillard, *Simulations*, p. 53.

26 "End of . . . the space of signs, their conflict, their silence; only the black box of the code, the molecular emitter of signals from which we have been irradiated." Baudrillard, *Simulations*, pp. 104–5.

27 For Baudrillard's views on radical otherness, cf. *Transparency of Evil*, esp. p. 146ff.

28 Gilles Deleuze, *Cinema 2: The Time-Image* (Minneapolis: University of Minnesota Press, 1989), esp. pp. 68–97.

29 Cf. Douglas Kellner, *The Persian Gulf TV War*, (Boulder, Cal.: Westview, 1992). See also Christopher Norris, *Uncritical Theory: Postmodernism, Intellectuals, and the Gulf War* (Amherst: University of Massachusetts Press, 1992).

30 Paul Virilio, *Pure War* (New York: Semiotext(e), 1983).

31 The Cold War was no different in this respect, a war where simulation and deterrence endowed conflict with a sense of hyperreality and uncertainty, and which, despite our inclination to think otherwise, caused millions of deaths in the regional wars it spawned around the globe. The Cold War, Baudrillard said somewhere, was also over before it began.

32 Norris, *Uncritical Theory*, p. 5. Baudrillard's remarks on the war serve Norris as an entry point for an attack on "postmodern intellectuals" in general.

33 Baudrillard, *Fatal Strategies*, p. 13.

34 Cf. George Bataille, *Theory of Religion* (New York: Zone Books, 1989). Also his *Accursed Share, Vols. 1 and 2*.

35 Cf. Jean Baudrillard, "Consumer Society," in *Jean Baudrillard: Selected Writings* (Stanford: Stanford University Press, 1988), pp. 42ff.

36 Baudrillard, *Fatal Strategies*, p. 14.

37 Cf. Baudrillard's remarks on *trompe l'oeil* in *Seduction*, p. 67.

38 Baudrillard, *Seduction*, p. 162.

39 President's Address, Conference on Modern Communication and the Disappearance of Art and Politics, Missoula, Montana, 1989.

40 The exterior is not the "outside." The difference between "inside" and "outside" is constantly subverted in simulation, which remains, none the less, a fully

"interiorized" space. On the distinction between exterior/outside and interior/inside, see Deleuze, *Foucault*, pp. 94ff.

41 Baudrillard would deny this. Seduction, by his account, has nothing to do with desire, becoming, or being a nomad. Cf. his remarks on Deleuze in *Seduction*, p. 146. These are precisely the kind of images I get from his travel book *America* (New York: Verso, 1988), however.

42 Gane, *Baudrillard's Bestiary*, p. 160.

43 The postmodern, then, *is* the modern, that is, the *modern in simulation*. No fundamental or essential distinction is possible here and such a distinction is always subject to reversion. And, like the modern, like everything that is simulated, the postmodern is already over by virtue of being repeated in advance.

44 Baudrillard's latest exploration of these themes is in *L'illusion de la fin, ou la greve des événements* (Paris: Galilée, 1993), esp. pp. 23–8.

45 Cf. again, Baudrillard's remarks to Lotringer, "Forget Foucault," pp. 67–9.

46 This, for example, is Baudrillard's position on artificial intelligence, in *Xerox and Infinity* (London: Touchepas, 1988).

47 One which, we have seen, is also the end of imagination, or rather, its sacrifice to the assemblages of simulation. In the same way we sacrifice our attention to television, our capacity to think and decide to computers.

48 David Godfrey and Douglas Parkhill, *Gutenberg Two* (Toronto: Porcépic, 1980), p. 1.

49 Baudrillard, *Seduction*, p. 147.

50 Cf. Alexandre Kojeve, *Introduction to the Reading of Hegel: Lectures on the Phenomenology of Spirit* (Ithaca: Cornell University Press, 1969), p. 148.

51 Baudrillard does not, I think, abandon seduction in his most recent work. In fact, seduction as a principle of the disruption of dominant orders informs his latest allusions to "viral" strategies of rebellion and resistance. The virus, like the cyborg, is an object at the intersection of living and dead matter (it is no accident that the term applies to computers as well as biological organisms). It attacks the system of immunity via processes of recoding and duplication, that is, via simulation. The virus, like simulation, is simply another disenchanted form of seduction. And what else is seduction if not the overcoming of defenses (of one's "immunity")?

52 Baudrillard, *Seduction*, p. 133.

53 And in that way, Hegel would be like the anonymous man Sophie Calle follows in *La Suite vénitienne*, someone who, through another's repetition of his itinerary, has its meaning stripped from it, who has "his goal stolen from him: an evil genie has slipped surreptitiously between him and his self" (Baudrillard, *Transparency of Evil*, p. 156).

DATE DUE

ILL			
537 8382			
3 8 01			
DE 07 05			
ILL			
4 18 08			
GAYLORD			PRINTED IN U.S.A

WITHDRAWN